MERLIN

KNOWLEDGE AND POWER THROUGH THE AGES

STEPHEN KNIGHT

D1072855

CORNELL UNIVERSITY PRESS
Ithaca and London

Frontispiece: Merlin visits court as a stag in the Vulgate *Merlin.*
BN MSS Français 95, f. 262.

First published 2009 by Cornell University Press
First printing, Cornell Paperbacks, 2016
Printed in the United States of America

Library of Congress Cataloging-in-Publication Data

Knight, Stephen Thomas.
    Merlin : knowledge and power through the ages / Stephen Knight.
        p. cm.
    Includes bibliographical references and index.
    ISBN 978-0-8014-4365-7 (cloth : alk. paper)
    ISBN 978-1-5017-0569-4 (pbk. : alk. paper)
  1. Merlin (Legendary character) in literature.   2. Merlin (Legendary character)
3. Knowledge, Theory of, in literature.   4. Power (Social sciences) in literature.
I. Title.

  PN57.M4K58   2009
  809'.93351—dc22   2009017327

Cornell University Press strives to use environmentally responsible suppliers
and materials to the fullest extent possible in the publishing of its books. Such
materials include vegetable-based, low-VOC inks and acid-free papers that are
recycled, totally chlorine-free, or partly composed of nonwood fibers. For further
information, visit our website at www.cornellpress.cornell.edu.

MERLIN

For David, philosopher-son

Contents

Illustrations

Introduction

Merlin is an icon: a few lines will create him, sketching the pointed hat and the long beard, plus a magic wand and someone to teach. So T. H. White described him in *The Once and Future King,* Disney visualized the image in *The Sword in the Stone,* and Lerner and Loewe set it to music in *Camelot.* But that image is an illusion of modernity: medieval Merlin was not old and bearded, was wise rather than a wizard, guided countries rather than learners. The modern icon delineates an image not anciently mythic, but one we find both credible and consoling among contemporary anxieties. Modernity, though, is not the first period to refashion Merlin and his knowledge in its own terms and interests: Merlin and his knowledge have multiple and conflicted meanings, developed and varied over some thousand years in many differing genres, locations, and political contexts. This book will explore these many manifestations of Merlin.

Merlin's beard, wand, and pointy hat are recent phenomena with recent meaning: through those motifs the figure who possesses knowledge is deprived of both normality and vigor, made pointy-headed to match the hat. This reduction of Merlin and his knowledge seems a odd phenomenon in an age of science, which is the Latin for knowledge. In fact it is a dialectical reality, the modern version of the constant and age-old conflict between knowledge and power. This book will argue that when knowledge is most important, most close to taking control, that is when it is most vulnerable to some form of limitation or repression by power. Michel Foucault's underlying idea was that knowledge and power are mutually interwoven, apparently to the disadvantage of neither (see the interview on "Truth and Power" in *Power/Knowledge,* 1980), but this Utopian idea of the sanctity of the savant, inspiring as it might seem, is not supported either by French history or the Merlin tradition.

The comic hat, the druidic beard, the entanglement with Vivien (under whatever version of her name), even his sudden disappearances from the stories—these are all forms of Merlin's containment, they are maneuvers by which power, realized in the texts in many changing ways, attempts to limit the threatening force of knowledge—which itself has many forms. Merlin can appear as a peasant, an old woman, a small boy, a stag: but these manifestations will always bring some form of knowledge to bear on the text. The transformed Merlin will guide, help, save, predict, judge—that is, use knowledge on behalf of those in power, and so in some way, and ultimately in an unacceptable way, expose the limits of the power of the powerful.

The story of Merlin, and in his first realization Myrddin, has been proceeding for about a thousand years, and to trace its recurrent realization of the conflict of knowledge and power will not only unearth a mass of intriguing detail—in family terms alone, Merlin rescues his own mother from execution for fornication, he causes chaos at his wife's second wedding, he organizes the birth of Tom Thumb—but more importantly will show how the texts explore the mechanisms by which knowledge and power both face and confront each other over time.

Literature is where knowledge is given power, and the great writers, Merlins of their time, convey tensions and conflicts of all kinds, including those of knowledge and power. Those conflicts are not only found in the so-called great works: the Merlin dialectic can be exposed in disempowered genres like elusive early Welsh poems, eighteenth-century satires, German Romantic lyrics, as sharply as, and even more pointedly than, in the sonority of early medieval French or Latin, or the uncertain assertions of Victorian grand poetry.

The story unfolded in this study is not single or simple: various Merlins can co-exist. One thirteenth-century French tradition made him a semi-priest, another a coarse seducer; he appears on both sides in the English Civil War, and in the early eighteenth century Merlin is an ideologue for the new Whig royalty of King William of Orange, but for the Tory opposition a figure of farce. The key is the context, and what the creator of the Merlin text understands by knowledge and would like it to do for, or against, power.

Each identifiable context seems to start again with the Merlin story, picking some pieces from the past but relocating and redirecting them in improbable but apparently comforting ways: Romantic poets like Southey, Arnold, and Tennyson turned the wise Merlin of the twelfth-century tradition into a silly old scholar, easy pickings for a *femme fatale;* the German Romantics and American poets like Emerson and Robinson saw him as the noble spirit of the bard; modern New Age enthusiasts have imagined a druidic Myrddin to access mysteries beyond rational knowledge; in 1999 Merlin starred in his own television series, ending happily with a wrinkle-free Nimue and a talking horse, rewards for knowledge as imagined by the modern media.

To trace such an intriguing, elusive, meandering, and sometimes alarming story requires a whole range of assistance—which Merlin of course never needed. Time has been provided for me mostly by the genial decision of Cardiff University to make me a distinguished research professor, while the British Academy supported expenses for two years as I traveled around acquiring materials.

To gather the wide-ranging data for this project and resolve many tricky issues—just where did Wieland read about the medieval Merlin? Just when did Alfred Noyes write "The Riddles of Merlin"?—I have been even more reliant than usual on the resources of libraries and the skills and tolerance of librarians in a range of institutions. Thanks to the invitations of generous colleagues, I have been able to work at the New York Public Library and at the universities of Houston, Ohio State, Western Michigan, Melbourne, and Western Australia, each with its gleaming vein of Merliniana. A major source has been the British Library, still defending well its incomparable resources for knowledge, though London University's Senate House Library has also been highly helpful. A reliable base, excellent for Welsh and German, has been the Arts and Humanities Library at Cardiff: I thank Tom Dawkes and Helen Dartillac-Brill warmly for their contributions to this research. Academic colleagues have answered questions, looked at drafts, and been generally supportive as, in the manner of T. H. White's egalitarian geese, we trudge hopefully around the mud-flats of the modern university; I would like to name for special thanks Martin Coyle, John Frow, Rob Gossedge, Richard Green, Tom Hahn, Dawn Harrington, Andrew Lynch, John Morgan, Carl Phelpstead, Helen Phillips, Lorraine Stock, Andrew Wawn, and Richard Wilson. At Cornell University Press Bernhard Kendler, Peter J. Potter, Karen Laun, Rachel Post, and copyeditor Gavin Lewis have given generous and expert professional support. In the family I have benefited from the recurrent interest in the project of Lizzie and David, and specifically from their technical help: I feel I am improving at following instructions. As well as collegiality, you also need isolation and several forms of absence: I have been dependent on Margaret for tolerating that, and also for her positive support, while I have slowly spelled out this study in the Merlinesque locations of Wales and France.

There is a wider range of beneficent colleagues, those who have worked on the Merlin material in many periods and many forms. As universities became the parade grounds of knowledge, a substantial number of scholars made contributions without which work of this kind would be impossible. Gaston Paris, Lucy Paton, H. Oskar Sommer, J. S. P. Tatlock, and Eugène Vinaver were wide-ranging medievalists with a real impact on Merlin studies, as were the less well-known specialists Ernest Jones, Laura Keeler, John J. Parry, and Adelaide Weiss. Not only my Cymreig location leads me to value the ground-breaking Welsh scholarship of Ifor Williams, Rachel Bromwich, Alfred Jarman, Brynley Roberts, and John T. Koch. Recently, major strides have been taken in gathering, editing, and analyzing the medieval sources: Robert Baudry, Anne Berthelot, Fanni Bogdanow, Catherine Daniel, Anne Mac-Donald, Alexandre Micha, and Gilles Roussineau have worked revealingly on the French texts, while Norris Lacy has exercised Arthur-like leadership in both the translation of the twelfth-century Merlin texts and assembling reference materials on the Arthur myth with much on the international Merlin. Alan Lupack has transmitted Merlin material as part of his wide-ranging Arthurian activities; Christopher Dean, Raymond H. Thompson, and Charlotte Spivack have made important statements on aspects of Merlin studies; Glyn Burgess and Karen Pratt have edited the splendid *Arthur of the French* (2006), while Peter H. Goodrich's very substantial contribution includes a most helpful reader, a well-assembled collection of secondary essays with an excellent introduction, and perceptive accounts of many elements of the tradition.

Another area of Merlin representation and scholarship is visual: as with Arthur material (but sadly not Robin Hood), Merlin's interface with power means that many of the texts are luxurious enough to have illustrations, some magnificent, from the high medieval period to the pre-Raphaelites: Muriel Whitaker is a fine guide here. A full account of the visual realization, and interrogation, of the Merlin story is a topic for another book, with its own meanings and enigmas—for example it is, puzzlingly rare until the postmedieval period for Merlin to be depicted as seduced and immobilized by Vivien—but I have tried to indicate through some discussion and some illustrations what issues might be involved in visualizing Merlin as a focus of knowledge in the context of power.

All these sources, scholars, and colleagues have provided a mass of data, but as the Merlin myth indicates, it is what use you make of knowledge that counts, for ill or good. While I hope that this book can serve as an introduction to and a coverage of the riches of the Merlin myth, it cannot seek to be exhaustive. German poetry and drama, French fiction, American popular material—these all, like illustrations, deserve studies of their own to work out in detail what those societies have made of, and through, Merlin-related cultural data. I am aware of offering no more than sketches in those areas, and also of having, sometimes sadly, bypassed material of rich potential interest like the French repertory of Merlin-valet plays (led by the productive if also repetitive Florent Dancourt), the near-contemporary role Merlin has in the fiction of violence (such as David Drake's regrettable Hammer's Slammers series), or the elusively off-center role Myrddin, not unlike Arthur, plays in medieval Welsh poetry.

These condensations and omissions have, like the structure of the book as a whole, been made in the pursuit of an overall argument about the recurring and recurrently varied relation between knowledge and power as figured in the Merlin myth. The thematic titles of each section, Wisdom, Advice, Cleverness, and Education, state what seem to me the major formations in the sociocultural apprehension of the value—and accordingly the threat—of knowledge at different times and in different contexts.

It was not my planning, but perhaps some tricksterish force in the material, that, as I eventually realized, led my four thematic summaries to spell out initially the name of the major disseminator of the Merlin myth to Europe, the twelfth-century French poet Wace.

To write about knowledge and its contexts has its necessary techniques. Merlin, the French prose texts tell us, dictated his adventures to his master Blaise. Their house style might be useful today, as there are always decisions to be made about the mode of communication to select, the form of discursive disguise to deploy. In order to spare the page a rash of numbers I have used the author-date style of annotation, but have inserted endnotes when there is some comment to make that would seem disruptive in the text. Where good translations of texts are available, I have used those, and indicated the translators in the primary bibliography; in other cases within my competence, when I have felt the translations are not clear enough or wander too far from the text I have translated the material myself. I have only quoted from the original when this seems relevant to the discussion. In referring to characters I have normalized to Merlin and Vivien (except in quotations) but with others such as Gauvain/Gawain and Isolde/Esyllt have followed the version of the relevant text. In referencing quotations I have used line numbers where they exist, and in prose or where poems are not lineated have given page numbers.

Merlin appears in that monument to British identity, the *Oxford Dictionary of National Biography,* and in many other places. Often when you start on a topic, you notice it everywhere—one of the signs you have chosen well. The name Merlin is very widely used in the modern world: it basically connotes a valued form of knowledge as in the modern international charity, Medical Emergency Relief International. But there can often also be a dialectic, even resistant, element: the offensive-defensive Spitfire was powered by a Rolls-Royce Merlin engine, and aggression through knowledge and against liberty seems embodied in the large British firm making Merlin wire-fencing, sometimes electrified: Mark Twain would be amused, as that is what his Yankee used against Merlin and the knights of the Round Table. Equally attuned to the nervous present is the firm in Carmarthen, mythic home of the sage, called *Morgeisi Myrddin,* or, if you do not speak or invest in Welsh, "Merlin Mortgages."

No doubt a grasp of prophecy might illuminate financial affairs, but of wider impact today is the contemporary governmental obsession with automatized and unreflective modes of "training": power technologizes knowledge. Equally functionally, and simultaneously dysfunctionally, academic knowledge is now insistently quantified, whether in terms of the "research questions" you must promise (in your pre-research ignorance) to ask in order to receive your dole of research funding, or, at the end, the "technology transfer" you should achieve to turn your research into profitable functionality, like Merlin in the Vulgate raising a mist to confuse King Claudas's soldiers.

As with, and as part of, the managerial control of professionalism that haunts most allegedly advanced countries, the subsumption of knowledge by and into power is now well advanced. In the Vulgate, when a baron ignored Merlin's instructions not to sit at the Siege Perilous, he was melted into a ball of lead. While modern intellectuals may not plan to convert their manipulative masters into minor weapons of destruction in this way, we might well want to stake out territory where knowledge can remain at liberty, even if it is now and then, like the Cumbrian Myrddin, in exile.

But when modern intellectuals feel our present situation is critically embattled, that the power of governmentality is increasingly compressing the freedom of knowledge, what the story of Myrddin-Merlin tells us is that it was ever thus: the lords will want their dreams explained; the generals, or their heirs the businessmen, will want a few reliable predictions. A mildly encouraging thought remains, that the powerful have not yet learned to do without knowledge, nor yet the people who possess it. The more powerful the electronic tools, the more leverage is in the pale hands of those who can really use them. The bigger the quest for power, the more important knowledge will be, and its absence, as recent political and financial events show, is all the more debilitating. From Cumbria to Camelot in story, and in reality from the Iron Age to the global present, Merlin consistently transforms into a figure of knowledge separate from power: the distance between the two energizes the mystery that empowers his knowledge.

Merlin

CHAPTER ONE

British Myrddin-Merlin

Wisdom

Myrddin-Merlin

The origin of the myth of Merlin lies among the British Celts, in the language now called Welsh. They named him Myrddin and located him first in Cumbria, northwestern England, before this area was settled by the Anglo-Saxons: Cumbria is the same as Cymru, the authentic name for Wales. Material about the early British Myrddin is preserved in a number of poems in medieval Welsh (or Cymraeg), and there is some later material from southern Scotland. The Myrddin story is neither full nor fully clear: like most early Celtic poetry, these are reflective lyrics not narratives, but two things emerge. Myrddin is a man of special knowledge in relation with power; and this relationship can generate both dissent from and support for social authority. As in all its massive later development, from the start the myth of Myrddin-Merlin is both political and complex.

In one of these poems,[1] "Afallen" ("Apple Tree"), Myrddin speaks:

> Sweet apple tree, growing in a glade,
> a treasure hidden from the lords of Rhydderch.
> With a crowd round its base, a host around it,
> a delight to them, brave warriors.
> Now Gwenddydd loves me not, nor welcomes me,
> and I am hated by Gwasawg, Rhydderch's ally.

> I have destroyed her son and daughter,
> death takes everyone; why does he not welcome me?
> After Gwenddolau, no lords revere me,
> no sport delights me, no lover seeks me out.
> In the battle of Arfderydd, my torque was gold,
> today I am no treasure to a swan-like girl. (35–46)

After the battle of Arfderydd (a real one, in c. 573) Myrddin is no longer in the world of lords, warriors, and ladies, but alone, in nature; in self-chosen exile and weary melancholy he represents a wisdom that rejects his society and its values.

These early Welsh poems are condensed and referential: they often need interpreting in a sense of their context to see what they mean by knowledge and power. In "Apple Tree" each stanza, in opposed two-line sentences, states forms of isolation from a real historical world. The context and events are quite obscure,[2] but the names are recognizable. Gwenddolau, Myrddin's lord, may have been a real late sixth-century king of Cumbria (see Koch, 2006, 82–83 on Arfderydd), and it is possible that a Cumbrian lord called Myrddin did once exist. Rhydderch was a contemporary historical king of Strathclyde, in southwest Scotland: this and Rheged, covering most of Cumbria, were the last bastions of the Celtic British: the Welsh still call this world "Yr Hen Ogledd," "the Old North" (see fig. 1 for a map of Myrddin's Britain).

Myrddin is described as having fought, and Gwenddolau apparently died, at the Battle of Arfderydd (to the English, Arthuret), just north of Carlisle. The battle caused Myrddin's trauma and isolation: his distress is in part because so many are dead, but it is also personal. He has apparently destroyed the son of his sister Gwenddydd, who hates him now: he has also caused the death of her daughter. Gwasawg, another new enemy, and apparently a prince of Cumbria, was probably their father. That Gwasawg is called Rhydderch's ally does not prove that Rhydderch fought in this battle, or against Gwenddolau, as some have thought:[3] Rhydderch is later referred to as a friend of Gwenddolau and Myrddin. Whatever the participants or the exact events in the battle, Myrddin is alone, in misery. From his viewpoint outside the world of the powerful, he is still aware of its workings and now implicitly critical of its operations and values, bearing a special burden of wisdom.

Knowledge and power are in consistent dialectic in this myth—and, it suggests insistently, in reality as well. The myth explores how through centuries, to the present, the person who bears knowledge can be useful to, often crucial to, the operations of the powerful and is actively courted by them.

MYRDDIN'S
BRITAIN

DAL RIADA

● Glasgow

STRATHCLYDE

CALEDONIAN
FOREST   Arfderydd
          ●
          Carlisle
RHEGED

CUMBRIA

St Asaph
(Llanelwy)
              ●
Cyminod ●
        GWYNEDD
        ●
        Dinas
        Emrys
              ● Ieihon

● Fochno

DYFED Caerfyrddin   Brecon   Glywysing
      ●   ●   ●   ● Oxford
        GWENT ● Monmouth
      Caerleon   ● Marlborough
      ●
        ● Glastonbury

Tintagel ●

0   100km

1. Myrddin's Britain.

This is primarily a male role, but Myrddin-Merlin will often—again to the present—be advised by women who are his counterparts, and also in varying ways be threatened by women. Always in some way and to some degree he separates himself from the powerful and their values.

For a thousand years the Myrddin-Merlin figure has represented a conflict basic to Western societies—and no doubt to many others as well. Whether it is based on bard versus lord, magician versus monarch, scientist versus capitalist, academic versus politician, the conflict between knowledge and power is inherent to organized societies, and the many formations of Myrddin-Merlin and his story have represented the many versions of this conflict. These have been continually different in their detailed representations but the same in the underlying structural tension which they realize between knowledge and power. Though the story of Myrddin-Merlin will vary greatly over time, as the hero's social role, location, special qualities, and above all the nature of his conflict with authority will all change, and keep on changing, the myth's essential dynamic of knowledge versus power will not alter—it will just be reconfigured to be newly relevant in many varying contexts.

The Earliest Materials

Llyfr Du Caerfyrddin ("The Black Book of Carmarthen"), written in about 1250, places first in its varied content three poems that represent the early Welsh idea of Myrddin:

> Ymddiddan Myrddin a Thaliesin ("The Conversation of Myrddin and Taliesin")
> Afallen ("Apple Tree")
> Oian ("Little Pig")

The following poem, "Y Fedwen" ("Birch Tree"), has similarities in style and mood to "Apple Tree" and "Little Pig," but lacks the specific references to the Myrddin story found in the others, and so is not properly part of the tradition unlike the three others.

A long poem entitled "Cyfoesi Myrddin a Gwenddydd ei Chwaer" ("The Prophecy of Myrddin and Gwenddydd, His Sister") is preserved in the early fifteenth-century *Red Book of Hergest,* while "Y Gwasgarddgerdd Fyrddin yn y Bedd" ("The Diffuse Song of Myrddin in the Grave") appears both there and also in the fourteenth-century *White Book of Rhydderch.* The latest surviving of these poems is "Peirian Faban" ("Commanding Youth"), found in a fifteenth-century manuscript, which also has versions of "Little Pig" and "Myrddin in the Grave."[4]

Although the three earliest of the six Myrddin poems cannot be dated in written form before about 1250, and some are first recorded some time later (notably "Commanding Youth"), the language and style of the poems make it clear, according to two authoritative scholars, that much in them was composed by the end of the eleventh century. Rachel Bromwich states that "Myrddin and Taliesin," "The Song of Myrddin in the Grave," and "Myrddin and Gwenddydd" were "certainly composed before 1100" and adds that "At least the nucleus of *Afallen* ("Apple Tree") and *Oian* ("Little Pig") are probably as old" (1978, 470). A. O. H. Jarman agrees, saying that the oldest part (lines 35–65) of "Apple Tree" might be dated in the ninth or tenth centuries" (1982, xxxvi) and that "Myrddin and Taliesin" was written down "during the second half of the eleventh century, 1050–1100" (1951, 53).

These dates are crucial, because they place the Welsh literary formation of the Myrddin myth before the creation of the expanded and substantially varied Merlin story created by Geoffrey of Monmouth in the later 1130s. In the past, scholars could not be sure of this, as the dating of early Welsh texts was still uncertain. The influential American scholar J. S. P. Tatlock dismissed what he called "the mess of inaccuracy, vagueness and evasion which half-swamps Welsh literary history" (1950, 176 n. 23) and made the Oxford-based Latin-writing Geoffrey of Monmouth the effective originator of the whole myth. E. K. Chambers, himself at Oxford, similarly felt "Merlin seems to have been wholly a creation of Geoffrey's active brain" (1927, 95).

More recent scholarship has resisted this rejection of Welsh priority: the existence of a formed and literary Welsh tradition before Geoffrey of Monmouth is now regarded as certain (Jarman, 1976, 1991).[5] Indeed, when they discuss the text itself, even Tatlock and Chambers recognize that Geoffrey had native British sources, though they reduce them as much as they can—Chambers calls them "vague rumours of a British hope" (1927, 96–97) and Tatlock merely says there is "reason to surmise" that Geoffrey had "some lost account of Merlin" (1950, 173). The fact that the Welsh manuscripts are later than those of Geoffrey's text is not a problem: it is usual in a whole range of early poetry, from Homeric epic to Anglo-Saxon poetry, for texts to be preserved in oral form with some accuracy for long periods of time. Brynley Roberts, the most recent of the Welsh Myrddin experts, states that the Myrddin poems point to "the professional bards as authors," that "native Welsh literary tradition appears to have been oral down to the fifteenth century" and that

"The ability to compose poems in traditional style without recourse to pen and paper, to recall phrases, lines, and whole passages of verse is not uncommon" (1992, 5–6).

There are other signs of a formed tradition about Myrddin in early Welsh. *Y Gododdin* ("The Gododdin"), itself only preserved in Wales, is a lengthy eulogy to the warriors of a tribe based around Edinburgh. They were defeated by the Anglo-Saxons at Catraeth, modern Catterick in Yorkshire, in about 600. Each stanza speaks an elegy to a hero, and one of them had been praised by Myrddin. This is not in the oldest layer of the poem, which some scholars think may in fact reach back to the early seventh century, but Ifor Williams felt the spelling of the name was in an early form (Williams, 1966, 188), and it is very unlikely to be later than the tenth century in origin, so is well before Geoffrey of Monmouth. Another comment from the tenth century is in the poem *Armes Prydein* of c. 930 ("The Prophecy of Britain," in Williams, 1972), where Myrddin is spoken of as a prophet of Welsh political history. Another possibly early reference is in the fourteenth-century *White Book of Rhydderch* where a list of place names of Britain claims the earliest of all is "clas Myrddin," or "Myrddin's enclosure" (Bromwich, 1978, 228–31), but this reference has eluded credible explanation, and might just be a back-projection of Myrddin's later fame.

So far this discussion has spoken of "early Welsh tradition" as if it is unified, and most commentators, whether on Merlin or Arthur, imply that is the case—a culture can appear uniform from a distance. But the Welsh Myrddin material refers to two quite different figures and functions. One, the earlier, is the Cumbrian Myrddin, the conceivably historical nobleman whose new and terrible knowledge leads him to reject contemporary heroic society in favor of nature and contemplation. The second figure and function, which developed out of the first as Welsh culture became restricted to Wales and faced the Anglo-Saxons, deploys his knowledge fully on behalf of the Welsh to celebrate their successes against the invaders, and to encourage them by prophesying their future reconquest of Britain. Characteristic of the multiple meaning of the whole Myrddin-Merlin myth is the fact that the Cumbrian Myrddin opposes the values and power of his own heroic social context, while the early Welsh Myrddin espouses that Welsh warrior culture and defends it against Anglo-Saxon incursion.

A special complexity of the early material, and the main reason why these two figures have not been fully separated in the past, is that the Cumbrian Myrddin material is itself interwoven with the Welsh material in the same poems: as what had formerly been a Britain-wide Celtic culture was preserved in Wales, previous interests were overlaid with the new ones, not displaced by them. But it is possible to disentangle the two layers and see that in the six Myrddin poems there are elements of the Cumbrian figure, elaborated with his Welsh development—different deployments of the figure of knowledge.

Natural Wisdom: Myrddin of Cumbria

Traumatized in battle, rejecting the noble heroic life, selecting nature for its more enduring value, the Cumbrian Myrddin inevitably offers a critique of secular power. "The Conversation of Myrddin and Taliesin" involves a famous figure of the Old North: Taliesin was probably a bard at the court of Urien of Rheged, with some poems apparently deriving from about 500 (see Koch, 2006, 1652–53). He asks:

> The battle of Arfderydd—where is its cause?
> All their lives they prepare for it. (23–24)

Myrddin answers, detailing his trauma:

> A multitude of bloodflowing spears on a bloody field;
> a multitude of mighty warriors will prove mortal;
> a multitude when injured; a multitude when forced to flee;
> a multitude their retreat in battle. (25–28)

He reimagines the "Seven sons of Eliffer," led by Cynfelyn, fighting heroically for the Cumbrians:

> Seven stabbing spears, seven rivers full
> with chieftains' blood they fill. (33–34)

But all ends in trauma, not just for himself:

> Seven score generous nobles went mad;
> in Celyddon Wood they ended. (35–36)

The action of the poem deplores the result of heroic deeds and the question about Arfderydd—"where is its cause" (23)—itself points to a critique of heroic society: Welsh tradition records the view that this battle was fought for no good reason. The *Triads,* a medieval rhyming repository of condensed commentary on Welsh events and culture, record it as one of "The Three Futile Battles of the Island of Britain." Elsewhere it is said to have been "brought about by the cause of a lark's nest," but this might simply derive from the name of the nearby fortress Caerlaverock, meaning "lark's castle" (Jackson, 1977). Line 24, "All their lives they prepare for it," makes a classical statement of heroic training—the war band achieves identity in its military moment—but that ideal has bitter meaning against the brutal, even futile nature of this battle: the tone is negative, and the heroic tradition is rejected from the standpoint of the knowledge of the northern wise men, Taliesin and Myrddin.

But this is only the second half of the poem: it opens with Myrddin speaking about battle trauma:

> So sad I am, so sad,
> because of what happened to Cedfyw and Cadfan.
> There was dazzling, loud battle;
> there was a stained, shattered shield. (1–4)

Battle is bright, but the shield is stained with blood: this scene too is less than triumphant. The difference from the Cumbrian material is that Cedfyw and Cadfan cannot be identified as heroes of the Old North: Cedfyw seems unknown,[6] but Cadfan was prince of Gwynedd, in northwest Wales, and the next stanza speaks of his great-grandfather Maelgwn, a famous lord of Gwynedd, who died well before Arfderydd, in 547. The first half of the poem appears to celebrate and lament battles in Wales itself, in the mournful spirit of the Cumbrian Myrddin.

This poem as it stands juxtaposes the northern trauma and Welsh military events. In fact as Jarman suggests (1951, 54–55; see also Bollard, 1990, 17), it may be two separate poems, similar in meter and rhyme, which have been linked by their comparable themes, and the Welsh material placed first because Wales was where such combined poems were preserved. The northern material is found at the heart of a number of the other Myrddin poems, and Welsh material is used as a frame, or added at the end of stanzas, possible signs of its later and inserted status.

In "Apple Tree" the central stanzas deal with the Cumbrian experience: Jarman says this sequence "may legitimately be regarded as the oldest existing document of the Myrddin legend" (Bromwich and Jarman, 1991, 118). Myrddin thinks of "Battle in Pictland" (21), far in the north of Britain, and he remembers both his warrior past and his present isolation in the Caledonian forest:

> Sweet apple tree that grows beyond Rhun;
> I fought at its base to please a maiden,
> with my shield on my shoulder, with my sword on my thigh,
> and in Celyddon wood I have slept alone. (27–30)

Then, in the stanza quoted above, he remembers Gwenddydd, Gwasawg, and Gwenddolau, from whom he is now separated (35–46), and specifies a major element of his battle trauma:

> …by my hand came the death of Gwenddydd's son (52)

He states his long-lasting position of exile:

> Two score and ten years in outlaw misery
> I have been wandering with madness and madmen.
> After fine belongings and pleasing minstrels…(58–60)

In "Little Pig" the Cumbrian experience is much briefer. Myrddin remembers the heroic life:

> I saw Gwenddolau as a glorious lord
> gathering plunder on each border.
> Under the bloody earth he now is still,
> chief of the lords of the North, the most generous. (28–31)

The second mention of Cumbria is merely to validate the poem's greater interest in wars in Wales, when Myrddin says:

> After the battle of Arfderydd, it would not interest me
> though the sky fall and the sea flood. (214–15)

Finally Myrddin's battle-trauma is used as validation for the statement about the Welsh future that "war will come to Dyfed, to you" (219).

In much the same way the whole of the long poem "Myrddin and Gwenddydd" has two figures of the Old North, Myrddin and his sister, debate and predict the Welsh warrior future against the Anglo-Saxons. The Cumbrian context is remembered: he says "I will tell it, from Rheged" (62); she says "I am sick because of the battle of Arfderydd" (229). Myrddin was "eminent in battles," a phrase recurring through the poem, but is now "a pale wild wanderer" (38); he still has his knowledge, being "chiefest of fame for genius" (96).

In "Myrddin in the Grave" the Old North is only remembered at the very end: after many varied statements about "red blood on the cheeks of Saxons" (21) Myrddin recalls his Cumbrian experience, apparently to validate his voice as "the judgment of the North," that

> Gwasawg, I was told your cry to Gwenddydd
> by the mountain madmen in Aber Craf. (21–23)

There seem signs through this material that the later the poem, the less mention is made of the Cumbrian Myrddin, and his antiquity is increasingly used as a validation of the Wales-based Myrddin material. So it seems odd that "Commanding Youth," the latest recorded of these poems, is the one that deals most with the north, though not only Cumbria. The setting of this poem is after Arfderydd: Gwenddydd and Gwasawg are mentioned as present, but there is only "the memory of Gwenddolau and his companions" (32), and Gwenddydd says:

> Myrddin will come, with great purpose,
> because of the killing of my brothers and Gwenddolau (48–49)

The central recurring reference is to "renowned Aeddan," Aedan Mac Gabrain, a late sixth-century Scottish Gaelic king of Dalriada in southwestern Scotland: it seems that he is to fight Rhydderch, and the "commanding youth," a young warrior born to rule, is being urged to join this battle. The poem ends by asserting that "Myrddin sang it," and this is clearly the Cumbrian exile: he says

> Time was once I sat in a court;
> my body-covering was red and purple.
> And today fair is neither my cheek nor my body;
> a comely maiden easily ignores me. (40–43)

Late as its recording is, it is quite conceivable that this poem preserves early heroic material. Perhaps this is a result of oral transmission, like the late-recorded heroic poems of the historical Taliesin for the court of King Urien; or perhaps, as if in historical fiction, the poem re-creates the world of the Cumbrian Myrddin, which had been by then almost forgotten in favor of his role as a prophet of wished-for victory against the Anglo-Saxons.

There are other traces of the Cumbrian story from the early period. The idea of a prince who has been traumatized in battle and takes to the wild, even to madness, is well known in Celtic tradition, and the Myrddin story, through its connection to Arfderydd, seems to be the earliest. A well-known parallel is the Irish story of Suibhne Geilt, "Sweeney the Wild," who went mad after the battle of Magh Rath in the year 637. *Buile Suibhne* ("The Madness of Sweeney," 1913), in prose and fine poems, survives in a twelfth-century Irish manuscript, and appears to have been composed by the ninth century. It has had modern resonance in Flann O'Brien's novel *At Swim-Two-Birds* (1939) and provides the central figure of T. S. Eliot's "Sweeney Agonistes" and "Sweeney Astray" by Seamus Heaney.

Fuller evidence of the Cumbrian Myrddin's critique of power appears in a Scottish, that is Gaelic, version of the figure. Preserved in writing about the life of the sixth-century Glasgow-based Saint Kentigern are several versions of a story about a wild exile, but he is here called Lailoken, spelled in various ways.[7] He is said to be a fool who lived at the court of King Roderch (Rhydderch in another form); he had, like Myrddin, lived "like some furious savage" and also "was the cause of slaughter" at a battle fought "between Liddel and Carwinlow"—the location of Arfderydd (Forbes, 1874, 118, 371). The stories of Myrddin and Lailoken seem very similar in basis, and so the difference of the central name invites explanation. Scholars have speculated that Lailoken is a name of Gaelic origin (Jarman, 1939; Clarke, 1973, 194–95; Forbes, 1874, 371), and this would imply the Scots gave their own name to the hero of the noble exile myth, as did the Irish with Suibhne. Jarman believes there were two differently named heroes and "each had existed separately and independently in Scottish and Welsh tradition for several centuries before their relationship was perceived" (Bromwich and Jarman, 1991, 123). Rachel Bromwich, however, was less certain about this explanation, commenting that the name issue is "one of the basic problems of the Myrddin cycle" (1978, 470) and Clarke feels the name "has not been explained convincingly" (1973, 195).

The word "Llallogan," obviously a Welsh equivalent of the name Lailoken, is used on a number of occasions in the Myrddin poems, especially in "Myrddin and Gwenddydd." There the hero's sister addresses him repeatedly as "My famed Llallawg" (25, 31, 55, 88, 109, 115, 155, 162, 170, 176, 184, 264, 270), simply as "Llallawg" (348, 368) and even, revealingly, as "My Llallogan Myrddin" (7). The Welsh word "llallawg," or in diminutive form "llallogan," can mean "friend," and that appears to be its real meaning throughout this poem, but its frequent occurrence in a vocative form means that it can easily be taken as a name.[8] There are other probable examples of descriptive adjectives in Welsh being taken as a name, such as Vortigern, probably a title meaning "great lord" and the similar Rigotamus (Koch 2006, 865), as well as Pendragon, an honorific meaning "chief dragon." It is a real possibility that when Welsh had been largely forgotten in Scotland the story of "Myrddin and Gwenddydd" was remembered and the word Llallogan, perhaps because of its similarity to a Gaelic name, was taken as the hero's name itself.

The Llallogan/Lailoken story adds a series of trickster activities, which will appear in Geoffrey of Monmouth's *Vita Merlini* (to be discussed below), and recur through the tradition. Geoffrey's knowledge of them suggests they were in the early Welsh tradition, but that the brief, allusive nature of the surviving Myrddin poems had no generic room for a humorous form of the superiority of knowledge, whereas the Latin prose narratives did. The Cumbrian Myrddin-Merlin is the first realization of a Celtic nobleman, traumatized in war, whose knowledge presents a natural wisdom critical of the conflicts of human power. This story was known in the three languages of his region, Welsh, incursive Scots Gaelic, and Christian Latin: the future multicultural range of the figure is there from the start as well as the dialectical relation of knowledge and power.

Multicultural multiplicity can seem challenging to national and ethnic identity, even among scholars: the assertion of a separate Scottish wild man story is in itself a form of national appropriation, made by Scottish scholars such as A. P. Forbes and K. H. Jackson (a professor at Edinburgh University who, notoriously, entitled his 1969 translation of the certainly Welsh-language *Gododdin* as "The Oldest Scottish Poem"), and a pair of scholars who, for all their wide learning, had a special interest in Scotland, H. M. and N. K. Chadwick.

Other appropriations can occur. The fact that Myrddin is a figure of early Welsh tradition, coupled with the undoubted historical nature of some of the names in those early texts, has led to the speculation that he himself might be a figure of history, not a mythic hero. As with Arthur defeating the Saxons at Mount Baddon, the undoubted connection of a mythic figure with a historical battle invites empirical identification, and there is a persistent argument that Myrddin was a real prince of the northwest who actually fought at Arfderydd and suffered some kind of breakdown. Reputable scholars have been intrigued by the possibility of a historical Myrddin. Basil Clarke went so far as to speak of "the probably historical tradition" of a "sixth-century fugitive" (1973, viii); and Bromwich argued a case for the authority of the medieval Welsh belief in a historical poet Myrddin, in spite of the fact that his name is not found in the northern genealogies and "no fragment of his poetry appears to have been preserved" (1966; see also 1978, 471). Jarman's final comment was that despite "the strength of the medieval tradition for a historical Myrddin, the arguments against are too strong": unlike the probably historical earliest Welsh poets known as the *cynfeirdd,* "the first bards," Aneirin and Taliesin, Myrddin is not mentioned in the earliest material and there is no surviving poetry attached to his name, only material where he is a character (Bromwich and Jarman, 1991, 140). Medieval Welsh poets re-created him in accordance with their own idea of potent knowledge, poetry itself: for them Myrddin made a triad with Aneirin and Taliesin and they often refer to him (Bromwich, 1978, 471–74).

The issue has reemerged recently in popular writing determined to find, somehow, a "real" origin for a mythic figure, but as this is a modern re-formation of knowledge in the service of the modern power of individual identity, the phenomenon is discussed with other modern Merlin manifestations in Chapter 4. However, past and present popular historicists are far from the only people who have reused the idea of the hero of knowledge to validate their own interests. Myrddin is always being appropriated on behalf of some position, and that process was at work when the Cumbrian Myrddin was turned into a Welshman, serving Welsh interests in the face of conflict, not against other British lords as at Arfderydd, but against the invading Anglo-Saxons.

Prophetic Wisdom: Myrddin of Wales

There were contacts between Wales and the Old North, and regular contact by water between north Wales and southwest Scotland—as Nora Chadwick comments, "the Celtic peoples were habitual seafarers" (1963, 49). But as Jarman asserted, "Though linked in the Middle Ages, the legend of Myrddin and the Welsh prophetic tradition were originally distinct and separate." (Bromwich and Jarman, 1991, 117) The meaning of the Cumbrian Myrddin, the exiled hero of knowledge of the northwest, is in Wales re-created in the context of a new issue of burning interest to the Welsh, a new form of hostile power, the Anglo-Saxon invasions. That relocation would long survive, especially because Myrddin was given a new, and for many across time, convincing relocation. The name of Caerfyrddin (Carmarthen), the ancient capital of Dyfed, southwest Wales, combines *caer,* "castle" (from Latin *castra*) and the name

Myrddin, in its mutated form,[9] to mean "Myrddin's fort." But that is not the original name of the place: the Romans knew it as Moridunum, using the Old Welsh words for sea, *mor,* and fort, *dun,* to describe a hilltop fortress that was near the sea. When the word *caer* was added to the front of the place name (a common practice in the period for fortresses), the sound of the new name suggested a suitable new home for the Cumbrian hero when his stories were being relocated in Wales (Jarman, in Bromwich and Jarman, 1991, 137–38).

A crucial part of the Welsh reuse of Myrddin is to make him a prophet, encouraging the Welsh in their difficulties by predicting the defeat of the Anglo-Saxons and the eventual reconquest of Britain by the British. This use of knowledge is associated with bards, who proclaimed both the past grandeur and the even greater future glory of their lordly patrons, and Myrddin was re-created by medieval Welsh poets, like Taliesin and indeed themselves, as a far-seeing bard (Rowland, 2003, 43). The medievalized bardic Merlin will surface, linked with potent nature, in a much later and vaguer form in Romanticism (European and American rather than English), but in the early Welsh period, before the poetic development, Myrddin's prophecies are specific, and entirely supportive of the community his knowledge now serves. Myrddin of Caerfyrddin is basically a propagandist: the power he challenges is that of the Germanic invaders, not that of his own Celtic lords like the Cumbrian exile. This oscillation between criticizing and supporting local power is another feature that will recur through the whole myth, right to the present.

Prophecy had been a part, if not an emphasized one, of the Cumbrian Myrddin's capacity. In the late-recorded "Commanding Youth" Myrddin says to Gwenddydd, "when the light of day comes, there shall be prophecy" (18). With more emphasis, "Myrddin and Taliesin" ends:

> Since it is I, Myrddin, in the mode of Taliesin,
> my prophecy will be right. (37–38)

But this is a broader wisdom than the political vision that Wales gives to Myrddin. His Welsh prophecies are detailed and anti-Saxon. In "Apple Tree" the thoughts described above about Myrddin's Cumbrian situation are preceded by his Wales-based visions of the future and, in the opening stanza, by heroic triumphs against the invaders that could be spoken by a bard in any heroic culture:

> Rejoicing to the Welsh, very great battles,
> quick swords defending Cyminod,

death to the Saxons on ashen spears
and playing ball-games with their heads
and I will speak the truth without a lie,
a youth shall rise in the region of the South. (7–12)

Cyminod, near Trefdraeth, in Môn (Anglesey), in north Wales, is frequently named in the poems as a Welsh heartland, but a pan-Wales connection is implied when the young savior of the future—Mab Darogan, "the son of prophecy" well-known in Welsh tradition—is located in the south. This general prediction of a coming savior, conveniently unnamed, is mixed with real Welsh successes against the Saxons:

When Cadwaladr comes to his meeting at Rhydd Rheon,
Cynan before him advancing on the Saxons,
the Welsh will prevail; splendid their prince,
all will gain their rights; glad the honor of the British,
horns of delight will be sounded,
a song of peace and fair weather. (84–89)

Cadwaladr (d. 682) was the historical last king of the Welsh: though in fact less successful than his father Cadwallon, he was long remembered as a great leader and potential savior; Cynan, who is often coupled with him in these and later prophetic poems, is usually taken to be Cynan Meriadoc, also known as Conan, the great hero of the Bretons, though there are also some historical Welsh heroes named Cynan, notably the sixth-century Cynan Garwyn, prince of Powys.[10]

Cadwaladr and Cynan recur in the Welsh Myrddin prophecies, but as these poems were handed down the prophecies could also be updated, as in "Little Pig," which answers "fear of five leaders from Normandy" (33) by reference to

Llywelyn his name, of the lineage of Gwynedd,
the man who will overcome (8–9)

This prophecy celebrates Llywelyn, the last independent Prince of Wales, whose real successes against the English led to his eventual betrayal and murder in 1282, at Welsh hands on behalf of Edward I, who made his infant son Prince of Wales, a real political appropriation of power which has survived, not un-resented, to the present.

That tragic defeat is not foreseen in the poem: rather its recurrent tone is prophetic triumph:

> When Cadwaladr comes to conquer Môn
> Saxons will be driven from the lands of Britain. (152–53)

Not all is so world-shaking: the prophecy is often detailed, even obsessive, like an optimistic history lesson:

> And I will prophesy the battle on the Iddon,
> and the battle of Machafwy, and the battle of Afon,
> and the battle of Cors Mochno, and the battle in Môn,
> and the battle of Cyminod, and the battle of Caerleon,
> and the battle of Aber Gwaith, and the battle of Ieithon
> and when Dyfed may be made a borderland for stags
> a youth will rise, good for the Britons. (174–80)

Some of these references apparently refer to fighting against invaders—there were several battles in Môn against the Irish and possibly linked to that type of conflict is Cors Mochno, or Fochno, in west-coast Ceredigion; to the east Iddon is probably a river near the Anglian border in Montgomeryshire, and the Ieithon further south in Radnorshire. Other references are less specific: "the battle of Afon" just means "the battle at the river," Aber Gwaith just means "the estuary battle." It may be deliberate, a form of national self-consciousness that the references, like the setting of the four branches of the *Mabinogi,* cover the whole of Wales (see fig. 1).[11]

While this material concerns the trials of the early Welsh, knowledge as prophetic encouragement moves further forward with a reference in "Myrddin in the Grave" to the late eleventh-century and William Rufus:

> When the red one of Normandy comes
> to confront the English (17–18)

And the poem looks further to the future, though hardly with confidence, when it finally refers to a medieval King Henry, probably Henry II and his son, "the young king" who never succeeded him, making war across south Wales:

> And I will prophesy after Henry,
> a king who is no king, distress will come

> when there is a bridge on the Taf and the Tywi
> war will come to Dyfed, to you. (216–19)

Prophetic knowledge can merge into a forward-looking version of geneal-
ogy: in the long poem "Myrddin and Gwenddydd" in response to his sister's
questions Myrddin provides a lengthy account of the future Welsh princes,
including Cadwaladr and Cynan and coming up to the very early fifteenth
century with Owain Glyndŵr, "who will conquer as far as London" (229–30),
but also moving back and forwards through Welsh history, with occasional
triumphs and many defeats.

The Welsh past can also be detailed. The first part of "Myrddin and Taliesin," dealing only with Wales, refers to a battle where Maelgwn and his
north Wales host fought, apparently against other Welshmen. Killed there
were heroes who are known to be connected with southwest Wales, Elgan
and Dyfel fab Erbin. Maelgwn is very well known in Welsh tradition: he was
lord of Gwynedd, northwest Wales, a mighty sixth-century war leader with
a resplendent legend of his own, indeed one that in Welsh rivals the tradition
of Arthur himself, though unlike him Maelgwn never came into contact with
the wider European world.

It seems in "Myrddin and Taliesin" as if Myrddin is honoring the men of
Dyfed, where he is now localized, while Taliesin speaks on behalf of Maelgwn and his men from north Wales:

> Myrddin:
> So sad I am, so sad,
> because of what happened to Cedfyw and Cadfan.
> There was dazzling, loud battle,
> There was a stained, shattered shield.
> Taliesin:
> I saw Maelgwn fighting:
> his warriors before a great army are not silent. (1–6)

The Welsh appropriation of the Cumbrian Myrddin was not only as a
prophet: it also asserted a strong Christian context for the hero of knowledge.
This is hardly surprising in that writing texts in manuscripts in the Middle
Ages was a function undertaken exclusively by Christians, mostly monks, and
it is notable that the strong emphasis on the value of nature in the Cumbrian
material is much reduced in the later Welsh material: it may have been seen
as inherently pagan. The "Apple Tree" poem indicates clearly the power of
nature in the Cumbrian Myrddin context: each stanza starts by invoking a

"Sweet apple tree": with its "tender blossoms" (47). The tree is a focus of emotional attention and "its special virtue" (83) is evidently a symbol of Myrddin's desocialized natural wisdom. Nature, as a form of consolation, but also a sign of deprivation, is a recurrent theme in early Welsh poetry, and the "Birch Tree" poem is another example, though without specific links to Myrddin. This nature is usually inanimate: M. E. Griffiths comments there is "practically no animal symbolism" in the Welsh prophetic poems (1937, 106).

Though "Little Pig" begins each stanza addressing the animal, this is unusual: the pig is not Myrddin's familiar, just a natural point of reference. The pig appears twice in "Apple Tree," and stags and birds are mentioned in passing in "Little Pig," but compared with the wealth of animals in Welsh folkloric prose, especially *Culhwch ac Olwen,* Myrddin's world is remarkably bare of animal company. This is in part a generic feature of the pared-down tradition of early Welsh and Irish poetry, but it also places emphasis on the human intelligence in a lonely landscape—a hero of knowledge has little in common with animals, his natural context is a form of desocialization.

The Christian emphasis of the Welsh Myrddin is not entirely an innovation: in "Apple Tree" Cumbrian Myrddin laments in Christian terms:

> Oh, Jesus! that my death did not come
> before by my hand came the death of Gwenddydd's son. (52–53)

And he links his exile to Christianity:

> After suffering illness and grief in Celyddon Forest
> may I be a blessed servant to the Lord of Hosts. (64–65)

In "Myrddin and Gwenddydd" Myrddin's sister once clearly links Arfderydd and Christianity:

> My only brother, do not rebuke me
> because of the battle of Arfderydd I am ill.
> I seek advice.
> To God I entrust you. (228–31)

These references are not likely to be all later Christianizing insertions. While it is not certain that around the date of the battle of Arfderydd the British of the northwest were fully Christian, archaeology and history are increasingly aware of the very early spread of Christianity in Britain and Ireland.

Rhydderch Hael, mentioned several times in the poems, was certainly a practicing Christian of the late sixth century. The Taliesin poems linked to the early sixth-century court of Urien have a definite Christian element, notably the *Marwnad Owein* ("Owein's Death-song").

The Christian elements found in the Cumbrian Myrddin material are substantially developed in the Welsh Myrddin material, not always consistently. "Little Pig" offers the prophecy that "monasteries shall arise, not for the unfaithful" (16) in favor of the monks, but "Myrddin and Gwenddydd" has a formal Christian ending that is strongly anti-monastic:

> I entrust ever my brother
> to the best kind of Lord.
> To take communion before death.
> I will not take communion from cursed monks
> with their pouches on their thighs;
> God will commune with me himself.
> I entrust ever my brother
> into the supreme fortress.
> May God care for Myrddin.
> I entrust ever my sister
> into the unfailing fortress.
> May God care for Gwenddydd. (247–58)

Curiously, "Myrddin in the Grave," which is almost fully Welsh, not Cumbrian in its reference, and hence might be expected to be firmly Christian, has no religious ending, though there is a Christian viewpoint in one comment about a future world which is "intent on oaths, evil life and fault in churches" where "faith will be weak" (50–51, 54). "Commanding Youth," the late-recorded heroic poem set in late sixth-century Cumbria, has recurrent Christian references, from "May God protect you from Irish heathens" (2) to its ending, though it is notable that the Christian comments tend to come at the end of the lengthy stanzas, and so might be additions. While it seems that at least some Christian emphasis has been added to these poems during their transmission, it is probable that there had always been a Christian element in the legend of Myrddin, and the re-formation of the figure as a prophet has emphasized and developed that.

In this early period, appropriated and redirected as the Myrddin tradition is in various ways by various interested groups—including the embattled Welsh, devout Christians, those valuing the British prophetic tradition, and even modern Scottish scholars—there is clearly an ancient and mysterious story about an early British Celtic figure who represents disturbing and potent knowledge, who both separates himself from and criticizes the forces of secular power whether lordly Cumbrian or invading Anglo-Saxon, and who stands for the values of nature, isolation, wisdom. Myrddin-Merlin has his roots deep in the turbulent experiences and the imaginative power of Celtic Britain, and like the figure of the tragic monarch Arthur, with whom he will become inescapably involved, his story was transmitted to an ever-widening world by the most imaginative and influential of all the British Celtic writers, Geoffrey of Monmouth.

Wisdom at Court: Geoffrey of Monmouth's Historia Regum Britanniae

Geoffrey of Monmouth's *Historia Regum Britanniae* ("History of the Kings of Britain"), produced by 1138, was one of the most influential books of the medieval world. Most famous for disseminating the story of the British chieftain Arthur in the form of a warrior-king like William the Conqueror, it also, and with the same long-lasting and wide-ranging effect, transmitted the story of Myrddin to Europe at large, and eventually to international culture.

The British antiquarian scholar T. D. Kendrick summed up its impact:

> Within fifteen years of its publication not to have read it was a matter of reproach; it became a respected textbook of the Middle Ages; it was incorporated in chronicle after chronicle; it was turned into poetry; it swept away opposition with the ruthless force of a great epic; its precedents were quoted in Parliament; two kings of England cited it in support of their claim to dominion over Scotland; it was even used to justify the expenditure of the royal household; it became the subject of a noisy battle between modernist and medievalist scholars in the sixteenth and seventeenth centuries; even in the eighteenth century there were antiquaries who believed it to be truthful history, and it is still the subject of study and argument. (1950, 7)

Geoffrey found the visionary wise man Merlin even more interesting than the great king Arthur: towards the end of his life he returned to him in the *Vita Merlini* ("Life of Merlin"), which clearly goes back to the earlier Celtic stories, though, with his characteristic creative energy, Geoffrey added a great deal of other imaginative and intellectual material.

Because he lived in a time from which written records survive, we know that Geoffrey died by 1155 and was for much of his life a member of St. George's College in Oxford—not a teaching institution, nor a monastery, but a site of church service and learning, not all of it religious. Oxford was not yet the site of a formal university, though already an important center for both scholarship and political contacts. In the six surviving documents which Geoffrey signed as a witness he is twice described as *magister*, "master," implying not so much that he had a formal degree but that he was involved in high-level learning and teaching (Salter, 1919).

Four of the documents name him "Geoffrey Arthur": the second was an unusual name at that time and suggests a family interest in British myth—probably his father's given name. Evidently Geoffrey came from Monmouth, a busy town on the border of England and southeast Wales. Though his first name is Norman-French, that does not indicate his origin: many Welsh people, then as now, carried culturally borrowed names. Some scholars have felt that Geoffrey had Breton blood (Lloyd, 1939, 523–24; Tatlock, 1950, 443): there were certainly Bretons in the border area, deployed by the Normans as administrators because their language was close to Welsh, but the idea of Geoffrey's Breton origin stems from his frequent praise of Bretons over the native British—a naïve piece of reasoning, especially about the notoriously self-critical Welsh.

Geoffrey's work shows he knew and valued Welsh tradition; Wright calls him "normanised" (1984, x), and he was one of the scholarly British Celts, including the slightly later Gerald of Wales (who had Norman blood) and Walter Map, who served the new Norman lords of Britain in various intellectual ways. Like the English-educated Indians and Africans who faithfully, if also dividedly, served the British Empire, Geoffrey is in a colonized position and his work is as a result a hybrid mixture of the ancient traditions of Celtic Britain and the interests, and ideologies, of the Norman state. As new kings the Normans could revel in this new national myth that by appropriating and inventing a grandiose British past enabled them to match the dignity their rivals, the kings of France, found in the Charlemagne legend, and also by implication justified their defeat of the anti-British Anglo-Saxons: John Gillingham has summarized Geoffrey's "politics of cultural nationalism" (1991, 101).

The Celto-Norman figure of Arthur is an example of this cultural mix, but Geoffrey's new representation of Myrddin, and especially his new name, is a prime instance of postcolonization hybridity. In early Welsh spelling Myrddin is represented as "Merdin," and to Latinize this as "Merdinus" would produce a name redolent of the French word *merde,* "excrement," as Gaston Paris noted (1883, 375). So Geoffrey neatly revised the name as "Merlinus" to fit his new sociocultural context—and perhaps a little more. Many scholars and most later fiction writers feel that the name refers to the smallest of the European hawks, the merlin. But it is by no means clear that this meaning was known at the time: the Latin world *merula,* which is probably the source, means both bird and fish (modern French *merle,* blackbird and *merlan,* whiting, are both derived from it). It is entirely possible that Geoffrey found a name that suggested both natural liberty and wisdom. There are several bird-like flying shape-shifters in Celtic tradition, including Myrddin's Irish analog Suibhne, and the wisest of all the ancient animals in the Welsh Arthurian story *Culhwch ac Olwen* is a giant salmon. Geoffrey may have imagined Merlin's animal avatar as a winged water-serpent, an epitome of wisdom—and so a dragon, the creature Merlin first encounters and recognizes, perhaps as family.

Geoffrey acknowledges British Celtic sources when he says he was given by Walter, archdeacon of Oxford—himself a canon of St. George's—"a certain very ancient book written in the British language" (1966, 51). He refers twice more to "this little treatise": the second reference comes as he begins to describe Arthur's final battle, in many ways the climax of his story (258), and the third is in the epilogue (only found in some versions), where the book's British nature is reasserted. Scholars have long debated what this source might be. Though Thorpe's "Introduction" does favor the zero-source interpretation (1966, 15, 42–43 n. 18), it also offers a summary of the most probable situation:

> It is now accepted that he had at his disposal something closely related to MS Harl. 3859 in the British Museum, the contents of which are Nennius's *Historia Brittonum* with the *Cities and Marvels of Britain,* the *Annales Cambriae* and the medieval Welsh king-lists and genealogies. (1966, 15)

On the basis of the varied early British sources and his own wider knowledge of Welsh-language material, Geoffrey wove his extraordinary fabulous history. He also had a deep familiarity with both biblical and classical tradition: the narrative makes links to contemporary events in Christian history, and Hammer, who has most closely studied Geoffrey's classical learning, identifies references to twenty-five classical authors (1951, 265–69).

The *History* was probably widely available by 1138, though some scholars think elements of it were in circulation a little earlier. It was very popular—the extraordinary number of seventy-five manuscripts or part-manuscripts survive from the twelfth century itself and over two hundred in all (Crick, 1989): no other nonreligious work of the period had such success.

Most scholars agree that the first part Geoffrey produced was the sequence given over to "The Prophecies" made by his version of Myrddin. This then became a section in the full *History*, which traces the British back to their mythic origin. Deliberately paralleling Virgil, who in the *Aeneid* gave Rome its origin in Troy, Geoffrey relates the escape of the Trojan Brutus (no relation to Caesar's murderer) to the land he named, after himself, Britain. After him there were centuries of development and conflict, especially between members of the royal warrior families, until the at least partly historical story of post-Roman Britain begins, and first Merlin and then Arthur appear so famously on the scene. Those who smile at Geoffrey's apparently naïve imitation of Virgil may not be aware that in Welsh, still, the name Brutus is pronounced "Britis," with a final sound close to "sh." Geoffrey's names are often deep.

In the full *History*, Merlin's "Prophecies" immediately follow the Saxon onslaught on Britain, and after them comes the major British resistance, at first led triumphantly by Arthur, then under later leaders falling into decline and defeat. Merlin's wisdom empowers the British Celtic state at its finest. Geoffrey clearly knows the British Myrddin material—as even Tatlock grudgingly accepted (1950, 173). But Geoffrey also extended the period and range of Merlin's power by adding an entirely different British story about wisdom and prophecy. While the Cumbrian Myrddin was linked to the late sixth century, Geoffrey begins Merlin's career over a hundred years earlier, as a wise boy at the court of Vortigern, the British Celtic ruler who in Welsh tradition, as Gwrtheyrn, both inadvertently assisted and then directly confronted the invading Anglo-Saxons in the mid fifth century.

Geoffrey drew the Vortigern-related material from a Latin prose text called *Historia Brittonum* ("The History of the Britons") which was compiled about the year 830: the work was formerly attributed to a north Welsh monk called Nennius, but scholars now doubt this (Higham, 2002, 119–21). The *Historia Brittonum* includes Irish stories such as the life of St. Patrick, bare historical records—the "Cambrian Annals," fifth-century material from the Kentish chronicle about the Anglo-Saxon invasion, and also the story that Geoffrey combines with the Welsh Myrddin (Morris 1980, 29–31).

In this version, under attack from the Anglo-Saxons, Vortigern builds, at the advice of his wizards, a stronghold in north-west Wales in the area of Eryri—Mount Snowdon. But each night the tower collapses. The wizards say that the blood of a fatherless boy must be sprinkled on the ruins, so Vortigern sends men to find one. In Glywysing, south-east Wales, they hear boys quarrelling and one says to the other "you have no father." His mother tells the envoys she bore the boy, but is still a virgin. They take the boy to Eryri and prepare to kill him. But he challenges the wizards to tell him what is in the stronghold's foundations. They do not know. He says there is a lake down there, with two vessels in it. They find this is so. He asks the wizards what is in the vessels; they do not know. He says there is a cloth in each, and in the cloths two *vermes* sleeping (*vermis* means both "worm" and "dragon"). The dragons fight on the cloth and eventually the red one defeats the white, and they and the cloth disappear. The boy asks the wizards the meaning: they do not know, so he explains that the red worm is "your dragon, the cloth is the world, the white worm is the dragon of the invaders." They "will reach almost from sea to sea but later our people will arise and will eventually throw the English people across the sea." He tells them to leave the fortress as it is unsafe, but he will stay there. In response to Vortigern's question the boy says he is called Ambrosius, that is Emrys Gwledig, "Emrys the Overlord," and his "father is one of the consuls of the Roman people." Vortigern gives him the fortress and the western part of Britain and goes to the north to build a city.

Geoffrey believed the *Historia Brittonum* was compiled by Gildas (Roberts, 1971, xv), an author and bishop of sixth-century Britain, who had both described the situation of his fellow Britons at a time of great danger from invasion, and had also passionately exhorted them to secure their identity and future. There were many reasons why Geoffrey, in similarly critical times for the Welsh, should identify with such a writer and be inspired to use what he thought was his book as an inspiration for his own masterpiece, his own complex response to the British people's loss of power.

The Emrys story combines the folklore motif of the wonderful child and a memory, or fantasy, of Roman-Celtic power in post-Roman Britain (much like the modern English myth of Arthur as a part-Roman war leader, to be discussed below, pp. 201–2). There was a historical Ambrosius, also called Aurelianus, fighting in Britain in the mid to late fifth century, and the still popular Welsh name Emrys goes back to him. The story of Emrys also brings into confrontation a figure of natural wisdom with a royal court marked by hostility and incompetence: there are clear resonances between this situation and the earlier Myrddin tradition, and Geoffrey of Monmouth simply condenses the two, as follows.

King Vortigern has been forced by the invading Saxons into north Wales. There he builds a tower but it keeps collapsing. His wizards say he must sprinkle the blood of a fatherless child on the foundations. He sends men out to search. One group arrives at Carmarthen and finds boys squabbling before the town gate. One named Merlin is abused for not knowing his father. They find his mother is the daughter of the king of Dyfed (Demetia), south-west Wales, and she says a handsome youth appeared to her regularly, and she became pregnant. A man called Maugantius, summoned by Vortigern, asserts this was a diabolic incubus. Taken to north Wales and learning he is to be sacrificed, Merlin asks the wise men what lies beneath the tower's foundation. They are silent. He tells the king there is a pool below, and two hollow stones with dragons sleeping in them. The king has the pool drained and the dragons appear, red and white. They fight and finally the red one wins. Ambrosius Merlin—his full name—laments and prophecies. The red dragon, representing the British, will be at first defeated, but eventually "the downtrodden people," led by "the Boar of Cornwall," will triumph. But there will follow trouble: he gives apocalyptic prophecies, many involving symbolic animals. Among these some are political: the Germanic (white) dragon will be assailed by "a nation dressed in wood and iron corselets" (the Normans) and Cadwallader and Conan will defend the British. But many prophecies are only vaguely symbolic—floods and fires will occur, the Forest of Dean will arouse all Wales and Cornwall, or just mysterious—a hedgehog loaded with apples will rebuild Winchester. Finally large-scale astrological conflict is predicted.

Geoffrey must have known of the Myrddin connection with Caerfyrddin, not mentioned in the surviving early Myrddin poems: as he does not call him Myrddin it would seem very odd if he had invented the move to that place. But he clearly also knows the Welsh poetic tradition of the prophetic Myrddin because he substantially extends in a mode very similar to the early Myrddin poems the prophecies that Emrys made for Vortigern. He also offers some subtle rehandling of his source. Where Emrys was the son of a virgin and a Roman consul, Geoffrey leaves the fathership in doubt. Merlin's mother reports that "a most handsome young man" came to her in the nunnery often and made love to her. It is Maugantius, one of Vortigern's incompetent advisers, who says that this must have been a diabolic incubus. Every later commentator seems to accept this as true, no doubt influenced by the French treatment of Merlin's diabolic birth, starting with Robert de Boron: even the meticulous translator Thorpe agrees that Merlin is "the soothsayer son of an incubus" (1966, 20). But Geoffrey leaves it quite possible that Merlin's father is in fact an angel, or at least the child is like the major Welsh saints, David and Dyfrig (Dubricius), both of whom were born to a nun and no known father. In another change Geoffrey specifies this is Dyfed, southwest Wales (not the broader "south Wales" used by many translators and commentators), and so he pushes the story further into Norman-free Welsh Wales than his own by now colonized southeast Wales, where Emrys's Glywysing is to be found. While the source has the two *vermes* inside a cloth inside a vessel, and so makes this sound like an ancient burial with symbolic meaning, Geoffrey more strangely—perhaps even alchemically—has the dragons magically embedded in hollow stones and then a supernatural event taking place as they fight in the lake.

This story has been so influential that the red dragon has become the symbol of Wales: but the origin of the dragon motif in Geoffrey's source is less clear. As the vases suggest a burial, it appears that these dragons, like Fafnir in the Sigurthr story and the dragon that Beowulf climactically fights, are versions of the serpents that in many traditions, Eastern and well as Western, guard a great treasure and must be defeated by the hero, often, as with Hercules, when very young.

The Welsh Myrddin tradition and other Welsh political prophecy, like that in the *Armes Prydein,* are now known to predate Geoffrey, so he is evidently, as Roberts notes, developing this Welsh material in a post-Conquest context (1971, xxxvi): Echard comments "this is the stuff of Welsh nationalist prophecy" (2005, 21), but projected into the Norman Middle Ages. Some scholars in the past doubted Geoffrey's capacity to do this, either feeling the text's innate difficulty implies a misunderstood source, as Griffiths argues (1937, 59), or in Tatlock's case, simply out of skepticism that Geoffrey could produce something so "fanciful" as the "Prophecies" (1950, 407). But it is now held not only that Geoffrey produced the entire "Prophecies," but that he published them, like a trailer, before the *History* was complete. This was first argued by Faral (1927, 10–11), and Meehan has recently claimed that a version of the "Prophecies" was available several years before the *History* appeared (1980). The separate status of the "Prophecies" is indicated in the text of the *History* by a new dedication to Alexander, bishop of Lincoln—who would have been Geoffrey's superior, as Oxford was then in the diocese of Lincoln.

Geoffrey recognizes his artistic power in his own text: having made Merlin resolve the problem of the crumbling fortress, he says, at the opening of his new chapter on "The Prophecies of Merlin": "I had not yet reached this point in my story when Merlin began to be talked about very much, and from all sorts of places people of my own generation kept urging me to publish his Prophecies" (1966, 170).

Geoffrey says he is translating the "Prophecies" from "the British tongue into Latin" (170). Presumably a separate version of the "Prophecies" alone would have started with the discovery of Merlin, but this has already occurred in the *History* and the book of "Prophecies" begins with the battle of the dragons and Merlin's extended visions. The "Prophecies" start with a sign of Merlin's capacity to act as a medium for an external prophetic spirit, a point Geoffrey makes several times. This changes his role as a producer of prophetic knowledge to something like that of a medium, a priest of knowledge, not a direct source of it. Not a feature of the Welsh Myrddin poems, this may simply be using the priesthood as a model of the transmission of knowledge. It appears in the action: when Vortigern asked him what the dragons meant "Merlin immediately burst into tears. He went into a prophetic trance, and then spoke as follows" (171).

The red and white dragons signify the British and the Anglo-Saxons; the latter will win but the British "shall prevail in the end" and the Boar of Cornwall will "trample their necks beneath its feet" but its "end will be shrouded in mystery" (171–72). This clearly refers to Arthur, born as he will be in Cornwall, and the boar was the biggest and boldest of the British wild animals of the period. For over ten more pages the prophecies follow—conflict in Britain involves mysterious figures like "the German Dragon," "The Prince of Brass," "the She-Lynx of Normandy," "the Boar of Commerce," "the Ass of Wickedness." The symbolic animals are radically different from the Welsh Myrddin tradition, and Tatlock links this to Old Testament symbolic prophecies (1950, 407), but there are still continuities with the earlier British material. Cadwaladr and Conan reappear, and there are many battles, terrible events, natural disasters, and a conclusion of astrological and climactic apocalypse ending with:

> In the twinkling of an eye the seas shall rise up and the arena of the winds shall be opened once again. The winds shall do battle together with a blast of ill-omen, making their din reverberate from one constellation to another. (185)

Among this wide range of tones and topics, Eckhardt (1982, 41) identified five separate themes, each of about the same length:

The Red and White Dragons
The Normans
The Succession of Symbolic beasts
The Restoration of Celtic rule
The Apocalyptic Conclusion

These prophecies were widely translated, long remembered and often reinterpreted: for example, a fifteenth-century English version, among many other details, identifies "The Man of Brass" as Cadwaladr's father Cadwallon,

"The German Dragon" as the Anglo-Saxon King Egbrit, "the Lion of Justice" as Henry I, and "the Lamb of Winchester" as Henry III (Eckhardt, 1982, 43–44). From this exotic material stems the long-standing tradition of Merlin as a political and all-purpose visionary, which lasts into the eighteenth century. In the *History,* though, Vortigern is merely amused by "the young man's wit and his oracular pronouncements" (186) and asks for clarification of his own future, which is grim indeed. Merlin predicts that, after the king's own "violent death" (172), the history of the British will continue with the arrival of the brothers Uther Pendragon and Aurelius Ambrosius (the latter, in Welsh form as Emrys, had been Geoffrey's own partial source for Merlin). At this point Merlin leaves the story, and the wars against the Anglo-Saxons continue as he predicted.

But Geoffrey has much more for Merlin to do. After these events occur, Aurelius wants to build a monument to the men who have died in his battles and decides that only "Merlin, the prophet of Vortigern" can achieve this: Merlin is found among the Gewissei, at Galabes Spring "where he often went" (196). Tatlock locates this in Gwent, southeast Wales (1950, 74–75). He is brought to Aurelius. He refuses to predict the future as there is no "urgent need" and if he did that "the spirit which controls me would forsake me in the moment of need" (196). But he suggests that as Aurelius wishes to build a monument to the men fallen in the war he should bring from Ireland "the Giants' Ring" (196) from Mount Killare. The king laughs at the idea. Merlin says they are valuable healing stones, moved in the past from Africa by giants. Uther and an army go for the stones, with Merlin's advice. Uther's army defeats the Irish and attempts to move the stones. After they fail, Merlin himself laughs and "with "all the gear he considered necessary" (198) moves the stones to Britain. Geoffrey sums up that Merlin so proved "that his artistry was worth more than any brute strength" (198).

Here Geoffrey develops crucial and long-lasting elements of the politics of the myth of Myrddin. He may be like a priest of knowledge, but he is a discerning and critical one, not simply at the beck and call of a king, however powerful. He decides when to prophesy and when to use his special knowledge on behalf of the secular power. It appears that only Geoffrey had the idea of extending Myrddin's fairly limited Welsh wisdom into the wider knowledge of science and engineering, itself linked closely to power at a time when the Normans were building stone castles all over Britain. Geoffrey suggests that great lords are particularly reliant for their own continuing power not on their own soldiers but on men of special gifts—Merlin is a supreme engineer, and his supremacy is symbolized by the mysterious power of the ancient

British who built Stonehenge and nearby Amesbury: Geoffrey no doubt thought of them as Celts, as many did afterwards. That the stones of Aurelius's monument come from Ireland in itself implies a greater realm of Celtic power, and also seems to re-create the Welsh myths of war in Ireland, like that fought by Bran the Blessed in the second branch of *The Mabinogi.* The Celticity of this scientific power is confirmed by the presence at Amesbury of the major Welsh saints Sampson and, Latinized as Dubricius, Dyfrig. But Merlin's power is not magic, it relies on a mastery of engineering "gear"—an early illuminator of the scene shows him as a mason, not a wizard (fig. 2).

A mysterious force of knowledge, close to royal authority but not cowed by its power, Merlin has one more role to play in Geoffrey's story—to usher onto the stage of British mythic history the unforgotten figure of King Arthur. This is the major strategic purpose of Geoffrey's use and augmentation of the Myrddin tradition in his *History.* Merlin has prophesied Arthur as "the Boar of Cornwall" and when a mysterious dragon-shaped comet appears before Uther's army, Merlin interprets its arrival as indicating the death of Aurelius Ambrosius but also in its dragon shape as foreshadowing Uther's son "who will be a most powerful man" (201).

2. Merlin builds Stonehenge without magic. From Wace, *Roman de Brut,* British Library Egerton MSS 3028. By permission of the British Library.

In the birth of this son, Merlin will play a major role. Uther desires the wife of Gorlois, Duke of Cornwall, "the most beautiful woman in Britain" (205) and presses his attentions on her, so Gorlois takes Ygerna to his distant fortress. With "a huge army" (205) Uther attacks Cornwall: Gorlois leaves Ygerna safe in Tintagel and himself fortifies Dimilioc, a short distance away—Geoffrey evidently knew the geography of this area, distant from England but, by water, quite close to Monmouth. Royal military power is useless, but Merlin's knowledge can find a way: "By my drugs I know how to give you the precise appearance of Gorlois" (206–7). Knowledge, not magic, is stressed: Tatlock even argues it may be just a matter of disguise and make-up (1950, 363). So "The King spent that night with Ygerna and satisfied his desire by making love with her" and "That night she conceived Arthur, the most famous of men" (207).

At this climactic moment of his whole *History,* Geoffrey dispenses with Merlin's services. Later writers will continue his career to the very end of Arthur's reign and even beyond, but Geoffrey's Merlin merely foresees the end of Celtic British power and predicts a later renewal of Welsh power in Britain: this "British hope" will fascinate the Welsh poets and even prove useful to some English kings. The idea briefly emerges at the very end of the *History* when Geoffrey says that "God did not wish the Britons to rule in Britain any more, until the moment should come which Merlin had prophesied to Arthur" (282). In fact Merlin never meets Arthur in Geoffrey's story, and this late comment may suggest a second thought on Geoffrey's part which he never went back to realize in the narrative—though one Welsh translation of the *History* actually corrects the text at the appropriate point, and Merlin does make this prophecy to Vortigern (Thorpe, 1966, 282–83 n. 1).

Merlin leaves the *Historia,* it seems, because his task is done: the special British prince, Arthur, can take the stage, and the future British role in history is foreseen. Where the Welsh Myrddin was a politicized and nationally focused version of the Cumbrian exile and thinker, both of them negative to power in their different ways, Geoffrey's Merlin has become closer to royal power itself. Geoffrey's merging of Myrddin and Ambrosius, which might be seen as simply a bold transhistorical fiction, is actually a condensation of the key roles of knowledge, both outside and inside the domain of power. Much will flow from this formation in the tradition, and it may well be that this is also why here, as often in the future, Merlin leaves the text early. How could the story be a tragedy, for Britain or for Arthur, if he were there, with good advice, to the end? And conversely, how could power, which acknowledges its need of wisdom—including by sponsoring texts like this—accept the continued and powerful presence of knowledge? Geoffrey not only creates a masterpiece of European literature and a source for story for centuries: he also encapsulates dialectically the two key elements of the Merlin tradition, the power of his knowledge and the difficulty of his engagement with power.

Geoffrey also spoke to his own twelfth-century context, in part by denigrating the Saxons, now an under-race to the dominant Normans. But more subtly, by using Merlin and then Arthur to realize the glories and also the cessation of Celtic British civilization, and so in a subtle way suggesting to the Norman lords both the possibilities and the limitations of their own authority, Geoffrey had created a text with a contemporary meaning of Arthurian grandeur and tragedy. That potent combination would fascinate a medieval world constantly aware of both the splendor and the fragility of military rule, as well as its reliance on and resistance to the power of knowledge, represented by Merlin.

This might suggest that Geoffrey was not fully committed to the Norman project, in spite of his unctuous dedications and his apparent success among the grandees of feudal Norman Britain. His next work, his fullest treatment of the Myrddin-Merlin tradition, indicates that he retained a deep commitment to the traditions of the British culture he had used and elaborated to create his most successful work. In the *Vita Merlini* he returned to the British Myrddin tradition, in his own characteristically rich and elaborated style.

Twelfth-Century Natural Wisdom: Geoffrey of Monmouth's Vita Merlini

Geoffrey must have finished this work between 1148, when the bishop of Lincoln to whom it is dedicated (formerly another canon of St. George's) took office, and 1155, when Geoffrey died. Basil Clarke, the most recent editor of the text, felt that when Geoffrey became bishop of St. Asaph's in north Wales in 1151 (a limited reward for his efforts), this might have led him to discover some of the Welsh material that he now used much more fully than before (Clarke, 1973, 41–42). But St. Asaph's was often inaccessible, in anti-Norman Welsh hands, and there was, as Wright notes, "no evidence that he ever visited" (1984, x): the dedication stresses Geoffrey's delight at the bishop's election, which implies the event was fairly recent: the most likely date for the *Life* is 1150 or even earlier, such as Parry's suggestion of "about 1148" (1925b, 193).

One striking difference from the representation of Merlin in the *History* is that the *Life* uses much more Myrddin material, including stories that are only preserved about Lailoken. This has led scholars to assume that Geoffrey discovered more about the Celtic sage after writing the *History* and now gave, as it were, an update on the situation (Chadwick and Chadwick 1932, 1:131; Clarke, 1973, viii; Haycock, 2004, 899). This relies on an academic model of knowledge—you deploy all you know at any one time. Writers of fiction are more selective: it is just as likely that Geoffrey previously used only the material that helped him structure Merlin as the buildup to Arthur, selecting from a wide range of details known to him, including, as he indicated at the start of the *History*, Welsh material. Merlin's personal life or trickster identity would have been irrelevant to the politically targeted "Prophecies" of the *History*, just as that material is not used in the early Welsh poems. It is entirely credible that Geoffrey, more like a novelist than an academic, used as much of the British tradition as was relevant to the *History*—and then imagined a place for the rest in his later work.

The other difference from the *History* is the comparative rarity of the *Life*. Only one complete manuscript survives, against over two hundred of the *History*. Six fragments suggest a reasonable number of versions of a twelfth-century work, but this relative paucity has led Clarke to suggest it was not a public work, rather a text passed around among Geoffrey's acquaintance (1973, vii). The fact that it is written in complex Latin poetry suggests it might well have a less limited appeal than the lucid Latin prose of the *History*, yet Tatlock argued, largely because of the later influence of the *Life*, that there was "no reason to doubt that plenty of manuscripts existed in its early years" (1943, 275).

The story is rich and complex, both the summation and the development of the British tradition of Myrddin.[12] It runs as follows.

Merlin was famous as a king and prophet to the people of Dyfed. He and Rhydderch of Cumbria fought with Peredur of Gwynedd against Gwenddolau of Scotland. Though the British eventually beat the Scots, Merlin grieved at the slaughter of "his companions" (55). After burying them he went mad and took to the woods. In winter he suffered, and addressed a wolf, his "dear companion" (59). A traveler heard him lament, and told a man sent to look for Merlin by his sister, Ganieda, wife to Rhydderch. He searched for Merlin and found him on a mountaintop where he was watching the wild creatures. He heard Merlin lamenting the savage winter and sang to him about the grief of Ganieda and Guendoloena, Merlin's wife. Merlin came to himself and returned to Rhydderch's court. They welcomed him, but the crowds at court drove him mad again. The king detained him in chains, and tried to calm him with music. One day the queen entered, and the king took a leaf from her hair. Merlin laughed. The king pressed him for an explanation, and in return for a promise of freedom, he explained—the leaf was there from the queen's encounter with her lover in "the undergrowth" (67). The queen said she would prove Merlin wrong. She had a boy brought in and asked Merlin to predict his death: he would die by falling from a high rock. She had the boy enter again, disguised, and Merlin predicted he would die in a tree. Then she had the boy brought in again, in woman's clothing, and Merlin said "Girl or not, she will die in a river." (69) Believing Merlin a fool, the king was reconciled to his wife. Merlin was determined to leave for the wilds. He said his wife could remarry, if the husband avoided him, and he would attend the wedding "with fine gifts" (73).

After many years, the boy died: when hunting he fell from a rock and was caught in a tree with his body immersed in a river. He died a threefold death as Merlin had predicted. In the forest Merlin realized from the stars and planets that his wife was remarrying. He mounted a stag, drove stags, does, and she-goats in three lines before him and went to court. The bridegroom laughed at the sight: Merlin ripped off the stag's horns and threw them through the man's head, killing him. Merlin was pursued and taken bound to his sister. He was wretched at court and the king had Merlin taken into the marketplace to cheer him up. Merlin laughed at a beggar, then laughed at a man buying new shoes. The king asked why he laughed: he said the beggar was sitting on a treasure, and the man who bought shoes would drown before wearing them. Both statements proved true. Merlin left for the woods, despite his sister's pleading him to stay. He asked her to provide for him a house with seventy doors and seventy windows so he could watch the stars, and seventy secretaries to record his words.

In his house, with his sister visiting him, Merlin prophesies: he foresees the death of Rhydderch, conflict and defeats for the Britons, the coming of the Saxons and Normans and further conflict: he refers back to his earlier prophecies to Vortigern and asks his sister to send Taliesin to him, who has returned from Brittany where he has been studying with Gildas. Ganieda goes home and finds Rhydderch dead: she mourns.

Taliesin visits Merlin and first, at his request, explains wind and rain, at some length. From explaining the role of the sea he goes on to describe fish types, then the topography of Britain and, briefly, other places, ending with the Island of Apples, where Morgen and her eight sisters cured Arthur after Camlan. Merlin and Taliesin discuss British history, and Merlin reviews the conquest by the Saxons, the role of Arthur and the aftermath.

Suddenly they are told a new spring has broken out; they go to it. Merlin is made sane by the spring, and praises God. Taliesin explains types of health-giving waters around the world. Chieftains and leaders come to see the new spring, and Merlin is asked to resume his kingship. He says he is too old and will remain happily in the forest of Calidon. Merlin explains the nature of many birds. Then a madman appears: Merlin knows him as Maeldin, a Welsh prince: he was driven mad by eating poisoned apples meant for Merlin (by a rejected lover). The spring water heals Maeldin, who decides to stay with Merlin, as does Taliesin. They are joined by Ganieda. She at times prophesies—about Oxford and Lincoln beset by soldiers and government, and apocalyptic horrors through Britain. Merlin comments that she is chosen to foretell the future, and the spirit "has curbed my tongue and closed my book." (135)

This summary abbreviates the scholarly description of the natural world provided by both Taliesin and Merlin, which Geoffrey, in the spirit of twelfth-century humanism, draws from a wide range of Latin scholars, using as his main source the early seventh-century authority on the natural world, Isidore of Seville (Parry, 1925a, 20). That the *Life* links with the Myrddin tradition is clear—M. E. Griffiths only saw "a resemblance" (1937, 68) but the Chadwicks were "convinced" of the link (Chadwick and Chadwick, 1932, 1:108, 126): both Parry and Clarke, editors of the *Life,* take the same view (Clarke, 1973, 2–3; Parry, 1925b, 194). Geoffrey makes no claim to have a specific British source as he did in the *History* (perhaps because poetry tends not to claim sources as history does), but much in the *Life* makes it clear that he was familiar with material like that found in the Myrddin poems and also with stories recorded about Lailoken. What form the latter came to him in is a puzzle. Such detailed narratives do not occur in the condensed, lyrical form of early Welsh poetry, and Geoffrey must have known them through prose, either Welsh or Latin. Both Clarke and the Chadwicks felt that he must have somehow had access to a learned Glasgow source (Clarke, 1973, 42; Chadwick and Chadwick, 1932, 1:126), but Parry argues convincingly for a version of the story in all the surviving Celtic languages (1925b, 198), and if, as argued above, the Lailoken story is just a renamed Scots Gaelic version of the full Myrddin myth, it is just as likely that this material was preserved in Welsh with the name of Myrddin attached to it, and was available to Geoffrey.

From the start of the *Life* there are variations from the account found in both the Welsh Myrddin poems and the Lailoken material. In interpreting these, it must be remembered that the versions of the poetic material Geoffrey knew might well have been different in details from what has survived in

Wales, and the Lailoken-related material has in its surviving forms been re-used for the purpose of aggrandizing Saint Kentigern. Nevertheless it seems possible to discern several areas where Geoffrey's imagination has been at work to appropriate the preexisting Myrddin story to his own Merlin and his own interests.

The politics of the battle of Arfderydd and Merlin's own position are new in the *Life*. As in the *History*, he is from Dyfed, southwest Wales, not a lord of the Cumbrian northwest, and now he is in league with Welsh princes: Peredur, king of Gwynedd, northwest Wales (who will return in romance as Perceval), leads the battle against Gwenddolau, who is here seen as a Scot and therefore Gaelic, not, as the Cumbrian poetry implies, a Welsh-speaking ruler of the Old North and Myrddin's overlord. Also fighting against the Scots is Rodarcus, the Latinized version of Rhydderch, here transplanted from his historical Strathclyde across the modern Scottish border to be king of Cumbria. The Chadwicks thought these variations arose because Geoffrey was being "vague" (1932, 1:126), but it is clear that this reorganization of the politics of the Myrddin tradition is being made from a medieval Welsh view-point: the Scots have become enemies and Gwenddolau, in spite of his Brit-ish name, has become their leader. Myrddin has been transplanted to south Wales as a prophetic quasi-bard, completing the process of appropriation to Wales visible in the poems, and the north Welsh Peredur completes a Welsh alliance with the Rhydderch of the Old North, as part of this anti-Scottish British Celtic coalition. While it is conceivable that such a process might have been made in Geoffrey's sources, these maneuvers are entirely consistent with the imaginative narrative reorganizations for which he was obviously responsible in the *History*, such as the condensing of Emrys and Myrddin into his wide-ranging prophetic hero and also the shaping of Arthur's own coalition.

Whereas in the poems it seems that Myrddin grieves for having himself killed men, notably his nephew, Gwenddydd's son, here he is free of guilt and his grief derives more generally from the slaughter he has seen, principally from the death of "three brothers of the prince" in the battle (55). Geoffrey's complex Latin word-order makes it at first obscure whose brothers they were. As they "had followed him to the war" they must have come from Wales with Myrddin, and *sodales* (54) implies they are from his family. From the self-lacerating family-killer of British myth, Merlin has become in Geoffrey a hero bereft of his brothers. This seems a euphemizing move: Parry argues that the *Life* deliberately rejects the guilty trauma Merlin suffers in the wide-spread Celtic battle-madness story (1925b, 205–6), and Geoffrey's Merlin is a figure of generalized sad knowledge, not a personally traumatized figure like the Cumbrian Myrddin: this distancing and depersonalizing of intense knowledge is parallel to Geoffrey's representation of Merlin in the *History* as a prophetic medium rather than a personal source of prophecy.

That distancing is compensated for by Geoffrey's interest, in the *Life* at least, in Merlin's semimythical trickster capacities, realizing the earlier Celtic figure recorded in the Lailoken material. A major element in this formation is the new character, Guendoloena, Merlin's wife. Ganieda, the Gwenddydd of the poems, is still his sister and is still married to Rhydderch, but Guendoloena plays an important role. As Lloyd suggested (1939, 527 n. 161), it sounds as if she has been invented from the name of Gwenddolau (here itself Latinized as Guennolous). There is a Guendoloena in the *History,* but she was a warlike queen of early Cornwall: Clarke's suggestion that Merlin's wife is linked to the Welsh "Gwen Teir Bronn," "Fair one with three breasts," seems very unlikely (1973, 186). The creation of Guendoloena both enables Merlin to mourn like a classical hero separated from his wife and also, with Geoffrey's typical flair for condensation, permits him to introduce later on the strange story of her second marriage.

When Merlin causes trouble at his former wife's wedding he in part plays the mysteriously contradictory role of a trickster. But, with his lines of creatures he resembles the lord of the animals, the threatening yet friendly figure whom Arthurian knights like Yvain meet on their self-testing and self-proving journeys, and Jung and von Franz have developed this scene in a symbolic and alchemical direction (1986, 357–60). But in riding a stag and using its horns to kill the bridegroom he also seems to reference Cernunnos, the god-figure of at least largely Celtic origin (Koch, 2006, 857), represented on a silver cauldron preserved in Denmark from the second or first century BC. He both bears horns himself and also has beside him a stag with the same horns (fig. 3). It may not be accidental that the horned god's other animal familiar is a ram-headed serpent, representing wisdom.

This incident, without trace in the earlier material, whether about Myrddin or Lailoken, and redolent of the mythic world of ancient Celtic story, is a cumulation of Geoffrey's deployment of the teasing tricksterism of Merlin found in the Lailoken stories. In disrupting a royal marriage he actually assaults the court and its rituals, but in an earlier sequence he disrupts the order of another royal marriage when he identifies the source of the leaf in the hair of his sister Ganieda, telling King Rhydderch that the leaf got there while she was making love with her paramour in the forest. The insight of Merlin, and even the incursive role of the forest, are signs of the challenge that his special

3. Cernunnos the Horned God on the Gundestrup Cauldron. Courtesy Lennart Larsen, the National Museum of Denmark, Copenhagen.

wisdom makes to secular power: centuries ahead the image will intrigue the German Romantics.

Ganieda, to discredit Merlin's analysis of the origin of the leaf, arranges a cunning test of his powers which leads him to predict three different deaths for the same boy, the last two times when he is disguised. The text neatly suggests Merlin's command of the situation: on the third occasion, when the boy is "in woman's clothing looking like a girl," Merlin describes him crisply as *Virgo nec ne,* "Girl or not" (68, 69). And of course Merlin's foresight comes true as, in a memorable sequence, the boy is killed simultaneously by falling from a rock, hanging from a tree, and drowning in a river.

Geoffrey has strengthened Merlin's challenge to secular royal power by inserting his weird, stag-related violence and transmitting the story of his detective powers and the boy's threefold death. Merlin's tricksterish knowledge is less challenging and more entertaining in the incident of the poor man who, known only to the seer, is sitting on a treasure and the gruesome detail of the man who buys shoes only to make Merlin laugh as he foresees his death by drowning, with the shoes never worn. In all these cases, and notably that of the leaf in the queen's hair, Merlin's laugh is important. In the mournful, highly charged context of the Welsh Myrddin poems, this feature is never found—nor is there laughter, even ironic laughter, in the other early Welsh poetry.

Through his deployment of and evident relish in the trickster stories, Geoffrey has substantially intensified the challenge that Merlin's knowledge makes to existing power and its systems of authority. Whether this is due to his own position as a clerical scholar, as a colonized servant, or just as a wit and free spirit, is not clear—probably all three are involved—but this essentially comic intensification of the conflict between knowledge and power is something that enlivens his text and reverberates through the tradition down to the present.

In a range of ways Geoffrey redirects what came to him in the Myrddin tradition, often in the light of and with the use of other Celtic materials, but perhaps his boldest piece of development is Taliesin's role. Presumably stimulated by the short poem that made their conversation a medium of transmitting the Myrddin myth into both Wales and prophecy, here Geoffrey presents the two wise men as a combined force of intellectual authority among the Celts. Taliesin had his own developed tradition as a mysterious magical figure: the *Chwedl Taliesin,* "The Story of Taliesin," does not survive in prose before the sixteenth century, but it evidently transmits the ancient folkloric development of the probably historical bard of early sixth-century Rheged into the first and greatest of the Welsh prophetic heroes, still a name of power in Wales. He has remained an authority for myth-interested writers, whether off-stage as in Tennyson's *Idylls of the King* or, in the hands of especially learned authors like Thomas Love Peacock and Charles Williams, actually replacing Merlin as the major Celtic prophet.

For Geoffrey, Merlin is the senior: he asks his sister to send for Taliesin as "I have much I wish to discuss with him" (89), but Taliesin is a young scholar who "has only recently returned from Brittany, where he has been enjoying the sweets of learning under the wise Gildas" (89). Gildas was, in Geoffrey's view, the author of his source for the *History* and here, in a parallel role, he is the ultimate authority, via Taliesin, who enables Geoffrey to inject a good deal of serious contemporary science into the *Life*. It is presumably an accident that Geoffrey's idea of the relative ages of Merlin and Taliesin fits closely to their notional historical identities in Cumbria and Rheged.

On Taliesin's arrival, we are told, Merlin "had sent for him to learn what winds and rain-storms were" (91), and on this topic (still of great interest to the British), Taliesin discourses at length. For several pages he describes the Creator's plans for weather, moving from the climatic effects of the sea to some unusual fish, and then on to other aquatic features—springs, rivers, islands in Britain and beyond. Finally he comes to "The Island of Apples," which, as the Welsh for apple is *afal,* is undoubtedly a reference to the region that became known as Avalon, usually identified as the formerly water-surrounded site of Glastonbury (see Bromwich, 1978, 267–68). While he begins with the beauty of the place, Taliesin moves quickly on to its famous inhabitants, nine ruling sisters, led by the most beautiful and the most skilled at healing, named Morgen: she is a shape-shifter, capable of flying, learned in astrology, and—as the *History* has already said—it was to Avalon that Arthur was taken after his final battle. This is of course the enchantress, at various times Arthur's sister, half-sister, lover, enemy, and finally his carer, usually known in the French mode as Morgan La Fée. As Clarke points out (1973, 203), her function in the narrative is to link the Emrys-Merlin of Arthur's time to the Myrddin-Merlin of the later period. He feels that in this context she "seems Geoffrey's invention" (1973, 203), and he canvasses a range of possible origins of the name.

There was an Irish queen Mugan, wife to King Conchobar of Ulster, who was in part a learned shape-shifter, but she seems to play no role in Welsh consciousness and the name is crucially different in lacking what would have been a strongly pronounced consonantal *r.* A closer possibility seems the Irish water spirit Muirgein (both in Irish and Welsh her name signifies "born of the sea"); Clarke favors her as the source of Geoffrey's Morgen, but she was not a healer and ended under Christian protection. Loomis argued for Morgan's relationship both to the Welsh "mother-goddess" Modron and to a figure exercising both more power and more malice, the Irish Morrígan, whose name appears to mean "great queen" and who was the ultimate enemy of the great Irish hero Cúchullain (1949, 51, 91, 270–73, 310). Bromwich has questioned the relation to Modron (1978, 471), but Morrígan, both healer and killer, seems the ultimate source for the range of powers that gather in the developed Arthurian myth under the name Morgan.[13] Geoffrey, like some early French romance writers, did not envisage her as the hostile figure who would haunt Arthur and the later romantic imagination. She is the climax of Taliesin's scholarly disquisition, and yet another initiating moment in Geoffrey's rich gathering of mythic possibilities that his inheritors made so much of in narrative terms.

After this, taking the cue of the reference to Arthur, Merlin gives an extensive summary of the Arthurian period as outlined in the *History,* so firmly linking the *Life* to Geoffrey's masterpiece, and then he visits a newly emerged spring. He praises God, part of the recurrent Christian theme of the *Life,* and then asks Taliesin, the water expert, to explain the power of this spring. As

Goodrich has commented, Taliesin's discourses do have some "symbolic correspondences to events during Merlin's life" (1990, 72), notably his exposure to weather and his being healed by a spring. But basically the spring has a narrative function: the widely spreading story of its power brings "chieftains and other leaders" (121) to see it. They describe to Merlin the state of affairs in Britain and ask him "to resume his kingly position" (121). He refuses, as he wishes to spend his old age in the Scottish wilderness where "its riches shall be my delight" (121): he has a special interest in birds, and describes them, their origins and capacities at some length, and the classical nature of the learning adds to British birds exotic species like the ostrich and even the mythical phoenix.

The final sequence of the *Life* begins when a madman named Maeldin, formerly known to Merlin as a royal prince, joins Merlin and Taliesin, is healed by the spring, and decides to stay in this idyllic world of wisdom and nature. They are joined by Ganieda, now a widow, who is also "from time to time exalted in spirit to sing of the future of the kingdom" (131–33). She prophesies about Britain and Merlin finally passes to her his gift and mission: "Sister, is it you the spirit has willed to foretell the future? He has curbed my tongue and closed my book" (135). Like a medieval Prospero, he abandons his learned prophetic mission and finally Geoffrey says, before asking the Britons for his own praise, "We have brought the song to an end" (135).

He might well end the poem with satisfaction, having combined the disparate elements of the British myth of Myrddin into a unified narrative, enriched with the natural wisdom of the classical world. Where in the *History* knowledge became involved with authority and so strangely vanished from the world of power, here pure wisdom manages to keep clear of power and so survives to, and beyond, the end. This position can be read in simplistically ideal terms: Howard Bloch has called Geoffrey's Merlin "the patron saint of letters within the Arthurian world" and "as powerful an image of the writer as the Middle Ages produced" (1983, 1, 2). Shichtman and Finke more materially argue that Merlin "illuminates Geoffrey's own anxieties about competition for patronage by focusing attention on the circulation of intellectual property within the Norman political and economic hegemony." (1993, 29–30)

But exile and court life are not the only possibilities: Merlin has a contemporary clerical context, which seems consciously realized in the text. Though Merlin prophesies in a Scottish forest, there is a recurrent strand of Christian fraternity, like that of the scholarly Augustinian canons of Oxford among whom Geoffrey lived. Merlin and his colleagues survive in simple, natural ways, away from the temptations of the world, the court, riches, and the flesh.

When Merlin rejects his sister's pressing request to return with her to the court of Rhydderch, he asks her instead to construct for him a fantasy research center: a house "with seventy doors and as many windows...through which I may watch by night the stars wheeling in the firmament." While the stars "will teach me about the future of the nation" he, like a good monk, or a good academic, wants to hand on his learning and he also asks for "as many secretaries to record what I may say and let them concentrate on committing my prophetic song to paper" (81).

Clarke comments that the *Life*, however rich its reference to the past and to "legends native and exotic," also

> reflects its own day—the intellectual speculation, the interest in the past, the civil war of Stephen's reign, the unfinished struggle between Welsh and Normans and the special moment of the establishment of a new bishopric in an area where these two clashed. (v)

The comment catches well the sense of contemporaneity that is Geoffrey's ultimate concern, and that finally takes on a note of drama and urgency. The *Life* is not as massively learned and as much a work of international reference as was the *History*—Clarke comments that its classical allusions "are such as would easily have been encountered in an ordinary advanced latinate education" (1973, 11). Geoffrey's interest is ultimately to speak about his own world, not to show off his learning. Just as Merlin's prophecies are concerned with the political future of medieval rather than ancient Britain and the learning he and Taliesin convey is at the cutting edge of medieval natural science, so Ganieda's own final vision is as concerned with the pressures of Geoffrey's own contemporary situation, caring for the liberty of the cities and the people most dear to him, the clergy and the Welsh:

> "I see the city of Oxford filled with helmeted men, and holy men and holy bishops bound on the decision of the Council....I see the city of Lincoln walled in by a fierce army...Normans, go! No longer take your armies of violent soldiery through our native kingdom." (135)

The contemporary bite and political daring of the comment matches the learning and imagination of the whole *Life*. Geoffrey's Merlin represents a wisdom that has been adapted to the period, context, and concerns of the author, here asserting the challenge that knowledge should advise and admonish power rather than serve it.

The *Life of Merlin* had an elusive impact, not only through its apparently restricted circulation, but also through the subtle nature of its effects. As Clarke notes, the French scholar Ferdinand Lot at first called it "facetious bizarrerie" (Clarke, 1973, v) and Tatlock's first impression was that it was "incoherent, unaccountable and uncertain in mood" (1943, 265): in the same dismissive spirit the Chadwicks regarded it as the work of "a literary dilettante" (Chadwick and Chadwick, 1932, 1:128). But both Lot and Tatlock came to recognize the poem's power, though the Chadwicks remained impervious to its imaginative essence. They are not the only academics to have offered a narrow account of Myrddin-Merlin. Religion has been a frequent instrument of reductivism: for Penelope Doob he is no more than a variant of heroic grandeur run wild, in the tradition of Nebuchadnezzar (1974, 153–58); to Nikolai Tolstoy he represents nothing more interesting than a "pagan druid or bard surviving in a predominantly Christian culture" (1985, 29); with even less focus, he was to the Celtic myth–questing R. S. Loomis, however improbably, a version of the undying Celtic sun god whom he named Celidoune (1927, 130, 144).

Literature and the poetic imagination are not so single in their meanings, nor so unrelated to their contexts. Geoffrey's genius was to reimagine the figure of wisdom in a way that refracted both the political and the intellectual nature of his own world. Through that remarkable achievement he passed on to succeeding writers, especially in the great expansion of French secular literature of the early Middle Ages, but also to the imaginative artists of later centuries, a dynamic, complex, and intensely fertile representation of knowledge beset by the pressures of human existence, and confronting the social, political and oppressively governmental forces to which it opposes both vitality and wisdom.

Medieval Merlin

Advice

From Prophecy to Advice: Wace

In feudal medieval Europe, where rule was personal, by a king or a great lord, and the role of knowledge was to guide and advise power directly, the wise prophetic Merlin was reshaped in the French language as a grand vizier.

Geoffrey of Monmouth's *History* spread across Europe: the historian Henry of Huntingdon was astonished when he encountered it in France as early as 1139 (1996, 559). He did not mention Merlin, perhaps because he was more interested in Geoffrey's work as history—he omitted other supernatural elements (see Wright, 1991, 77). Even earlier Ordericus Vitalis, writing in Normandy, used the Merlin prophetic material, perhaps in the separate book form that Geoffrey implies had existed as his first effort, in his *Ecclesiastical History* (1978, 6:387).

Henry and Ordericus were scholars and fluent readers of Geoffrey's Latin, but that was a rare skill: it seems surprising that translations of the *History* were not made more quickly and in greater numbers. Presumably, just as oral performance of adventures was an early mode of Arthurian entertainment, oral translation from the Latin was a common mediation of Geoffrey's *History*. A French translation by Geoffrey Gaimar was so little copied it has been lost, but Wace's popular *Brut* appeared soon after 1150.[1] The title, referring to the Trojan Brutus as the founder of Britain, indicates that this is an example of *translatio studii et imperii* ("the transference of culture and power") as the

West both admired the grandeur of the classics and also indicated its own new quasi-imperial authority (see Baswell, 2000). But it is also the reverse of that, implicitly asserting that Western Europe has stories—here Celtic ones— just as exciting and intriguing as those of the classical world. As Françoise le Saux notes (2005, 1), Wace's often-cited first name Robert is an error (see Keller, 1990) and though his surname has been held to be of Germanic origin, it could come from the British Celtic "gwas," "servant," itself the origin of the Norman-French feudal term "vassal"—a possibility that might explain Wace's interest in Arthur.

Wace's *Brut* transmitted the Arthur material to French and European sto- rytellers: few of them look back to Geoffrey's Latin as a source. Wace wrote in Anglo-Norman, the version of French that was used and preserved in England, and he belonged to that mixed culture, having been born on the Channel Island of Jersey. As a scholar, perhaps even a tutor, he worked for the English royal house and then was employed in Caen as a "clerc lisant"— which may imply an oral reader of texts, including the *Historia*. As Margaret Houck notes, Wace's audience seems to have been lords and ladies who knew no Latin (1941, 162), and while he gives a fairly faithful translation of Geof- frey's text there are variations which both fit that audience and look forward to French romance. Where Geoffrey's genre is historical, if also highly inven- tive, there is a stronger literary feeling to Wace's work, as he elaborates scenes and to some degree the feelings of characters: Margaret Pelan has shown that he gives a more glamorous account of life in Caerleon, a vivid narrative of Arthur's stormy voyage, a moving depiction of a country in ruins after war and a closer representation of the roles of women (1974, 165). Paul Zumthor sums up that Wace adds "picturesque and psychological finesse" to the story (1943, 51).

Wace began the advice-oriented reshaping of Merlin that following French writers would substantially develop. Françoise le Saux notes Wace's "barely perceptible, but real, erosion of the independence of Merlin" (2005, 24) and "the relative downgrading of the figure of Merlin when he goes to Ireland with Uther to fetch the Giants' Circle" (2005, 24 and 137 n. 23). She feels this is because Wace tends to focus directly on one central character, here the king, but there seem wider reasons for the restriction of Merlin's role. Jean Blacker- Knight has written about Wace's "depoliticization of Merlin," making him a mere "instrument" of royal power (1988, 71, 72).

The emphasis on royal advice is partly created by the absence of political prophecy: Wace says of Geoffrey's "Prophecies," "I do not wish to translate this book, since I do not know how to interpret it; I would not like to say anything, in case what I say does not happen." (1999, 7539–52) Wace's apparent caution rationalizes the fact that his essentially French audience had little interest in Merlin's visions of a future Britain. This is a far-reaching change: Wace's rejection of Merlin's British political prophecies starts their continental decline, and wider Europe only rarely uses the political prophecies of Merlin. It is equally notable that several British scholars put them back into their versions of Wace, as in the manuscript preserved at Lincoln Cathedral (Blacker, 1993, 56–58).

Though Merlin will remain famous as a prophet, and French writers from Robert de Boron to Paul Zumthor will emphasize this role, for them his prophecies stay within the text, predicting what will happen to Arthur, Lancelot, or the grail—Merlin's visionary role on the continent is restricted to literary structure and morality, not the future politics of Britain. A major outcome of this change is that later on, when royal advice was of little interest, continental Merlin was, especially in France, best known as an enchanter.

Wace did know British motifs not in Geoffrey. As Arthur dies a Merlin prophecy is quoted, that Arthur's death is "dutuse" ("doubtful") (13286). Merlin also speaks in prophetic mode about Cadwallader's departure and Wace adds the figure of Teleusin, or Taliesin, probably from the *Historia Brittonum* as there is no other sign of Wace knowing Geoffrey's *Life.* He does seem to have spent time in Britain, because his knowledge of its geography, especially in the south, seems quite good. He also famously inserts the story of the Round Table for which he seems to suggest a Celtic source: "Arthur had the round table made, about which the British tell many a tale" (9751–52).

But if Wace transmits, even enlarges, Merlin's ability to know and foresee the truth, it is still on a smaller stage, just to do with the narrative, not history and the British future. When he acts alone, and not to glorify the great, his power seems similarly circumscribed. As he moves the stones to Stonehenge, he may be praying: "He looked around, his lips moving like a man saying his prayers. I don't know if he said a prayer or not." (8148–49) Similarly, when he transforms Uther's appearance, it is done "par nuvels medecinemenz" ("by new potions," 8702), though also by "enchantemenz" (8727).

Wace seems little interested in magic—in his *Roman de Rou,* a history of the dukes of Normandy, he speaks of visiting the Breton forest of Brocéliande to check on magical stories, but found no basis for them there (1970, 2:6393–98). In the same distanced way he makes Merlin more an instrument of the narrative than a figure of crucial interest: his age is not given when he first appears, and when Uther sends for Merlin Wace speaks dismissively: "He sent for him at Labanes, a far-off spring in Wales (I don't know where, because I was never there)." (8013–16). A sense of distance from the Celtic world, shared no doubt by his Anglo-Norman gentry audience, epitomizes Wace's reduced role for Merlin: in this version the prime role of his knowledge is as an instrumental assistant to the extraordinary Western monarch. Merlin has no separate status as he has in Geoffrey's "Prophecies" and *Life;* he has become primarily a royal adviser.

But Wace's reduction and instrumentalization of Merlin's knowledge in the service of power, however influential, was not the only French medieval reshaping of the Celtic figure. In the space created by the absence of political prophecy another writer, as imaginative and influential as Geoffrey of Monmouth in his different way, would radically reshape the nature and direction of Merlin's knowledge and the power it served.

Christian Advice: Robert de Boron

The best-known author of the Arthurian development was Chrétien de Troyes, creator of the new genre of romance. Substantial peace and prosperity in western Europe and the development of new ideas of heroism, including personal integrity and the possibility of love, not just brutality and warrior bonding, were the context for the new journey of the romance hero to fame, love, and happiness.[2] The romances picked out heroes from the Arthurian throng, and from elsewhere, using a biographic trajectory to glory as the structure, and close-up on feeling as the technique. Focusing on morality, gender, and identity, knowledge here is involved with personal adventures that resolve problems such as Yvain's sense of failure, Lancelot's conflict between honor and love, Perceval's quest for a value higher than secular chivalry. In these personalized dramas there is no place for Merlin either as royal facilitator—the king does almost nothing anyway—or as repository of any useful knowledge, historical, scientific, or religious—the hero knights do it all on their own, with occasional specialist advice from wise men or maidens. Like many later romance authors, Chrétien only mentions Merlin once, in passing and the past: sterlings had been currency in Britain "since the days of Merlin" (1970, 5531).

But if single-hero stories ignored Merlin, before long the Arthurian chronicle as a genre, the kingdom as a stage, and Merlin as a figure of authority were to return. This time, however, his knowledge was different and in the service of a higher form of power. Chrétien had in the 1180s in his *Perceval* created the idea of the grail as a symbol of a value beyond worldly chivalry. He had neither finished the poem nor conceived of the grail in a fully Christian way, but his continuers and followers were to make the holy grail a central Christian symbol, with an authority and fascination that would survive to the present. This too had a context. It can be argued that Chrétien's grail, a lightly sketched symbol of personal charity, became the focus of intense interest after the battle of Hattin in 1187, when Saladin annihilated the Crusader army and shortly afterwards took Jerusalem (Knight, 1994). In fantasized compensation for the shattering loss of the holy places, the grail became for the West a potent symbol of the truly holy: Christianity espoused it as the focus of a myth suggesting that the most potent of all the mysteries had in fact been saved and was to be found, if we really concentrated and were really pure of heart, somewhere in the West. It was as if we had not needed the crusades after all.

Robert de Boron involves Merlin in this new religious knowledge and its supernatural domain of power. In his *Joseph,* Robert first tells the story of the rescue of the holy grail from the Holy Land, and then his *Merlin* recounts its journey to Britain. This dramatic and powerful idea, rich in both compensation and exculpation for the West, caught on remarkably: grail stories flourished in the early thirteenth century with a speed, energy, and range that seems quite out of keeping with what we think of as the leisured pace of medieval cultural development. Some commentators have disparaged Robert's technical skill: Pierre le Gentil said he was "endowed with boldness and piety but with mediocre talent" (1959, 251) and Richard O'Gorman has called him "a sorry poet" (1996, 386). It is true that his poetry lacks the limpid clarity of Chrétien, but so did everybody else's: Robert's work is a triumph of content, not of form.

In a discussion of sources, Alexandre Micha makes it clear that as well as Wace and Christian material, Robert knew something of Merlin the trickster and possibly also the prophet (1980, 30–58)—perhaps only, as Gaston Paris suggested, via oral transmission (1886, x, xv). Through his skill in combining and refocusing this varied material Robert reestablished Merlin in a new form and a new function: Geoffrey's underlying sense of a quasi-priestly role in Merlin's transmission of prophecy becomes a means of transmitting the Eastern religious power of this story into a decidedly Western and modern context. Merlin's new Christian knowledge about the grail realizes a power beyond the secular: he is an adviser, but on spiritual perfection, not worldly success.

Robert worked for a Burgundian lord, Gautier de Montbéliard—Boron is a small town near Montbéliard—who went on crusade in 1202 and died, still on crusade, in 1212; Robert says he read the poem to his lord "in time of peace" (1995, 3490). The language and style and the relation with other texts make good sense if the *Joseph* is dated around 1200. Anglophone scholars have traced some connections between a Robert de Boron—not necessarily this one—and England (Nitze, 1953, 282), but while there was a good deal of cultural contact between Anglo-Norman England and France itself, there seems no interest in Britain to speak of in Robert's text and this connection is either untrue or at most insignificant. It is more credible to take Robert as a French writer, as do French scholars from Gaston Paris to Richard Trachsler (Paris, 1886, x; Trachsler, 2000, 38).

Robert's work is quite short: Nigel Bryant's recent translation (2001) is a slender book, and even then the later sequences are merely attributed to Robert. The *Joseph of Arimathea* is certainly his, a fairly short poem in the rhyming couplets used by Chrétien. There is also the beginning of a *Merlin* in the same poetic form,[3] a complete prose version of the *Joseph* and the *Merlin* (the latter presumably based on a once complete verse *Merlin*): both the prose texts are dated at about 1205–10. The prose versions were quite popular, with fifteen versions of the *Joseph* surviving and over fifty of the *Merlin*. This popularity seems to relate to a change of genre and audience: E. Jane Burns has discussed the process of this development (1993, xxviii–xxx) and Thierry Revel has suggested that the genre of the royal chronicle is being developed for Arthurian moral narratives (2000, 107), and the audience appears to be the great aristocratic houses of France, not the royal court.

The role of Merlin and his knowledge is central to this re-formation of a moralized story of great deeds written down in French prose: Merlin becomes primarily a serious royal adviser speaking directly to the powerful and interpreting their ambience in the light of Christianity, a symbol of the contemporary clerics who as learned, Christian men, disseminated their views on worldly matters, both political and sexual, in secular forms (Gaunt, 2000; Kay, 2000). The interface, even hostility, between a clerical viewpoint and that of a secular court is a consistent focus of attention in the texts, particularly through the role of Merlin: Corinne Denoyelle has explored this area of medieval realpolitik of knowledge (2000).

After the *Joseph* and the *Merlin* there follows in two manuscripts a prose *Perceval*, known as the Didot *Perceval*, after an owner of one of the manuscripts. This is a short version of Perceval's achievement of the grail, here supervised by Merlin, concluded with a brief *Mort Artu* detailing the end of Arthur's world. The Didot *Perceval* was not popular, presumably because fuller and quite different versions of the grail story became widely accepted, with many more adventures, without Merlin appearing and before long with

Galahad, not Perceval, as the grail achiever—a much fuller *Mort* was also available. But the four stories that Robert either wrote or initiated are in fact the first version of a coherent and complete French redevelopment of the saga of Arthur, a new genre that would find its fullest form in what is widely known as the Vulgate Arthuriad, also called the *Lancelot-Grail*. As Burns notes (1996, 497), Robert's work has not been widely acknowledged as being effectively a pre-Vulgate cycle, a first, potent, and very influential rationalization of the existing Arthur story, and the Merlin material is woven together with the grail story as its moral dynamic.

Robert's plan was bold and ambitious. Having obviously read at least one completion of Chrétien's *Perceval,* which makes the grail the symbol of full Christian knowledge and love of one's neighbor, Robert amplifies the ideological force of the grail by linking it back directly to Christ's crucifixion. He makes it not the flat meat dish, suitable for the Paschal lamb, that Chrétien seems to have had in mind, but in a story Robert draws from the apocryphal Gospel of Nicodemus it is the chalice used at the Last Supper and then by Joseph of Arimathea to collect Christ's blood, so the archetype of the cup of the Eucharist, the recurrent and intense focus of medieval Christian worship. The resurrected Jesus visits Joseph in prison and validates the chalice; after a dramatic series of apocryphal events, including Pilate's repentance, Veronica's cloth-borne image of Christ and the conversion of the emperor Vespasian to Christianity, the grail is sent overseas to western Europe with Bron, Joseph's brother-in-law. At the end of the *Joseph* the narrator says there are four stories to be told about the people involved, but he will leave those till later to tell the fifth, which will be about Merlin. So the *Joseph* story, including a lengthy sequence involving Christ himself, is essentially a potent introduction to a story focusing on Merlin in modern chivalric time, and leading to a convergence of the stories of the grail and King Arthur.

Both Geoffrey and Wace had kept Merlin and Arthur separate: Robert is the first to link them, making Merlin return after Arthur is made king, and supervise many activities of the Round Table world. Merlin connects the Gospel of Nicodemus with Chrétien's grail and Wace's Arthur story, and Robert adds material about Merlin's trickster spirit, ultimately from Geoffrey's *Life*. Perhaps it is because scholars in the past have been more interested just in the grail or just in Arthur that they have not seen Robert's full originality: to follow the threads of his treatment of the Merlin story is to see a remarkable new creation of a potent adviser, and though Merlin did not survive as a Christian authority, his newly central advisory function answered in secular form the interests of feudal power.

The Merlin story starts on the same high Christian level as the *Joseph,* just after Christ has harrowed hell—more material from Nicodemus. The devils are furious: they feel Christ's rescue of Christian souls is unfair, as they earned them along with Adam's soul in Eden (they were wrong: they had lied to Eve). So they decide to create an Anti-Christ, the child of a human mother and a devil who will, they hope, further their cause in the world as success-fully as Christ has represented his own father. Robert has taken Geoffrey's suggestion that Merlin can be thought of as half-demonic, but by then saving him for Christ he has developed this into a characteristically big idea, creating a figure who can act as a major interpreter of God's plan for the world—so giving Merlin a new and extensive kind of knowledge and proximity to a far-reaching range of Christian power. Micha goes so far as to see Robert as making strong and positive links between Merlin and Christ himself (1980, 297–300) and Burns has seen Merlin as "a master of artifice" parallel to the Creator (1985, 17)—but Merlin's future is to be quite un-Christlike.

Not only does Merlin now move in terms of Christian history: he is also geographically generalized. His location is no longer simply Carmarthen and the Celtic world—while Robert accepts the idea that Merlin and Arthur op-erate vaguely in Britain he has none of Geoffrey's or even Wace's geographic specificity. It is true, as Baumgartner comments, that in some ways this is an "eastern" Merlin, because of the origin of the story in the Holy Land (2001, 30), but the location of the narrative is essentially, if now generally, western. Zumthor comments that Robert's world is one of "fully feudal society" (1943, 132): the woman who is selected for the diabolic birth is the daughter of a wealthy merchant, and the story deploys familiar features of town life, mod-ern vices, the law, a priest, a judge, a tower. Like the grail itself, the narrative is located in the here and now.

In a lurid sequence the devils assault the family of Merlin's mother. They brutalize her father and mother to death, reduce her sisters to disgrace, then harass her and, when she is too distressed and exhausted to cross herself at night, manage to impregnate her: the scene was often illustrated (fig. 4). Imprisoned for fornication, to await execution after childbirth, she remains faithful to the church, and especially to her wise confessor. When he absolves her of sin she "proceeded to lead a good and honest life" and as a result "the devil realised he had lost her" (Robert de Boron, 1979, 53). The child still in her womb is rescued for Christ, and the mother's agency is crucial: Merlin himself will later say "through my mother's repentance they lost me" (62). It is not, as some commentators think, just his baptism that saves him: the role of women's agency in the developing French version of the Arthur story is to recur. But Merlin's mother, now in jail, still suffers. The child is born and baptized: he is christened Merlin, after his grandfather, Robert says in a moment of human domestication. At eighteen months, much younger than his first triumphs in Wace and Geoffrey, Merlin promises to protect his mother, and a little later when she is to be stoned to death, he takes on the judge.

Though Robert is following the familiar "wonderful child" pattern, common to heroes of all kinds, some of his plot detail comes from the trickster Merlin tradition. Merlin insists on questioning the judge's own mother and reveals that the judge is in fact the son of a sinful priest. Not only is Merlin's mother freed, but the priest drowns himself, as Merlin has predicted to the judge. This story both creates Merlin's authority in a world far different from the British politics of the Vortigern sequence and also establishes Merlin as a sternly moral figure, appropriate to his grail-related future. This authority is closely linked with literacy: the confessor "gladly" (61) agrees to write down Merlin's account of the Joseph of Arimathea story. He is called Blaise, and these two are to work together in this way through the whole French Merlin narrative.

Some feel this name comes from Welsh *blaidd,* Breton *bleizh,* meaning wolf, and they relate this to the old gray wolf that Merlin befriends in the *Life* (see Walter, 2000, 138, and Baudry, 2000, 179). More likely is a better-recorded Celticism, tracing Blaise to a figure usually known in French as Bleheris, in Latin as Bledhericus, and in Welsh as Bleddri, who was a real person, a famous twelfth-century storyteller, an archetype of the oral dissemination to France of British Celtic story.[4] In Robert, and the Vulgate authors, Merlin regularly visits Blaise in wild Northumberland, remembering Merlin's own northern past. Blaise occasionally advises Merlin, but crucially he is the person who records the stories Merlin has experienced, a hero of the clerical, the figure of the author, and a sign that clerical activity has now supplanted the oral activity of the past: the mediation of the stories has gone from Bleddri to Blaise.

It is only now, with Merlin established as the figure of Christian knowledge and authority, that Robert takes up Geoffrey's account, via Wace. Vortigern's men "scoured many lands" (68) looking for the sacrificeable seven-year-old: Merlin who knows "everything that had been happening" (68), takes them to Blaise and explains all to them. On the way to Vortigern Merlin demonstrates his trickster capacity by laughing first at the man buying shoes—he will die before he can wear them—and then at the priest burying his unrecognized son. He meets Vortigern, sorts out the tower, and prophesies much more briefly than in Geoffrey, just speaking about Vortigern's death.

Unlike Wace, Robert does not feel the need to explain the absence of the future prophecies: no doubt his continental French audience had even less interest than Wace's in obscure British political prophecies, and Arnaud de la Croix has suggested that prophecy itself as a mode of knowledge was in some disrepute in the intellectually rigorous world around 1200, notably in the context of the growth of harder-edged philosophy and science in the new universities (2000, 29). Robert finds in the deeply Christian grail story a powerful new role for Merlin's prophecy, though most future writers will reject this in favor of a merely secular form of advice.

Robert, combining narrative energy with thematic profundity, keeps his grail prophet in touch with the folkloric tricksterism of the *Life* figure, just as the *Life* combined that element with substantial Christian wisdom. To facilitate this Robert exploits another folkloric element: transformation—here too, his originality has been under-noticed. Pendragon and Uther, Robert's splitting of Geoffrey's hero (Wace, like Geoffrey, has Uther Pendragon as Aurelius's brother), are advised to find Merlin for advice in the war against Hengist. Merlin knows this and approaches the royal messengers "disguised as a woodcutter—a great ax on his shoulder, big boots laced, and wearing a tattered jacket—with his hair lank and matted and his beard very long" (78).

This is the first of many similar instances. Although Geoffrey's Merlin and before him Myrddin had different avatars—prince, warrior, exile, madman, prophet, child, even a peasant archer (fig. 5)—these were in fact identities created in the narrative. Merlin the shape-shifter is new, asserting powers of magic which previously—as in moving Stonehenge, transforming Uther— have been hedged with some doubts. Paris felt the shape-shifting was just "diverse metamorphoses where Merlin amuses himself" (1886, xv): but others feel that they arise from his being a half-devil: de la Croix notes that shape-shifting is strongly associated with the devil's ways of testing people (2000, 86–87). The first time Merlin appears transformed, that is in fact the instinctive response of Pendragon's men: "We've been talking to a demon" (79). But like Merlin himself, shape-shifting has been saved for God's purposes, and the text consistently shows it having a benign outcome. It also has a specific and complex meaning.

In part the transformations emphasize Merlin's power. The thirteenth-century French development will make a good deal more of Merlin the magician and shape-shifter, and this emphasizes his knowledge. The idea of deep learning in the medieval period easily merged into magic. From Pope Sylvester, through Roger Bacon, Albertus Magnus, and on to John Dee, the idea of the magus who was also a magician is familiar. The mysterious powers of Merlin are themselves to be linked both to his pure knowledge as it realizes itself in a new context, and also, as the narrative shows, to his relationship with power. In this process shape-shifting is a central feature. It should not be called disguise, as that implies a real person who is briefly unrecogniz-able, like Uther as Gorlois. What Merlin does is transform: these manifesta-tions realize the multiple possibilities of knowledge in its complex relations with power.

Merlin consistently transforms when he is being sought by the powerful. The knowledge that permits him to transform enables him to give a sign to power that the figure of knowledge has his own power, which must be respected. This process of challenge has social meaning: characteristically he is transformed as a person of low status—in the sequence of narrative involv-ing Merlin and Uther and Pendragon and Hengist, as Robert rewrites Wace, Merlin is at first a woodman, and then an ugly deformed herdsman from Northumberland, an old white-haired man, Uther's mistress's serving boy, an old man, a boy. The dialectic of knowledge and power seems clearly under-stood by the illuminator who shows Merlin addressing a row of tall dignitar-ies as a small boy—but only he carries a weapon (fig. 6).

Anne Berthelot sees the essence of the pattern of transformation when she describes Merlin as representing "a deformed, marginal humanity, at the limit of bestiality," yet she only sees this as part of a "masquerade" (2000, 16). But these recurrent marginal realizations, all outside adult masculine authority, express the elusive location of Merlin and the potency of his knowledge. The challenge is parallel to the knowledge-based laughter of the trickster at and against a corrupt priest or judge, and this challenge may well mesh with and gratify the curious position of a learned clerk in a royal or baronial court. As Micha notes, Robert "has multiplied these sudden bursts of laughter" (1980, 300), but critics have sometimes diminished their role. For Bloch Merlin merely "incarnates the persona of the writer" (2000, 50) while Walter finds it just an example of "the demonic spirit" (2000, 148). But there is more here: Merlin's transformations are outside the power elite and yet they transmit information crucial to the powerful. The value of the knowledge floats free of social institutions, and by implication would be threatened if enclosed in them, unable to transform.

Merlin's many shapes are not necessarily crude. After being the Northum-berland herdsman, Merlin appears as a "very smart man in fine clothes and shoes" and then one day as "a handsome and very well dressed gentleman"

(80)—and the king's men recognize him in that form. This is his default role at court—another transformation of knowledge, not an identity, and it is this Merlin who says to the king "I wish to be a friend to you and your brother Uther" (81). There will be later instances of Merlin appearing as a gentleman when he is in fact strategically locating himself as, at least, an equal to the powerful.

Robert seems conscious of the knowledge-power interface. He transmits Geoffrey's suggestion that Merlin is consciously controlling his knowledge and its use by the powerful when he says to Blaise that there are "those I do not choose to enlighten" (62). This guarded, even rationed, knowledge is triumphant in the war with Hengist, and then the king accepts Merlin's advice to spare the Saxons if they leave the country. Here too Merlin's knowledge is successful and his reward is the highest place for a man of knowledge: "So, as you have heard, Merlin knew the Saxons' thoughts and had them driven from the land, and so it was that he became the king's chief counsellor" (85).

The image of Merlin as hero of advisory knowledge is Robert's new development, drawing on hints in Wace and Geoffrey, and it is a concept that will remain fascinating to authors in the thirteenth-century French material after Robert. As Robert's story continues he makes Merlin as important in the secular world of Uther and Arthur as he is in commenting on the meaning of the grail, and it is this later advisory development that will survive as the dominant mode of medieval Merlin.

Knowledge has a lot to do in Robert, as compared with Wace and Geoffrey. In the next sequence of action it is Merlin, not Uther, who decides the military response to the Saxons who have arrived to avenge Hengist and it is he, not Aurelius, who plans that the cemetery at Stonehenge will be "something unheard of" that "will be talked of for ever" (91): he has a quasi-royal interest in creating fame. Yet this grand and carefully constructed para-royal authority still has some of the tricksterish skill of the old Celtic Myrddin: a baron is jealous of the king's reliance on Merlin and, being "a cunning and a wicked man" (86), he is made the focus of a version of the threefold death prophecy. Three times he pretends to be sick and Merlin gives three different death predictions: but here, whether to shorten the story or magnify Merlin more—or perhaps both—Robert makes Merlin explain it all to the king, and the predictions rapidly become true (86–87).

Triumphant in both military strategy and court intrigue, Merlin now extends his authority over time to bring together the strands of Robert's ambitious plan. To the king, here known since his brother's death as Uther Pendragon, he explains God's plan, referring back to Christ's instructions in

Joseph to make a second table in memory of the Last Supper, which Robert named the Table of the Grail. Now, he says:

"If you'll trust in my advice, you'll establish a third table in the name of the Trinity, which these three tables will signify. And if you do this it will greatly benefit your body and your soul, and such things will happen in your time as will astound you." (92)

Robert, with his characteristic bold condensation, absorbs Wace's casual interpolation of an apparently Celtic round table at Arthur's court into his grand plan for a scheme both spiritual and secular. The fact that it is Uther who establishes the table seems to recall the lack of links between Merlin and Arthur in Geoffrey and Wace, and the link back to the Last Supper briefly stops this table being round. Robert stresses the grandness of the design and Merlin's authority in transmitting it; at Carduel Merlin chooses fifty knights to sit at the table and predicts the grail-related filling of the empty seat by Alain's future son.

The establishment of the table is honored by Merlin's return to Blaise to record the great event (99). While Merlin is away the Uther-Igraine affair develops, with Robert laying a good deal more stress on Igraine's hurt feelings and anger than Wace, for all his increased humanism, had done. As Baumgartner notes, Igraine is treated basically as Merlin's mother has been (2001, 40); the text provides some sense of Igraine's agency and a clear suggestion that she is mistreated, a theme which will develop in later versions. Eventually Merlin returns, in teasing form as an old man, and then as a cripple, and agrees to arrange matters for Uther: here, going beyond Wace's possible euphemization of the magic, Merlin produces a herb for the king to rub on his face. But he takes the child to its foster-father as "a most handsome man" (104): caring for a future king and so acting as a courtier, he is represented as one.

This is his last intervention in Arthur's establishment as king. Arthur effectively becomes king through drawing the sword from the stone (actually from an anvil on the stone), a supernatural device that has since become dominant in the story but first occurs here, apparently another of Robert's potent inventions. Merlin is not involved, though he predicts that God will send a sign to reveal the proper king: Christian faith rather than prophecy is his mode now, and certainly not magic. The sword and its drawing are highly religious in their context: it appears on Christmas Day and Arthur is finally accepted at Pentecost. That epitome of Christian history is supervised by an archbishop (his British location is unnamed in this French-oriented version) and the whole context is richly Christian.

Merlin returns briefly after Arthur has become king, to confirm his right to the throne by explaining his lineage, but adds to that secular validation an insistence on a religious orientation: "I will never give you any advice that is contrary to Our Lord's will" (112). Then Merlin operates as the agent of God's plan, urging Arthur to maintain the Round Table in its Christ-linked context through to the achievement of the grail. At that time, he says enigmatically, "the enchantments of the land of Britain will vanish" (113). As if he is himself linked to such enchantments, Merlin announces his departure, in spite of Arthur's wish to keep him, with "his deepest affection" (114). Merlin leaves for Blaise and the renewal of the written record.

The great sage will do little more in the story, though that will be crucial. This first of the French prose Arthurian cycles moves on, with the Didot *Perceval* telling the story of the achievement of the grail. It is basically a summary of Chrétien's story and its continuations, but seen in the light of Robert's version of Christian history as found in the *Joseph*: scholars still do not agree whether Robert wrote it or not.[5] Merlin plays little active role but, consistent with being the prophet of the grail, on a crucial occasion he fills the role of adviser. Perceval fails to ask the right question and so heal the maimed king, he has wandered through the country with various adventures; but suddenly, he meets an old man dressed as a reaper (presumably an ominous prediction of the tragic end of the Arthur story). It is Merlin: he briskly advises Percival how to find the house again, and all rapidly comes right.

Finally Merlin takes Blaise, as he had long promised, to the Fisher King's house where Blaise too joins the grail company—a projection of his clerical mastery into a spiritual conclusion. Merlin comes to court to explain what has happened, and then leaves for the grail castle, but not for his own spiritual release: clerical as ever, especially in the sense of being an author, he gets Blaise to "set everything down in writing" (156).

The enchantments have indeed ended, and Arthurian adventure with them: the Didot *Perceval* succinctly concludes the story with the European military adventures against France and Rome that were the glory of Geoffrey's monarch. It is a skeletal account, by Merlin's choice: "Blaise says nothing about their daily marches and what befell them, for Merlin did not care to mention it" (166). First comes the successful attack on King Frollo of France (a major enemy in Geoffrey's *History*) and then the great assault on Rome in response to its demand for Arthur's submission, but as in Geoffrey and Wace the military triumph ends with the news of Mordred's betrayal. The tragedy is very rapid, and this brief *Mort* leaves only Perceval alive of the Arthurian military personnel: spiritual values have superseded the secular enchantments of Arthur's world.[6] Here as in so many places Robert, or his successor, is condensed and suggestive, and his ideas will be massively developed by followers.

But the *Perceval* ends with one feature which looks back rather than forward, and restates Robert's fascination with the figure of knowledge who was so central in his story. Much as Merlin in the *Life* basically retires and leaves wisdom to his sister Ganieda, so here he gives Perceval and Blaise a modified farewell:

"I shall make my dwelling-place outside your house, where I shall live and prophesy as Our Lord shall instruct me. And all who see my dwelling-place will call it Merlin's *esplumoir.*" (172)

Later writers will dispose of Merlin and his troublesome knowledge in a range of revealing ways. Robert, who has used Merlin as a royal adviser both spiritual and secular, as the messenger between Christ's Jerusalem and the chivalric present, and also as the image of redemption by deeds (or by his mother's deeds), finally presents him in an active wise retirement. The word *esplumoir,* it is generally agreed, refers to a molting cage, as would be inhabited by a real merlin in its inactive time (see Nitze, 1943, and Adolf, 1946): the word is by now in use for a small hawk. With symbolic linking back to the wild, animal-related Merlin of the *Life,* there is also, it seems, an affectionate and positive reference to the clerical world that Merlin has so strongly represented. Just as in the *Life* Ganieda provided seventy scribes for Merlin in his learned retirement, so this image of him as a molting bird will also of course generate plenty of *plumes*—the feathers and pens which are so central both to the clerical world and its powers, and to the frequently foregrounded transmission of this story itself. And that is where Robert ends: "Merlin prayed to our Lord to grant mercy to all who would willingly hear his book and have it copied for their remembrance of his deeds" (172).

Through Robert's energetic imagination Merlin has become deeply Christian, though still capable of looking after himself with the cunning of a true trickster, and he has also risen from the level of a wonderful boy and mournful exile whose wisdom combines present critique and future prophecy to the position of learned adviser in a medieval Christian realm. The new Merlin, a super-cleric who deploys his knowledge on behalf of the powerful, is a projection of learning such as Robert's own into the courts of the highest contemporary power, and in this transformation, especially in its secular version, Merlin will attract the attention and the variation of many more medieval writers.

Grand Vizier: The Vulgate Merlin

The early British Myrddin was difficult to trace because of the paucity and lateness of the documents; thirteenth-century French Merlin is the opposite. Both Arthur and Merlin, and the many stories, religious and secular, attached to them and their associates were widely recorded as two overlapping but essentially different impulses drove forward the development of the Arthurian myth, both of which gave Merlin a major role. One of these impulses was to elaborate the stories and meanings of the Arthurian world. The narrative of Chrétien's Lancelot was developed to include the birth, upbringing, and many adventures of the great romantic hero. Robert's brief grail story was both enormously extended and refocused on the perfect Galahad, not the humanly errant Perceval, in the *Queste du Saint Graal.* The tragic love of Tristan and Isolt was brought into the Arthurian world, and in extended romances authors gave knights, both existing and invented, adventures in love and war. Robert de Boron's development of Merlin as an authoritative adviser was, in the secular context, itself substantially developed to outline just what Merlin did for Arthur and the Round Table.

The second main impulse of thirteenth-century Arthurian writing was the desire to link and rationalize these separate and massively developed stories. The Vulgate Arthuriad, also called the *Lancelot-Grail,* connected the independent and itself huge story of Lancelot (developed by about 1220; *Lancelot do Lac,* 1980) and the new grail *Queste* achieved by his son Galahad with equally extended accounts of Robert's *Joseph* and *Merlin* and the *Mort Artu,* all of this being focused as a narrative of human aspirations and sins. The Vulgate Arthuriad (*Vulgate Version,* 1908–16; translation, *Lancelot-Grail,* 1993–96) was completed, for all its length, very rapidly, by about 1225. A triumph of clerical work, it testifies both to the fascination with the topics of Arthur and the grail—both involving Merlin—and also the compelling power of the new medium, vernacular prose fiction.

The Vulgate's continuation of Robert's *Merlin* is sometimes known, especially in France, as the *Suite,* or continuation; but this term is also used for the later revision, the post-Vulgate *Merlin,* to be discussed below. The stories' interrelations are complex enough without this confusion, and the name will be avoided here in both cases. The Vulgate *Merlin* survives in fifty-five manuscripts, some of them fragmentary, and was clearly widely known in its period and later. The author starts by covering the material offered by Robert de Boron. As Lacy says, it "borrows the text of the *Merlin* intact" (1993, ix), with a few differences. The Vulgate *Merlin* can be a little more elaborated and emphatic than Robert: it makes the newborn Merlin very hairy (presumably through his devil heritage) and the judge threatens to burn Merlin as well as his mother. Where Robert has Merlin, when accepting the baby, disguised as "a most handsome man," in the Vulgate he is "very old and weak": the Vulgate does not see this as an instance of Merlin operating as a courtier but as one of his socially marginal transformations (trans. Pickens, 1993–96, 1.209).

A major change directly emphasizes the challenge Merlin's knowledge makes to the power he advises. Where Robert passes straight from Merlin's establishment of the Table to Uther's passion for Igraine, the Vulgate author inserts a double confrontation. While Merlin is away, people begin to doubt his authority, and a rumor goes round that he is dead. One baron, "high born and very wealthy," who had been refused the Siege Perilous by Merlin, decides to take it anyway:

> He had just the time to put his thighs on the seat when he melted away, just like a ball of lead, and was lost from sight right before everyone, so they did not know what had happened to him. (1.198)

When he returns, Merlin is angry with the king for letting this happen, and refuses him an explanation:

> "It is not your place to ask. And it would be worthless to you even if you knew. Think instead about those who still sit at the table and how to keep up in the most honorable way what you have started.... Be careful to do just as I have told you."
> The king said that he would very willingly do so. (1.199)

This dramatic insertion positions Merlin as a figure whose great knowledge means he need have no awe of the powerful, and he is aware of this. In the Vulgate when Merlin encounters royalty, discussions are fuller, details are dwelt on more, and as a result his impact is more fully realized. The startling scene of the melted baron brings to a head the issue of the real secular power which the Vulgate bestows on Merlin: advisory knowledge can become a real challenge to royal authority.

As Robert's *Merlin* ends, Arthur is ruling in peace among his people and barons, but the Vulgate opens its continuation by deploying Merlin's knowledge in state politics: as in Robert, he steps in to explain Arthur's right to rule through his lineage but then, when rebellion breaks out, he keeps on helping, giving Arthur advice—to ally himself with King Leodegan of Carmelide, to arrange for the archbishop to excommunicate his enemies, and to "stock the main strongholds in every city and castle with food and arms" (1.219).

Here the image of Merlin and his knowledge is substantially extended, from the confidant to kings he has been in Robert's *Merlin* to a figure who is central to the management and continuance of the kingdom: it is the image of a grand vizier to the throne. But there are limits: as in Robert, the Vulgate Arthur's sword-drawing is not arranged by Merlin. All he does is predict that God will provide a sign on Christmas Day: the installing, like the passing, of a king is not a matter for human knowledge, or for Merlin, however much modern writers will involve him in these events—even the Vulgate author later says that Arthur pulled the sword out "on Merlin's advice" (1.307), which is not what actually happened earlier.

The Vulgate brings many new adventures into the context of Arthur and Merlin. Its author's tone is less religious than Robert's, less widely referential than Geoffrey's: as Putter comments, it is "closely modelled on chronicle material" (1994, 10), telling a story of a king and his kingdom, and his greatest adviser, Merlin. Micha's analysis of the sources (1976, 319–65) identifies four areas of borrowing: military events of the period; literary memories of *chansons de geste;* folklore, in which he includes Merlin as a trickster; and also narrative threads already in the Vulgate stories of the *Graal, Lancelot,* and the *Mort.*

The most innovative area is Merlin's military involvement. Robert's very limited venture into this field expands hugely in the Vulgate and Merlin's strategic advice acts as a substitute for his previous capacity to prophesy the outcomes of future battles. He does not actually use weapons, but his advice goes a long way. Regularly he helps Arthur strategically, such as arranging for Ban and Bors to come to Britain with their army, and also tactically, advising Arthur to hide their forces in a great ambush against the rebel barons. He offers detailed planning in the battles, and some supportive magic: as Arthur faces the rebel barons for the first time Merlin sets their tents on fire by means of a spell. In the major battle that follows, the king's enemies face "a great wind and storm that Merlin sent against them and a fog" (1.229). Later he raises a river and also a fog to help defeat the ten thousand Saxons who have renewed their attack on Britain in Arthur's realm (1.298).

Merlin's power extends to reinvigorating warriors: twice he accuses Arthur of cowardice and shames him back to fight (1.217 and 1.291); on another occasion he rebukes Arthur, Ban, and Bors in the same acerbic way (1.317), and at Salisbury he sends Ban back into battle in disgrace (1.386). Magic aside, there were contemporary models: nobly born churchmen could ride to war like Archbishop Turpin or William I's cousin Bishop Odo, and when Merlin brings the Breton army to Arthur he, in the spirit of those famous warrior-priests, "led them riding in front on a great black horse" (1.228).

The location of these battles has often shifted across the Channel. King Leodegan's Carmelide borders on Arthur's realm and is in the southwest of Britain, which meshes with Geoffrey and British mythic history. But when King Rions attacks Leodegan's fortress, named Carhaix, it is undoubtedly in Brittany—though a credible Celtic connection, this is still a strange relocation. The British rebel kings seem comfortable on both sides of the Channel. After fighting in Britain, they fortify "Nantes in Brittany, near Cornwall" (which may be the Breton region Cornuaille: 1.236) and later they also occupy Wissant, in northern France.

If the traditional Arthurian warfare against rebel kings in Britain and even Leodegan's British Celtic war with Rions have drifted over to France, another Vulgate development is more firmly located there. This is the war in which King Ban and King Bors of Brittany, supported by other forces, notably King Leodegan and King Arthur himself, fight King Claudas and King Frollo. Frollo is a familiar enemy, the king of France Geoffrey of Monmouth showed Arthur trouncing, and Claudas is known from the *Lancelot*, where he is the king of Berry (based at Bourges in central France), a natural enemy to kings and lords located in northwestern France.

The *Lancelot* conflict between Arthur and his Breton allies against France is extended in the Vulgate *Merlin*: Anjou, Poitou, and Normandy are now also ranged against Claudas and Frollo. Part of the innovative force of the extended Vulgate *Merlin* is to imagine war between the noble British and their allies against royal enemies in central France. This evidently relates to the real situation in France at the beginning of the thirteenth century: King John of England, duke of both Normandy and Aquitaine (the latter a huge duchy which included at this time both Poitou and Anjou to the north), and also overlord of Brittany through his nephew Arthur, was consistently maneuvering and fighting against the French king Philippe Augustus, though the uneasy truce of 1206, followed by defeat in northeastern France at Bouvines in 1214, basically ended English involvement in France on this scale for over a century.[7] The Vulgate *Merlin* is usually dated at about 1210–15, and it would seem likely that the continuing Anglo-French wars have been absorbed into the story, with a distinctly Anglo-Norman perspective, which overlooks the loss of Normandy in 1204: this even attracts a rare old-style political prophecy in animal mode back into a French text, as Merlin speaks of Claudas as a wolf and Arthur as a British lion (1.280). Micha has seen a connection to contemporary war (1976, 320–21), but from his French viewpoint he believes Arthur here represents Philippe Augustus himself in his recurrent conflict with the great barons of France. But none of that fighting took place in the areas of the Arthurian battles, which, as J. Neale Carman shows (1973), focus on the contemporary frontier between France and the Anglo-Norman coalition.

With its heightened interest in warfare in France, the Vulgate *Merlin,* like Robert de Boron, shows no sign of a detailed interest in Britain, nor any familiarity with it. Arthur's hall is located at Caerleon, said to be beside the Thames, while Brocéliande is thought to be near the Severn (where Caerleon actually is). Merlin visits Bredigan, said to be "the chief city of Great Britain" (1.234) somewhere near Salisbury—but if that implies Winchester, it elsewhere appears, as both a forest and a castle, a good way further north: a later English version gives it as Breckenho, suggesting Brecon in southeast Wales. An important place called Clarence is near Salisbury Plain (1.382), but though this provides a medieval ducal title in England, there is no location with that name except a village in northeastern France. Yet in spite of this distance from Britain, the originally Celtic elements that Robert has inserted are preserved and even extended: before the battle at Bredigan Arthur meets a churl who tells him about buried treasure and gives his source as "a wild man named Merlin" (1.234); during the battle against the ten thousand Saxons Merlin behaves as if at Arfderydd: "Then the fighting grew heavy and wondrous, and Merlin went back into the forest, wherever he wanted to go, and he stayed there a very long time" (1.300). But Merlin's exile is brief: he returns to help the king win a victory. With the same mix of older patterns and new commitments, he says to Arthur, after telling him the story of his own birth:

> "I want to keep going back to the woods; and this is by the nature that came to me from the one who sired me, for he does not seek out any companionship that might come above from God. But I do not go into the wood for fellowship with him, but to keep company with Blaise, the holy man." (1.221)

Though originally Celtic, this self-exile can have medieval religious implications: as Corinne Saunders comments, "Merlin's life of solitude in the forest also clearly parallels that of the anchorite" (1993, 119).

More clearly in contact with the Celtic trickster are some digressions later in the Vulgate version, exotic stories brought into the narrative through attaching them to Merlin. The longest begins with him suddenly appearing in "the wide and deep forests of the country around Rome" (1.323) as "black-skinned, wild-haired, bearded and shoeless" and in "a ragged tunic" (1.324): shortly he will run into Julius Caesar's palace in the form of a stag and interpret his dream about a sow and twelve wolf-cubs. Merlin's appearance as a stag was visually popular, as in a lively manuscript illumination (see frontispiece) and in the deluxe 1505 version of the 1498 printed text (fig. 7): Lucy Paton has explored how the story's connection with the *Vita Merlini* and with folklore in general helps to construct its "complex nature" (1960, 241). Following this startling opening comes a summary of what will be the plot of the romance *Silence,* only found today in one manuscript from the later thirteenth century (*Silence,* 1992). A young woman called Avenable ("Lovely") has taken service disguised as a man, but the empress desires "him." Merlin, with satiric laughter at various ironic situations, explains the sinful adultery of the empress who is executed, with her twelve lovers—the sow and the wolf-cubs from the emperor's dream. In the midst of this classicized Celticity Merlin makes another rare prophecy in French about the British lion versus the Roman dragon (1.327), presumably retained with the Celtic trickster elements. The story is an example of *translatio studii* reversed, as the Celtic story is sent into the classical world.

The other digressive episodes are less interesting. Merlin visits Jerusalem briefly to interpret a dream for the Saracen King Flualis and the major point of this story is to predict the Christian reconquest of the holy city. A retrospective digression involves Merlin taking Arthur, on his anti-Roman European military tour, to Lausanne, where he tells him about the devil cat of that region—a story itself reminiscent of the giant Cath Palug of Welsh tradition which survived in French and Creole myth as "le chapalu," and made a reappearance in film in 1965 in the form of Jane Fonda as *Cat Ballou,* the female gunslinger.

Interested as the Vulgate is in both contemporary warfare and tricksterish elements of Celtic origin, through its new material it nevertheless maintains in general the learned, advice-oriented figure of Merlin as he was established by Robert. Merlin's prophecies are almost always in the new material, in which he foresees the coming of Lancelot (1.320–21) and the ending of Arthur (1.380), and makes some minor prophecies, such as one about the death of a dwarf who becomes involved in the story (1.401). Zumthor reports finding only three Geoffrey-style future prophecies and recognizes that Merlin has here been "domesticated": he deploys the compensatory phrase "prophet of the Round Table" to try to redeem at least some visionary power (1943, 77, 207, and 263).

The grail is only foreseen twice (1.176 and 1.280): the whole Vulgate *Merlin* is written to fit into a sequence where the grail will later enjoy its own full narrative, and so the author seems much more reticent in this context than Robert, who was going on to the grail narrative as his main purpose. On a few occasions Merlin sees outside the story, in addition to the limited, Celtic-related prophecy to Caesar and the equally restricted, Anglo-Norman–linked one about Claudas. Once he speaks to Blaise about the future of Logres (1.342); later, when he foresees a lion and she-bear overrunning Logres (1.398), this may only refer to Mordred's rebellion, but it does use the animal language of the original prophecies.

If Merlin's knowledge in the Vulgate relates to royal power rather than Christian wisdom through time, a distinct reduction of his authority in Robert, his knowledge is accordingly secular and courtly in several ways, involving Merlin in a surprising range of chivalric adventures, sometimes as more than a mere observer. The adventure of a single knight, testing himself, proving himself, sometimes failing and needing help, was the pattern of most of the romances, and in the Vulgate *Merlin* the knights often engage in tournaments and single combat, frequently supervised or at least guided by Merlin. Such detailed and genial involvement in knightly affairs seems to mesh, on a limited scale, with his enhanced capacity as a military strategist: this is a worldly and martial Merlin.

But he is still learned, and still in several senses a cleric. The Vulgate *Merlin* clearly shares Robert's interest in the powers of clerical knowledge and develops it substantially. Merlin visits Blaise regularly in order to keep him up to date with events and have them committed to writing: there are fourteen such visits in the narrative, mostly short ones to dictate new adventures: many manuscripts illustrate this—no doubt the scribes found it of special interest (fig. 8). The value of writing is asserted in the story: Merlin has a document written about the details of Arthur's conception (1.205) where in Robert he merely asks the king to note the date when he was with Igraine; a sealed letter about the events is written by Ulfin after Arthur's birth (1.217); the amazing Roman adventure ends with Merlin writing an account of it in magic letters above a door, though they will later fade when the emperor Hadrian reads this account (1.329). Literacy goes further: Vivien writes down the spell Merlin uses to make a river appear and harass his enemies (1.332) and, more importantly, she writes down the sleep-inducing charm she will use against him (1.322). Female literacy also seems implied when Guinevere first appears: not only is she beautiful but she is "one of the cleverest women in the world" (1.218).

The triumphs of Merlin's knowledge are a major feature of the Vulgate development: as Arthur says, stressing the literate character of Merlin's knowledge, "he knows everything he wants at a single word, and nothing can be hidden from him" (1.227). He can offer random information like the history of the Cat of Lausanne, the underdeveloped matter of the treasure hidden on the battlefield (1.305), or the mystery of the dwarf-knight, which he also explains to Blaise (1.416). More important to the plot, as explanation if not control, is his understanding of the false Guinevere threat (1.334 and 339) and various dream interpretations—for Arthur, Caesar, King Flualis of Jerusalem, and Queen Elaine of Brittany (1.410, 327, 399, 320–21).

Secular as his main advice may be, there is still a recurrent recognition of Merlin's role as a cleric in the Christian, even priestly, sense. He invokes God in the move to crown Arthur, saying "Our Lord means to give back to the son what is rightfully his" (1.217) and Blaise urges Merlin to work "for God's sake to keep Christendom from shame and destruction" (1.280). These dangers are recurrently related back to problems in religion: the false Guinevere problem is caused by "the breach of faith" (1.339) and, more forcefully, Merlin tells Arthur "as long as you are steadfastly in our lord and believe in him, you will have victories over the enemies of our lord" (1.380). When he finally leaves he says to Arthur "I commend you to God" (1.414), and his last word to Gawainet, from his own entombment, is "May God keep King Arthur and the kingdom of Logres" (1.422).

This devout tone, however, does seem somewhat swamped by the amount of secular activities, battles, loves, deceptions and impostures in the Vulgate extension of Robert's story of Merlin and especially by his direct and largely supportive relation with royal power. Robert's Merlin was decisive in his authority against Uther and Pendragon, and the Vulgate emphasized this with the story of the melted baron, but although Merlin reacts ferociously against the Arthurian barons who make fun of him (1.218), and tells the new king "You must do as I advise" (1.218), the relation with Arthur is mostly one of concord and friendship, not of challenge. Merlin is, Arthur says, "the best friend I have" as "It was through him that he had won all the wealth and honour he had" (1.333). Uther and Pendragon had also been "fast friends" with Merlin (1.190), but they, in a relationship already structured by Geoffrey, had faced the exercises of his power more sharply than Arthur.

However, if knowledge and power can seem harmonious, the Vulgate author is also aware of their potential conflict: he not only enjoys Merlin's transformations but stresses their element of coded challenge. At Bredigan, there appears before Arthur

> a huge peasant, a lowborn freeman.... The freeman had great cowhide shoes
> on his feet and was dressed in a tunic and coat of burlap and a cape, and around
> his waist was a knotted sheepskin belt. He was big and tall, black, and hairy,
> and he looked ruthless and evil...(1.234)

Merlin then appears as a blind beggar with a dog and asks to carry the ensign in battle. Having been refused, he reappears as an eight-year-old boy with no breeches but carrying a cudgel (1.395): a focal image of knowledge versus power, appreciated as such by an illustrator—see fig. 6. Merlin can, when appropriate, transform into less humble guise. As a royal messenger he has a "garland of flowers on his head" and "low buckled shoes...and black silk hose," but he still is "swarthy" and the elegance seems ironic (1.271–72). He can also be a courtly lover: he becomes a fifteen-year-old youth to cast a love spell on a beautiful girl whom King Ban desires (1.390) and he turns himself into "a most handsome youth" in order to attract Vivien (1.281).[8] Although Ulfin suggests shape-shifting can be self-protective, saying "Merlin changed shape because there were many people in the country who wanted him dead" (1.234), the text maintains generally the sense that knowledge can transform its bearer as a way of testing and teasing the powerful, as well as providing spectacular demonstrations of magic.

Merlin's courtly-love transformations signal the secular courtly context of the Vulgate *Merlin,* and the great sage can become something like a pander for his friends: his spell helps Arthur consummate his (prenuptial) love for Lisanor (1.235); he arranges, with some magic, the liaison between King Ban (who is married) and the unnamed daughter of Agravadan—whom he finds very attractive himself (1.389–90). This secular and courtly departure for the presentation of Merlin goes much further in the striking innovation of his love for Vivien, and its even more drastic result.

The fatal relationship with Vivien represents a major containment of Merlin's knowledge, both as an authority figure and in the story. Where in Geoffrey he just faded out, here he is magically immobilized. In Robert's reconstruction he stayed until the end of the Didot *Perceval,* but here there is no final appearance as Arthur's world collapses, no last acknowledgment of his role in the grail story. From the beginning of the Merlin myth to the present, there are two structural categories: whether the great sage survives to the end or not. The difference appears to relate to the extent of conflict in the text between the knowledge Merlin represents and the power with which it is involved: this topic will recur throughout this study.

The idea that Merlin was fatefully involved with a beautiful and powerful woman first appears in the earliest, pre-Vulgate, *Lancelot,* where Ninianne (as she is there named, and also Nimenche), linked with the Lady of the Lake, is Lancelot's protector. Her magic is explained as derived from Merlin, whom she has put to silence. This would seem a myth of female power, and the role of superseded authority is all Merlin will play in the massively extended Vulgate *Lancelot.*[9] The Vulgate *Graal,* which was attached to the expanded *Lancelot,* similarly uses Merlin as an emblem of long-past knowledge: there are occasional references to prophecies of his about events in the Arthurian world which have or will come true, but he does not appear as a guiding and judging figure as he had in the Didot *Perceval.*

One explanation of the Vulgate's major change to Merlin's role in Robert is straightforward. Because the Vulgate *Merlin* was to be inserted into the Vulgate as an explanatory prequel, the author, already knowing that the Vulgate *Graal,* unlike the Didot *Perceval,* gave the great sage no role in the achievement of the grail, had to dispose of him, and just as the Vulgate *Merlin* was fitting in before the *Lancelot,* it also used its way of dispensing with Merlin.

Yet Merlin's extended departure in the Vulgate, even if simply a technical necessity, is also complex in its meanings. Where Robert used Merlin as the agent of satirically revealing the dangers of sexuality, as in the judge's father and his own mother's sister, the Merlin of the Vulgate is not only friendly to male sexuality—in Ban, and in Arthur with both Lionors and Lot's wife (the latter event occurring when Merlin is away, and is not criticized by him at all)—but he is also a practitioner of it. He admires Agravadan's daughter even after he has fallen heavily in love with Vivien, with whom he will share a "Haven for Joy and Happiness" (1.283). They are in fact presented as a pair of courtly lovers, and later we are told how "his love for her grew and became stronger, so that he found it hard to leave her" (1.376). As in courtly love, this commitment is reciprocated: "she loved him with a deep love, because of the great nobility she had found in him" (1.391), and so she says "the great love I feel for you has even made me leave my father and mother to hold you in my arms day and night" (1.416). Even when she has finally been taught everything, and imprisons him, it is still a prison of delights, and she says "'Dear friend, I will come here often, and you will hold me in your arms and I you, and you will do forever whatever you please.'" (1.417)

In the same fairly positive way Diana the huntress, who was godmother to Vivien's father Dyonas, foretold and essentially blessed, if in proto-feminist terms, the love affair, wishing that

> "your first girl-child be sought after by the wisest, most learned man on earth, that he may show her the greatest part of his learning, and that he may teach her everything she asks—all through the power of necromancy, so that he might be so much under her sway from the moment he sees her that he lacks the power to do anything against her will." (1.281)

Merlin, like Lancelot in Chrétien's romance, is enmeshed in the silken web of courtly love: Nitze has seen a link with the "joie de la court" episode in *Erec* (1943, 69), while Pelan has linked this with the hidden love sequence in *Cligés* (1974, 160). More generally, the model for the relationship is that of a fairy mistress who keeps a knight with her in the otherworld.[10] But whatever her origin, Vivien is not here shown as a fatal temptress of an unwary cleric, a dark monastic threat. It is as if the author, accepting the structure conveyed by the *Lancelot,* has given it as positive a shape as possible, not as an austere moralistic account of the dangers a mature man of intellect might run with an entrancing young woman: illustrations of Vivien and Merlin as courtly lovers are not rare (fig. 9).

The Merlin of the *Life* and the Welsh Myrddin were also visited by a woman, whether wife or sister, or conceivably both. Scholars have speculated that Vivien is a revenant from the Celtic past and some have even argued that her name is to be related to the word *hwimleian,* found in the Myrddin poems "Apple Tree" and "Little Pig." But it seems more likely that Paris was right to argue that the Breton-oriented author of the pre-Vulgate *Lancelot,* seeking a name for the new fey, used a familiar enough Breton name, Ninian, which became altered through simple scribal misreading to Vivien, where the minims are simply misread, and to Nimue, where the minims are misread and a final nasal abbreviation is not noticed (1886, xlv).[11]

Valuing the female, as in admiration of Merlin's mother and irritation at Igraine's treatment (see 1.199, 208), is evident in the early French Merlin texts, and that itself is part of Vivien's meaning. She is not alone as a positive and intelligent woman: Morgan is a friend of Merlin, learns from him, and is "endowed with great learning" (1.307), but she plays no part, for good or bad, in the story except to annoy Guinevere (herself learned) with an amatory interest in one of her young male relatives (1.354). There were, of course, scholarly women about in the period and the milieu, some of them in the audience, and some of whom probably supported this kind of literature, as Chrétien's Comtesse de Champagne had done.

Another context for the story of Merlin and Vivien is more negative. As Nitze mooted (1943, 79) and Carolyne Larrington has discussed (2006, 99), there are parallels with the medieval story of Aristotle, notably the comic *Lay of Aristotle*. The myth of Alexander's great wise man brought low by lust was well known, and the parallel may well be a response to the rise of the man of knowledge to the role of grand vizier. Rosemary Morris suggests that Merlin's fall stems from the fact that he "exults in his power" and shows "God-like infallibility" (1982, 116), but it seems to have a more complex mix of causes. While structurally a way of excluding him from the text, the immobilization of the man of knowledge seems also to be a way of gratifying courtly reservations about a powerful adviser and may also be, both prurient and negative at once, a way of expressing clerical anxieties about the power of women over the celibate male.

But Vivien is far from a vicious enchantress: Larrington calls her "Merlin's sincerely loving partner" (2006, 103). When Vivien has, through Merlin's willing help, learned enough, she makes her move to hold power for herself:

Then they tarried together for a long while, until one day came when they were walking hand in hand through the Forest of Brocéliande looking for ways to find delight, and they came upon a beautiful bush, green and high, that was a hawthorn loaded with flowers. They sat down in its shade, and Merlin laid his head in the lady's lap, and she began to rub it until he fell asleep. And when the lady felt that he was sleeping, she got up carefully and with her head-dress drew a circle all about Merlin and the bush, and she began to cast her spells. Then she sat down again beside him, took his head in her lap, and held him there until he awoke. And he looked about him. And it seemed to him that he was in the most beautiful tower in the world, and he found himself lying in the most beautiful bed he had ever lain in. Then he asked the young lady, "Lady, you have indeed tricked me if you do not stay with me, for no one but you has the power to undo this tower."

And she said to him, "Dear friend, I will come here often, and you will hold me in your arms and I you, and you will do forever whatever you please."

And she kept her oath to him faithfully, for few days or nights went by when she was not with him. Merlin never thereafter left the stronghold where his lady love had put him, but she came and went as she wished. (1.416–17)

The Vulgate scene of Merlin's end will have many variations in the continuing myth; they will activate the power of woman as an element in the dialectic of knowledge and power. There had already been elements of this in the Celtic Myrddin, through his wife and his sister, but the dramatic nature of Merlin's entombment intensifies the issue, with some remarkable, and remarkably varied, results in the future.

In the Vulgate, Merlin is not only a courtly lover: he is also chivalric, especially supportive of young knights, notably Gawainet, Yvonet, Sagremoret. Macdonald sees a distinctly paternal side to his representation (1990, 85), and Morris finds it "heavy-handed patriarchalism" (1982, 103), but these seem post-Freudian readings of what would have been seen in the medieval period as lordly and laudable patronage. And if Merlin has protégés, he also has avatars: there are several references to other wise men. Whereas Ulfin in his attempts to resolve the problem of Uther's passion for Igraine is clearly meant to be a failure as a man of intellect, Ban and Bors have a brother called Guinebol, sometimes Guinebaut (the name clearly once began with *gwyn,* meaning "white" or "pure" in Welsh and Breton),[12] who is "a very learned clerk who knew more about astrology than anyone except Merlin" (1.224):[13] he will later have a beautiful lady he entertains with magic, and for whom he makes a magical chessboard and a spinning castle (1.302).

There are other rivals to Merlin: later in the Vulgate there appears Doon of Carduel, a "most worthy and clever man" (1.279) who knows of Merlin and his qualities; and others appear outside the Vulgate, notably Helyas of Toulouse, "the wisest of Arthur's clerks," who appears in the *Lancelot* and is often remembered, even as a possible author or at least like Merlin a transmitter of texts; similar is Master Antoine in the late thirteenth-century *Prophécies de Merlin.* They all represent to some degree clerical advisory knowledge in the context of royal power, but none as strongly, or as threateningly, as Merlin does himself.

Written remarkably soon after Robert de Boron's *Merlin,* but also fitting into the Vulgate's massive scheme, the Vulgate *Merlin* both transmits the clerical, wise, and sometimes tricksterish Merlin, and also curtails him finally, and substantially. Yet even in his own fate, there is beauty and tolerance, and the Vulgate *Merlin* has, rather like the work of Chrétien de Troyes himself, some of the largeness of mind and elegance of approach that is characteristic of romance at its finest: its Merlin is volatile, energetic, loyal, and endlessly positive, and his knowledge is consistently placed at the disposition of a secular power that is highly valued. Knowledge and power are realized fully in their own terms and the strains that are inherent between the two

4. Merlin's diabolic conception in Robert de Boron's *Joseph*. BN MSS Français 95, f. 113v. By permission of the Bibliothèque Nationale de Paris.

5. Merlin as a peasant archer with the king in the Vulgate *Merlin*. BN MSS Français 9123, f. 149. By permission of the Bibliothèque Nationale de Paris.

6. Merlin as a ragged but club-bearing boy before the king and courtiers in the Vulgate *Merlin*. BL MSS Add. 100292, f. 200v. By permission of the British Library.

7. Merlin as a stag visits the Emperor of Rome: *Prophécies de Merlin*, 1505 reprint of 1498 ed., on vellum, BL C 22 c 6, vol. 2. f. 23 v. 2.16. By permission of the British Library.

8. Merlin dictates the Arthurian story to Blaise in the Vulgate *Merlin*. BN MSS Français 749, f. 264v. By permission of the Bibliothèque Nationale de Paris.

9. Merlin and Vivien as courtly lovers in the Vulgate *Merlin*. BN MSS Français 9123, f. 285. By permission of the Bibliothèque Nationale de Paris.

forces are here at their least forceful and least damaging. The hero of the Vulgate *Merlin*—confident with Arthur, serious with Blaise, informative with everybody, devoted with Vivien—is a substantial figure, no longer just an instrument of plot or a contributor of data. All the major medieval narrative variations of the figure from now on will stem from what he became in the Vulgate, in the richly dynamic and secular but also learned and clerical culture of early thirteenth-century France.

Darkening Advice: The Post-Vulgate Merlin

Scholars believe that in the 1230s a major and serious reworking of the Vulgate material was undertaken, but a heavily revised "post-Vulgate" *Merlin* is the only major survivor in French of this postulated revision (see Bogdanow, 1966 and 2006). It starts by following the Vulgate closely—though it omits the scene that climaxes with the melted baron, including Merlin's following strictures to the king—until the moment when Arthur takes the throne by drawing the sword from the stone, without Merlin's intervention or assistance. When he soon reappears, Merlin at once has a more challenging, moralistic tone: as a four-year-old child he rebukes Arthur for his sin in fathering Mordred. Arthur thinks he is "a true devil" (trans. Asher, 1993–96, 4.169) and rejects his words, but he returns as an old man and Arthur accepts what he says, with what turns out to be good reason.

This version makes Arthur commit unwitting incest with his full sister, not his half-sister as is usual—the first of many darkenings of events by its author. At once, Arthur has a terrible dream about the destruction of the kingdom and his own death, which Merlin explains as foreseeing the harm to be caused by one "who is begotten but not yet born" (4.170)—obviously Mordred. Arthur has already seen and heard the strange questing beast, a large animal with the sound of baying, or "questing" hounds in its stomach: Merlin identifies this as "one of the adventures of the Grail" (4.171), and related events, involving King Pellinore and his illegitimate son Torre, are juxtaposed to the new story of Balin and the dolorous blow.

The author has drawn this austere material from varied sources. Torre and Pellinore are derived from one Chrétien grail continuation, the questing beast draws on another and also on a different grail story, the *Perlesvaus,* while the story of Balin has several general sources, including a Chrétien continuation.[14] These stories look forward ominously in what Vinaver called "a complex but eminently coherent system of echoes and anticipations" (1990, 1269).

Bogdanow subtitled her book on the post-Vulgate cycle "The Romance of the Grail" (1966), seeing the notional whole as a set of adventures directed consistently towards the need for spiritual regeneration and giving a somber and unrelenting account of sinfulness. The post-Vulgate *Merlin* foresees ultimate Arthurian collapse but also possible redemption through the grail.

The structure of the whole story works with some subtlety over some distance to make its powerful points. The first knight to have an adventure is Girflet and at once Merlin predicts to Arthur that Girflet will be the last of all them, who will attend Arthur at the end of his final battle—a role usually played by Bedivere. In a similarly far-reaching way, when Arthur breaks the sword he drew from the anvil Merlin advises him that the Lady of the Lake will find him another, so preparing for the final throwing of Excalibur back into the water. When Merlin places Balin's sword in a stone, he foretells it will eventually be drawn out by Lancelot and one day used to kill Gauvain. The rewriter is constructing for the audience's edification the overall moral meaning of the ill-fated interaction of the members of the Arthurian world: the lack of such meaning in the melted baron story may have led to its omission.

In most of these scenes Merlin watches and comments, possessing knowledge of the outcome of sins in the context of a power beyond human time and place. While he is no longer the initiator of the grail adventure, as in Robert de Boron, the advisory role to which he was largely restricted in the Vulgate *Merlin* is now developed to include moral meanings for Arthur's court, especially about the grail. But at times he operates in his simply helpful Vulgate mode. After Arthur has arranged his own massacre of the innocents, and of course misses Mordred, Merlin intervenes to calm down the barons who have lost children, and even assures them that the children are in fact still alive and will return before long (4.185). But in the post-Vulgate he is much less involved with military matters. In the Huth manuscript, one of the two that survive, the early rebel kings' wars against Arthur are not even covered, and in the Cambridge version Merlin's role is reduced, as he is not involved in the later throne-defending war with the five kings. The obsession with early thirteenth-century war in France is also absent: a fight against Claudas is mentioned, but only as an aside in the relationship of Merlin and Vivien (4.216), and he is eventually defeated off-stage (5.60).

Geographically the story is as vague and French-oriented as the Vulgate, with Northumberland located in Brittany, presumably because what was once Myrddin's northern forest has become Brocéliande. Issues of British politics interest this author no more than the wars in western France: there are no Merlin prophecies dealing with future British politics, only internal narrative predictions, and the British military imperialism that Geoffrey cherished so much is only briefly noticed when the author introduces the messengers from Rome early (4.176–77), and disposes of them quickly: Macdonald describes the tone here as "quiet diplomacy" (1990, 130), but the key moment is Arthur's commitment to God's will. Though the war with the Romans eventually takes place, it is contained in one paragraph towards the end of the fragmentary post-Vulgate *Mort Artu* (5.301–2).

The major innovation of the post-Vulgate *Merlin* is its powerful, dark and far-reaching account of the story of Balin, a further grail prequel showing how an inherently well-intentioned but unduly aggressive young knight came to strike the "dolorous blow" which turned the land waste, maimed the king, and so necessitated the achieving of the grail. The Balin story powerfully combines the ideas of possible social destruction with a critique of undue ferocity in knighthood itself. Merlin's role is different from his benign engagement with the follies and weaknesses of the kings and knights of the Vulgate: he watches appalled, but unable to intervene, as the terrible story unfolds:

> Merlin went on all the while from room to room until he came near the room containing the Holy Lance and the Holy Vessel that men called the Holy Grail.
>
> He knelt at once and said to those who were near him: "Oh God, how foolishly he acted, the wretched, unfortunate sinner who with his soiled, low-born hands, befouled by the base venom of sexual indulgence, touched such a noble, precious shaft as I see here and with it wounded such a noble man as King Pellehan. Oh, God! How dearly will this great outrage and forfeit be paid for, and how dearly will they pay who have not deserved it, and how much misery and torment the nobles and the good knights of the kingdom of Logres will suffer for it, and how many marvellous, perilous adventures will yet happen because of this Dolorous Stroke that has been struck." (4.213)

Not everything is so negative. The Round Table knights do attempt to bring order against a world of crime, and this is referred to as the "custom" of knightly adventure. Girflet is the first knight to fulfill this custom and Merlin is specific about this, saying to Arthur: "this custom will be practiced all your life, but afterwards there will be nobody in your land so valiant that he can maintain it, for men will not be worth so much." (4.275) This theme is mentioned earlier, when the "custom of adventures" is discussed (4.227). Critics seem to have missed the legal implication of the term "custom" in medieval

France: as with Chrétien's Yvain and "the custom of the fountain"; the customs of a region were the codifying practices which reenacted the authority of the lord over his people (see Köhler, 1960). As Asher comments, "What Merlin is introducing is the idea that the government's obligation to right individual wrongs should be executed by knights who owe feudal service to the throne" (1993–96, 4.175, n. 2).

Girflet does his best, though against Pellinore, and in the general context of the questing beast and the dolorous stroke, he is overmatched. Later, though, the text returns to this chivalric ideal: on the day that Arthur and Guinevere are married, and the round table is filled with knights, Merlin states that there will follow "three of the most marvellous adventures you ever saw' (4.227)—but "marvellous" here means astonishing, not necessarily excellent. In a sequence of three adventures Gauvain, Pellinore, and Torre are involved in complex action with results ranging from depressing to dreadful. Gauvain, rash and young (even younger than he was in the Vulgate), manages to behead an innocent maiden; Torre does well but is exposed as Pellinore's son by a cowherd's wife; Pellinore reveals serious failings, and his tragic death is predicted by Merlin. This set of misadventures is followed by further dark events: Morgan's theft of Arthur's sword, war with the five kings (by its lateness and the absence of Merlin showing the French author's lack of interest in British politics), and then Merlin's disastrous entanglement with Vivien, here named Niniane. But the Round Table world struggles on, and as something of a respite a fairly positive sequence follows in which three young knights, Gauvain, Yvain, and Morholt, accept adventures supervised by three symbolic maidens, one aged fifteen, one thirty, and one seventy. Evidently meant to represent the processes of chivalric development, this includes positive recognition of Merlin's own knowledge: the oldest of the maidens says "Merlin knows whatever is done or thought" (4.240)—there are no major outcomes of this knowledge in the narrative.

Not yet entirely despairing, the post-Vulgate *Merlin* prepares for the final parts of the cycle by telling of the rise of Lancelot and Perceval, the two knights who in their opposite ways will take the Arthurian story up to its final fatal sequence. Grimly and also subtly coherent as it is, the post-Vulgate is also a new reading of the figure of Merlin and of the possibilities of knowledge in the context of power. Where the Vulgate was written to fill in the story of Merlin, but was also constrained by the shape of the *Lancelot* and the *Queste* to get rid of him, here Merlin is himself involved in the processes which will lead to the quest, not, as in Robert, as an instigator and interpreter, but as a representative of the secular world. Merlin watches in apprehensive horror as the retributive Christian powers start to operate, and comes to act foolishly himself, and to suffer his own retribution.

A feature of Merlin which is least changed, but still darkened, by the post-Vulgate author is his capacity to prophesy within the narrative. Early on he is chased by peasants, angry because he has just prophesied their deaths. He predicts events within the immediate narrative—Arthur will gain land through marrying Guinevere (4.222), Torre will turn out to be noble (4.226)—or across the overall Arthurian story: Tristan and Lancelot will fight later on (4.190), Pellinore will die (4.244), Gauvain will kill Bagdemagu (4.202). He foresees the deaths of himself and Arthur (4.199, 223; 4.176, 223). But the emphasis of many of his predictions is moral, not merely narrative anticipation, and the climax is his recurrent prediction of the achievement of the grail.

Another gloomy element in the post-Vulgate is that Morgan is activated as a supernatural threat. Just mentioned in Robert de Boron as a clever woman and never hostile in the Vulgate, here she is a beauty who it seems has become ugly "because the enemy entered her" (4.172) Merlin loves her but she repays him by getting close enough to Arthur to steal the sword and the scabbard. The problem is averted, in part through Merlin's powers, but he still allows her to get away.

Not only the tone of the text is more religious: Merlin is "in the white robe of a convert" (4.206) as he sees the Dolorous Blow struck, and there is a much more strongly Christian atmosphere to his activities. He celebrates Arthur's baronial victory like a bishop, but it is a church militant to which he belongs. He has a statue made of the twelve kings, all holding a lighted candle, while Arthur's much finer statue holds a raised sword "seeming to threaten those around him, while they were bowing as if begging forgiveness for some misdeed" (4.199).

The courtliness common in the Vulgate is here not tolerated, and leads to Merlin's dire end. When Merlin desires Morgan, this is an innovation that clearly shows dangerous weakness, and then he forces his attentions on a quite unwilling Niniane. She comes to court with Pellinore—one of the many ways in which this random-seeming opening adventure has resonance—because she is a "maiden huntress" he has rescued (4.244). The link to Diana is a good deal more negative than in the Vulgate, where the goddess indirectly approved of the relationship, and Niniane has become, as Macdonald says, "a much more mysterious character" than in the Vulgate (1991, 12). Merlin takes her to the lake of Diana, where they see the tomb of Faunus, who was killed by Diana with, Merlin says, "the greatest treachery in the world" (4.246)—she persuaded him to enter the tomb to be healed of a wound, then had it sealed and filled with molten lead. But Niniane feels "the place pleases and attracts me so much that I'll never leave it until I have made a home as beautiful and rich as once was made" (4.247). So Merlin has a house built—by craftsmen, not spells, one of the post-Vulgate limits on his power—and conceals it among waters, this time by magic: in the post-Vulgate Niniane is frequently herself called the Lady of the Lake.

He is totally in her power, itself expressed as hostility: "he did not dare ask her to do anything for him, for he dared not anger her" (4.248). But she is already angry:

> ...there was nobody in the world she hated so mortally as she did Merlin, because she knew well that he desired her maidenhead; and if she had dared to kill him, either by poison or in some other way, she would have undertaken it boldly, but she dared not, for she feared that he would know about it. (4.248)

Merlin has taken her to Brittany, where she sees the young Lancelot, and they then return to Britain, at her urging, because Arthur has lost his sword to Morgan—a telling narrative interconnection, honoring and exculpating Niniane. In the following sequence, she makes clear the seriousness of her objections: she hates Merlin "because he is the son of the devil and not like other men" (4.259), and he speaks not in the language of courtly love, but of an old man's folly: "I have left, for your company, King Arthur and all the noblemen of the kingdom of Logres, of which I was a lord, and I have had no profit out of following you." (4.259)

In this version he does not, as in the Vulgate, end in a lover's exclusive paradise, but is brutally sealed alive in a room that becomes a tomb and is itself a site of previous tragedy. This is where a king's son brought his lower-class lover to escape his father's wrath; they both died, but to Niniane this is not a moving tragedy of love, but an opportunity for relief:

> When the maiden heard this story, she was full of joy, and she thought then that she would put Merlin there, if she could, and if magic and the power of words could help a woman, she thought she could accomplish it. (4.259)

There is female self-empowerment, even aesthetic value, about her disposal of him, but no sympathy or affection, as in the Vulgate. She notes that "it is a rich and beautiful place" (4.260) and proposes that they spend the night there—in separate beds. She enchants him, then calls in her retainers: she reviles him as one "who follows me, not for my honour but to degrade and deflower me" (4.260). There Merlin stays. Baudemagu, this story says, later tries to let him out when he hears his cry but Merlin tells him only Niniane could release him, and she chooses not to do so.

Far from the almost positive tone of the Vulgate, and much more austere than Merlin's relations with women in the *Vita Merlini* and the Welsh poems, this sequence is a major element of the darkening tone of the post-Vulgate. The Merlin-Niniane relationship may also represent a view about the mistreatment of woman that is more critical than the hints found in Robert de Boron. In the post-Vulgate Igraine cries "Oh Merlin, damn you" for his intervention (4.173), and even Torre's mother is angry with Merlin for his investigation into Torre's fatherhood. Dissent is converted into female agency in the case of Morgan and her challenge to Arthur, and though Niniane is hostile to Merlin, her power seems otherwise entirely positive and purposive. Indeed after Merlin's entombment she to some degree supplants him: in disguise as an old woman she saves Arthur from a poisoned mantle sent by an enemy and sees the king as the pillar of chivalric ideology, saying "I love you, for you love the flower of chivalry of the world and hold it up to honour and respect" (4.276).

The Vulgate represented Merlin as a secular-friendly figure of knowledge. The Merlin of the post-Vulgate is without that propinquity to royal power, and though the text is seriously religious, his voice does not mediate that force as it did in Robert de Boron: the tone of the text seems closer, as Bogdanow suggests, to the austerity of the *Queste* (2003, 46–50). In the post-Vulgate, Merlin's knowledge is largely limited to observation and commentary, and he seems to represent the limits of knowledge when it is not devotedly allied to Christian faith, and its exclusion from any lasting power as a result. The deracination of Merlin in the post-Vulgate, with no roots in British politics, religious history, or secular advice, looks forward to the isolated and vulnerable cleverness of the Renaissance mage.

Though manuscript survival suggests no success for the post-Vulgate *Merlin* in France, this version of the myth had some further life in both Spanish and Portuguese (see Lida de Malkiel, 1959; Michon, 1998, 51–69, and Miller, 2000). The late fifteenth-century text *Merlin y Demanda* ("Merlin and Queste") combines a Galahad grail-quest with the *Baladro del Sabio Merlin* ("The Cry of the Wise Merlin"); the latter, focused on the entombment of Merlin and its aftermath, appears to be a version of the poem referred to in the post-Vulgate as the *Conte du Brait* ("The Tale of the Cry," 4.261), an amplification of Merlin's end which has not survived in French.[15] The *Baladro* is a serious Christian text as in the early grail stories, making Merlin's fate in part a punishment for his mistreatment of Igerne. In this and its general seriousness it shows a real audience for the conceptions of the author of the post-Vulgate *Merlin.*

Not only Spain was interested. Vinaver's finding of the Cambridge manuscript of the post-Vulgate was appropriate, because it is this version of the developed story of Merlin events which became very well known in England through Malory's use of it as his major source in the first part of the *Morte Darthur,* the section which Vinaver in his edition called "The Tale of King Arthur." But this was only the conclusion of the English-language medieval tradition about Merlin and his world. In order to understand that tradition and its development it is necessary to return in time to consider the aftermath of Geoffrey of Monmouth in medieval Britain.

Advising a Nation: from Layamon to Malory

In England the stories of Arthur and Merlin took a path different from their sophisticated courtly and Christian development in French. The English-speaking audience was much less likely to be aristocratic and leisured, even learned, and there was almost no interest in massive structures using Merlin as a Christian and moral authority, as in the early grail stories and the post-Vulgate, or a social and military adviser as in the Vulgate. Robust single-hero romances were the English favorites, and in these stories, as in those of Chrétien and his followers, Merlin had very little role. For the English his strength still lay in political prophecy, and the favored genre was quasi-history in chronicle form: Geoffrey's tradition persevered.

The earliest of the English Arthurian texts remains one of the most powerfully imagined and confidently written of all. Layamon's *Brut* is dated around 1200, and only survives in two thirteenth-century manuscripts, one a shorter version that has been damaged by fire. Where Geoffrey appropriated Arthur and Merlin for Norman culture, Layamon goes a step further and reshapes the story and its interface of knowledge and power into a distinctly Germanic, and English, pattern. This heroic context does not permit Merlin to develop as a feudal grand vizier, and its location in Britain retains the interest in him as a political prophet. But prophecy is now not tied to Celtic Britain: just like the Arthur who had formerly fought the invading Anglo-Saxons, Merlin here becomes merged with their culture and concerns as a mythic hero of England.

Anglo-Saxon religious culture survived vigorously after the conquest in the potent sermons of Bishop Wulfstan of Worcester, and it was in his region that Layamon flourished. He tells us he was a priest at Arley Regis, a village on the River Severn. His long poem, in the Old English style of alliterative meter and rich with the tradition and vocabulary of Anglo-Saxon heroic values, has the essentially French title *Brut* (Layamon, 1989). More than the title is hybrid: Layamon sets out to make Geoffrey's story, taken from Wace, available not only in English, but also to an audience consciously identified with that language. At the start he says of himself:

> It came into his mind and his fine intention
> That he would of the English the nobleness tell
> What they were called and where they came from
> Who the land of England first owned
> After that flood that came from the Lord. (6–10)

Arthur, formerly a Celt, is the centerpiece of this English story, and Layamon displaces Merlin by relocating Arthur's birth in the context of the elves of northern myth:

> The time came that was chosen, then was Arthur born
> As soon as he came on earth elves took him over
> They enchanted that child with very strong spells
> They gave him strength to be the best of all knights
> They gave him another thing, that he would be a great king
> They gave him a third, that he would live long
> They gave him, that king's child, very good qualities
> That he was the most generous of all men alive.
> This the elves gave him and so that child thrived. (9608–15)

Layamon makes other changes to Wace. His text is much longer, partly because scenes are more detailed—his account of the Round Table develops Wace's hints into a complex social reality—but also because new material is added. The fine formal description of the arming of Arthur is a heroic set-piece both classical and Germanic (10542–62). Some additions are developed from the text itself: Barron and le Saux have discussed as "reduplication," rather than invention, moments like Layamon developing a new scene where Uther sends for Merlin on the basis of the previous scene where Aurelius has done much the same (1989, 34).

Layamon also selected material from elsewhere to amplify his text and develop his own meanings. Le Saux has argued that he had access—perhaps in oral form—to material in Geoffrey of Monmouth that Wace did not pass on, such as his comments on the Orkneys and Caerleon, and she feels there are "definite signs of indebtedness to Geoffrey's lesser-known *Vita Merlini*" (1989, 110). She refers to the scene where Merlin is spoken of as being in the wild (9379–86), and other Celtic-aware instances exist—Layamon gives Merlin's grandfather a Breton name, Conan; he amplifies Arthur's mysterious end considerably in the direction of the Celtic idea of his survival, and even consigns Arthur to Avalon, as in the *Vita Merlini,* with a fairy healer called Argante, whose name appears to be a version of Morgan.

Layamon knew something of Wales and its culture, living as he did on the Severn, in a region where the Welsh language and its traditions were current. The fairly accurate Welsh names, as le Saux notes (1989, 143–44), could come easily from one of those latimers who, like Bleddri himself, moved freely around this multilingual, multicultural world and would have transmitted Celtic stories along with names. But there are also some errors to indicate distance from the Celtic world. Layamon locates Vortigern's castle on Mount Reir, while Wace's name for Snowdon, Eir, is much closer to the Welsh Eryri; Layamon, unlike Wace, feels the reeve of Carmarthen can run to meet Vortigern, some hundred miles away in the mountains of the north.

The poem's treatment of the Germanic peoples is not simple. I. J. Kirby argued that Layamon represents "the Angles, untouched by Saxon guilt, as the true successors of the Britons" (1964, 62), and James Noble went further to suggest Layamon casts the Saxons as like the Normans, the wrongful invaders of his own period (1992, 175). Neil Wright has doubted this, arguing the author is just careful in historically distinguishing the names, if finally favorable to the less aggressive Angles (1994). Whatever interpretation is preferred, Arthur is being appropriated one step beyond Geoffrey's move from Welsh to Norman values: he is now a hybrid figure of English grandeur, a heroic warrior whose nobility has nothing to do with the Norman-French of Geoffrey's patrons, or indeed Wace's source, but lives on in the contemporary form of English heroic culture. The idea that Arthur, validated by Merlin's prophetic knowledge, is king of a country both Celtic and Germanic will recur in sixteenth-century nationalism and twentieth-century historicism, and Benedict Anderson has explained this process as one element in imagining a nation. In the revised edition of *Imagined Communities* a sequence called "The Reassurance of Fratricide" relates how, in order to validate national unity, countries will rewrite their history and represent a past conflict that was a real national or ethnic struggle for possession of a land as no more than a civil war between fractious parts of an already existing national unity (1999, 199–203). This is exactly how Layamon and some later English writers redeploy the Arthur myth, often with Merlin as the ideologue of this new national unity.

No doubt to strengthen this political maneuver, Layamon does rather more with Merlin than Wace did. First, he makes him seem a little more independent—he is angry with Uther and the wise men (7904–5); he sternly says three times to Uther: "King keep your promise" (7931, 7937, 7950); and he even teases Arthur (8586–87). Merlin's cleverness is stressed as he raises the stones (8705) and he refuses riches on several occasions (8510, 9444–60)—like a bard, a saint, or even a humble Severn-side priest. There is more mystery about him than in Wace when he creates Stonehenge (8601–4), and in the striking new scene where Merlin quakes with prophetic power Layamon represents the mysterious power of a Celtic bardic or shamanic trance:

> Merlin sat silent for a long space of time,
> As if in a dream he laboured deeply.
> They said, those who saw with their own eyes,
> That often he shook as if he were a snake,
> Then he started to wake, he began to quiver,
> And he said these words, Merlin the wise... (8935–40)

This enhanced Merlin offers power to the imagined English state through the knowledge in his prophecies: his advice is more for the whole English nation than to the king alone. Layamon does not amplify the merely military prophecy made to Vortigern, where Geoffrey located major future predictions, but he does omit Wace's doubts about the prophecies in general; he also has the bishop of Caerleon recommend Merlin to King Uther as a prophet (8478–79). His most important move is to remind the audience of Merlin's prophecies after he has, as in Geoffrey and Wace, left the text—and these are not simply narrative predictions as in the Vulgate, but long-lasting political and national prophecies. These recurring prophetic references have been seen by le Saux as a "leitmotiv" through the text (1989, 135), and Barron and le Saux discern Layamon making a "periodic return to Merlin as the prophet of Arthur's destiny" (1989, 37–38).

Merlin is remembered at 11492–517 as prophesying in general about Arthur's grandeur and his large-scale prediction that Arthur would destroy Rome is twice mentioned (13530–39, 13964–65). This British Celtic nostalgic fantasy was to have increasing currency in the Middle Ages, as English kings struggled increasingly with the influence of Rome. Two more Merlin prophecies are cited: the first briefly foresees the battle of Winchester (14200–2), and finally comes a memorable concluding statement of the future glory of Arthur and his unified kingdom:

> Then was it brought about what Merlin said before
> There would be untold care for Arthur's departure.
> Yet the Britons believe that he is alive
> And dwells in Avalon with the fairest of all elves
> Never a man born of never so fine a lady
> Knows how to say more truth about Arthur
> But once a wise man—Merlin he was called
> Prophesied in words—his sayings were true
> That an Arthur would again come to help the English. (14288–97)

Very limited though its direct influence was, Layamon's *Brut* exemplifies the way that England and English culture over the next centuries made a powerfully nationalistic use of the Arthur myth in its saga forms: the national vision—or ideology—of Merlin's Celto-Norman prophecy in Geoffrey's *Historia* is redeployed with potent meaning for power, both symbolic and real, in the triumphs and tragedies of a great British, but also specifically English, monarch. Barron and le Saux comment that Layamon's *Brut* is "the nearest thing we have to an English national epic" (1989, 25) and this was the major impact of the text, and Merlin's contribution to it, in following centuries, when "the reassurance of fratricide" was often redeployed.

The Anglicization of Arthur and Merlin in saga form is not a dominant theme in medieval English literature, but Layamon's initiative did have parallels. The Auchinleck manuscript of about 1320, which preserves so much of early English romance—by no means only Arthurian—also contains what Lee Ramsey called "the earliest Arthurian romance composed in England" (1983, 71). *Arthour and Merlin* appears to have been written by the end of the thirteenth century and, drawn from the Vulgate *Merlin,* it had considerable popularity.[16] Versions which abbreviate the story and stress the "reassurance of fratricide" element survive in fifteenth-century manuscripts, an early print by Wynkyn de Worde in about 1510, and as late as the mid-seventeenth-century Percy Manuscript.

The author probably also wrote *Kyng Alysaunder* and *The Seven Sages of Rome:* some think he also produced *Richard Coeur de Lion.* Experience shows: Helen Newstead described the poem's "clearly presented narrative and its smooth competent handling of the couplets" (1967, 48), and considerable confidence is clear from two early sequences in *Arthour and Merlin.* The context has become English history, separating itself from the chivalric and religious adventures of the Vulgate. Catherine Batt sees the text using English legal systems in the trial of Merlin's mother and smoothly merging the concepts of Britain and England (2002, 16–22). The structure of the story does the same, beginning at the crucial English (no longer just British) date of the conflict between King Constans and Vortigern. It is only when Vortigern's tower keeps collapsing and the blood of a fatherless boy is prescribed as the cure that the author turns back to Robert de Boron's story of the devils and the birth of Merlin, and amplifies the narrative. Merlin explains to Vortigern's messengers that their king has a chamberlain who is really a woman, that the queen was in love with this "man," and when "he" rejected her she accused "him" of rape. When the king heard this, the chamberlain was brought from jail, stripped, and found to be a woman. It is of course the Vulgate story of Avenable, elaborated in the romance *Silence,* but the only outcome here is Merlin's brilliance: the queen is not executed, the female chamberlain does not marry the king or his son.

This amplification emphasizes what Geraldine Barnes has shown is the author's strong interest in Merlin's role as a provider of advice to the king, extending "beyond the functions of political adviser and military strategist to those of priest, father-figure and, effectively, ruler of the kingdom" (1991, 62). The advisory Vulgate Merlin is merged with the British, now to be English, prophet. The author feels able to omit less royally focused action, including building Stonehenge and the threefold-death sequence. Not surprisingly, this English version has almost no French wars—Claudas is very briefly mentioned, but Frollo never appears, and consistent with the insular viewpoint is a rationalization of place names: the Vulgate's Vambrieres becomes English-sounding Wandlesbury (perhaps referring to Wendlebury near Bicester), but when Sorhaut becomes Schoreham this can be neither of the actual southeastern places of that name: as it is Urien's stronghold it must be far to the north; Bredigan appears once as Breckenham, twice as Breckenho (both may refer to Brecon, or Brycheiniog, in southeast Wales), and several times as the genuine forest of Rockingham. Logres (the Welsh for England) is, as in the source, London, and that suggests no knowledge of or interest in Wales, a view supported when it is "Inglond" that is searched for the fatherless boy (614).

But this is an updated version of England, at times euphemizing Layamon's "reassurance of fratricide" into something like simple xenophobia. The historical Saxon invader and father-in-law of Vortigern Hengist is now Angys—in the Vulgate he was called Hangus—and this Gaelic-sounding enemy leads in war an army from "Denmark and Sessoyne," Saxony. But before long Angys is more dramatically said to be supported "with mani Sarrazin" (1315–16). In the Vulgate the Saracens only appeared once, fighting with the Romans against Arthur (1.410), but here they are the enemy. As Turville-Petre comments, "English readers are therefore shielded from their unfortunate descent from the pagan enemies of Christ's knights" (1996, 126). This is the first of the Arthur stories in English to translate Saxons into Saracens—presumably the similarity of names permits the expression of the recurrent anxiety about the Islamic threat to Europe, both in Spain and the Holy Land. Diane Speed has argued that the slightly earlier martial romance *King Horn* transmitted the idea, because it locates Saracen enemies in Britain by adapting its French *chanson de geste* source, where Horn, like Roland, fought more realistic enemy Saracens (1990).

In all this Merlin plays a part different from that in the source. As the editor of the text, O. D. Macrae-Gibson sums up, "Merlin's part is somewhat reduced by elimination of some of his wonders and mystifications" (1979, 34). Prophecy is treated in the same way as Wace: Merlin does predict briefly to Vortigern, including some things that have not yet happened (1694–1704), but:

For it is alle thester thing	[obscure]
Nill I make therof no telling	[I will not]
Ac forth ichil with mi tale—(1705–7)	[I will]

If that seems brusque, then terse to the point of obscurity is the only mention of Vivien in the text, when it discusses a witch called Carmile who knew a great deal about witchcraft and villainy:

Withouten Arthurs soster abast	[illegitimate]
Morgein forsothe was her name	
And woned withouten Nimiane	
That with hir quaint gin	[clever trick]
Bigiled the gode clerk Merlin. (4444–48)	

On this reference to Nimiane, Macrae-Gibson says the poet "has been misled into treating her as a place" (1973, 118). He evidently reads the third line as "Morgain 'woned' (i.e. lived) outside (a place called) Nimiane." But the text actually uses "withouten" twice, of Morgaine and Nimiane, and surely means "except" in both cases: they are two magicians better than Carmile.

The phrase "hir quaint gin" describes the Vivien and Merlin story much better than anything that happened between him and Morgan.[17] But if not quite as dismissive as Macrae-Gibson suggests, this is still the only reference to Nimiane in the text; it breaks off before Merlin and Vivien have their final encounter in the Vulgate, but not before they had in the source met for the first time. Macrae-Gibson states that the author had "little interest" in the Merlin-Vivien story and "would not have treated it" (1979, 8): while it is just possible that there might have in the uncompleted or lost material have been a late meeting and rapid encounter, it still seems that Merlin's personal life is of very little interest. The thrust of the second half of the story is Arthur's busy fighting against the rebel kings and the Saxons turned Saracens, and while Merlin is at times helpful, as in the Vulgate, the emphasis is on knightly adventure, sometimes of real confusion—the text manages to assemble no less than six knights under the name of Ywain.

The earliest of the Middle English Arthur poems, *Arthour and Merlin* has a clear resemblance to Layamon's *Brut* rather than its own French sources, and a consistent concern with English national ideology—Cooper sees the author's central concern with Arthur as "reclaiming him for the English" (2003, 150). He does not employ Merlin as a national prophet, as Layamon does, because this is not part of his Vulgate source, but the manuscript insists that Merlin's name is part of the title: the hero of knowledge validates the hero of unified English power, and this support is without the tensions of the earlier texts—and so there is no need for Merlin to leave the story.

Other texts from its period had little use for the great sage. His political significance brings him a mention at the start of a mid-fourteenth century patriotic war poem by Laurence Minot (1996, 51), and the subtle author of *Sir Gawain and the Green Knight* mentions him very late, apparently to suggest a historical perspective, as the intensely personalized Gawain-favoring viewpoint begins to pull back ironically. The title *Brut,* code word for the historical Arthur genre, is used only in the very last line of that poem, apparently to remind us that the *Brut* saga was referred to and then generically withdrawn in the first lines as well. Though that great artist signaled what he was not choosing to write, most romancers had no awareness of or interest in the Arthurian saga and its involvement of Merlin.

Even in the alliterative *Morte Arthure,* the late Middle English follow-up to Layamon's *Brut,* there is no Merlin. Only preserved in a single manuscript, this is long, rich, heroic, Christian, and all in the powerfully fulfilled English, though not now Old English, alliterative tradition. The grand poem marches on through heroic conflict, noble fraternity, brilliantly evoked bold fighting, and wretched feeling, to a heroic end far from both Celtic and French traditions, where Arthur is as dead and as noble as Beowulf ever was. Taking the tradition of Geoffrey and Wace as its structural source, and favoring military events in the Germanic and classical traditions that Geoffrey also observed, the poem has no place for a magician, nor even, in this sealed heroic world, of a prophet.

But there is one striking use for knowledge, when Arthur dreams. Usually this is the moment when Merlin steps forward to explain all, past and future alike. Here after the king's "dredefulle drem" (*Morte Arthur: A Critical Edition,* 1984, 3224), he sends for his "phylosphers" and tells them the dream. Then it is just "the philosopher" (3394) who expounds the dream in terms of Arthur's future fame as one of the nine Christian worthies, and that he should in the present repent of sin and seek mercy for his soul (3305–3455).[18] The shift between a group of advisers and just one real one is strongly reminiscent of Merlin's performance before Vortigern, and dream-reading is a regular Merlin activity. It is as if even when he is absent, the Merlin role as a provider of knowledge to advise power is so important it must be filled, albeit anonymously.

The reverse structure, when a Merlin story is told in a non-Arthurian context, appears in *The Seven Sages of Rome,* by the author of *Arthour and Merlin*—and one of the nine English versions of the poem also appears in the Auchinleck manuscript. This poem is an anthology of tales, and the creator of its French source shows familiarity with the Merlin and Vortigern story in one of them. Herod lost his sight and asked his wise men to explain; they could not, but the child Merlin identified a cauldron deep beneath Herod's bed full of boiling bubbles, representing the wise men whose corruption had effectively blinded him. When they were executed the bubbles subsided, and Herod could see again. Here Merlin is named as a source of advisory knowledge, but is basically insignificant in the whole shape of the story, whereas in the alliterative *Morte Arthure* he is unnamed, but implicitly central to the heroic king and his fame.

Up to the fifteenth century a full Merlin story or an Arthur saga are in England exceptional phenomena, exotics against the mainstream of single-hero romances. In the fifteenth century this no longer seems the case. Helen Cooper has seen "a new surge of popularity" for the French prose romances in fifteenth-century England, and "a cult of chivalry to encourage their reading" (1998, ix). In the context of a weightier cultural role for the language and a new reading audience, not now institutionalized in monasteries, nunneries, or great courts, three different writers in the relatively short period of fifty years attempted to deliver an English version of at least part of the massive French Arthur saga.

An archetype of the new secular author was Henry Lovelich, a Londoner and a prosperous member of the skinners' guild. He never completed a verse translation of the Vulgate *Merlin* but he did finish his *Quest of the Holy Grail,* though its beginning is now missing. He wrote the *Merlin* for Henry Barton, master of the skinners' guild and twice mayor of London, who died in 1435: Lovelich's poem is dated, with some uncertainty, to about 1425.[19] He states he is translating from French, evidently a Vulgate *Merlin* manuscript, but expansions appear. In the scene where Merlin first meets Vivien, here also Nymiane, there are very few changes other than occasional amplifications for rhyme, but then, as Merlin displays his magic to impress her, Lovelich elaborates with some skill. His sequence from 21385–21424 is just one paragraph in the Vulgate, and the same is true of 21425–21468: the whole scene is rich and quite fluent, possibly with some reminiscence of the magician's demonstration in Chaucer's "The Franklin's Tale":

> Tabowrers with chymbys so merye gonne rynge,   [bells]
> Therto many jogelowrs to-forn hire pleynge.
> Alle these with-inne the cerne they weren in fere,   [magic circle]
> Which that Merlyn with his rod made there. (21391–94)

Lovelich transmits with clarity the Vulgate's interest in warfare: Merlin has the same strategic and leadership functions and even appears to engage in military action: as the marginal summary at 27505 says, in the final battle against Claudas in France Merlin, with the men he leads, "bears down whomsoever he meets." Lovelich also elaborates Vivien: she warns Lancelot, after Arthur's death, to frustrate a plot by Claudas to murder Bors and Lionel, which is not in the source (27213–36).

The poem has never been highly regarded. Newstead said Lovelich had "no talent for writing and no ear for verse" (1967, 49) and Ackerman called it "undeniably bad poetry" (1952, 477). Roger Dalrymple has recently identified its "dullness" (2000, 157), but he also argues for the poem's special interest in urban affairs and activities, and links this to Lovelich's own base in London and the patronage of the future mayor. The failure to finish the English verse *Merlin* may well have been in part caused by problems with Lovelich's health and his patron's support, though Ackerman feels Lovelich may just have lost interest: he comments that there are far more errors in translation in the *Merlin* than in the earlier *Grail* (1952, 483). Lovelich did not vary or develop the material in any substantive way: power and knowledge and their interrelationship did not have any dynamic new meaning, and that lack of energetic innovation may have itself been a cause for the abandonment of the project, as it has been for the general lack of interest in Lovelich's work in succeeding periods.

The other unfinished saga is the English prose *Merlin,* though only a few pages are missing at the end. Dated to about 1450, it exists in one manuscript and a one-page fragment of Merlin prophecies. In his edition John Conlee calls the text "a straightforward and fairly accurate translation of the Vulgate *Merlin*" (1998, 1) and it lacks the structural changes found in *Arthour and Merlin.* Though W. E. Mead found the text dull (1865/99, cxlii–viii), Karen Stern has more recently defended it (1986), and Carole Meale has shown how an early woman reader was intensely interested in the text, and marked passages where women were closely involved in the action (1986).

The source is taken to be a Vulgate *Merlin* manuscript, but, as Karen Hodder notes (1999, 81), this and Lovelich's *Merlin* have not yet been carefully compared. Mead's table comparing names in Lovelich and the English prose *Merlin* shows many similarities between the two (1865/99, lxv–lxvi) and the word choice in translation of the English prose *Merlin* is very often the same as Lovelich's; there must be a possibility that the author of the prose *Merlin* used the English poem as a guide to his French source. Other similarities exist—for example, both English texts recount the story of the rebellious baron who takes the seat at the Round Table forbidden by Merlin, but neither makes him disappear like molten lead: rather he just drops out of sight as if as heavy as lead.

At times the prose translator foregrounds human activities and feelings more than the Vulgate original: here it is stressed that Merlin's mother herself saves him from the devil:

> And ther the devell was dysseyved of his purpose, that he hadde ordeyned the child to have his art and witte to knowe alle thynges don and seide, bothe that were paste and that were to come. And oure Lorde, that alle thynges knoweth, when he sye the repentaunce of the moder and that it was not her will that was so befelen, He wolde have hym on Hys parte…(1998, 27)

Igerne is also given more emphasis as a wronged woman, and Merlin confesses that "I helped to disseyue the lady" (87). When Merlin tells Arthur that he is leaving, but will return when Arthur needs him, the king is more upset and anxious than in the source:

> And the kynge was stille a longe while and began to stodie sore. And whan he hadde be longe in this thought, he seide all sighinge, "Ha, Merlin, feire swete

frende, in what need shull ye me helpe?" I praye yow tell me, to sette myn herte in more ese." "Sir," seide Merlin, "I shall yow telle, and after I shall go my way. The lyon that is the sone of the bere and was begeten of a lepard shall renne by the reame of the Grete Breteigne; and that is the need that ye shall have." With that Merlin departed and the kynge belefte in grete myssese and sore abaisshed of this thinge, for he knew not to what it might turn. (303–4)

In the Vulgate all the king says before Merlin speaks is "Ah Merlin dear friend, please tell me in what time of need you are to help me" (1.398) and there is no comment about the king's anxiety after Merlin speaks. If this magnifies not only Arthur's feeling but also Merlin's mysterious power, the English author also touches in more memorably the power used against him: as Vivien (still as Nimiane) finally enchants him,

> She aroos softly and made a cerne with her wymple all aboute the bussh and all aboute Merlin, and began hir enchauntementez soche as Merlin hadde hir taught, made the cerne nine tymes and nine tymes hir enchauntementes. (321)

In the source she simply "got up carefully and with her wimple drew a circle all about Merlin and the bush, and she began to cast her spells" (*Lancelot-Grail,* 1993–96, 1.416).

The added color of Arthur's anxiety and Vivien's magic indicate that this is a highly capable author. He includes uncut the French battles that the author of *Arthour and Merlin* dispensed with, but he continues that poem's updating of the Saxons to Saracens, apparently thinking these are essentially the same, as when "That day Gawen slowgh many a Sarazin of the Saxons" (127). For all its solid detail and capable work, the prose *Merlin* is one of the forgotten texts of English literary history—perhaps because its titular hero in French style exhibits so little of the prophecy that England had, through the chronicle tradition, come to expect of him and also fewer grand vizier features than in the Vulgate. In a period when learning and writing, and advising kings, were now largely secular matters, the tensions focused on the potent clerical adviser of the Vulgate *Merlin* must have seemed of much reduced interest; in the same way the idea of divine foreknowledge and punishment Merlin mediated in Robert de Boron and the post-Vulgate is by this time not as interesting as human apprehension of sin.

More related to the late medieval English context was the more humanist, though still firmly Christian, reworking of the Arthurian saga by Sir Thomas Malory. He is now identified as a Warwickshire man who had been involved, mostly in the Yorkist cause, in the upheavals of the mid-fifteenth century (see Field, 1993), and known only from rather embarrassing accusations, though not convictions. C. S. Lewis was skeptical about his criminality (1963, 8–10), and at least some of Malory's activities seem to have been a mixture of rough politics and dirty tricks characteristic of the period.

Like Geoffrey and Robert, Malory used no single source but assembled very varied materials, probably from the fine library collected by Anthony Wydville, brother-in-law to Edward IV (see Griffith, 1981, 172), and he exhibits a power to select and order material that matches the major Arthurian redactors. He did not find Merlin interesting enough to develop or even recreate at any length: that disappointment and his great success both derive from his originality in his restructuring of the existing material.

Malory was the first English writer to condense the structure of the Arthur saga and the riches of knightly romance, turning the expanse of the Vulgate into one book (*The Works of Sir Thomas Malory,* 1990): Cooper calls it a "unique redaction" (2003, 155). Starting with the post-Vulgate account of Arthur's early reign, he deployed the adventures of Lancelot, the non-Vulgate Tristan, and many other figures into the overarching story from Arthur's mysterious birth to his equally mysterious death. He even, like the Vulgate, fitted in the holy grail, though there is a strained transition from his unfinished Tristram to the Galahad story. He gave full value to Geoffrey's story of Arthur defeating Rome, but, with a patriotic emphasis, placed it early and showed a link to the English saga tradition by using the alliterative *Morte* as his source in that sequence.

What Malory did not do was make Merlin in any way a dignitary who supervises the long series of knightly adventures. This had been the pattern of the Vulgate *Merlin* and to some degree the Didot *Perceval,* but there is no sign he knew them. The stories he selected from the *Lancelot* and the *Tristan* and the *Queste* all lack Merlin: evaluative commentary is provided in the chivalric narratives largely by the king and queen, and in the *Queste* by recurrent Christian hermits and maidens. His choice of the post-Vulgate as a source for his opening sequence may seem surprising, as there were so few manuscripts of this—though the only two survivors have long been in England. It is conceivable that Malory deliberately chose the more austerely religious opening as he already knew that his story would have, especially in the repentance of Guinevere and Lancelot, a powerfully Christian ending as in the English stanzaic *Morte Arthure,* which he clearly knew—a late text which, like its alliterative parallel, is also without a role for Merlin.

The most striking thing as Malory starts writing is his bold confidence. Elizabeth Archibald has commented that the tone "may well seem abrupt" (1996, 139), and this is partly Malory's driving style, partly the authorial assumption that we know this story well. Merlin is present at first, and then advises Arthur, but much of his mystery is reduced. Here are none of the Vulgate (and post-Vulgate) elaborate disguises and teases by which Merlin approaches Uther: as Dean remarks, in Malory Merlin's magic "is much played down" (1992, 25).

There is no detail about the king's transformation into Gorlois—it just happens: Merlin says "'ye shalle be like the duke her husband'" (1.9), and he is. Just as his knowledge has direct impact, so Merlin is firmer as a figure than in the source: he braces up the sick king Uther for battle in an irresistible way:

"Sir," said Merlyn, "ye may not lye so as ye doo, for ye must go to the feld, though ye ryde on an hors-lyttar. For ye shall never have the better of youre enemyes but yf youre persone be there, and thenne shall ye have the victory." (1.11)

In the events around the choice of Arthur as king, Merlin conveys a firm aura of contemporary practices as, like a fifteenth-century senior bureaucrat, he writes busily and repeatedly with instructions to the archbishop: in earlier versions he had just urged people to pray. Another modernization—what Field calls "one of the rare flashes of political realism" (1998, 54)—is that where in the source the feudal barons agree to Arthur's election, in Malory "alle the comyns cryed at onse 'We wille have Arthur unto oure kyng.'" (1.16)

As the story continues Merlin moves into the morally advisory role that the post-Vulgate created for him as commentator on the beginnings of the turbulent future of the Arthurian world. Here too Malory is essentially brief: he wants to get the kingdom working so he can move on to knightly adventures. The elaboration of the post-Vulgate is reduced in various ways. On a few occasions Merlin is involved in what Vinaver describes as Malory's "practice of solving a mystery at the earliest possible opportunity" (1990, 1333–34). He clarifies the mystery of Torre's birth at the start of the sequence here (1.100) and is similarly demystifying about whom Pellinore has killed (1.119). In a more direct style of abbreviation, Merlin's rebuke to Arthur is cut right back (1.44.16–19, 26–27); he never explains why he was being chased by the churls (1.49.7–8); his prophecy to Arthur about his own end is reduced to two lines (1.44.28–30). The questing beast appears but, as Batt comments, "it participates in but does not necessarily clarify the narrative" (1989, 152).

When speaking of Girflet (1.47.13), Merlin omits the prophecy about his being the last of all the knights, which had in the post-Vulgate set up the time-transcending meaning of the story.

Merlin still has evaluative force. To Balin he says

"…because of the dethe of that lady thou shalt stryke a stroke moste dolerous that ever man stroke, excepte the stroke of our Lorde Jesu Cryste. For thou shalt hurte the trewyst knight and the man of moste worship that now lyvith; and thorow that stroke three kyngdomys shall be brought into grete poverté, miseri and wrecchednesse twelve yere." (1.72, 25–31)

He sternly sums up Pellinore's misdeeds:

"Truly ye ought sore to repente hit," seyde Merlion, "for that lady was your owne doughtir, begotyn of the lady of the Rule, and that knyght that was dede was hir love and sholde have wedded hir, and he was a ryght good knyght of a yonge man, and wolde a proved a good man." (1.119.29–33)

At this early stage Malory is giving weight to secular human values, even if like Lancelot on the grail quest they will fail, and he is not as fully focused on the Christian vanishing point for which the post-Vulgate author used Merlin as a guide. As Jill Mann has argued, Malory explores "the late medieval obsession with chance and destiny" in a world where the interlinked customs and adventures are no longer, as throughout the Vulgate, supervised in a Christian context by Merlin (1981, 88).

Malory does not even seem very involved in Merlin's own story: Merlin's end does not escape the habit of drastic cutting. Merlin meets, loves, and pursues Vivien, here Nenyve, and is entombed by her, all in two pages—which also provide his prophecy to Arthur about his own entombment and his prediction to Queen Elayne of Brittany about her young son Lancelot (1.125–26). Vinaver suggests in a note that Malory offered "the virtual suppression of the Merlin-Niviene theme" (*Works of Sir Thomas Malory,* 3.1279), but it is still a memorable sequence and there are also some slight changes to the source. Merlin seems a little more aggressive to Vivien: the comment that he "wolde nat lette her have no reste, but allwayes he wolde be with her" (1.125.5–6) is brusquer than the source's "he did not want to be with her without knowing her carnally" (*Lancelot-Grail,* 1993–96, 4.259), and her own hostile response is understandable—as Holbrook comments, in Malory's version "she has more to excuse than to blame her" (1978, 769). Because "allwayes he lay aboute to have hir maydynhode" she was "ever passynge wery of hym, and wolde have been delyverde of hym, for she was aferde of hym for cause he was a devyls son, and so she cowde not be skyfte [*free*] of hym by no meane" (1.126, 18–21).

In Malory there are relatively few later references to Merlin and his prophecies after his entombment, and they tend to be perfunctory, referring to Merlin's dealings with King Melodyas (2.373), the questing beast (2.717), and twice, deep in the Tristan book, the stone he set up in the Balin episode (2.562, 595); a little more important is a reminiscence of his grail prophecy (3.906–7). Merlin is not remembered at the achievement of the grail, nor at Arthur's end, nor in the moral context of Guinevere's adultery or Mordred's treachery. Malory seems to have no interest in Merlin as a figure whose knowledge, past and future, could run through the whole story and who could act as a transmitter of Christian morality; rather he uses him effectively early in the story to establish the Arthurian platform on which both knightly adventures and the strongly moralized late action will develop. Merlin's knowledge establishes Arthur's power, but does not go very far in supervising or, especially, criticizing it.

The reduced role for Merlin's knowledge relates to historical changes in the way power has come to use knowledge. The Merlin as grand vizier role had already been diluted in the post-Vulgate, but though, when Malory wrote, English had become the language of the court's business, there was no longer any direct feudal and personal link between the king's decision-making and his advisers: the structure of power had made knowledge valid only as prophecy.

Because of his primarily chivalric and moral interest in the story, Malory's unhistorical emphasis on English politics did not involve Merlin as a prophet, but only manifested itself in limited, if also potent, elements of contemporary realization, like the guns with which Mordred menaces the Tower of London or the growth of friction between lords and their affinities into outright civil war, so vivid a fifteenth-century reality.[20] But while Malory was at work on the first proto-humanist version of the Arthurian story, which was to speak strongly to later contexts, Merlin was still very important in a national and political mode in the chronicles, especially as the prophet of English national politics, and these were to be a continuing element, among many new forces, in the representation and the value of Merlin in England in the next centuries.

CHAPTER THREE

English Merlin

Cleverness

Prophecy and Advice in Decline

When the medieval French re-created Geoffrey of Monmouth's Merlin in various forms as an adviser to social authority, this role largely restricted his prophetic powers to within the narrative, but there were exceptions. In four Wace manuscripts future prophecies were reinserted (see Wace, 1938–40, 1, vii–xiv, and Matheson, 1984, 216) and some were included in the second and third versions of Richard of Cluny's late twelfth-century Latin Chronicle (Fletcher, 1896, 145–46). New prophecies could serve continental interests. About 1170 Étienne of Bec produced the *Draco Normannicus,* a visionary chronicle which included Geoffrey's prophecies as well as some material from the *Vita Merlini,* notably the association of Arthur with Avalon (Fletcher, 1896, 171). Gunnlaug Leifsson's poem *Merlinusspá,* from the late twelfth century, was close to Geoffrey's *Prophecies,* but added material directly from its Icelandic context (Lavender, 2006). A wider impact was made by the extensive Latin commentary on Geoffrey's prophecies attributed to the French writer Alanus de Insulis, which, appearing as early as 1167, was long known across Europe. The influential *Prophécies de Merlin* was written in French in about 1276, probably by a Franciscan friar from Venice. Paton comments that the text combines "historical prophecies and teachings drawn from the stock of encyclopaedic material of the Middle Ages" with anecdotes on "the weaknesses of the clergy" and also "romance episodes" (1913, 122); new prophecies serve the interests of the

Guelf faction in Italian politics and deal with "political events that occurred in Italy and the Holy Land in the thirteenth century" (Bogdanow, 2006, 353; see Daniel, 2006, 280–81); another version of the *Prophécies* added romance material, mostly from the Vulgate (*Prophécies de Merlin,* 1992).

In Britain Merlin prophecies largely continued, as what Chris Given-Wilson calls "part of the stock in trade of the majority of English chroniclers" (2004, 40)—like the English-language texts discussed above they tended to validate an England-led Britain and Geoffrey's work was a major stimulus. Lesley Coote comments that prophecies were "extremely popular in the second half of the twelfth century" and she details their role as being "above all, concerned with power" through to 1485 (2006, 50, 238). Richard Moll calls Merlin prophecies "an integral part of the Brut tradition" (2003, 200): the *Flores Historiarum* from St. Albans about 1200 gives the whole of Geoffrey's *Prophecies* and sees Merlin as "a thoroughly supernatural person" (Fletcher, 1896, 189), while Thomas of Castleford's English-language chronicle of about 1325 reproduces the whole of Geoffrey's *Prophecies* in verse (Johnson, 1999, 46), and as late as the mid-fourteenth century the Latin *Eulogium Historiarum* did the same (Keeler, 1946, 36). Adam of Usk's early fifteenth-century Latin *Chronicle* includes Merlin prophecies, some linked to Glyndŵr (Yarndell, 2001, 90). The fifteenth-century Lambeth Palace *Brut* manuscript 84 gives an expansive account of Merlin, even extending to the Welsh folkloric story of "King Arthur and the Wildcats" (Matheson, 1990, 255). Merlin prophecies appear in the "Long Version" of the Anglo-Norman prose *Brut,* which in English translation became enormously popular: Matheson speaks of over 170 examples from the beginning of the fifteenth to the sixteenth century, and they all handed on an idea of Merlin as a national prophet of importance (1990, 253–54). Not surprisingly, as Glanmor Williams comments, "the prophetic tradition remained vivid and resilient among the Welsh poets" (1979, 72), but English interest was also wide. Rossell Robbins commented that "Because of their doggerel and obscurity, many Merlin prophecies are still unpublished and even uncatalogued" (1975, 1521–22): that elusive popular aspect of the Merlin tradition would surface in print in the almanacs of the seventeenth century.

Royal power had specific use for Merlin's validation: his prophecies were deployed in the fourteenth century to support the English ambitions to rule France and in the fifteenth century to justify the Yorkist claim on the throne (Thomas, 1971, 397–98); Edward IV made at least some use of Merlin as part of his claim to power (Eckhardt, 1982, 116, 117). The *Annals of Worcester* offer Merlin as a prophet of the death of King John (Keeler, 1946, 69), while the early fourteenth-century *London Annals* state that Edward I's deeds fulfill Merlin's vision (Keeler, 1946, 60). Prophecies in the Long *Brut* directly validate the power of Henry III, Edward I, and Edward II (Fletcher, 1896, 218; Matheson, 1990, 254), while the best-known of these king-specific deployments of Merlin was "The Six Kings to Follow John." First appearing in Anglo-Norman in about 1312 (Smallwood, 1985), this explanation of English royal history was both popular and polemical: Henry IV was abused for being the "mouldwarp" last king (that is, a mole). As late as 1535 John Hale, the vicar of Isleworth, was executed for using that name for Henry VIII (Thomas, 1971, 400) and an Exeter lawyer, John Bonnefant, died for the same reason in 1539 (J. P. D. Cooper, 2003, 110).

But against the credibility of Merlin prophecies in opportunistic royal propaganda, some chroniclers remained doubtful about their value as real history because of their elaboration and unclarity. Fletcher notes that Robert of Gloucester, writing in about 1300, "omits the greater part of the prophecies of Merlin, on the ground that they are not easily understood by the unlearned." (1896, 194). Sir Thomas Gray, in his Latin *Scalachronicon* of about 1355, leaves out Merlin's prophecies as "not credible" (Fletcher, 1896, 225), yet he had at least some interest in them (Given-Wilson, 2004, 48). In the same spirit John of Whethamstede, abbot and chronicler of St. Albans Abbey, writing in Latin around 1435, felt this material was "poetical rather than historical, fanciful, rather than real" (Keeler, 1946, 88). Especially dubious about Merlin's role, no doubt because of his association with English royalty, are the late medieval Scottish chroniclers. John of Fordun's *Chronicon Gentis Scotorum* of the 1380s "has little respect for his pseudo-prophecies" (Keeler, 1946, 79), while Andrew of Wyntoun in *The Orygynale Chronykil of Scotland* of about 1420 is overtly "distrusting...Merlin's prophecies" (Fletcher, 1896, 242), and John Major, whose *Historia Majoris Britanniae* was published in 1521, simply "disbelieves" both the stories and the prophecies (Fletcher 1896, 244–45).

Some writers in England had a sense of historiographical method that resisted Merlin. As early as 1198 William of Newburgh regarded the prophecies as "mendacious fictions intended to gratify the curiosity of the undiscerning" (Dean, 1992, 17), though he still sees them as antique (Fletcher, 1896, 92). In the same double way Gerald of Wales was consistently "uncomplimentary" (Thorpe, 1978, 280) about the value of Geoffrey's work as a whole, but did make use of it and wrote knowledgably about both Merlin Ambrosius—the Latin king-advising figure—and Merlin Sylvestris, the northern British exile (Thorpe, 1978, 192–93). Some voices were more skeptical. As early as about 1150 Alfred of Beverley was cautious in his *Annales,* accepting Geoffrey's account in general but puzzled that there was no corroboration in other historians, notably Bede (Kendrick, 1950, 10). In the early fourteenth-century *Vita Edwardi* the Monk of Malmesbury comments dryly that Merlin's prophecies are "yet to find fulfilment" (Keeler, 1946, 62).

Other historians retained elements of the story of Merlin's royal services in spite of their doubts about the value of the prophecies. In his early fourteenth-century *Chronicle* Robert Mannyng omits the prophecies because "I haf no witte / to open the knottes that Merlyn knytte" (Mannyng, 1996, 8109–10), but does describe Merlin's "Quoyntise" ("subtlety"), his "sleght and connyng"("skill and knowledge") and his "coniurisons" ("spells") at Stonehenge (8683, 8686, 8786), as well as his use of "charme through vertue," presumably "white magic" (9314), in the conception of Arthur. Ranulph Higden, in his mid fourteenth-century *Polychronicon,* as translated by John of Trevisa, is skeptical about the story of Merlin and Vortigern: "I wolde putte it to this storie yif I trowed that it be i-holpe by sothenesse" ("helped by trueness") (Higden, 1874, 279). He does accept that Uther erected Stonehenge "by helpe of Merlyn" (1874, 313), but does not involve him in the conception of Arthur—Uther just kills "Gorulus," husband to "Yngerna." However, in an earlier description of Wales Higden goes much further with Merlin than Geoffrey did, not only linking him with Arthur but saying he is buried on Bardsey Island, Ynys Enlli, traditional home for Welsh saints (1865, 416–18).

In the early fifteenth century John Hardyng, after summarizing the story of Vortigern and his tower, says about Merlin's birth, the dragons, and his prophecies "I cannot wryte of suche affirmably" (Hardyng, 1812, 115), but also that Stonehenge was built by Merlin's "aduise" and that he made Uther look like Gorlois "by coniurisons" (1812, 116 and 119), sharing Mannyng's word. Robert Fabyan, in his *New Chronicles of England and France,* written by 1493 and not published until 1516, merely mentions the story of Merlin and Vortigern's tower, omits any mention of magic in the building of Stonehenge, and, while he does say Uther gained Igraine through Merlin's help, he dismisses any faith in such "fantastycall illusions" (Fabyan, 1811, 75.)

In this increasingly skeptical context, it is hardly surprising that when Polydore Vergil in his *Historia Anglica* (published in 1536) brings to British history both an outsider's eye and the classical tradition of critical scholarship he is critical of the value of Geoffrey of Monmouth's account: the seventeenth-century translation says Geoffrey "published the sowthesaieings of one Merlin, as prophesies of most asseured and approved trewthe" but "always addinge somewhat of his own": Vergil implies his own low valuation by adding that "The common sort of menne" say Vortigern relied on "a certain soothesayer called Merline" (1846, 1, 29).

The chroniclers' growing doubt is reflected in a diminishing reliance on Merlin in royal propaganda. When Henry VII flew the red dragon banner on his march to victory at Bosworth there is an implicit reference to Merlin's revelation of this in Geoffrey of Monmouth's story as the British and then Arthurian symbol of victory (Michelsson, 1999, 35), and Henry's general claim as the inheritor of Arthur clearly implies the force of the Merlin prophecies (Summers, 1997, 92). But there is little substantial role for Merlin in the Tudor use of the Arthurian myth as part of their self-legitimation. When Henry named his first son Arthur and insisted that his heavily pregnant wife be moved to Winchester for the birth, it was the royal status of the famous warrior king he was claiming, not the support of the ancient prophet.

But even the impact of Arthur was not of lasting or deep political value for the Tudors. Though Millican has spoken of an "obvious Arthurian ferment in connection with the Tudors" (1932, 5) his evidence emphasizes Welsh sources: as Sidney Anglo has argued, the political use of Arthurian medievalism in the sixteenth century has been overestimated. He notes that when Prince Arthur was married in 1501, Geoffrey of Monmouth's Arthurian tradition "was completely overshadowed by the wider cosmological implications suggested by the parallelism of Arthur/Arcturus" (1961, 32): the change to Arcturus shows that classicism and science were now more potent than medieval magic and Merlin will be largely reshaped in the image of a new cleverness rather than an ancient wisdom or feudal advice.

Decreasingly credible as his prophecies were, Merlin's words and works were still available, but to a scholarly rather than to a wide lay audience as before. The commentary attributed to Alanus de Insulis was reprinted in Frankfurt in 1503; in Paris there appeared in 1498 Vérard's two-volume edition of the Vulgate *Merlin* with the Italian-oriented *Prophécies* as a third volume: as Hoffman discusses (1996), it had dramatic woodcuts (fig. 10) and in 1505 a version was printed on vellum with fine illuminations (see fig. 7): Henry VII had a copy (Crane, 1919, 8; Winn, 1997, 152). Wynkyn de Worde printed a reduced version of *Arthour and Merlin* as *A Lyttel Treatyse of Merlyn* in 1510, perhaps as early as 1499: there was another edition in 1529 (Macrae-Gibson, 1980). But as Helen Cooper has shown (2004, 409–29), the wealth of sixteenth-century romance included no stories or quasi-historical adventures about Merlin. Rather they offered elaborate and ahistorical chivalric adventure, like Lord Berners's *Arthur of Lytel Bryteyne,* written by 1520, which translates a Merlin-free late fifteenth-century French story about a son of the duke of Brittany named after the great king.

Merlin can even be seen as illusory and negative, to be rejected with the medieval past. In *The Mirror for Magistrates* of 1559 he is cited as a misleading authority for both Owen Glendower and the duke of Clarence, the murdered younger brother of Richard III. Part of Owen's confessional self-criticism is that he

> toke on me to be the prynce of Wales
> Entiste therto by many of Merlines tales. (1938, 69–70)

While Clarence does express respect for "learned Merline, whom God gave the sprite, To know and utter princes actes to come" he also asserts that the obscurity of the prophecies led people to create "false named prophecies" such as that which said "a G, Of Edwardes children shold destruccion be," and this led to his own downfall (211–12, 225).

At a time when there was great anxiety about political threats internal and external, dubious prophecies seemed to play into the hands of enemies of the fragile state, and there were many to dismiss them. Merlin stories were among those described by Sir Thomas Elyot in 1545 as "incredible fables" and by John Speed as "deceitfull conjectures and foretelings" (Kendrick, 1950, 42–43; Merriman, 1973, 164). Gabriel Harvey called Merlin "impious, monstrous and hellish" and found "all prophecies fraudulent" (Dobin, 1990, 22–23). William Perkins in 1588 attacked "Merlin's drunken prophecies" and Henry Howard, the highly placed earl of Surrey, denounced "the rubbish of unsound interpretation" (Dobin, 1990, 109–10).

Up-to-date European intellectualism also had little time for Merlin. Both Cervantes and Rabelais made fun of him,[1] and Inns of Court Arthurian drama, whether serious like Thomas Hughes's *The Misfortunes of Arthur* (1587) or satirical like *Tom of Lincoln* (in two parts, 1599 and 1607), found no room for the character; Shakespeare only mentions him in Hotspur's rant against Glendower in *Henry IV Part I* and the fool's mock prophecy in *King Lear*.[2] Roland Smith's argument (1946) that Lear himself is modeled on Merlin as a Celtic wild man has not convinced scholars.

On the rare occasions when Merlin did appear close to power, he had only a secondary role. At Kenilworth House in 1575 the earl of Leicester greeted the queen with a major pageant by George Gascoigne figuring the earl as Arthur: the queen, through her personal perfection, rescues the Lady of the Lake, who has been imprisoned by Sir Bruse Sauns Pittie, "in revenge of his cosen Merlyn the Prophete (whom for his inordinate lust she had inclosed in a rocke)." (Gascoigne, 1907–10, 2, 102)

Merlin played a somewhat more elevated but harmlessly loyal part in 1592 at an Accession Day pageant, where the earl of Cumberland, the Queen's Champion, appeared as "The Knight of Pendragon" (the name of a castle in Westmoreland owned by his family) and where Merlin, who appeared riding the red dragon of Wales, related the glory of Arthur (anachronistically located at Vortigern's castle) and then that of the Virgin Queen.[3]

In spite of the decreasing interest in him, Merlin the political prophet devoted to British interests would not be forgotten, especially under the Stuarts, but his role would be limited to mere royal validation not national prophecy. But in Renaissance culture he would return in a highly idealized form as a symbol of newly sophisticated knowledge: no longer a king's advisor or national propagandist, but a representative of the new learning itself—and yet here too there would be limitations. The new Merlin would signify a limited cleverness, rather than the positive advisory wisdom, secular or Christian, which he had previously represented.

Renaissance Cleverness

Like so much in Renaissance culture, a major element in the re-formation of Merlin derived from Italy. In *Orlando Furioso* Ariosto reshaped the figure "to do the work of the prophets and oracles of classical literature," as Blackburn comments (1980, 183), and this developed him as a magus, already envisaged in the frontispiece to the 1498 printed version of the *Prophécies* (fig. 11). *Orlando Furioso* was translated in 1591 by the scholar, wit, and eccentric, Sir John Harington (1972).[4] In Book 3 the distinctly classical and Sibylline "sage Melissa" and the Amazonian Bradamant (in Italian Bradamante) visit Merlin's tomb, but Ariosto makes his afterlife more extended and positive than in the Vulgate or in Boiardo's *Orlando Innamorato*, which briefly transmits this motif. He not only prophesies "things both present, past and future" but acts as a general adviser "Resolving men of ev'ry doubtfull case / That for his consell come unto this place" (3.12, 6–8). The tomb itself combines magic and modern learning: its creation is either "done by magike art alone" or perhaps "by helpe of Mathematike skill / To make transparencies to meete in one" (3.52, 3, 4–5). Harington has added the idea of mathematics to Ariosto's original.

Merlin's prophecies about Bradamant are not lengthy, though they do refer to the grandeur of the d'Este family, which Ariosto consistently praises, as Goodrich notes (2003, 20). Melissa takes over with an extended prophecy in, Harington's side-note indicates, the style of Virgil: the fully classical overrides the medieval. A little later in Book 3 Bradamant spends time in Merlin's tomb, where his "voice with talke did her still entertaine" (3.52, 4) but all he does is urge her to commit her love to Rogero, acting more as plot device than prophet.

In his notes to the "Storie" of this book, Harington, like many contemporaries, is skeptical about Merlin without dismissing everything. He comments that "manie are hard of beleefe" of the stories, but he holds it "verie likely" that Arthur did have such a counselor—though he doubts his connection with "the great stones at Stonage on Salisburie plaine which the ignorant people beleeve he brought out of Ireland" (3.47) and claims the nearby town of Marlborough is "Merlin's Borough," an English appropriation of the Caerfyrddin story that will recur.

Ariosto recalls Merlin's medieval prophecies at his tomb, but develops his Renaissance cleverness in the context of political prophecy and art. In Book 26 Rogero and Bradamant visit a cave "that famous Merlin wrought"—not where he was buried—and here he

> in milke white marble did engrave
> Strange stories which things future strangely taught.
> The verie images seemd life to have,
> And saving they were dumbe, you would have thought
> Both by their looks and by their lively features
> That they had mov'd and had bin living creatures. (26.2, 3–8)

Merlin becomes a sculptor of prophetic images when Bradamant sees carved murals about Italian wars against France (fig. 12) created not by Michelangelo, Raphael, or Titian but by "the British Merline": (33.3, 7):

> He made by Magicke art that stately hall,
> And by the selfe same art he causd to be
> Straunge histories ingraved on the wall (33.4, 1–3)

Even before Harington's translation appeared, Ariosto's image of Merlin as technically highly skilled was of interest in England. In 1582 the preface to Robert Robinson's English translation of John Leland's *Assertion of Arthur* patriotically insists on Arthur's historical reality, in response to Polydore Vergil's doubts. Robinson adds a prefatory reference in support of the credibility of Merlin as a truthful "scientist," "especially in the science mathematicall" (Robinson, 1925, 86).

This new creation of Merlin as a figure of Renaissance technical skill, clever rather than wise, is developed, among many other elements from the Italian epic, by Edmund Spenser in *The Faerie Queene* of 1590–96. David Summers calls this idealized Merlin, far from a political and historical prophet, an "apotheosis from history, his transformation into a cultural icon" (1997, 201) and Fletcher identifies him as "a Renaissance culture hero" (1896, 111 n. 67). While Merlin can still prophesy, there are limits: his major role, as in Ariosto, is only linked to knowing the future greatness of the powerful and amounts to no more than useful cleverness.

Spenser retains some medieval resonance: Merlin's first appearance recalls the figure who resolved the problem of Vortigern's tower and erected Stonehenge. We see the splendor of Arthur's shield and also the engineering skill behind it, but, separated from prophecy, these only reveal the powers of a great Renaissance artificer:

> But all of Diamond perfect pure and cleene
> It framed was, one massie entire mold,
> Hewen out of adamant rocke with engines keene.
> (1912, 1.7.33, 5–7)

The shield dismays monsters and daunts armies with its "glistring ray" (1.7.34, 5); it can resist hostile magic, turn enemies to stone, stones to dust or blind the proud and all to serve a lord:

> Both shield, and sword, and armour all he wrought
> For this young Prince, when first to armes he fell; (1.7.36, 4–7)

Merlin is not only a great armorer. As Prince Arthur explains to Una, the sage supervised his education in northeast Wales near the river Dee, appointing a tutor (whom Spenser uniquely calls Timon).

Spenser later locates Merlin in southwest Wales at Carmarthen and this has some political resonance: as Summers notes, Spenser reuses the old Welsh idea of the unity of the island of Britain as a political notion (Summers, 1997, 164), and it also permits Prince—never King—Arthur and his realm to be parallel with, in some way anterior to, yet also not in conflict with, the realm of the real and royal Elizabeth of England. In an opposite but equally one-kingdom direction, Redcrosse is clearly intended to be of Saxon origin as he is "borne of English blood" (1.10.64, 6) and "from ancient race / Of Saxon kings" (1.10.65, 1–2).

Spenser's limitation of medieval myth and Merlin's part in it is clear when Arthur, in the House of Temperance (2.9.59), finds and reads a book of "Briton Moniments." A version of Geoffrey's *Historia,* this tells throughout a whole canto the story of the British kings from Brutus to Vortigern. But it omits the story of Merlin, the tower, his prophecy, and even the building of Stonehenge. Book 3 will make it up to Merlin, but as a technician. First we hear of the magic mirror he made "By his deep science and hell-dreaded might" (3.2.18, 7) for King Ryence, father to the warlike heroine Britomart. Through the magic glass Britomart sees Artegall and his situation and then in the next canto she and her nurse Glauce visit Merlin's "hideous hollow caue" (3.3.8, 3), filled with infernal industry:

> And there such ghastly noise of yron chaines,
> And brasen Cauldrons thou shalt rombling heare,
> Which thousand sprights with long enduring paines
> Doe tosse, that it will stonne they feeble braines,
> And oftentimes great grones, and grieuous stoundes,
> When too huge toile and labour them constraines...(3.3.9, 2–7)

Merlin had been working on a "brazen walle" around "Cairmardin" and, later, when the Lady of the Lake took him away for good, these fiendly laborers could not stop, "So greatly his commaundement they feare" (3.3.11, 5). The romantically immobilized Merlin of the Vulgate is condensed with the part-devil, part-artificer figure found between Geoffrey and Robert de Boron—and an implied image of Vulcan enmeshed by Venus. Yet Spenser seems concerned not to weaken unduly the figure of his enchanter, because he goes on to aggrandize him as one who "had in Magicke more insight, / Then ever him before or after liuing wight" (3.3.11, 8–9), stating his power to "call out of the sky / Both Sunne and Moone, and make them him obay" (3.3.12, 1–2).

Here Britomart and Glauce find Merlin, and Spenser, acknowledging medieval tradition, lets him take over the full duty of prophecy that Melissa appropriated in Ariosto, though it has distinct limits. To Britomart he reveals her future with Artegall and the results of their union. His powers may sound grandiose—he can predict "the streight course of heauenly destiny, / Led with eternall prouidence," (3.3.24, 3–4)—but he, unlike medieval Merlin, can go no further than the Elizabethan present: cleverness useful to royalty has replaced prophetic vision. He describes Welsh, then Saxon and Norman rulers until the return via Wales of the Tudors creates the "eternall vnion" "Betweene the nations different afore" and the present "sacred Peace" under the "royall virgin" (3.3.49, 1, 2, 3, 6). But this is eulogistic history, not prophecy, and as Schwyzer points out, Spenser's source is not Welsh but English Latin scholarship (2004, 41–42).

The present is not the only limit to Merlin's power. After expressing the triumphs of the royal virgin the text goes on:

> But yet the end is not. There Merlin stayd,
> As ouercomen of the spirites powre,
> Or other ghastly spectacle dismayd,
> That secretly he saw, yet note discoure... (3.3.50, 1–4)

This "suddein fit and half extatick stour" (3.3.50, 5) alarms Britomart and Glauce, and has puzzled scholars. Howard Dobin thinks Merlin has foreseen the death of Elizabeth (1990, 6), which would be a daring and bizarrely unresolved move on Spenser's part; Harry Berger felt Merlin foresaw the war in Ireland depicted in Book 5, which seems contrary to Spenser's own understanding of those dark events as justice in action (1988, 130). In terms of the Vulgate, Merlin would be foreseeing his own end, and that seems the most likely meaning, though it too is unresolved. Essentially the sequence limits his knowledge: he is a servant not a subject of the narration and does no more in the poem. Britomart discusses her future with Glauce, who then arms her; they leave for Fairy Land, and Redcrosse, and the complex allegorical future.

For Spenser, Merlin is the creator of the fantastic diamond shield, the commander of a diabolic force, but his powers are also restrained before royal authority. Spenser's re-formation of Merlin, building on Ariosto, creates for the first time in English an archetype of profound technical and intellectual skills beyond the mere magic of medieval imagining and not involved in advising the powerful so much as in shaping the world of intellect and culture. It is an archetype, the first in English, of Merlin as cleverness, concerned with its own interests and displays. This Merlin is useful to royal power but distinctly limited in comparison to his past authority.

That major change in the meaning of Merlin is related both to the new models of power, the aggrandization and separation from ordinary activity of the powerful, notably the near sanctification of the ruler, and also to the administrative specializing of his, and her, forms of advice into what are effectively ministries of state. In a late overview of the subject, G. R. Elton speaks of the sixteenth-century move "towards the elimination of the purely

personal in favour of bureaucratic control" and the Privy Council's development of "direct executive functions" instead of "merely being able to advise
the monarch on what he should do" (1991, 480). Accordingly, the figure of
Merlin is contained, dispensed with, not only because he seems to be too powerful, as in the Vulgate tradition, but also because his knowledge, now refor-
mulated and specialized as cleverness, has a distinctly restricted role in the
service of power: he is a useful specialist not an all-purpose authority. Spenser
has set up a figure of contained cleverness who will dominate, and also re-
strict, the representation of Merlin in high culture in England for nearly three
hundred years.

Cleverness High and Low: The Seventeenth Century

The Renaissance cleverness of Merlin existed alongside the surviving medieval British figure, now treated with some skepticism but also capable of
validating power, both royal and more generally national. In *Albions England,*
first published in 1586 and republished in extended forms, William Warner
notes that Merlin was the son of a "Feend" and recounts Geoffrey's Vortigern's tower story in a decidedly unconvinced manner, saying that Merlin

> Bewraied more then I beleeue, or credit seems to beare:
> As shewing how the Castell worke, rear'd daily, fell by night,
> By shaking of two Dragons great that underneath it fight,
> With other wonders, tedious if not trothlesse to resight. (1589, 3, 19)

Merlin also shows useful cleverness as he "transfigured by skill" Uther, so he
could possess the wife of Carolus (a classicized version of Gorlois), and then,
to entertain Arthur, "the British Prophet," "half of humane seede" presents
visions of "sixe long after-Kings" and "many things that came to passe indeed" (3, 19).

This scholarly caution and restricted interest in Merlin remained common
in the seventeenth century, but the end of Elizabeth's rule and the need to
establish the validity of the new dynasty revived the value of prophetic justification for taking power. The Stuarts sought to link themselves back to
British tradition—the deliberate political use of the term Great Britain dates
from James I—and Merlin prophecies were useful in support of this idea, but
they consistently adhered to Spenser's major limitation by being backdated:
prophecy ends with the triumphant Stuart present.

In 1603, the year James came to the throne, there appeared several editions of *The Whole Prophecies of Scotland* attributed to "Marvellous Merling," or even "Marling," and other prophetic figures: they remained popular. As if to trace his authority back into English popular tradition, Merlin's first prophecy is in alliterative verse. Nothing so crass as a specific justification of James's claim to power is made, but the general implication of his Arthurian right, transmitted by Merlin's prophecy, is as clear as it was to be in the frequently repeated anagram "Charles Iames Steuart Claims Arthurs Seat." Also in 1603, presumably not by accident, the substantial Latin Merlin commentary attributed to Alanus de Insulis was reprinted in London, and it appeared again in 1608.

Literary writers followed the same royalist path, at times with increasing authority for Merlin's useful cleverness. Robert Chester's *Loues Martir* appeared in 1601 as a romantic anthology, subtitled *Rosalind's Complaint,* including in the middle a lengthy section introducing "Merlin the wise that shall content your mind" (Chester, 1878, 40). Uther's fathering of Arthur is given a newly romantic turn—Merlin comments to Uther that "the faire-fac'd lady Igrene is unkind" (41), as if she is a difficult beloved, and then the text describes Arthur's birth, crowning, defeat of Rome, death, and discovery at Glastonbury. James I knighted Chester soon after he became king, and in the 1611 version of the poem-sequence the Arthur section, as the text's nineteenth-century editor Grosart comments, "becomes (on the title page) the main poem" (Chester, 1878, lxii). With the same propagandist spirit, in *The Masque at Lord Hays Marriage,* produced in 1607, Thomas Campion includes a Merlin prophecy where the sage is corrected, and advised that his proper subject is not Arthur but James (Michelsson, 1999, 151).

The usefulness of Merlin's knowledge to the Stuarts is central to an elaborate masque performed in 1610, *The Speeches at Prince Henries Barriers,* designed by Inigo Jones and written by Ben Jonson. Henry, heir to the throne, himself insisted on a medieval and Arthurian event to celebrate his coming of age, and Jonson, who had wavered between an interest in using Arthur as the basis of a "Heroick poem" and a certain skepticism towards this, like other medieval English topics,[5] was able in lucrative royal service to link medieval and Renaissance ideas: John Peacock comments that he combines Prince Henry's enthusiasm for chivalry with praise of his father's commitment to peace (1987, 172). As at Kenilworth, and probably referring to that earlier royal propaganda, the Lady of the Lake appears to praise with conspicuous loyalty this present time when "the Iland hath regain'd her fame Intire, and perfect" (Jonson, 1941, 17–18), and "a monarch aequally good and great...claimes

Arthurs seat" (19–20). Arthur himself is present, but in Renaissance mode as Arcturus, "Translated to a starre" (67). As Peacock notes, Jonson "classicizes wherever possible" and Inigo Jones takes this further by imagining Arthur as a Roman (1987, 175, 179–80), a motif to be much deployed in the twentieth century. This quasi-classical authority is recruited to Stuart politics as Arthur proclaims: "since the times are now devolv'd That Merlin's misticke prophesies are absolv'd" (74–75): no future prophecy is required.

To celebrate this present greatness, Merlin is revived. Arthur criticizes the Lady for having buried him, because of his high propaganda value:

> ... when thou shutst him there,
> Thou buriedst valure too, for letters reare
> The deeds of honor high, and make them liue. (102–4)

Beginning his lengthy career in political theater, Merlin rises from his tomb and his first act is to call up Prince Henry under the name Meliadus, derived from the French *Prophécies*. Merlin admires the architectural splendor of the scene, notably the young hero's shield that is theatrically "Let downe from heauen" (166), and embarks on a selective prophecy of national history, leading quickly up to the triumph over the Armada. This history of a glorious past points to the even more glorious and securely powerful present of "Royall, and mightie James" who has "fixed fast The wheele of chance" (353, 364–65): even fortune, like prophecy, has come to a stop with the Stuarts.

Meliadus receives the shield and then Jonson, adding allegory to his revisionary version of Merlin's power, has the sage identify and call up to life the figure of "Cheualrie." This is not just medievalizing talk: Henry was himself fascinated by the now distant glories of the past, and a real—or rather, theatrical—tournament follows, in which the prince of course performs magnificently. After such spectacle, and such vigorous poetic royalism, Merlin is finally permitted to prophesy the future—but not very far, and very loyally: he foresees to "you, great King and Queene" that

> this yong Knight, that now puts forth so soone
> Into the world, shall in your names atchieue
> More ghyrlands for this state, and shall relieue
> Your cares in gouernment; (419, 424–27)

In the spirit of Spenser, but without his sense of the anxious complexities of the interface of knowledge and politics, and in the power-enhancing context of magnificent display, Jonson has deployed Merlin as a voice of political authority with a propagandist confidence and a lack of even implicit dissent. The trickster, the magician, the puzzling prophet, the challenger of royal power, even the rash lover—they have all been elided as medieval untidiness in the process of creating this skilful master of royalist ceremonies. Merlin, like the people, is fully subjected to royal power. In this role as royal and national mouthpiece, as cleverness under royal control, he will reappear throughout the following century.

Events and public attitudes were not so simple. Prince Henry would soon die; monarchic certainties would dissolve in civil war, and there were already other seventeenth-century re-formations of Merlin to be found. For Michael Drayton, Merlin was part of the deep-laid and wide-spread traditions of Britain that he made the basis of mythical geography in *Polyolbion,* a poem expressing the overall, and ultimately political, unity of both the island and its self-consciousness.

The Merlin references come in the first version of 1612, with eighteen songs interweaving myth, patriotism, and topography. In the fourth song, dealing with Monmouthshire, Drayton relates from Geoffrey the story of Arthur, adding, ultimately from the *Historia Brittonum,* the battles against the Saxons, all without—faithful to both sources—any Merlin activity. But Arthur's death calls up reference to

> How Merlin by his skill, and Magiques wondrous might
> From Ireland hither brought the Stonendge in a night...
> (Drayton, 1933, 329–30)

Drayton goes on to say that Merlin "for Carmardens sake, wold faine have brought to passe / About it to have built a wall of solid Brasse" (331–32). He paraphrases Spenser on the diabolic labors involved, and mentions Merlin's entombment through "loving of an Elf" (335).

In "The fift Song" the "Muse" moves on to "Camarden" and "Merlins wondrous birth shee sings" (97): Drayton gives full honor to the sage:

> Of Merlin and his skill what Region doth not heare?
> The world shall still be full of Merlin everie where.
> A thousand lingering yeeres his prophecies have runne,
> And scarcely shall have end till Time it selfe be done...(159–62)

The song tells how his mother was "a British Nymph" who "plaid / With a seducing Spirit" and so was born the "Prophet" who "from his Mothers wombe Of things to come foretold until the generall Doome" (163–64, 168, and 173–74). But the Protestant and deeply English Drayton backs away from the idea of a "fayned birth," especially that "this dreamed Incubus" should in fact "licentiouslie subsist," and at length defends himself against a possible charge of being a "humorous Platonist" who might believe in such spirits (175, 176, 177 and 179–202). The note provided by the antiquary John Selden is also skeptical, paraphrasing Polydore Vergil on Merlin, "So is the vulgar tradition of Merlines conception" (107), though also appearing to agree with a suggestion imputed to "Nennius," that Merlin's father was a Roman consul.

Committed as he is to reading both the topography and the myths of Britain, Drayton returns in "The tenth Song," about north Wales, "To Merlins ancient prophecies, / At Dinas Emris" in Snowdonia, the location of Vortigern's tower (201). He merely comments that it was here:

> Prophetique Merlin sate, when to the British King
> The changes long to come, auspiciously he told. (14–15)

The song's opening says that the River Conway heard Merlin "first relate / The Destines Decree, of Britains future fate" (24) but only the dragons beneath the tower are mentioned and then one line refers to Merlin's comments on "The Britains sad decay then shortly to ensue" (37). By restricting prophecy in this way Drayton perhaps merely means to shorten his text, but he also fits in with the historians' skepticism about Merlin's prophecies—not to mention the new seventeenth-century idea that there is no need for any doubtful prophetic remarks about the future. Selden's note adds a doubting comment about Merlin that "learned men account him but a professor of unjustifiable Magique, and that all prophecies eyther fall true, or else are among the affecters of such vanity perpetually expected" (211). While Drayton and Selden know of the wise and the advisory Merlin, they both reduce him to a cleverness of doubtful status and value.

Merlin descends further in esteem in William D'Avenant's masque *Britannia Triumphans* which, like Jonson's *Barriers,* was designed by Inigo Jones and actually performed by the court for Twelfth Night 1638. This represents Jonson's royalist ideology without either his literary energy or his valuing of Merlin. In Act 2, Scene 1 Britanocles, a figure of imperial and maritime glory, oversees an allegorical debate between Action and Imposture, the latter supported by a Merlin whom J. D. Merriman describes as "a foppish parody of a necromancer" (1973, 21). Britanocles transforms the stage into a "horrid hell" (D'Avenant, 1872, 273) of London vulgarity, rebel leaders, and parasitical courtiers: but Bellerophon, famous for defeating monsters, rides in on

Pegasus, and joins Action in banishing both Imposture and Merlin with the words: "How trivial and how lost thy visions are!" (282)

This negative reading of Merlin as old-world, irrelevant, having only a trivial cleverness, matches a dismissive moment in Sir Aston Cokayne's play *The Obstinate Lady,* written around 1630 (1986). A pompous fool called Lorece launches into a very elaborate speech in honor of Merlin as "an intricate prognosticator of firmamental eclipses, and vaccinated future occurrences by the mysterious influences of the sublime stars and vagabondical planets" (2.1, 130–36). The wisdom of Merlin has become a parody of the new learning, seen as wordy nonsense.

At the popular level, Merlin's status survived as a vigorous demotic cleverness. An entertaining pamphlet by Richard Johnson, as "R.I.," survives from 1621 (and was probably written earlier) telling the comic and folkloric story of Tom Thumb. The author states at once that his "merry Muse" will not speak of familiar stories ranging from the romances of Guy of Warwick or Bevis of Hampton, through Robin Hood and Little John to "Garragantua, that monster of men" but will address the story of "Little Tom of Wales" (Johnson, 1965, 1, 2).

In King Arthur's time when "the World was in a better frame than it is now" (3) an old man sent his elderly barren wife to Merlin in quest of a child, even a tiny one. Merlin has a wide range:

> …he is a man, rather a diuell or a spirit, cunning in all Arts and Professions,
> all sciences, secrets and discoueries, a coniurer, an inchanter, a charmer, hee
> consorts with Elves and Fayries, a Commaunder of Goblins, and a worker of
> Night-wonders: hee can shew the secrets of Nature. Calculator of childrens
> Birthes, and no doubt, but discover the cause of thy barrennesse…(4)

Merlin offers a verse charm, which the text calls, in mock-heroic mode, an "Aenygma, or mystical riddle" (5); Tom is born and has a lively career at Arthur's court. This story will be persistent, and have special antiheroic, even antiliberal, political meaning in the eighteenth century, but here it just indicates the cross-cultural potential of popular Merlin in the early modern period.

This is most strikingly developed in *The Birth of Merlin,* a play by William Rowley written by 1612. On the title page of the 1662 printed version (fig. 13), Shakespeare is claimed as the co-author, but although Mark Dominik has argued for this as a fact (1991) and Joanna Udall does see some similarities to *Henry VIII* (1991, 101–2), most have thought it just a bold claim for publicity. It is true that the play thematically combines comic and serious material, but it lacks a Shakespearean interrelation of modes, just interweaving the vulgar and the patriotic, in an uneven tone looking forward to Victorian pantomime.

The setting is Geoffrey of Monmouth's world of Vortigern, with some names borrowed from *King Lear*—the earl of Gloster and a nobleman called Oswald, as well as a Clown. But the Clown is no incisive Fool: he is Merlin's doltish uncle, brother to his mother, a peasant girl with the vulgar name Joan Goe-too't. The play also has heroic elements, opening with war and intrigue in an Anglo-British world reminiscent of *Arthour and Merlin*. King Aurelius is seduced by the cunning Saxon princess Artesia and wants peace, but Uter, who also likes her, is for war. At the comic level, Joan is pregnant by a gentleman she met in the woods. When she and the Clown arrive at Aurelius's court in quest of her child's father, a courtier and lawyer named Sir Nicodemus Nothing, offers to help, for a fee, and suddenly, as if produced by his name and profession "Enter the Devil in mans habit, richly attir'd, his feet and his head horrid" (Rowley, 1991, 2.1, 195).

Joan seems to recognize her "dear friend" (3.1, 202) and he predicts:

> The fatal fruit thou bear'st within thy womb
> Shall here be famous till the day of doom. (3.1, 209–10)

The political plot lumbers on, but in a scene borrowed at some distance from *Macbeth* (and with a nod to Spenser's brass wall) Lucina, attended by Hecate and the three Fates, prophesies that

> In honor of this childe, the Fates shall bring
> All their assisting powers of Knowledge. Arts,
> Lerning, Wisdom, all the hidden parts
> Of all-admiring Prophecy, to fore-see
> The event of times to come: his Art shall stand
> A wall of brass to guard the Brittain Land. (3.3, 25–29)

The Devil agrees, adding that

> . . . envy shall weep,
> And mischief sit and shake her ebbone wings,
> Whilst all the world of Merlin's magick sings. (3.3, 37–39).

Merlin is born, "with a beard on his face" (3.4, 55); the Clown says "This is worse than Tom Thumb" (3.4, 65). Merlin meets the devil—hence the play's subtitle and recurring joke "The Child Hath Found Its Father"; the devil sends his son to Wales to help Vortiger with his tower and—very unusually— asserts that "Yet still I will be near at Merlins call" (3.4, 142); Merlin, the Clown and "a little antick Spirit" are then found in Wales in a scene that multi-tonally combines comic conjuring, Merlin's solution of the tower problem, his mother's rather fine speech about her female vanity, and a final prophecy of Vortiger's fate.

After Aurelius's death, poisoned by the treacherous Artesia, Uter arrives, Merlin predicts his triumph and the wider glory of his son: all the while— Rowley's contrasts are both extreme and condensed—his Clown uncle mumbles because Merlin, annoyed by his babbling, has made him silent. Joan is pursued by the amorous Devil; Merlin with a long Latin charm encloses his father, Merlin-like, in a rock and takes his mother off to be penitent in Merlin's Bower until, after her death, he will raise Stonehenge in her memory. Uter, now king, and his supporters decide, after a grisly debate, to bury alive Artesia the royal Saxon villainness—she is rudely unrepentant—and Merlin predicts the glory of Arthur.

Ranging widely, even wildly, across the many tones of the Jacobean stage, the play indicates the vitality of Merlin and the dual use in this period of his cleverness as that of both a patriotic-historic seer and a folkloric comic trickster. Critics have been hostile: Mungo MacCallum called it "a miserable fabrication" (1894, 124) and Goodrich a "burlesque portrayal" (1990, ed., 203); Dean says it "degrades Merlin further" and has "virtually no literary merit" (1992, 20); while Dobin more analytically feels it strains across "unbridgeable chasms" (1990, 194). Udall however, notes that it had a successful professional production by Theatr Clwyd in north Wales in 1989, and provides a scholarly account that makes it possible to see the play as a realization of the political and discursive range of the Merlin tradition in this period and a clear sign that Merlin's power was not weakened at the popular level (1991, 88–89). Rowley manages, and in this sense at least he is Shakespearean, to combine the dialectical forces of knowledge and power that the tradition can offer into one strange, untidy, but also potent play.

The popular vigor of clever Merlin could be appropriated for a conservative position, as by the royalist Thomas Heywood. In 1609 in a Draytonesque treatment of British myth, the stanzaic *Troia Britanica or Great Britaines Troy,* he had been as dismissive of Merlin as any rigorous chronicler or classicizing aristocrat, but very late in his career Heywood produced a lucid prose version of Geoffrey's story with an emphasis on the development of the prophecies and a strong commitment to royalism. For *The Life of Merlin Sirnamed*

Ambrosius, published in 1641, Heywood drew heavily on Fabyan's chronicle (published in 1516) and seems to have used the commentary on the *Prophécies de Merlin* attributed to Alanus de Insulis. The first sequence synopsizes Geoffrey, via Fabyan, in a "Chronographical History" of Britain from Brutus to Vortigern. Then Heywood begins his real task by discussing the nature of prophecy with extended reference to prophets in the Old Testament and the classical world, refers to Alanus de Insulis, and launches into a detailed version of Geoffrey's story: Merlin is envisaged as a fairly young scholar in the frontispiece (fig. 14): he impresses Vortigern "as having a quick and piercing eye, and ingenious and gracious countenance, and in his youthful face a kind of austerity and supercilious gravity" (Heywood, 1641, 21).

Heywood creates lengthy and poised speeches and Merlin prophesies in rhyming couplets with some vigor, if not much subtlety:

> For out of Cornwall shall proceed a Bore,
> Who shall the Kerk to pristine state restore
> Bow shall all Britaine to his kingly beck,
> And tred he shall on the whit Dragon's neck. (23–24)

Arthur is foreseen as a nationally unifying monarch, in itself attractive in the period, but also as a restorer of the church, which as Keith Thomas notes makes Merlin "not only a Christian but a Protestant" (1971, 414). Heywood recognizes a possible negative to Merlin: "by some authours it is affirmed of him that he was skilfull in dark and hidden arts, as Magic, Necromancy and the like" (24). But Heywood also envisages a popular side: to cheer up Vortigern Merlin would "present him with stately Masques and Anti-Masques; and againe for variety sake, with Rustick Dances presented by Swains and Shepherdesses" (28). Verging into the world of fairyland, this Merlin could offer aerial hunting, with flying hares and dogs, and a tournament enlivened by pigmy archers, but he was too sensitive to stay with Vortigern when the king's fate was close, and having "fained occasions abroad" he left a final prophecy in the form of "a paper which hee put in the King's Closet" (30).

Heywood covers in some detail the military affairs of Aurelius and Uter, and the story ends abruptly with the marriage of Uter and Igerna "by whom hee had Arthur and Anna, by which match the fame of Merlin spread farre abroad" (41).

In the lengthy following pages, Heywood uses prophecies, decreasingly attributed to Merlin, as an introduction to sections of royal history derived from Fabyan, with some emphasis on religious affairs, notably in the Anglo-Saxon period. The prophecy-introduced summaries come up to Elizabeth and the arrival of James I. A full account of the Guy Fawkes plot is offered and a strongly royalist summary about Charles I—but, as usual now, no prophecies of the future.

Royalist Merlin returned at the end of the Civil War when in 1660 the name of Martin Parker, the veteran balladeer and pamphleteer who had in fact died before 1656 and has been described as "a symbol of traditional royalist alliance" (*Oxford Dictionary of National Biography,* 42, 706), was added to a *Famous History of that most Renowned Christian Worthy ARTHUR, King of the Britaines* (Parker, 1660). Strongly royalist, or, by now, restorationist, it tells how "that learned clerk Merlin" was "in great favour with King Uter" and so "to him was committed the tuition and education of the young prince" (2). This, presumably a simplification of Spenser and the tutoring of Prince Arthur, is a very early educational redirection of Merlin, a theme to be potent in the twentieth century. But for Parker Merlin's major commitment was royal rather than pedagogical, proclaiming "Fidelity to his Nation and his Soveraign" (2).

Merlin also appeared on the parliament side. Keith Thomas comments that there was, "an unprecedented amount of prophetic advice before the lay public" (1971, 409) and as Dean notes, prophecies could be associated with sedition (1992, 63): Cohen suggests that the possible insertion of a Merlin reference in *King Lear* was "linked to radicalism" (1985, 352). The classic figure is William Lilly, a republican with some royalist friends, notably the scholarly Elias Ashmole: in the pre–Civil War years Lilly was arrested nine times but survived the Restoration (see *Oxford Dictionary of National Biography,* 33, 795–98). He produced several "almanacs" called "Merlins": they held some political prophecies but also a good deal of useful advice about sunrise and sunset, tides, and likely market prices. The almanacs were very popular, with many imitations, and other names including "Mercuries." Lilly's *Merlinus Anglicus Junior,* a collection of new prophecies, sold out in a week in 1644. The second volume, published in 1645, was held to have predicted the outcome of the battle of Naseby later in that year and in 1647 he started his long-running series of *Merlini Anglici Ephemeris: ephemeris* being a Greek word for calendar or almanac. Almost as successful was Richard Saunders, using the quasi-bardic anagram Schardanus (sometimes Cardanus) Rider, starting with his *Brittish Merlin* in 1656. As is clear from Bernard Capp's study (1979), Lilly and Saunders had many rivals, including an anti-Merlin, George Wharton's *No Merlin, nor Mercurius, but a New Almanacke* of 1647; the more trickster-ishly titled *The Mad-Merry Merlin or the Black Alamanacke* of 1654; and anti-republican almanacs like *The Royal Merlin or GR's Loyal Observater* of 1655.

The notional link between Merlin and republicanism was not enough to attract Milton. Even though he had once considered the possibility of writing

a heroic epic based on Arthur, which no doubt would have made some reference to Merlin,[6] by the time he came to write his *History of England* (finished
in 1655, though not published until 1670) he had been thoroughly disenchanted with the idea, in part no doubt because Arthur was both a king and a
Catholic but especially because his attitude to Geoffrey of Monmouth's work
had become what French Fogle describes as "bemused scepticism" (1971, 5,
9 n. 25). In his *History,* Milton did, like Polydore Vergil, refer to the account
of Vortigern building a castle in "Nennius" "with the advice of Ambrosius, a
young prophet whom others call Merlin" (150), but otherwise shows even less
interest in Merlin than in Arthur.

Milton's position is the logical development of the cool attitudes that had
evolved over the previous two centuries among chroniclers and historians
who felt the Merlin story was based on Geoffrey's fantasies alone. However,
as Ernest Jones shows, there were still some like Archbishop Ussher who felt,
writing in 1639, that "beneath the fable there may lurk some truth"; and even
those like the undoubtedly learned Robert Sheringham, publishing in 1670,
"who took almost the whole of the *Historia* seriously" (1941, 362–63, 376). But
they were now in the minority. Displaced as a prophet of the political future,
Merlin had survived in royalist high culture as a royal propagandist and also,
even more visibly, in popular culture as an all-purpose figure of useful, if also
trivial, information.

These two strands of the meaning of Merlin were to run in parallel, and
sometimes in collision, over the next hundred years. Essentially he was still
the figure of clever usefulness which had evolved in sixteenth-century England, rather than the British fount of obscure but natural wisdom or the inti-
mate adviser to princes that the French had made of him. But as cleverness his
knowledge could only operate either as a mundane guide to the populace at
large or as a validator of national English power, now increasingly conceived
along party lines.

Merlin the royal propagandist had work to do with the Revolution of 1688.
John Dryden, a Stuart loyalist, had planned for some time to use either Arthur
or the Black Prince "for the Honour of my Native Country" (1974, 22) when
in 1684 he started work on what became *King Arthur, or The British Worthy.* But as with Jonson's *Barriers,* the fate of princes took a hand: Charles II
died in 1686 and the "dramatick Opera" was not finished until 1691.

As a royalist Tory and from 1687 a Catholic, Dryden was displaced as Poet
Laureate when the Whig House of Orange took over. His position was deli-
cate and his preface first appealed to fellow loyalists: "This Poem was the last
Piece of Service, which I had the Honour to do, for my Gracious Master, King

CHARLES the Second" (1996, 1–3). Then he both appealed for tolerance and lamented the impact of political change on literature:

> But not to offend the present Times, nor a Government which has hitherto protected me, I have been obliged so much to alter the first Design, and take away so many Beauties from the writing, that it is now no more what it is formerly. (12–16)

The detail of Dryden's changes and lost "Beauties" has not survived. He had reused his original first act to begin *Albion and Albianus* (1685): it rejects the parliamentary past, pillorying forces like Democracy and Zeal as hostile to true order, and showing Albion, the spirit of Britain, in triumph. The Arthur opera is more subtle, focusing on a new peace between warring factions, re-working the "reassurance of fratricide," and suggesting that the invading forces—William and Mary as the Anglo-Saxons—have been acculturated by the British: noble Arthur and clever Merlin represent the Stuarts.

Like Ariosto and Jonson, Dryden disdained the medieval structures of Geoffrey of Monmouth and his French developers. His clearest influence is the *Grande Chroniques de Bretagne* by Alain Bouchart, an early sixteenth-century resume of the Arthur story, and his main interest is to combine wonder and theatrical vigor, with Merlin as master of propagandaesque ceremonies.

Restoration theater entails major roles for women, and often adds Henry Purcell's splendid music. For his romantic lead Dryden creates Emmeline, a blind beauty loved by both Arthur and the Saxon leader Oswald—her name probably derives from the "redoubted Emmeline," the martial daughter to Charlemagne mentioned by Spenser (1912, 2.3.54, 8),[7] but she is passive and potentially productive, as both Tories and Whigs would like the ordinary populace of Britain to be.

Merlin is soon at the center of the plays emphatic theatricality. After a first act setting out the conflict in war and love between British Arthur and Saxon Oswald, Philidel, the "Airy Spirit" who helps the British against the Saxon-oriented "Earthy Spirit" Grimbold, is lamenting alone when the magus materializes:

Merlin, with Spirits, descends to Philidel on a Chariot drawn by Dragons

MERLIN: What art thou, Spirit, of what Name and Order?
                 For I have view'd thee in my Magick Glass,
                 Making thy moan, among the Midnight Wolves,

> That Bay the silent Moon: Speak, I conjure thee.
> 'Tis Merlin bids thee, at whose awful Wand,
> The pale Ghost quivers, and the grim Fiend gasps. (2.1, 7–12)

In the glass and the wolves Dryden calls up earlier images of Merlin, but his opposition to "the grim Fiend" firmly aligns him with Christianity, not the murkier contacts that Rowley had enjoyed putting on the stage. Merlin assures Philidel "a great Power protects thee" (2.1, 8), evidently God's, and he leaves his spirits behind to help when he and his dragon chariot ascend.

Merlin's authority would seem to suggest an easy victory for Britain and true love, but, as in seventeenth-century political reality, things are not as simple as faith might hope, and Merlin's power is reduced to useful cleverness in spite of his imposing initial appearance. After Act 2's seesawing conflict in war and romance, Act 3 begins with the British close to despair in the face of Grimbold's Saxon magic. Arthur attacks anyway, but Merlin reappears with less bravery, pulling Arthur back by the hand: "Hold, Sir, and wait Heav'ns time; th'Attempt's too dangerous" (3.1, 26–30).

No longer a deus ex machina, this Merlin is not even master of the magical situation:

> There's not a Tree in that Inchanted Grove
> But numbred out, and given by tale to Fiends;
> And under every Leaf a Spirit couch'd.
> But by what Method to resolve those Charms,
> Is yet unknown to me. (3.1, 26–30)

Merlin does announce that Emmeline shall no "longer want the sun" (3.1, 38) because "This Vial shall restore her sight" (3.1, 45), but such scientistic cleverness is not powerful action. It is Philidel who takes the vial and restores Emmeline's sight, so that she can see Arthur, and their love is semi-erotically celebrated by Airy Spirits singing "O Sight, the Mother of Desires."

Osmond appears and seizes Emmeline, but Philidel again intervenes. Brad Walton has suggested Dryden emphasizes Philidel's agency simply as a "solution to the lack of suspense" in a drama that must have a happy ending (1991, 48), but the author seems aware of the need to limit Merlin to cleverness, making him say to Arthur:

> Merlin: Thus far it is permitted me to go;
> But all beyond this Spot, is fenc'd with Charms;
> I may no more; but only with advice. (4.2, 1–3)

In Merlin's weakness Restoration theatricality flourishes. Some no doubt very lightly clad sirens tempt Arthur and when he attacks the tree they surround, what seems like Emmeline emerges, apparently disenchanted, but with her arm bleeding from Arthur's attack. He cries for illumination: "O Love! O Merlin! Whom should I believe?" (4.2, 122), but again Philidel comes to the rescue, revealing that the tree-bound siren Emmeline was in fact Grimbold.

As the last act begins, the leaders exchange insults and theatrically "Fight with Spunges in their Hands dipt in Blood" (5.2, 44). Merlin appears, and gives Arthur his sword. The battle goes well and Merlin as master of ceremonies leads in the triumphant Britons, banishes Osmond to a "loathsome Dungeon," and sums everything up in ways both medieval and modern:

> Merlin to Arthur
> For this Days Palm, and for thy former Acts,
> Thy Britain freed, and Foreign Force expell'd,
> Thou, Arthur, hast acquir'd a future Fame,
> And of three Christian Worthies, art the first:
> And nowe at once, to treat thy Sight and Soul,
> Behould what Rouling Ages shall produce:
> The Wealth, the Loves, the Glories of our Isle,
> which yet like Golden Oar, unripe in Beds,
> Expect the Warm Indulgency of Heav'n
> To call 'em forth to Light (5.2, 76–85)

In the absence of "foreign force"—which has a conveniently wide reference, from Parliamentarians or Catholics to just France—the productivity and profit so dear to William and the Whigs can flourish, and this ideal state is immediately imperialized:

Merlin waves his Wand; the scene changes and discovers the British Ocean in a storm. Aeolus in a cloud above. (5.2, 89)

Aeolus sings to persuade the winds to "let Britannia rise in Triumph o-er the Main" (5.2, 92–93): she appears "seated in the Island," then follow a fishermen's dance, a classically authorized chant by Pan and a Nereid devoted to farming riches, and a robust harvest song ending "And Hoigh for the Honour of Old England" (5.2, 149). This celebration of nation, productivity, and wealth comes to a sublime climax as Venus honors Britain as "Fairest Isle, all Isles Excelling" (5.2, 155)—Roger Savage calls it "a minuet-prelude...of the most tender poise and elegant gravity" (1995, 376).

Charming idealization gives way to real power as "A Warlike Consort" appears and Merlin steps forward in his knowledge-as-service role to explain the origin of this authoritative group:

> These who last enter'd, are our Valiant Britains,
> Who shall by Sea and Land Repel our Foes. (5.2, 197–98)

Even when so directly involved in potent propaganda as at the end, Merlin still represents knowledge serving, not directing, or even advising, authority. The delegation of action to Philidel and the use of music and song to express the messages of restoration and harmony, both royal and simply profitable, clarify theatrically the subjugation of knowledge to power characteristic of this period. The text does not dramatize any plot-based rejection of Merlin—there is here no Vivien—but his self-limitation is noted when Arthur, no doubt speaking for Dryden, who knew a good deal about knowledge and power and had personally experienced how power could see artistic knowledge as a threat, tells Merlin he has been wise to be cautious:

> Wisely you have, whate'er will please, reveal'd,
> What wou'd displease, as wisely have conceal'd. (5.2, 195–96)

Not all Restoration writers who dealt with Merlin were as memorable as Dryden. Richard Blackmore, a doctor and prolific author knighted by William III for his medical activities but also for his support as a loyal Whig and energetic ideologue, produced in 1695 *Prince Arthur,* "a heroic poem in ten books," lauding the new king and his party. The opposition, both Tory and talented, took immediate aim. John Dennis, in a full-length book called *Remarks on a Book entituled Prince Arthur, an Heroick Poem,* was trenchantly negative: "Mr Blackmore's Action has neither unity, nor integrity, nor morality, nor universality"(1696, A.1). A little later Dryden called him a "Pedant, Canting Preacher and a Quack" (1952, 1759); Pope made him a recurrent target in his literary satire *Peri Bathous* (1727), and pilloried him with elegant irony in *The Dunciad* (1728) as "everlasting Blackmore" (1993, 2.302).

Blackmore's critics had grounds beyond politics. His ponderous preface dismisses Ariosto and Spenser for their "lack of epic decorum" (1695, unpaginated), and proclaims his own link with Virgil. His poetry seeks an English epic style in its Miltonic weight of language, but unwisely, and often clumsily, adds couplet rhyme. He adopts the story that Geoffrey of Monmouth offered, but does not share Geoffrey's interest in Merlin: for Blackmore his knowledge is presumably too medieval and too Catholic to be anything but suspect. Merlin's knowledge role is shared between a group of "orators" led by the Greek-sounding Tylon, and, varying the earlier limits on prophecy, it is Uther himself who in Book 5 foresees at length the future royal glories of Britain. Merlin is eventually noticed as a "Sorcerer of wondrous Fame" but he is both "pagan British" and a traitor, helping the Saxons with "baleful herbs," "Familial fiends," "Nocturnal Feats," and "infernal Company" (7.202).

Although Blackmore in this way develops the negative cleverness of the diabolic Merlin, there is hope: Merlin's evil cursing of Arthur turns, through divine intervention, into "Heavenly Fury" (7.206) in which he blesses the king. The whole poem allegorically praises King William III and his Protestant Whig rule: Uther's lengthy historical prophecy omits the Stuarts entirely and proclaims a "brave Nassovian" as "the great Deliverer to come" (4.122)— William was connected with Nassau in Germany. The evil Saxon Octa clearly represents James II, and the Saxons in general are thought of as Catholics: the side-changing Merlin may well refer to Dryden himself.

Blackmore's value to the new political power must have helped the poem's success: it went quickly into three editions, and in spite of Tory ridicule he moved straight on to produce *King Arthur* in 1697, this time in the full Virgilian form of twelve books. An even more pompous preface criticized his critics, but the sequel was less successful, neither new as Whig propaganda nor interesting in itself. Though claiming Geoffrey of Monmouth as its source, it ignores most of his story, especially Merlin, merely plodding in great detail through the contemporary attraction of bloodily triumphant wars as "The valiant King the haughty French subdued" (12.347).

Cleverness High and Low: The Eighteenth Century

Merlin was at his weakest at this time largely because of his new servility to power: reduced to a clever producer of useful propaganda, he had no greater role. Even when Geoffrey of Monmouth was translated into English by Aaron Thompson in 1718, and the introduction argued strongly and at great length, if not very credibly, for Geoffrey's historical and patriotic value, Merlin was basically dismissed:

> Merlin's Prophesy, for the Nonsense and unintelligible Jargon it contains, should have been omitted, but that Jeffrey has so connected it with the History,

that the Thread of the Story would not be entire without it. (Geoffrey of Monmouth, 1718, v)

In these negative contexts, with Merlin caught between scholarly doubt and political servility, the idea of using him as a major figure in high culture seems, as Dean comments, to fade for the whole of the eighteenth century (1992, 89). But Merlin as a source of useful knowledge remained alive in the popular mind: Rowley's *Birth of Merlin* was revived in "a droll" in 1724, at Southwark Fair in London (Allen, 1937, 137; Udall, 1991, 2), and Merlinesque prophecies were still very popular. In the Restoration period both Lilly and "Rider" had continued to publish and they had many imitators like *Merlinus Verax* ("Truthful Merlin") of the late 1660s, *Merlin Reviv'd* in the 1680s, *Merlinus Rusticus* of 1685, and Joseph Partridge's *Merlinus Liberatus,* first appearing in 1680 and becoming regular from 1689 on. Merlin was not the only figure: Mercurius was still a popular pseudo-author and others ranged from the long-famous Nostradamus to the locally English Mother Shipton.

This seemed to conservative people both ignorant and also a troubling exercise of the populist voice. One response was Jonathan Swift's entertaining attack on Joseph Partridge (1713). In a pamphlet under his querulous pseudonym, Isaac Bickerstaff, he confidently predicted Partridge's death in 1707; he followed up by announcing both the astrologer's death and then the humiliating impact of his having to meet the costs of a funeral, coffin, and grave when he protested he was alive (though the protesting pamphlet may also have been a Swiftian hoax). Swift never made direct fun of Merlin: perhaps because he was no more than a name in the almanacs, but possibly through a greater respect for knowledge than Partridge held.

The longest-lasting conservative mockery of Arthur and the propagandist Merlin was Henry Fielding's inspired development of the ironic potential of the Tom Thumb story. In 1730 appeared *Tom Thumb: A Tragedy,* a short, hilarious satire on the pomposities of Restoration drama, including Dryden's, which Fielding expanded and sophisticated by 1731 into *The Tragedy of Tragedies: The Life and Death of Tom Thumb.* The jokes flow from the start: in the dramatis personae Arthur's queen is Dollallolla, "a woman entirely faultless saving that she is a little given to Drink; a little too much a Virago towards her Husband, and in love with Tom Thumb" (1731, 1). As Tom Thumb arrives in victorious triumph we are told he was "By Merlin's art begot" (4), but Merlin plays no part in the ridiculous plot until early in Act 3. Then, like a witch in *Macbeth,* he calls Tom thrice from a storm-ridden plain, introduces himself as "Merlin by name, a Conjuror by Trade," and sings a farcical ballad about "the mystick getting of Tom Thumb" (50), harking back to Johnson's pamphlet of 1621.

This parodic clever Merlin reveals to Tom his terrible fate, to be eaten by a red cow: but he also gives him heroic consolation with a theatrical prophecy:

> For lo! A Sight more glorious courts thy Eyes;
> See from afar a Theatre arise;
> There, Ages yet unknown shall Tribute pay
> To the Heroick Actions of this Day; (51)

For Fielding that is all Merlin contributes; the play ends in dire parodic tragedy as, after Tom Thumb's bovine fate, everybody is killed in a ludicrous frenzy of revenge: Arthur, the last left alive, stabs himself, crying "And take thou this" (57).

The piece was extremely popular, then and after. Some politics was involved: it expressed in parody the Tory dislike of Italianate heroic tragedy, a mode which, like the new Handel opera, had been supported by the new Germanic Whig royalty, and the tiny Tom Thumb the Great was clearly a burlesque of Sir Robert Walpole, the Whig prime minister, often called "The Great Man." But it is the sheer comedy that made this remain a theatrical standard into the nineteenth century. The most innovative version was by the actress and playwright Eliza Haywood, with her partner William Satchell: *The Opera of Operas* of 1733 directly mocked the Italian opera form. Exploiting skilfully the musical possibilities of the comic setting, this remained for some time in the repertoire. It was reworked by Kane O'Hara as *Tom Thumb: a Burletta* in 1780, which also lived on, being revived and published in 1805.

Haywood revises Merlin's prophecy to Tom Thumb from a general vision of the theater to ironic reference to recent Italianate productions:

> Be not dismay'd; for this heroic Act
> Shall gain thee fame immortal;
> Ages unborn shall warble this soft theme,
> In tunefull Opera,
> Exceeding far *Hydaspes, Rosamond, Camilla or Arsinoe.*
> (Haywood and Satchell, 1999, 210)

The plot follows Fielding to its grotesque end, but then two fashionable commentators, Sir Crit-Operatical and Modely, deplore such a tragic end for a modern opera, and foresee Merlin's help. So, to "solemn Music" he "waves his wand" (216) and addresses the "rav'nous Cow" in a couplet that even Fielding must have admired:

> Now, by emetick Power, Red Cannibal,
> Cast up thy Prisoner, England's Hannibal. (217)

Tom emerges from the cow's mouth and all the others are revived from their tragic deaths. Tom and Huncamunca, or Hunky as he calls her, are betrothed, and the hero offers appropriate thanks to Merlin: "Conjuror most blest! Among the Faculty of Quacks the best" (219).

But if the politicized Merlin could, as a clever clown, be a tool of Tory mockery, he could also be an approved element in Whig culture: power still battled for control and use of knowledge. George II's queen, Caroline of Anspach, was a rare creature, an intellectual in the English royal family: before coming to London she moved in learned circles in Berlin and knew the philosopher Leibniz. In 1732 she established in the royal estate at Richmond, under the design of the garden architect William Kent, a "Hermitage" dedicated to learning: it included busts of the modern thinkers Isaac Newton, Robert Boyle, and John Locke (Allen, 1937, 135–36), and was intended, as Judith Colton puts it, "to make an artistic statement of her belief that natural religion and the new science could be reconciled" (1976, 1).

By summer 1735 Kent had built nearby for the queen a cottage with Gothic doors and windows and thatched roof, set into a hill, and known as Merlin's Cave (figs. 15 and 16). It had a library of English books and six life-size wax images: Merlin was central, studying books and scientific instruments, with a wand nearby. The five other figures were Merlin's male secretary, Queen Elizabeth, Henry VII's queen, Margaret, and two women. One is variously named as Britomart, Bradamant, Britannia, or Minerva—clearly meant to be a powerful woman; the other is variously described as Glauce, Britomart's wise nurse, or a prophetess, either classical Melissa or folkloric Mother Shipton. They are all figures of applied knowledge, not just cleverness. The female emphasis must owe much to the queen, and may in itself have sparked some of the substantial criticism Merlin's Cave attracted.

Merely ironic towards the male and respectably accredited thinkers honored at the Hermitage, the Tory press ridiculed the Cave, especially when the queen made Stephen Duck, the peasant poet, its custodian. *The Craftsman* said it was like "an old Haystack" and "a Cave above Ground" (Allen, 1937, 136–37; Jones, 1941, 404). But there was also positive interest in the Cave as a symbol of modern knowledge. The Welsh poet Jane Brereton, an enthusiastic supporter of Hanoverian culture (Prescott, 2005), writing under the prophetic pseudonym Melissa (herself probably one of the Cave figures), published *Merlin: A Poem* (1735). Merlin thanks "Lerning's Patroness" and lays his own claim to scientific modernity. Wearing astronomical signs on his gown, he asks:

> Why shou'd not British Merlin, grace thy Page,
> In Mathematicks, once esteem'd a Sage? (5)

He claims Stonehenge as his work "by meer mechanick Pow'rs atcheived" not, as most think, "th'Effects of Magick" (6), and he insists that "other sciences to me were known" including "the Wonders of the Sky" (6, 7), but he acknowledges Newton's superiority in this field.

Though more than just clever here, Merlin is still, as so often, contained: he is only a forerunner of modern science. The present, embodied in Newton, is superior and Merlin also has a primitive role as a sort of Celtic bard, the first sign of the bard/druid identity which will later become a common way of reinterpreting Merlin.

> I study'd Nature, through her various Ways;
> And chaunted to this Harp, prophetick Lays (7)

A positive Whig Merlin emerged when Horace Walpole—Sir Robert's son—involved Arthur and Merlin in a lost poem honoring the British naval triumph at Quiberon Bay in 1759. Loyalist Merlin is also a feature of what starts as a guidebook, Edward Curll's publication in 1736 of an illustrated volume on *The Rarities of Richmond*. First it offers an "exact description of the Royal Hermitage and Merlin's Cave" but its subtitle continues "with the Life and Prophecies." Most of the book is a full sequence of numbered Merlin prophecies up to James I, drawing on Heywood's 1641 *Life*. In 1755 there was a version of the same book entitled *Merlin's Life and Prophecies*, without the Richmond Cave material but bringing the prophetic story up to the glory of George II. Whig loyalty then confronts resistance to royalty when Curll adds at some length a Merlin prophecy about, and then legal details of, a case from 1754 where residents of Richmond challenged the royal right to enclose the park, and lost.

Merlin's Cave caught the imagination, both among the wealthy—Smiles comments on the number of similar buildings aristocrats were to erect (1994, 198)—and the wider public: *Merlin in Miniature* was a display "at the Crown coffee-house in King Street near Guildhall" which lasted until 1760, not long before the Richmond Cave was destroyed in a new landscaping maneuver by Capability Brown about 1765 (Colton, 1976, 4 n. 11). "Merlin's Cave" was the name for a famous tavern in the Farringdon district of London which seems to date from 1737 and, as knowledge became a potent force for change, was to become a meeting place for radicals in the early nineteenth century.

Theatrical Merlin remained popular. The Dryden/Purcell musical play was reperformed, in at least one version renamed as *Merlin: The British Inchanter.*[8] In the same period the London theater saw a production of *The Royal Chace or Merlin's Cave* by Edward Phillips (1736), which was revived in 1740 (Allen, 1937, 138). It opens with claims to seriousness as Merlin, much like Queen Caroline, welcomes Diana the huntress to his "Solitude, O pleasing Solitude" where

> Contemplation holds her sacred Seat
> And to her studious Scions the Knowledge deep
> Of Nature's Laws unfolds (3–4)

But the play becomes more popular as Diana calls up "pleasing Shapes," a dance of lightly clad female graces and male zephyrs. Then Jupiter, who is also Harlequin, performs, without the need for words, the story of Europa— the god raped her, with the two transformed as cow and bull. This erotic theater uses the contemporary name of Merlin as a mere starting point and stresses his limitations, even rejecting cleverness: he is both "humble" and "an old, but honest heart" (20 and 18).

The general Merlin-mania of the mid 1730s included a revival of Rowley's *The Birth of Merlin* in 1736, and Lewis Theobald's new play *Merlin or the Devil of Stonehenge,* staged and printed in 1734, with a preface praising, presumably with tongue in cheek, "Our British Merlin" as "an excellent Mathematician, . . . having wrote an allegory on the Philosopher's Stone" (1734, unpaginated). The preface goes on, in the spirit of fake scholarship, to refer to Alanus de Insulis, Ariosto, and Cervantes and the notion that Marlborough is "Merlin's Bury"—a sixteenth-century English appropriation reinforced by the recent military fame of the Duke of Marlborough. Merlin "formerly an Enchanter" is "now an Infernal Spirit"—and so is the devil of Stonehenge. As in Rowley, Merlin buries his mother at Stonehenge, and he also has powers that include what is now simply disguise, but that tricksterish memory does no more than provide some theatrical surprises and early Gothic melodrama for a fairly lightweight piece of theater, essentially an early harlequinade.

A compatible comic cleverness guides Aaron Hill's *Merlin in Love, or Youth against Magic* (1760), a pantomime opera written in 1737 but apparently never performed, possibly because its scenic elaborations would have strained even the remarkable production capacities of the period. The story of Merlin and Vivien, here Nimue, is reworked as farce, with Merlin being outwitted by Columbine and rejected for her Harlequin: there would be many other versions of this conflict, notably Charles Dibdin's *Wizard's Wake: or Harlequin and Merlin,* performed at London's Sadler's Wells in 1802 (see Simpson, 1990, 121–22). In more elevated mode, David Garrick's play of 1766, *Cymon,* deriving from a Dryden poem, made Merlin curiously both weak and strong. He is obsessed with the enchantress Urganda, but when she rejects him for Cymon, he defeats her power because he is "mischievously angry," makes Cymon happy with Sylvia, and then leaves in his dragon chariot (1766, 10).

In spite of the Whig interest in him as a precursor of modern disciplinary knowledge, and the continued popular interest, Merlin had relatively little to offer in the world of new practical learning and nonautocratic government. Not much use to princes in royal propaganda, for they themselves now had little decisive power, he had largely lost his popular prophetic role and was reduced to limited deployments of cleverness. Where "Melissa" found Merlin a noble but very limited predecessor of modern science, for Hill he is not nearly as clever as Harlequin. While for Dryden his greatest achievement was to interpret the self-conscious grandeur of Restoration England, Blackmore could make no more of Merlin than a sort of Caliban of the world of magic, and for Fielding he was no more than a nursery trickster. Merlin's strongest supporter in the period, Queen Caroline, located his value in a cottage annex supervised by a peasant—a sign at best of quaint and distinctly constrained cleverness, really a code for female knowledge, only marginally linked to the new learning of his neighbors in the Hermitage. Like his own creation and master, Arthur, in the world of classical learning, parliamentary power, and mercantile profit, where wisdom lay in shrewdness and negotiation, not deep insight, Merlin and his knowledge were very much at a discount as no more than instrumentalities of cleverness. They would essentially remain so for another century, especially as individual moral judgment came to be seen as the key element of human knowledge.

The Dangers of Cleverness: The Romantics

Romanticism, so revolutionary in so many ways, did not substantially change or elevate the reduced role of seventeenth- and eighteenth-century Merlin.

From R. S. Loomis's medievalist distance it looked different: he said that "with the Romantic Movement Arthur and Merlin heard the magic horn pealing through fairyland and returned once more to the fellowship of men" (Loomis and Loomis, 1938, 144). But Arthur was of limited interest in this period (see Gossedge and Knight, 2009), and Merlin had his own disadvantages. His Gothic cottage, even if they knew of it, would not have attracted the early Romantics. Under thatch and in the Middle Ages they found the values of simplicity and authenticity, tokens to resist the intensely formal behavior that they felt had masked political and personal corruption in the eighteenth century, but Merlin did not represent those values. Michael the road-mender or the experience-scarred Ancient Mariner represented their idea of natural wisdom and—the key value which clever, complex, possibly diabolic Merlin could hardly represent—simple morality.

Attraction to and avoidance of Merlin is clear in that deeply learned, and even more remarkably overlooked, harbinger of Romanticism, modern scholarship, and criticism, Thomas Warton. Familiar directly with Geoffrey of Monmouth—he said "his Latinity rises far above mediocrity" (1774, 1, g2)—and very widely read, he also responded to the emotive appeal of medieval myth. In his poem "The Grave of King Arthur," which Mungo MacCallum thought one of his finest (1894, 176), he relates, from apparent familiarity with Geoffrey's *Vita,* and combining Augustan precision with Romantic feeling, how the story goes that an "elfin queen" bore Arthur's body to Avalon:

> In Merlin's agate-axled car
> To her green isle's enamel'd steep
> Far in the navel of the deep. (1777, 65)

But Warton's scholarship resists his Romanticism: drawing on a story he found in both Leland and Gerald of Wales, he then tells how another bard denies "Merlin's potent spell" (69) and claims that Arthur is actually buried at Glastonbury. Royal power is as important to Warton as learning, and both outweigh romance: Henry II sends men to dig, and they find Arthur and Guinevere buried there.

Emotive insights into the mythic power of the past are sidelined by Warton's scholarly analysis of romance, which he sees in a world light: he finds Merlin's transformation of Uther "a species of Arabian magic" (1774, 1, b2), identifies the Merlin prophecies as having an "oriental growth" (1774, 3, 146), and understands Arthur as being parallel to Charlemagne as "the first and original heroes of romance" (1774, 1, 1c). For Warton, Merlin is little more than a reference to the intriguing but still outdated power of the medieval.

Warton's friend Thomas Gray moved further towards the emotional power of the past in "The Bard" (1757), but he by-passed Myrddin/Merlin for the more genuinely Welsh bardic tradition of Taliesin as an image of resistance to modern so-called civilization. Gray's bard was a figure whom the Romantics, drawing on the new energy in Welsh scholarship, would often condense with Merlin, now provided with a beard and visionary passion, and a strong visual image: Horace Walpole himself recommended illustration of the figure to Gray (Smiles, 1994, 50–51), and the best known depiction was Thomas Jones's dramatic 1774 painting "The Bard" (fig. 17). In this spirit the young Cornish-raised scientist Humphrey Davy, in a poem of about 1795, saw "mighty Merlin," "The Master of the spell" to be a figure of "anguish" with a "dull dark eye," and suffering a Gothic death in "a dark cave upon the flinty rock"(Davy, 1988, 196).

The Romantic rejection of Merlin is, like that of Arthur, the more striking because the medieval Merlin material had become increasingly well known by the early nineteenth century. A widely read source was George Ellis's *Specimens of the Early English Metrical Poems* of 1805, including synopses and translations from Geoffrey's *Historia* and his *Vita Merlini,* as well as lengthy passages from *Arthour and Merlin* and Lovelich's *Merlin;* another was John Dunlop's very popular *History of Fiction* of 1814 which offered, among many other medieval texts, a full synopsis of the Vulgate *Merlin* up to the death of Uther and a short account of Vivien. The preface Robert Southey wrote for the handsome two-volume Malory of 1817, *The Byrth, Lyf and Actes of Kyng Arthur* (which Southey did not, contrary to many opinions, edit: it was basically a reprint of Caxton's edition) summarized Robert de Boron's story up to Merlin's departure to Northumbria. The notes to the preface gave a synopsis of the Vulgate story of Merlin and Vivien (as Nimue), as well as of Heywood's *Life*—but, much more negative than the source, the preface makes Vivien into a dangerous temptress.

Yet available as it was, the Merlin story lay fallow. For many of the major Romantic writers, first and foremost modern humanists, Merlin's wisdom was either inappropriately unsecular or suspect as insufficiently internal and moral: he was as a result only deployed as an occasional point of reference, as a mere and malign bearer of cleverness.

Blake used Merlin's name eight times, among very many others, in the immense *Jerusalem,* and his "Merlin's Prophecy" is just a four-line ironic jotting (1972, 620–747 and 177). Coleridge in "The Pang More Sharp than

All" mentions Merlin's "crystal orb," drawing on Spenser, as an image for his own troubled memory (2001, 4.1.39, 82); Shelley in the unfinished play *Charles the First* has the Fool parody a Merlin prophecy (obviously a *King Lear* borrowing) (1923, 366). Southey, setting the early Celtic scene for the Welsh-American voyage of discovery by *Madoc,* speaks of "Old Merlin, master of the mystic lore" and also associates him with a "band of bards" (2004, 1.11, 104–5). Slightly more weight is involved when Keats deepens the atmosphere of "The Eve of St Agnes" by saying "Never on such a night have lovers met / Since Merlin paid his Demon all his debt" (1970, 270–71). Rather than diabolizing Vivien, the lines suggest that Merlin is internally compelled to destroy himself: humanizing the fallible man of learning, it offers an idea that Tennyson would develop.

Merlin, like Arthur (see Gossedge and Knight, 2009), was to some degree used by non-English British writers in this period, but even here there were limits to his value. Scott knew the medieval material better than any of the other Romantics, though he too never adventured the full Arthur story he once seriously considered. He does purloin the potent name and concept of "The Lady of the Lake" for his own very different Scottish mythic and national purposes, and *The Bridal of Triermain* (1813) is a new Arthurian narrative that employs Merlin in a negative role. He enchants Arthur's illegitimate daughter Gyneth to sleep to revenge the death of his young kinsman at a tournament to select her husband, only for her to be revived centuries later by a heroic Scots laird.

Another medievally learned Romantic, who knew Welsh well, largely through his wife, and at least noticed both Arthur and Merlin was Thomas Love Peacock. His *Sir Calidore,* written in 1817, is a witty but unfinished sketch of an updated romance: Calidore is a pure-minded knight baffled by the paper currency of modern Britain, and there is a brief glimpse, drawn from Spenser, of Merlin inscribing on the sand some puzzles in geometry; in Peacock's amusing poem "The Round Table," also of 1817, "old Merlin" stands near Arthur "Drawing circles, triangles and squares on the sand" (1926, 321). He then invites guests such as Pluto and Robin Hood to join them, and British monarchs from Arthur to the present, to feast at the Round Table— Merlin as master of ceremonies again. Even in *The Misfortunes of Elphin* (1829), where as Gossedge notes (2006) Peacock follows with some accuracy early Welsh material, Taliesin is the major figure of poetry and wisdom and Merlin appears briefly, and eclectically, in three Welsh forms: in a bardic competition, as Myrddin Wyllt, and finally as the possessor of an all-providing hamper (like Gwyddno in *Culhwch and Olwen*). It seems a clear sign of the general cloud under which Arthurian studies largely lay in this period that a scholar, wit, liberal, and Celtic sympathizer like Peacock found no focal use for Merlin.

The Cornish loyalist John Magor Boyle, in *Gorlaye* (his version of Gorlois), offers in the context of Igraine's seduction only a negative mention of the clever enchanter, stating that "Merlin's guile, and Uter's gold / Had won the guardians of the hold." (1835, 115). Other diminished accounts of Merlin were frankly comic. John Moultrie's "La Belle Tryamour" (1837) is a creditably Byronic treatment of the medieval fairy-mistress romance *Sir Launfal* where Merlin, who combines magic and mathematics, cures Arthur of "the blue devils" (in Latin, st. 50) by giving him a magic glass, as in Spenser. Further reduced is the hero of *The Cat's Tail: Being the History of Childe Merlin,* from 1831, dedicated "To the Infant Public." Merlin is a black kitten who has many perilous domestic adventures and ends, like Tom Thumb, by being eaten, in this case by a mare: the author's name, the Baroness de Katzleben, is equally fantastic.

There were two areas of fuller activity in the Merlin myth in the Romantic period, though neither of them was entirely positive about the great sage. The first strand, where Merlin is more than just clever, which has had little impact on either literature or public attitudes, and which seems completely unrecognized, is an English version of the nationalist Celtic interest, where Merlin validates masculine and military narcissism in an unusual English imperialism: the Arctic Arthur.

Richard Hole published in 1789 *Arthur, or The Northern Enchantment.* Merlin has some scientific status—he retires into the wild "to study nature's secret laws / And trace her wonders to the primal cause" (31). The story starts in the far north where Arthur is shipwrecked among weird sisters, but Merlin appears from a cloud, and explains that the fleet is safe and that this is all illusion. The plot goes back in time to Arthur's struggle with Hengist, including a conflict of love over Merlin's daughter Inogen—slightly different from Shakespeare's Imogen in *Cymbeline.* With the help of Lancelot, and Merlin's magic bark, Arthur fights and beats Hengist, much of the action taking place in Scandinavia, including Lapland. Eventually all is well and Arthur becomes Merlin's royally triumphant son-in-law, charged by the scientist-cum-magician to a rule which hybridizes modern liberalism with Roman imperial nobility:

> Crush stern oppression, and the wrong'd redress;
> Fight to protect, and conquer but to bless. (253)

This "cultural pot-pourri," as Merriman calls it (1973, 108), combining Shakespearean and Gothic elements, owes a good deal to the recurrent English fascination with Northern exploitation, often linked to the Arthurian myth, going back to Geoffrey of Monmouth. John Dee's recently discovered *The Limits of the British Empire* (2004) explicitly recruited Arthur as a precedent for Elizabethan imperialist claims to the Northwest Passage and the Arctic generally. Blackmore has material on this theme, and Dryden's "frozen Genius" scene may be a version of it. Apart from imperial validation, there is no special role for knowledge alone in this context, and so Merlin is no more than a plot-assistant and anxious father. As in Dryden and *Arthour and Merlin,* this weakened and power-compliant Merlin can remain through the whole text, rather than being disposed of as a knowledge-rich challenge to power.

Another essay in this northwards-looking masculinist imperialism that deploys a politically useful Merlin is Henry Milman's twelve-book blank-verse epic *Samor, Lord of the Bright City* (1818). The city is Gloucester, and its hero is Eldol, both praised by Geoffrey of Monmouth, in honor of the royal-born Count Robert of Gloucester. As the preface notes (vii), Milman chose to rename the hero Samor, as found in some early chronicles—perhaps that seemed more exotic, even oriental.

Overall the poem is a sluggish epic about British military triumphs including, as in Blackmore and Hole, many in the northern maritime areas. Part of Samor's education in manliness and imperial ferocity is his visit to north Wales in Book 8 where he encounters a highly druidic and bardic version of Merlin who provides good advice about the value of freedom on this "Peerless Isle" (8.126) where "fruits on earth Shower'd" (8.478–79), and ends his vision with an account of contemporary order:

> A Throne, an Altar, and a Senate-House.
> Upon the throne a King sate, triple-crown'd
> As by three kingdoms; voices eloquent
> In harmony of discord fulmin'd forth
> From that wise Senate.... (8.491–95)

As this is published in 1818, when both hunger and civil unrest were widespread in England, when the mythic resistance of Captain Swing and Ned Ludd stalked the land, and Merlin's Cave in Farringdon had become a center for rousing radical speeches, quite a few of whose makers were jailed for treason, this vision of a "harmony of discord" seems strikingly complacent, even for an Oxford don like Milman, destined to become dean of St Paul's Cathedral.

The same mix of epic grandeur and a somewhat sadomasochistic interest in war and suffering, including in the north, with Arthur supported by Merlin's knowledge, is central to Edward Bulwer Lytton's *King Arthur* of 1848.[9] Another quasi-classical epic, and by someone who, like Blackmore, was closely involved in politics, it offers Arthur as a warrior leader against the Saxons, and once more the chieftains of the Northern world, but as Mark Cumming outlines (1992, 36), Lytton maintains a multiple allegorical image of Arthur as not only "the perfected Man" (12.173) and "the Christian Prince" (12.174) but even "the great Archetype of Chivalry" (7.51). This might sound as if Lytton is reaching for French medievalism here, but, following Thomas Percy's views,[10] he claims in his introduction to the second edition that it is "The Great North from which Chivalry sprang" (xii), and there is nothing of the Mediterranean about Lytton's Arthur and his bracing world.

Merlin is Romantic in mode: Arthur finds him in "a lone turret," where "sate the wizard on a Druid throne" (1.38 and 41). But there is more to the image: he has also been Arthur's quasi-paternal educator in "the young hopeful day / When the child stood by the great prophet's knee, And drank high thoughts to strengthen years to be" (1.41). This may be the seed of the future educational Merlin, but he retains a Celtic-Gothic grandeur:

> Vast was the front which o'er as vast a breast
> Hung, as if heavy with the load sublime
> Of the pil'd hoards which Thought, the heavenly guest,
> Had wrung from Nature, or despoil'd from Time... (1.46)

This awesome Merlin sends Arthur forth to organize his military kingdom, and prophesies long-lasting, wide-spreading British success, until lands "broader than Caesar ever won, / Shall clasp a realm where never sets the sun" (1.87). English imperial politics are specific as well as general: Simpson records in detail many resonances found by contemporaries, such as identifying the Vandal King Ludovick as Louis Philippe of France (1990, 147–49).

Lytton was familiar with the Vulgate grand vizier tradition through Ellis's *Specimens,* and Merlin also has a strategic role, but not one of such authority that it leads to his early dismissal from the text. For Lytton, like the Tudors and their successors, knowledge serves power, not challenges it, and the early version of an educational relationship between Merlin and Arthur may itself

explain why Merlin can remain through the whole story in a consistently supportive and non-challenging role.

He is also an adviser, in the Vulgate mode. When after his imperial adventures to the north Arthur has wandered into a luxurious, sexualized Happy
Valley, Merlin sends a raven messenger to tell him "The Saxon's march is in
thy father's soil" (4.96). Many adventures and complexities ensue, including
a prophetic Phantom who suggests Lytton's interest in sensational fiction;
but he also was adept at manly sentiment, which is deployed at length when
Merlin sends off the Cymrian warriors, including his quasi-son, the young
bard Caradoc (a memory of Scott's *Bridal,* it would seem), to fight, and die,
in "One strong effort more / For God, for Freedom—for your shrines and
homes" (12.14). Continuing to speak for Victorian ideology, Merlin finally
offers the long-lasting one-nation theory as he celebrates a Britain in which
"Celt and Saxon rear their common throne" (12.190) and whose empire wid-
ens until "new-born nations speak the Teuton's speech" (12.191). Cumming
comments that "laissez-faire economics, geology and the extinction of species, utilitarianism, and democracy" also appear in the densely packed epic
(1992, 33).

Extremely ambitious, at times deeply learned, and often showing real interest in a range of issues—for example Lytton does not hesitate to use the
Welsh name Cymri for the Welsh, an authenticity still very unusual among
the English—Lytton's epic, which he felt to be "the grand effort of my literary life" (see Alexander, 1913, 2, 97), itself ultimately fails partly through his
mediocre poetry and also because it celebrates rather than interrogates power.
Though Merlin is empowered by magic and Gothic mystery, his role is just
to facilitate war, to utter imperialist prophecy and English national ideology
with no contestation. For Lytton the popular novelist and successful politician, there was no separation between knowledge and power.

These versions of English imperialist politics did enlarge Merlin's role
above cleverness but not above royal servility. The other strand of Romantic Merlin also depended on substantial additions and changes to the older
story, as the authors reshaped the figure to deal with the moral complexities
of inner motivations and their outcomes in action. This new and inherently
negative humanist reading of Merlin as merely clever and as lacking moral
knowledge produced at least three texts of real interest, and led further in the
mid-nineteenth century.

The thrust of Anne Bannerman's "The Prophecy of Merlin," published in
1802, derives from her capacity to limit the action, and to create a controlled
emotive effect in a brief suggestive narrative—a central feature of the ballad

genre she used. Arthur and Merlin meet before the battle of Camlan, rather like Hamlet and his father:

> That monk had Merlin's giant form,
> The other was the king. (126)

Broadly following Malory—who had been out of print since 1634—Bannerman gives Arthur a "witched sword" (the adjective is euphemized to "wizard" in later editions) that is used in an attempt to heal him after the battle:

> They wav'd it twice in Merlin's name
> Before they touch'd the king...(131)

But he still dies and is borne away to the "Queen of Beauty" (136) with her "demon-smile" (138), who entombs Arthur beside the sea, and, in a reference to the Merlin story, "He too must slumber in the cave" (139). Yet the story has a positive, if enigmatic, ending:

> Arthur knew he would return
> From Merlin's prophecy. (139)

While Scott admired Bannerman, he thought this poem "perhaps too mystical and obscure" (*Oxford Dictionary of National Biography,* 3, 708). But her notes refer to Selden's comments in Drayton and to Ellis's *Specimens* and justify her own innovation, claiming that while in her poem "legendary tradition has been violated in the fate and disposal of this great national hero" this is in fact "all fairy-ground, and a poetical community of right in its appropriation has never been disputed" (1807, 227). Claiming the right, and need, for artists to re-create both plot and meaning in revivifying myth, as had been evident in both the medieval and Renaissance transformations of Merlin, Bannerman in fact achieves a minor but potent Romantic version simply by imaging self-knowledge in the context of Romantic Merlin and transferring it to the individualized vulnerability of the king.

Wordsworth had the same innovative boldness, but by 1828 lacked the verbal and imagistic clarity to bring off successfully that kind of revisionary maneuver in "The Egyptian Maid," the only product of the early interest he—like so many others—had in developing "some British theme" (1959, 168). While the story does involve Merlin, Arthur, the Lady of the Lake, and several knights, and takes place in part at Caerleon, Wordsworth's central figure is far from Arthurian. His prefatory note (1946, 3, 232) states that the idea of the maiden representing the Lotus or Water Lily "was suggested by the beautiful work of ancient art, once included among the Townley Marbles, and now in the British Museum": the Townley Vase, bought by a rich Lancashireman in 1805, is thought also to have been the "Grecian Urn" that inspired Keats.

This Merlin is very clever but also very negative, and far from positive or moral in his knowledge. Wordsworth had spoken in *Artegal and Elidure* of "The sage enchanter Merlin's subtle schemes" (1946, 2, 51), but here, though he is an "Enchanter" (3) and a "Sage" (14), he is also "a Mechanist, whose skill / Shames the degenerate grasp of modern science" (19–20): his cleverness suggests the intellectually degraded nature of the present. When on "Cornish sands" (1) Merlin sees a beautiful ship coming, through his "freakish will" he is "Provoked to envious spleen" (22, 24), and decides to destroy it. By his art the clouds become like "spiteful Fiends" (34)—the diabolic Merlin is implied, and also the devil who sinks a ship in the well-known ballad "The Demon Lover" (which Wordsworth would have known from Scott's 1812 *Minstrelsy of the Scottish Border*). The elegant boat struggles bravely but finally founders, casting ashore "a meek and guileless Maiden" (66).

A voice accuses Merlin of "the blindness of thy malice" because the boat carried "a Damsel peerless" (79), a princess coming to Caerleon for her "bridal hour." The Lady of the Lake speaks, here given the modern-seeming name Nina. Merlin flees guiltily to a cave—the medieval pattern of Merlin's knowledge is reversed as he is negatively involved, as Romanticism requires, in personally focused moral issues. Another reversal follows. The dead maid will be carried in a boat to court like another "lily maid," Malory's Elaine of Ascolat, but it is Nina who arranges this. Her own "pearly Boat, a shining Light" (103) will bring the maid from the island and then Merlin, "to expiate thy sin" (98), will fly her to Caerleon in "The very swiftest of thy cars" (109), drawn by "two mute Swans" (179, 177): Wordsworth clearly knew Warton's "The Grave of King Arthur."

When Merlin arrives at Caerleon he announces the dead Maid of Egypt, and says that though "joy is turned to sorrow" he hopes, in a jingle, that "grief may vanish ere the morrow" (206, 21). King Arthur attacks his "mockery hateful" (212)—another reversal of the authority of knowledge—laments the maid, and blames himself for the sad event: when he freed her father's land, the king agreed to turn Christian and send his daughter to marry a knight of Arthur's choice. A repentant Merlin steps forward; not mentioning his part in her death, he asks, with presumably unironic wordiness, that the one, evidently God,

... whose skill
Wafted her hither, interpose
To check this pious haste of erring duty. (244–46)

Now fully Christian in his strategy, Merlin arranges "a high attest" to establish "What Bridegroom was for her ordained by Heaven" (249, 250). One by one the knights must touch "the cold hand of he Virgin" (254) and "for the favoured One... the Flower may bloom / Once more" (255–56).

The knights try to heal her (a sequence borrowed, and varied, from Malory's "The Healing of Sir Urry"), but not even for the pure Percival does the test work. In Malory Lancelot triumphed in spite of his sins, but the saintly Galahad saves the maid he will (only here) marry. All ends happily, but Merlin's mix of cleverness and malice is more of a threat in Wordsworth's eyes than the sexual passion or the tricksterism with which medieval Merlin used to make trouble.

While this is not Wordsworth at his limpidly commanding best, nor an Arthurian reworking of major interest, the poem clearly positions Merlin's knowledge and his quasi-scientific status as a potentially dangerous force: his envious malice can only be contained by, at first, firm moral rebuke and a sense of guilt, delivered in the modernized and schoolmistressy person of the Lady of the Lake and reinforced by royal authority. Yet ultimately only devout Christianity will work against such an agent of disorder. The danger of free-floating, whimsical human intelligence is clear in this poem: firmly rebuked as Merlin is, he offers no challenge to the moral power wielded equally by Nina and Arthur—and so, again, he can stay to the end of the text.

This rejection of Merlin's knowledge because of his moral failure is even clearer in a striking poem by Reginald Heber. A man of many talents, literary and priestly, who died at forty-two when working hard as Bishop of Calcutta, Heber combines in his poetry a bookish traditionalism with Romantic fluency—at times he reads very much like Tennyson, and like him he celebrates feeling within a carefully conservative frame. He had a real sense for the medieval, both in style—his undergraduate comedy "Book of the Purple Faucon" of 1803 brilliantly re-created early medieval English romance (1840, 262–66)—and also in theme: where for Wordsworth Merlin was a clever but selfish fellow, for the more classically learned and more religious Heber, the diabolic potential was closer to the surface.

In his *Morte D'Arthur: A Fragment,* he had written, starting in 1810, of the "perilous decay" of "Celtic glories" (1840, 3.1), but though Arthur is well treated—not even the father of Mordred—Merlin is less admired: he attempts to curse Ganora, a version of the name Guenevere that Heber could have found both in Ellis and in Scott's *Marmion,* but she is "guarded by prayer" (2.12). This seems to be in line with the general Romantic negativity about Merlin, but Heber also responded to the figure with more excitement and less constraint.

"Fragments from the Masque of Gwendolen" (Heber, 1840) was written in late 1816, probably as one of the Christmas entertainments Heber produced for family and friends (Amelia Heber, 1830, 1, 448). Merriman calls it "a pleasant enough entertainment" (1973, 173), but it seems more substantial, even darker, than that. At the start Merlin's goblins bring gifts to his chosen bride, Gwendolen: the name is that of Merlin's wife in Ellis's account of the *Vita Merlini,* though as Taylor and Brewer note (1983, 63) Scott had used it for Arthur's own fairy mistress, mother of Gyneth, in *The Bridal of Triermain.* "Good angels guard me!" she prays (205), but the only arrivals are sylphs, sea nymphs, and then two genii of fire. They display their powers and Merlin arrives to ask Gwendolen "Am I proud who lay, / Mine empire at thy feet?" (207) Like a Celtic Lucifer, he offers her

> ...a regal throne
> Of solid adamant, hill above hill,
> Ten furlongs high, to match whose altitude
> Plinlinmon fails, and Idris' stony chair
> Sinks like an infant's bauble. (207)

Evidently this menacing wooing builds on earlier acquaintance, and Gwendolen regrets "my folly" because she "play'd with such a visitor" (208), but any sexual implication is withdrawn as she indicates she just enjoyed getting him to show off his magic.

Told to leave, Merlin is threatening: "Ah, do not raise the fiend within my soul, Nor arm" (208) and claims experience:

> In love unmatch'd, in hate unmatchable,
> I have done that ere now which mine own eyes
> Have wept to look upon. (208)

He is on the brink of a truly Gothic frenzy:

> ...One little moment more
> I feel the demon rush into my soul,
> And prayer will then be vain. (209)

She rejects him, preferring death, which she herself imagines in sadomasochistic Gothic form: "throw me / To the wild boar, or where the lioness / Seeks for her brindled young their human banquet" (209). Merlin is still lover and monster combined and accordingly he curses her to roam the woods as a hideous medieval-style loathly lady, until "a youth of form divine" shall woo and kiss her (210).

His role as troublemaker complete, Merlin as diabolic rapist fades away, as is common with Gothic threats. Titania (used as a female authority) reports that his "elfin paramour" (unnamed, but evidently Vivien) has entombed him because—in an ironic moral touch—she was "Jealous of his late wanderings," like his wooing of Gwendolen (213). But his spells still have power and Gwendolen is still in the forest and hideous. As it continues, the story is now based, with Shakespearean additions, on "The Marriage of Sir Gawain," which Heber apparently knew from Percy's *Reliques,* rather than from Chaucer's subtler "Wife of Bath's Tale."

Gwendolen wakes; she has dreamed of freedom and even hears an armed man coming, but then the scene changes to Arthur's court. Llewellin is in chains, about to be executed to fulfil Arthur's "cursed oath! / Which stops the mouth of mercy" (216). Arthur has sworn he will free Llewellin only if he explains "What women mostly crave" (218). In Chaucer, a genuinely interrogative writer, it was Guinevere who with ironical awareness imposed the question herself as a penalty for rape: four centuries later it is male authority that sets the puzzle. Gawain gives the answer: "Power is their passion" (218), and Llewellin is freed—no one asks any women if it is true, again unlike in Chaucer.

Arthur notices a "ghastly spectre" (218): the plot rapidly unravels. When Gawain plans to leave, the hideous woman who gave him the answer complains: he recognizes his duty to kiss and then marry her. The text dwells on Gawain's horror as this grotesque enthusiastically embraces him, and the poem ends as she says the words "Turn, Gawain, turn" and the stage direction is "Loud Thunder" (221).

A magical transformation to the beautiful Gwendolen is apparently to be the masque-like end of an effectively complete poem, but the text does not confirm this: Heber's widow Amelia referred to it as "some extracts" from the poem (1830, 1, 448); no more appears in the 1840 collected poems and lines of asterisks are inserted at times in the text in both the *Life* and the *Poetry.* It is, as Simpson suggests (1990, 116), conceivable that Amelia Heber censored the poem, though it seems unlikely she would have cut out a happy ending and left the quite sensual earlier material. The text can be taken as it stands, with a masque-like celebratory ending implied.

Where Wordsworth restrained his dislike of Merlin to moral distaste for selfish knowledge and power, Heber has used Merlin's fiendish connections to elaborate the idea of sadistic assault and also, as a sort of male exculpation, has deployed the medieval loathly lady story to provide the image of woman as monster. This powerfully imagined poem relies on Merlin's knowledge and magic powers at their most negative as truly dark cleverness, and uses them to liberate and express nineteenth-century male attitudes to and anxieties about women, revealingly produced by a devout and deeply serious Anglican. It also looks forward, in its medievalism, its focus on moral duty, and its sense of disastrous opposites, and indeed in its initiatory use of a rapidly rejected Merlin, to the enormously influential reworking of the tradition by Tennyson.

The Dangers of Cleverness: The Victorians

The accession of Queen Victoria in 1837 gave an old-fashioned if limited royalist role to Merlin: George Darley, a minor poet and critic, published in the *Athenaeum* "Merlin's Last Prophecy" where "wise Merlin's potent daughters" bring coronation gifts of symbolic power to the young queen (1838, 495). The fact that they are also "Morgan-le-Fay's handmaidens" indicates this is a token flourishing of Arthurian myth as vague national propaganda, not a close working through of its meanings, while rhymes like "kept her" and "sceptre" have their own debilitating effect.

More detailed treatments of Merlin continued to be essentially negative, seeing his cleverness as the opposite of moral force. In Matthew Arnold's *Tristram and Iseult* (1852), after the tragic end of the lovers, Tristram's wife, Iseult of Brittany, tells their children (a Victorian innovation) the story of Merlin and Vivien. In a parallel to what she sees as the seduction of their father, a man of great quality is distracted from his proper honorable course by a temptress:

> She looked so witching fair, that learned wight
> Forgot his craft, and his best wits took flight;
> And he grew fond, and eager to obey
> His mistress, use her empire as she may. (1979, 3.181–84)

The narrative diabolizes Merlin in terms of Victorian morality: "fond" means "foolish" as well as "amorous," and both "mistress" and "empire" are words of special power in the period. Taylor and Brewer suggest Arnold represents Merlin as "imagination that escapes ordinary passions by means of the peace, beauty, and permanence of art" (1983, 84), but in the voice of the widow Iseult to her children, moral criticism remains weighty.

The attitude of this poem may have influenced Tennyson in what was to be the major representation of Merlin in Victorian literature, his seduction by Vivien in "Merlin and Vivien" in the *Idylls of the King*. Tennyson started the *Idylls* in 1853 and returned to it after writing and publishing *Maud* in 1854. He had long held plans to write a major Arthurian poem and also harbored negative feelings about Merlin. A variety of sources, assembled and discussed by Roger Simpson (1990, 190–226), indicate that in the 1830s Tennyson was thinking about a major Arthurian work, which would include "Merlin Emrys," a name he drew from a range of Welsh-informed sources. But this figure was not to be authoritative or successful: a summary of "The Ballad of Sir Launcelot" written by Tennyson's friend John Kemble (the text of the poem has not survived) records that "Merlin's downfall" would occur in Avilion, as he was "miserably floored" in argument with Lancelot. Though "wise and gray," he is also foolish in appearance: he rides a lean horse and "His legs were thin as legs of pies," meaning "magpies" (Simpson, 1990, 191, 194).

In more serious mood Tennyson composed in about 1833 a plan of an Arthurian epic with allegorical roles for characters: they include "Merlin Emrys, the enchanter. Science. Marries his daughter to Modred." As Modred represents "the sceptical understanding" the marriage suggests to Simpson "the development of modern rationalist and anti-supernatural scepticism" (1990, 194–95).[11] Kemble's summary of this plan states that Tennyson thought of Merlin as "Worldly Prudence," a characteristic of distinctly doubtful value. He plays no role in the early frame-story "The Epic" which Tennyson used (like one of Scott's introductions) to justify an Arthurian theme, nor in the early poems "Sir Launcelot and Queen Guinevere," "Sir Galahad," or "The Lady of Shalott," though the Lady's mirror may derive from Merlin's magic glass in Spenser. The early references indicate Tennyson, like his predecessors, thought of Merlin as representing a cleverness that lacked moral weight, but when he came to write an idyll about Merlin he made central Merlin's vulnerability to female sexual seduction, apparently building on the moves in this direction by Southey and Arnold.

In order to unravel the meanings of *Idylls of the King* and the characters involved, it is crucial to grasp the order in which they were written. What would become, with some additions, "The Passing of Arthur" was published first in 1842 as the "Morte d'Arthur," using Malory's final battle, and much of Malory's language, in sonorous blank verse to celebrate both the mythical king and, in a potent condensation, Tennyson's beloved friend Arthur

Hallam. A negative review by John Sterling in the influential *Quarterly Review* put Tennyson off Arthurian writing (Simpson, 1990, 231–34), and when he returned to the theme it was in the context of his developed concern—or anxiety—about the role of women in society, as seen in the contemporary poems *The Princess* and *Maud*.[12] His first four Arthurian idylls, published in 1859, all had women's names for titles and debated different kinds of female role. The strongly moral thrust of this discussion was clear in the title given to a book including the first two, which was never published: there Tennyson combined "Enid" and "Nimue" as *The True and the False,* but he withdrew the book, apparently because "a comment reached him" about "Nimue" suggesting that it would "corrupt the young" (1987, 3, 260). But when the two, linked with "Elaine" and "Guinevere," were published as *Idylls of the King* in 1859, it sold extremely well: Tennyson was on his way—it was to be a long one—as a major Arthurian writer.

The idyll became "Merlin and Vivien": her name was probably changed from Nimue to ensure people gave it three syllables (Staines, 1982, 26 n. 10), and Merlin's appearance in the title for the 1870 edition is matched by the addition then of male names, presumably to contain the power of the female, to all but "Guinevere." "Merlin and Vivien" was not only the first idyll to be worked on in the 1850s; its theme, or at least the menace of Vivien, seemed to obsess Tennyson. The idyll was later expanded, to darken Merlin's gloom (see below); the whole idyll was so negative in impact that Tennyson later had to write the rather tame "Gareth and Lynette" as a preceding positive idyll, and then the later-written "Balin and Balan" in part served as a prequel to Vivien's wickedness. One of the last things Tennyson did was in 1890 to insert a line into "Guinevere" to make it clear that Mordred's evil was in fact initiated by Vivien.[13]

From the start of "Merlin and Vivien" there is no doubt about the fateful theme: "A storm was coming" (1) and "At Merlin's feet the wily Vivien lay" (5). The idylls often start with a static scene full of predictive meaning—literally an "idyll" or image—and they will then trace the sources and implications of the opening image. Originally the idyll repeated the phrase "The wily Vivien" in line 6 (now 147) and went straight to her arrival at court, where people laughed at her attempt to seduce "the blameless King" (162), then "set herself to gain" Merlin (163). Tennyson gives him a powerful description:

> ...the most famous man of all those times,
> Merlin, who knew the range of all their arts,
> Had built the King his havens, ships and halls,

Was also Bard, and knew the starry heavens;
The people call'd him Wizard...(164–68)

Engineer, astronomer, and cultural polymath are all from the medieval tradition, but Tennyson also, as in the Romantic period, adds the role of bard, and the overall popular title, not actually justified in the description or the text, "Wizard." This seems, as Claude Ryals comments, "Western civilization's whole cultural accomplishment" (1967, 139), with some stress on scientific knowledge. But it is not to have positive impact: this knowledge is fated, both in the imagery of the opening lines and also in Merlin's sudden "great melancholy" (187) which leads him to leave court for Brittany, where Vivien follows, and eventually steals his power.

Effectively, Tennyson begins his *Idylls* by disposing of Merlin. As in his early plans, Tennyson has no role of value for Merlin's knowledge as mere cleverness: like Lancelot's warrior skills and Galahad's religiosity, such values pale beside the moral focus and the world-engaged faith represented by Arthur. Merlin is mentioned in the narrative elsewhere. In "The Coming of Arthur" he presents Arthur as king and recommends him to take Excalibur from the lake, but he has no agency in Arthur's birth—either from Igraine or the alternative mystical sea-borne arrival—and he is unable to explain Arthur's origin beyond an annoying "riddling" (411). In "The Passing of Arthur" the king does mention of Merlin's prophecy "that I should come again" (191), but that is already in the 1842 "Morte D'Arthur," and has no impact on the *Idylls'* negative image of Merlin.

Tennyson's dismissal of science, foreshadowed in the early plans, is obviously related to the rise of Darwinism, the weakening of Christian faith, and the types of sensual relativism that so much alarmed him. He was to present Tristram as the archetype of this "free love" in his highly original idyll "The Last Tournament"—another contact with Arnold—but he also makes Merlin, as in the Vulgate tradition he read about in Southey's preface, too much of a sensualist to survive as the hero of knowledge.

That is emphatically clear in the original version of the idyll discussed so far. But when Tennyson had written more, and particularly the two dark idylls "The Last Tournament" and "Balin and Balan," in 1874 he added a passage after Merlin's "great melancholy" summing up both the final action and the full meaning of the whole *Idylls:*

He walk'd with dreams and darkness, and he found
A doom that ever poised itself to fall,

> An ever-moaning battle in the mist,
> World-war of dying flesh against the life,
> Death in all life and lying in all love,
> The meanest having power upon the highest,
> And the high purpose broken by the worm. (188–94)

Merlin's medieval prophecies were never so negative: they either foresaw a British, or English, political future, or redemption through the grail. Knowledge without morality is, for Tennyson, without hope. That will be revealed in Merlin's encounter with Vivien, but the message is also relevant to Arthur's court. In the 1874 edition Tennyson also inserted a long passage to develop this link, now 6–146, which makes Mark's court the starting place of Vivien's malice, a link with "The Last Tournament," and brings her to encounter Mordred and also Lancelot and Guinevere.

The action of the encounter between Merlin and Vivien is slowed by lengthy speeches: as Gray notes, only King Arthur and the magic charm are silent (1980, 130). She talks with particular effect—he does not speak until line 262, but is steadily drawn into talking to her, laughing at, and with, her. She makes more references to the Bible than any other character in the *Idylls* (Gray, 1980, 53; Rosenberg, 1973, 133), and she also argues energetically: Eggers calls her "an accomplished sophist" who offers "feigned avowals of religion" and distortions of "Evangelical altruism," feminism, and utilitarianism (1971, 152–53). All of these Tennyson would have found spurious, and as Kincaid says, "crudely naturalistic" (1975, 184).

Vivien's assertiveness has strong physical support. She wears a robe "that more exprest / Than hid her, clung about her lissome limbs" (219–20), and she presses her body on Merlin by climbing onto his lap:

> And lissome Vivien, holding by his heel,
> Writhed toward him, slided up his knee and sat,
> Behind his ankle twined her hollow feet
> Together, curved an arm about his neck
> Clung like a snake... (236–4)

The snake image is well, even obsessively, prepared: the prominent and repeated adjective "lissome," the verbs "writhed," "slided," and "twined" all make the point synaesthetically. But Vivien is not only offering a natural physical invitation. While much of the subtlety of the language is the narrator's—like the emphasis on the prefix "over-" that Gray notes (1980, 78), there is more to Vivien than her body. Just as she can argue vigorously, she can be girlishly inviting: she is "smiling saucily" (266), calls Merlin "dear love" (322), and invites him to "caress her" (379).

It is clear enough that Tennyson does not approve of her or her behavior: when she is, or pretends to be, outraged by the muttered word "harlot," she

> Leapt from her session on his lap, and stood
> Stiff as a viper frozen; loathsome sight,
> How from the rosy lips of life and love.
> Flash'd the bare-grinning skeleton of death! (842–45)

Vivien's rejection by the language of the text is extreme, presumably related to the need Tennyson had to write this idyll first, and to rewrite it more strongly so often: a Freudian might well feel that the language is that of masculine neurosis and castration anxiety. All the more comforting to the male author, then, that when she reaches for a dagger at her belt, she has none (847–51).

Some commentators have accepted Tennyson's apparent account of Vivien and her actions: Staines finds her "a disgraceful wanton" (1982, 28) and Taylor and Brewer feel Merlin's response is "singularly noble and altruistic" (1983, 109). But others see her as a symbol, whether general, with Kincaid, as "the representative of the new and increasingly threatening natural world" (1975, 183), or human, with Shaw, as "the extraordinary power of ordinary female sexuality" (1988, 108). Both views indicate that Vivien is more a force to which Merlin responds than a successful and deliberate destroyer—Rosenberg in the same vein speaks of her "nihilistic exuberance" (1973, 110).

Whatever knee-jerk reactions there might be to Vivien—Tennyson does not fail to link her to Eve as well as the serpent (360–61)—there is an undercurrent of veracity to some of her views, at least about Lancelot and Guinevere. As Eggers comments, she is "nearer to the truth about the realm than her virtuous opposite—Enid" (1971, 150). And if Vivien can be right, she can also be not wrong. The plot tells us that she in fact fails in her schemes to excite, or attract, or convince Merlin: she succeeds not through her own doing but because "he let his wisdom go" (890).

What the text subtly shows is that the cause of the disaster is Merlin's own weakness: cleverness lacks moral knowledge. He can see quite well the threat: he senses that Vivien is herself the wave that will break on him (300); he knows how unwise he was to tell her of the charm (355–59); he dismisses her slanders, though he can only alleviate the one against Lancelot and Guinevere. But he does not enact his judgment of her: from the time they first meet at Arthur's court he tends to be "Tolerant of what he half disdain'd" (176). His own sensual participation in his seduction is shown recurrently: Vivien is able to "flatter his own wish in age for love" (183); when he finally speaks and she explains her servitude he "lock'd his hand in hers"(288) and speaks of his dark mood; he praises her "pretty sports" (302) and thanks her for her "dainty gambols" (307). After rejecting her request for the charm, he asks her "Why will ye never ask some other boon" (373); after her song, where faith is tellingly relativized away—Eggers calls it "new paganism" (1971, 199)—he "half believed her true, / So tender was her voice, so fair her face" (398–99); when he speaks of other and better songs, and she answers by offering love for fame, he takes her hand again (468); when she teases him about using the charm on lovers, he responds "merrily" about his own "youth and love" (543 and 546). After his story of the wizard, whose purity and unphysicality he cannot match, just as he cannot read the central text of his book, only the margins—a sign of cleverness, not knowledge—he laughs at her flirting (616), calls her "my pretty Vivien" (665), and even as her anger appears, he is "careless of her words" (698). Reed puts this all down to his "infirm mood, the result of his melancholy" (1969, 51), but the text is more critical than that, and the crisis of the idyll confirms a negative reading of Merlin.

His sensual weakness is central when, as the storm approaches and Vivien is in both real and mock despair, "he let his wisdom go / For ease of heart" (890–91): he responds both to her physicality and to his inappropriate need, and goes on to entice her with "tenderest-touching terms" (896): the alliterative intensity itself seems belittling. She has accepted defeat and merely claims never to have "schemed against thy peace" (928), asking to be struck by lightning if she lies.

When the storm breaks and the heavens appear to take up her offer, she panics, and begs him "Merlin, tho' you do not love me, save, / Yet save me" (942–43). This is not manipulation—"She shook from fear and for her fault she wept" (950). It is Merlin who acts:

> The pale blood of the wizard at her touch
> Took gayer colours like an opal warm'd. (947–48)

The myth that opals, through their color variation, are unlucky, is behind the image.[14] Fate and masculine vanity have stepped in: Merlin's wish for love in age is fulfilled in lust. It is evident that Tennyson means the storm, and the language he describes it in, to indicate that Merlin's heating blood has led to sudden sex between him and the gasping, even orgasmic, Vivien:

> ...she call'd him lord and liege,
> Her seer, her bard, her silver star of eve,
> Her God, her Merlin, the one passionate love
> Of her whole life; and ever overhead
> Bellow'd the tempest, and the rotten branch
> Snapt in the rushing of the river-rain
> Above them; and in change of glare and gloom
> Her eye and neck glittering went and came;
> Till now the storm its burst of passion spent,
> Moaning and calling out of other lands,
> Had left the ravaged woodland yet once more
>   To peace; and what should not have been had been (951–62)

He postcoitally tells her the charm; he lies as dead in the hollow oak, and is "lost to life and use and name and fame" (968): those terms have recurred through the idyll (212, 372) and in one sequence have seemed to suggest an identification between Merlin and Tennyson, as "use" is prized well above "fame" (499–503). The idyll ends, as it began, very rapidly, and with an image: Vivien, here directly called "the harlot," where Merlin had only muttered the word before, runs through the forest, shrieking "O fool" (970). and the final comment is "the forest echo'd 'fool.'" (972)

Some critics have felt that this means the poem judges Vivien as a fool for her villainy (Taylor and Brewer, 1983, 106). But the moment is complex: Shires calls it "one of Tennyson's most marvellous evasions" (1990, 64). The reference is clearly to Echo and Narcissus: and it seems more likely that the forest's echo is speaking to Merlin, notable for his own narcissistic weakness: Tennyson would have extended that charge to those who believed in the values of humanistic rationalism, including what Buckler calls "the myopia of scientism" (1984, 97), those values of science, engineering, and astronomy which his figure of Merlin has represented and which Tennyson has so early dismissed from the world of Arthur. Though Dean has argued for a more positive view of Merlin as a self-sacrificing tragic figure, and also against the sexual interpretation of the storm (1993, 30–33), contemporary interpretation matches the emphasis of the text: a prose summary published in 1879 described it as "an old, very old story, the weakness of wisdom."[15] Artists understood it the same way: Gustave Doré's grand illustration of 1875 shows physical nature, in the form of the oak, beginning to enclose Merlin (fig. 18), and Edward Burne-Jones's famous *The Beguiling of Merlin* expresses potently the physical nature of the encounter (fig. 19).

The exclusion of Merlin clears the space for a battle between dutiful faith, represented by Arthur alone, and a range of selfishnesses—Gawain's fickleness, Pelles's vengeful fury, Balin's despairing aggression, Tristram's self-indulgent free love, Galahad's obsessive religion, Guinevere's preference for the flesh above the spirit. Merlin's knowledge, being only secular, cannot help with any of these problems, and is itself shown to be vulnerable to that sensual force which the Victorians in general found so disturbing and so exciting, especially the Pre-Raphaelite painters Rossetti and Burne-Jones, though they sourced their Merlins to Malory. Beardsley, who provided many drawings for the 1893 edition of Malory, seems to have drawn on an early model for the entombment (fig. 20) but when he placed a tortured Merlin opposite the list of illustrations and isolated and emphasized the letters "ME" of his name (fig. 21), it seems he is offering Merlin as a fin de siècle figure of the lonely, suffering artist.[16]

Not everyone accepted Tennyson's judgments: in 1859 William Morris gave a very different account of the queen in his "Defence of Guinevere," as a sensually self-aware woman, capable of her own defense and deserving Lancelot's rescue, but he did not defend her himself. Robert Buchanan, a poet of some reputation and ability, published in September 1859 his *Fragments of the Table Round,* a set of narrative ballads from Malory but ending with one ultimately from the Vulgate, referring to Merlin, as Humphrey Davy had, as "mighty Merlin" and honoring him and "the Lady Viviane, His peerless paramore" (1859, 65 and 66). A less serious-minded immediate rejection of Tennyson's positions is evident in the "Original Travestie" entitled *Arthur: The Hididdle-diddles of the King,* by "Our own Poet Laureate," performed privately and published in 1860. Here Merlin appears as "The original British wizard, table-turner etc." and Tennyson's outcome is itself overturned: Arthur divorces Guenevere, who marries Lancelot; Elaine recovers and becomes the new queen; and the happy couples are in the finale joined by a third, Merlin and Vivien. This popular tradition thrived: the prolific E. L. Blanchard produced for Christmas 1860 *Tom Thumb or Merlin the Magician and the Good Fairies of the Court of King Arthur:* Merlin is described as "Wizard of the Early Ages and Professor of Parlour Magic" (1861, unpaginated).

Swinburne, never an admirer of Tennyson, reverses his and Arnold's moralizing use of the Merlin-Vivien story in *Tristram of Lyonesse* (1882; begun in 1869). He speaks in the highest terms of both "the great good wizard" (98) who has a "sacred voice" (24) and "holier Nimue" (29) with her "mystic mouth" (98). Taylor comments that he "reinvented Nimue as a saint of love," who brings Merlin to "the ultimate experience" where "passion and spirituality are one" (1998, 76). Two sequences (97–99 and, close to the end, 141–42) see

Merlin and Nimue as predecessors of Tristram and Iseult, enjoying now in Brocéliande, as they will soon at Tintagel, that "holier sleep" (140) that derives from tragic passion. Clifton Snider argues that, as the Jungian "Wise Old Man," Merlin provides for Victorian poets a way of compensating "for contemporary doubts about the supernatural, as well as Victorian prudishness" (1981, 51); he sees Swinburne's treatment in *Tristram of Lyonesse* as the only positive version of this Merlin. However, in the later "Tale of Balen" (1895/6) Swinburne returns to a less intense image of Merlin, part-medieval and part-Romantic, as the druid-like prophet and royal counselor who had "shown the king the doom that songs unborn should sing" (1990, 201).

Tennyson himself, intriguingly, did not hold implacably to his dark view of Merlin. He had never rejected the Wales-developed idea of Merlin as a bard—perhaps that is why it was not explored in the idyll—and just before starting "Merlin and Vivien" in 1852 he published two poems under the pseudonym Merlin (Staines, 1982, 26). Much later in life, in what he meant as his only autobiographical poem, he identified with the figure. Just before publication of his 1889 *Demeter and Other Poems* he added "Merlin and the Gleam," a survey of his poetic life. Its opening states:

> *I* am Merlin
> And *I* am dying,
> *I* am Merlin
> Who follow The Gleam. (1987, 7–10)

Tennyson identified "The Gleam" with Vivien (as Nimue) and "the higher poetic imagination," drawing directly or indirectly on W. F. Skene's *Four Ancient Books of Wales* (1868) in resurrecting Nimue, or Hwimleian, in a poetic guise.[17] The poem tells how through life he followed "The Gleam"—ever mobile, curiously like the grail in his own idyll—until

> At last on the forehead
> Of Arthur the blameless
> Rested the Gleam. (72–74)

This memory of his condensing King Arthur and Arthur Hallam as "The king who loved me, / And cannot die" (79–80) leads to his sense that he "Sang through the world" even when "Old and weary / But eager to follow" (98, 100–101), and finally, with a reference to his own "Ulysses," he calls the "young Mariner" to "Follow the Gleam" (123, 131).

Having, like writers from the medieval to Romantic periods deployed the knowledge of Merlin only to dismiss it from his text, Tennyson, in touch with the early Welsh tradition as well as the Romantic ideal of the poet as an "unacknowledged legislator," realizes another Merlin who stays not only to the end of the text but also to the end of his life, and who provides an unending source of inspiration. Tennyson is both traditionally Christian enough to reject the idea of Merlin the humanist scientist and modern enough to be fascinated by the idea of the power of the artistic intellect. As he looks back, and would have been pleased to think he did, to Ariosto and Spenser in deploying but also restricting the merely clever and scientific Merlin, so he also looks forward to the modern international use of Merlin's knowledge as a positive instrument of individual development in a new role as an all-purpose figure of both art and personal education.

10. Vivien entombing Merlin in Wynkyn de Worde's printing
of Malory's *Le Morte Darthur*, 1498. By permission of the British
Library.

11. Merlin as a Renaissance mage. Frontispiece to Vérard's 1498
printing of *Prophécies de Merlin*. By permission of the British Library.

12. Merlin's prophetic murals in Sir John Harington's translation of Ariosto's *Orlando Furioso*, 1591.

13. William Rowley's sub-Shakespearean *The Birth of Merlin*, 1664 edition.

THE

BIRTH

OF

MERLIN:

OR,

The Childe hath found his Father.

As it hath been several times Acted
with great Applause.

Written by *William Shakespear* , and
William Rowley.

Placere cupio.

LONDON: Printed by *Tho. Johnson* for *Francis Kirkman*, and
Henry Marsh, and are to be sold at the *Princes Arms* in
Chancery-Lane. 1 6 6 2.

14. Merlin as guardian of traditional order in Thomas Heywood's *Life of Merlin*, 1641.

15. Merlin's Cave in Richmond Park, 1735, exterior.

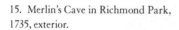

16. Merlin's Cave in Richmond Park, 1735, interior.

17. Thomas Jones's *The Bard,* 1774. National Museums and Galleries of Wales, Cardiff.

18. Gustav Doré's illustration of Tennyson's "Merlin and Vivien," 1866.

19. Edward Burne-Jones's
The Beguiling of Merlin, 1874.

20. Aubrey Beardsley's
Entombment of Merlin.
Le Morte Darthur, 1893.

21. Aubrey Beardsley's
self-representation as
Merlin. *Le Morte Darthur*,
1893.

22. André Derain's *Vivian
Dances over Merlin's Tomb*.
In Guillaume Apollinaire's
L'enchanteur pourrissant,
1909.

23. Dan Beard's "Merlin as Tennyson" in Mark Twain's *Adventures of a Connecticut Yankee at the Court of King Arthur*, 1889.

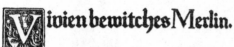

24. Howard Pyle's version of Merlin and Vivienne. In *The Story of King Arthur and His Knights*, 1902.

25. Nicol Williamson as Merlin. In *Excalibur,* directed by
John Boorman, Orion Pictures, 1981.

CHAPTER FOUR

International Merlin

Education

Continental Merlin: From Cleverness Back to Wisdom

While politics and popular culture kept postmedieval Merlin alive, to a degree, in Britain, his fortunes on the continent were to be more varied but also more propitious. At first he was merely a figure of limited cleverness: Cervantes made fun of him, like so much else, in *Don Quixote,* and in 1660 the two were linked in *Don Quichotte ou les enchantements de Merlin,* a play by Madeleine Béjart, Molière's lover and co-actor (Lacour, 1932, 264). Michael Glencross comments that Merlin then appeared in "light comedies, ballads and children's songs" (1995, 56–57). In *Les Amours de Merlin* (1691) by "Rozidor,"[1] Merlin is a valet to Lysandre, assists his master's love of Julie, and finally marries Julie's servant Marton. He also appears as a Figaro-like valet in five of Florent Dancourt's light comedies from 1690.[2] In *Merlin Dragon* by "Officier Desmarres" (1696), he resolves his master's love problems and also joins the dragoons: nearly a century later Claude Dorat revived this French image in *Merlin Bel-Esprit* ("Witty Fellow"): though he is a "flower of erudition," his "lightness" and "grace" (1780, v) are only deployed to manipulate a comic romance plot.

As Lacy comments, this kind of representation "contributed significantly to the decline of the sorcerer's reputation" (Lacy and Ashe, 1988, 154), but French rococo Merlin gained a German context that would move his cleverness back towards wisdom when in 1758 the Viennese imperial theater commissioned Christoph Willibald Gluck to write new music for a light opera called both *Le Monde Renversé* ("The World Turned Upside Down") and *L'Île de Merlin*. The piece was a success, but had little to do with the Merlin tradition. After a shipwreck two knights meet the nymphs Argentine and Diamantine; the ladies already have fiancés but Merlin, also stranded, ensures the success of his shipmates. He is basically a simplified Prospero: the new wise German Merlin comes from an older source.

The first real modern German link with the medieval Merlin is literary and scholarly. In his Quixote-like novel *Don Sylvio* (1764) Christoph Wieland makes a few comments on Merlin as a great magician—though Cervantes may be the intermediary, the references are not ironic. In 1777 Wieland published a short prose piece entitled "Merlin der Zauberer" ("Merlin the Magician"), a summary of the Vulgate Merlin story focusing on Merlin's birth, his links with Uther, and his support for Arthur's early kingship, and then jumping to the Vivien story and Merlin's end. The major source was the *Bibliothèque Universelle des Romans,* a French compilation of synopsized stories which included the Vulgate *Merlin* (1970, 109–34), calling it "the first Romance of Chivalry," and added a few of the Italian-oriented prophecies (109, 134–40).[3] But Wieland also researched the story himself, ending with several references to Merlin appearances after the Vulgate, both literary—Alanus de Insulis—and material, including Merlin's Cave in London.

In 1810, when he was old and German culture and society lay under the power of Napoleonic France, Wieland saw more in the figure. His poem "Merlins weissagende Stimme aus seiner Gruft im Walde Brosseliand" ("Merlin's prophetic voice from his grave in the Forest of Brocéliande") starts innovatively: Vivien has a son; she and her friends worry about his future, so she decides to consult Merlin in his tomb, and after a great storm comes the prophetic voice. Now Wieland combines the entombed Merlin of the Vulgate and the *Baladro* with the British political future prophet: "under the influence of favourable stars he shall grow quickly to a tree in whose shadow the grandsons of Tuiskon (i.e. the Germans), risen again, will one day grow with new vitality and make happy the earth's sphere with all blessings of harmony and industry" (1859, 103).

To this newly weighty Merlin the German Romantics were to add Celtic wisdom, shaping Merlin as a *Naturmensch,* a hero whose triumph and disaster came from internal conflict in the context of nature. They knew but rejected the medieval and Renaissance figure found in Friedrich Schlegel's 1804 summary of the French Vulgate *Merlin* (much of it by his wife Dorothea) and Ludwig Tieck's 1829 translation of Rowley's *The Birth of Merlin*.

It was the Celtic Myrddin found in Ellis's *Specimens of Early English Metrical Romances* which sparked Ludwig Uhland's interest in "Merlin der Wilde" of 1829 (1854, 308–12). Merlin sits "In Waldeseinsamkeit" ("In wooded isolation," 309), on a mossy stone by a lake and listens to the "Geist der Welt" ("the spirit of the world") (309). A universalized version of the Cumbrian Myrddin, this moves closer to its ultimate source: a hart hears a horn and carries Merlin off to the king's castle. The king seeks a demonstration of "die Sprüche" ("the words of wisdom") (310) Merlin has learnt in the wild, and asks him to explain something: last night the king thought he heard whispering, like lovers, by the linden tree. The king's daughter comes in: Merlin takes from her hair a linden leaf and comments that "where the linden leaves fall, / There is the Linden near" (311). The story of Myrddin identifying the queen's adultery is euphemized as the king's daughter kissing her lover. Uhland also stresses that it is nature that has answered the question, and Merlin returns to the forest, lying on the moss, where his voice still sounds.

Karl Immerman, both lawyer and playwright, had already in "Merlins Grab" ("Merlin's Grave"), written in 1818 when he was only twenty-two, also celebrated Merlin as a *Naturmensch,* though without the intensity Uhland found in the Myrddin story. In the spirit of Wieland, a young man goes to consult the sage: the grave now has a Romantic Gothic setting, in the forest, by a fast-running river, in a grotto, lit by a red glare. Merlin speaks about the conflict on earth between the clear-sighted brave and the narrow-minded deaf: to attain virtue requires hardship, faith, strength. The essential moment of Romantic transcendental humanism comes when the youth says "Die Welt ist ein verschloss'nes Haus" ("The world is a locked house") and he seeks the key (1936, 114–17). Merlin replies "Leer is das Wort, Leer is das Ort" ("Empty is the word, empty is the place") (140–41). Learning and society have nothing to offer: rather the youth's reliance on his own heart will find the way to open happiness and true success because "Alle Segen kommt dir von innen" ("All happiness comes to you from within") (154).

This positive idea of natural knowledge seems simple compared to Immerman's major work, *Merlin: Eine Mythe* ("Merlin: A Myth"), which roots this new wise Merlin in Christianity. A long verse play written in 1830–31 and published in 1832, it has apparently only once been performed, in 1918—a suitable date for a drama about pride, disaster, and final Christian humility. Drawing on Schlegel for its characters and story (Porterfield, 1911, 50–51), this long, intense play focuses throughout on "Widerspruch" ("conflict"). Satan and God are at odds; Satan fathers Merlin on a virgin and the child is, as Adelaide Weiss puts it, "the living *Widerspruch*" (1933, 113). The child buries his mother at Stonehenge (a memory of Rowley) and, looking further back, reveals the mystery of the grail which he is destined to rescue from its jealous guardians, led by Titurel. The influence of Wolfram von Eschenbach's *Parzifal* enters the story, as Merlin encounters and defeats Wolfram's Klingsor, or Clinschor, the false magician. Then he meets Niniane and cries that he is "ausgetauscht, verfälscht, vergiftet" ("completely changed, falsified, poisoned") (2.464), and so he is "nicht Merlin mehr" ("no longer Merlin") (2.464–65). Part of the change seems based on pride, as he now promises to bring Arthur and his knights to the grail and proclaims himself "Der Paraklet," the Holy Spirit.

Things rapidly turn worse: Merlin leads Arthur's army to Montsalvasche, the grail location, but Titurel moves the grail far to the east and in any case Merlin meets Niniane again, and she gains the power to imprison him. Arthur and his knights are left to die in the desert, without benefit of either grail or home. This tragedy of masculinity, through both pride and lust, leads Satan, in the epilogue called "Merlin der Dulder," ("Merlin the Sufferer"), to attempt to enlist Merlin again, but finally he resists and dies speaking the Lord's Prayer.

In 1833 Immerman wrote a short poem "Merlin im tiefen Grabe" ("Merlin in the deep grave") (1936, 439–40) which seems in effect a second epilogue to, almost an apology for, *Merlin: Eine Mythe*. Immerman says people do not hear Merlin's message from the grave—they come at the wrong time, presumably a recognition that the play has missed its mark. But if someone was able to "Empfinge mein Vermächtnis" ("accept my legacy"), then would come the "höher Freiheit" ("lofty Freedom") and "Die Kreatur erlöst" ("the Creature redeemed") (23, 25, 28).

With Immerman's Gnostic beliefs located in the godlike human Merlin, the play makes him more than just a man of knowledge: Porterfield comments that "*Merlin* is speculative mysticism" (1911, 92) and the true zeal of Romanticism, both spiritual and educational, is embodied in him. Too ambitious and serious for theatrical success, the play has many qualities, not least its vigorous and mobile verse, and it also is the first representation anywhere of Merlin as something like a character, a being with aspirations and limitations. Only a few later writers would match Immerman's deep humanization of Merlin and no one would dare to condense so many of the traditions of Christian culture into the Merlin context, but this reestablishment of him as a figure of massive, even tragic, knowledge initiated the Merlin of the modern age, with substantial dissemination around the world—but not yet in Britain.

Merlin: Eine Mythe had limited influence. It did stimulate two cut-down opera versions in 1886, one with book by Siegfried Lipiner and score by David

Goldmark (1886), the other written by L. A. Hoffman and with music by Philip Rüfer (1887). They are both less intense than Immerman, with endings influenced by the Tristan and Isolde story, where both Merlin and Vivien die in a religious spirit. Other nineteenth-century German Merlins are closer to Uhland: Heinrich Heine in the third of his "Katharina" poems, writing in 1835, sees himself as an "armer Nekromant" ("a wretched magician") (1983, 2) and links his own love to Merlin's fated feeling for Niniane:

> Like Merlin, the foolish wise,
> I am a wretched magician
> Now in the end firmly bound
> In my own magic circle. (1–4)

Heine also shares the *Naturmensch* concept, saying in 1851 in the postscript to his "Romancero" "I envy you, dear colleague Merlin, these trees and the fresh breezes blowing through them." (1982, 693): Weiss suggests he may have meant Merlin as an allegory of himself, ill and isolated in Paris (1933, 135–60).

In the same spirit "Nicolaus Lenau" (N. F. Nembsch von Strehlenau) starts one of his 1840s *Waldlieder* ("Wood-songs") with "Wie Merlin / Möcht' ich durch die Wälder ziehn" ("Like Merlin / I may move through the woods") (1878, 393). In what Weiss calls a poem "of extraordinary beauty" (1933, 129), he feels he can understand what the trees say, face the storm, and understand the magical and spiritual life of the forest: the poem ends by spiritualizing poetry itself: "Und in Kelch der feinsten Moose / Tönt das ewige Gedicht" ("In the chalice of finest moss, Sounds the eternal poem") (395).

Gottfried Kinkel, like Uhland a Rhineland poet, also finds consolation through Merlin. "In der Winternacht" finds him like Merlin "fest gebunden / Durch grauses Zauberwort" ("imprisoned / Through a dread magic word") and he too sings of freedom in "The forests distant and broad" (1851, 267–68). Weiss argues that he wrote the poem while imprisoned in Spandau in 1849 for his involvement in the radical actions of that turbulent period in the German states: at this time his friend Alexander Kaufman, who also mentioned Merlin in several poems, was in touch with his sister Johanna and addressed her as Niniane (Weiss, 1933, 135–36). A lighter version of the same idea of Merlin the *Naturmensch* is in *Merlins Feiertage* ("Merlin's Holidays") by "Robert Waldmüller" (Édouard Deboc) (1857): on "Weinacht-Abend" ("Christmas Eve") he sets out on his "Feiertage" as "ein freier Minnesänger" ("a free minstrel") (3). There is no trace of Arthur or the Celtic world, and this is just a lightly romantic Merlin: at the end it is only love which "liegt am Grab" ("lies in the grave") (150). A stronger version of the *Naturmensch* was behind Gerhart Hauptmann's long-nurtured plan to use Merlin as a "symbol of mystical rebirth" (Garten, 1954, 58) in his Romantic but also nationalistic mysticism. In 1917 he was planning a novel about Merlin, and he kept writing notes and plans (1970, 1064–67), but in time the figure merged with other symbols, the "Erdmann" ("Earth-man") and the Christ-bearing priestly Everyman, "the new Christopher" who was central to the major but unfinished novel published posthumously in 1956, *Der neue Christophorus*.

French writers responded to the substantial imaginative development of the newly wise Merlin by the German Romantics with a somewhat later and at first more nationalistic Romantic Merlin. The aristocrat-serving Figaro-type French Merlin vanished with the Revolution and after Waterloo the myth of King Arthur, being both royal and British, had little attraction. French historians in the mid-nineteenth century paid some notice to Merlin: as Glencross notes, the very influential Jules Michelet in his *Histoire de France* (1855–67) used Merlin's long sleep to suggest the lack of interest French people now had in French medieval splendor (1995, 105–18). In addition to this political historicism, the first stirring of literary interest was, parallel to the Cornish, Scots, and Welsh Arthurian revival, among Bretons. The aristocratic Bretonist Hersart de La Villemarqué included some comments on Merlin and Vivien in his *Contes populaires des anciens Bretons* (1842) and in 1862 he produced a major study on *Myrdhin ou l'enchanteur Merlin* which explored Arthurian romance from a Bretonist viewpoint.

A major contribution to the French Merlin tradition, both historicist and patriotic, was Edgar Quinet's long novel *Merlin l'enchanteur* (1860). Poet, essayist, and novelist, Quinet, like his friend Michelet, lectured at the Collège de France. He opposed Catholicism, but not religion, favoring for some time the new Protestant ecumenism of the Unitarians (see Crossley, 1983, 95–97). He was elected a member of parliament during the Second Republic of 1848, but after Louis Napoleon's coup of 1851 went into exile and wrote *Merlin l'enchanteur* in Geneva between 1853 and 1860: Simone Bernard-Griffiths comments that he "aspired to give France the monumental epic which it still lacked" (1999, 14) and as Geoffrey Ashe notes in his account of the novel, Merlin is represented as the "patron of France" (2006, 186), but he also possesses a wisdom across time and politics.

In keeping with his distaste for England, matched only by his dislike of Germany, Quinet did not initially link Merlin with King Arthur. The novel is a mythical picaresque with Merlin visiting various parts in various periods and forming opinions, mostly negative, about Europe at large. But this all points to the present: as Baudry comments, Quinet "enlists Merlin among the militants of his political battle" (2007, 284): he dedicates the book to "Mon cher pays" ("My dear country") and in his preface contrasts the cultural and political poverty of modern France with the "vastes inventions" of medieval French culture (ix). Grimbert and Lacy describe the novel as an "allegorical epic, with Merlin's exile representing both the author's own disillusion and the political and moral decadence Quinet perceived in a dispirited France" (2006, 548).

While the grandeur of medieval romance is remembered to relieve modern sociocultural poverty, Merlin's adventures can suggest a way forward. At times accompanied by Jacques Bonhomme, a French plebeian Everyman, he meets a wide range of figures involved in religion and authority, in a constant quest for what Ceri Crossley calls "a tolerant syncretism" (1983, 95), as Merlin's adventures expose the weakness and the potential that, from a French viewpoint, run through history. In Book 8 Merlin's wanderings take him to "Great Britain, then called Albion" (1.246). At Dover he meets three witches with their hair on fire proclaiming Macbeth as king; he smiles and passes by to find Robin Hood, a "grand braconnier de ce temps-là" ("great poacher of those days") (1, 246), but he is not a hero. In response to a huge public auction where everything is bartered, including people, Merlin complains to Robin Hood that "on vend ici l'espèce humaine" ("here one sells the human race") (1, 249). Robin, a typical English shopkeeper, "ne sachant que répondre" ("not knowing what to say") (1, 249), just whistles through his teeth. For Quinet nothing good can come from outside the French heart.

Not all is so stereotypical, and the resolution of the novel pursues a positive theme. Merlin does eventually meet Arthur, when he speaks for the assembled kings to invite Merlin "to enchant their countries so that the people will be submissive" (2, 231). When he addresses Arthur in the crisis of his kingdom it emerges that Merlin's form of enchantment would in fact be a general submission to the rule of love. It is Vivien's love that enables Merlin to deploy his magic and although they do separate, and this weakens him, she returns both out of love and to be protected by his power.

Vague—or deeply Romantic—as this program of public amatory conversion might seem, Quinet does not feel it is implausible, nor that Merlin's mission deserves a negative ending as so often in the past. Though Arthur is gravely wounded, he is only asleep, not dead, and at the end of the novel when Merlin manages to convert Satan and so destroy Hell—or, in terms of Romanticism's inner dualism, convert the Satan in himself and destroy negative attitudes—then Arthur wakes and the world reviews itself. This evidently prophesies the collapse of the rule of Louis Napoleon (who is represented as Hengist) and the Second Empire, but the unspecific nature of the scheme is both its strength and its weakness. Quinet spins a fine story and a charming dream, though Janine Dakyns sees it negatively as a "prolix utopian fantasy" (1996, 412). He also, more importantly, and not unlike Immerman, makes Merlin a central, positive character as a sage able to advise not only a king but also a whole country—the elements of Merlin the educator begin to appear. At the same time he is a character in his own story with, as in Immerman, his own problems, features appropriate for the modern genres of novel and drama. The humanist Merlin is coming into being: this is recurrently implied by his resemblance to Quinet's own position, and it is easy to extend this idea of personal authority to the role of the writer in modern society.

An artistic version of that position was developed by Rimbaud in the shadow of Quinet, focused on "the poet, leader of the world," as Margaret Clarke has shown (1945, 8), but it was most memorably linked to a spiritual and potentially educational Merlin by Guillaume Apollinaire in his prose poem *L'Enchanteur Pourrissant* ("The Decomposing Enchanter"), published in 1909, with bold black brush drawings by André Derain (fig. 22). Apollinaire—a pseudonym for Wilhelm de Kostrowitsky, a European wanderer who settled in Paris among the vibrancy of Symbolist art and literature in the early twentieth century—had read both Quinet and the French prose *Merlin* by 1898, when he was eighteen. He worked on his own version in 1899 when he was himself living in a forest, at Stavelot in the Ardennes (Burgos, 1972, ix). He published a draft in 1904 and then the revised and authoritative version in the 1909 illustrated volume, splendidly produced by Henry Kahnweiler at his Paris press.

In spite of his commitment to Symbolism and its inherently antirational processes—what Timothy Matthews has called his interest in "the purely, inhumanly poetic" (1987, 100)—Apollinaire also had a clear idea of Merlin as a figure of the deeply wise artist. Jean Burgos comments that he conveys "the impossibility of communicating in love, but also the solution that poetry alone can convey this distress" (1972, cxxi). In his own text for the subscription advertisement, Apollinaire himself described *L'Enchanteur Pourrissant* as "one of the most mysterious and most lyrical of the books of the new generation" (1972, 83), and its mix of verse and prose is designed both to elevate the concept of love and passion—the wisdom function—and also celebrate the mysterious inchoate coherence of feeling and identity—the newly personal element of Merlin. The beauty of the language, in delicate yet subtly vigorous French, establishes one domain of value:

Mais, soudain, la dame du lac s'elança, et, laissant derrière elle une traînée de sang, courut longtemps, sans se retourner. Des pétales feuillolaient, détachés des arbres aux feuillards, défleuris en l'attente de fructifier. La dame ne s'arrêta qu'au bord de son lac. Elle descendit lentement la pente que surbaigne l'onde silencieuse, et s'enfonçant sous les flots danseurs, gagna son beau palais dormant, plein de lueurs de gemmes, au fond du lac. (1909, 71)

(But suddenly the lady of the lake ran forward and, leaving behind her a trail of blood, ran for a long time, without returning. The petals fluttered, detached from the leafy trees, deflowered at the moment of bearing fruit. The lady only stopped at the edge of her lake. She descended slowly the slope over which the silent waves lap, and plunging herself beneath the dancing waves, reached her beautiful sleeping palace, full of the gleam of jewels, at the bottom of the lake.)

English, with its hard consonants and leaden prepositional phrases, cannot equal the fluidity of the French, which itself intensifies the mystery of the blood, the silence, the jewels. The idea that the enchanter himself is "pourissant" ("decomposing"), and that his deep knowledge only amounts to an awareness of human incommunication, gives all the more power to the art-effect of this powerful text and its vivid images. Apollinaire has transmitted the Romantic idea of the druid and the German idea of the *Naturmensch* into the claims of art itself. A little later he restated this in one of his finest poems, "Merlin et la Vieille Femme" ("Merlin and the Old Woman"). Collected in *Alcools,* but first published in 1912, this deploys Merlin to explore the poetic process:

> I made white gestures in the wilderness
> Lemurs ran swarming through my nightmares
> My leaps and twirls expressed that bliss
> Which is an effect of art and nothing more (1965, 97)

He identifies his own vitality in his art:

> The lady awaiting me is called Vivian
> And when comes a springtime of new sorrow
> Couched among coltsfoot and sweet marjoram
> For ever I live on beneath the hawthorn flowers (99)

Though French dramatic writing returned to Merlin the enchanter, Apollinaire's level of artistic intensity is not found in A. Le Franc's "drama-féerie"

("Drama-fairytale") *Merlin et Viviane* (1930), Edouard Schuré's Celto-mystical play *Merlin l'Enchanteur* (1924), nor in Jean Cocteau's *Les Chevaliers de la Table Ronde* ("Knights of the Round Table," 1937) where Merlin is both a trouble-maker and a Cocteauesque aesthete, saying "my only policy has been to clothe reality with flowers" (1967, 283). *La Grande Nuit de Merlin* ("The Long Night of Merlin," 1943), is, curiously for its period, only a light piece of theatrical magic by "Samivel" (Paul Gayet-Tancrède). Love and the self will return as French Merlin themes later in the twentieth century, then running in parallel with the medievalism and Celticism which had by then developed in both Britain and that other major location for international Merlin, North America. It was there that major steps were taken to develop a newly wise and ultimately educational Merlin in the English language.

Toward Education: America

Independent America showed itself aware of both the English and the continental European Merlins, and reshaped them with substantial success and impact. In 1807 Joseph Leigh, born, as he tells his readers, in Somerset and educated in south Wales, relocated the ancient mode of prophecy in *Illustrations of the Fulfilment of the Prediction of Merlin Occasioned by the late outrageous attack of the British ship of war the Leopard, on the American frigate Chesapeake.* In a short prose tract, with a good deal of political and military detail, he deploys eight Merlinesque animal prophecies, the Lion signifying Britain, the Cock France and the Dove America (this peaceful emblem is neatly derived from the name of Columbus). He analyzes the prophecies to show, as he concludes, that "I conceive the Lion's power to be at an end" (1907, 14).

The continental Romantic Merlin appears in Lambert A. Wilmer's three-act play *Merlin,* first appearing in a Baltimore newspaper in late 1827. Wilmer was a friend of Edgar Allan Poe and wrote the play about the distress Poe felt when the parents of his fiancée Sarah Elmira Royster intercepted his love letters and pressured her into marrying someone else. Poe's misery was productive: he wrote the poem *Tamerlane* about the events and his brother William used them as a basis for his melodramatic story *The Pirate.* Wilmer's response starts with Merlin in "An uninhabited country at the mouth of a Cave," calling up spirits to help the young Alphonso regain his cruelly alienated Elmira (1941, 1). After his triumphant restoration of true love, Merlin says farewell in creditable Shakespearean—and Spenserian—terms:

To Maridunum's caverns, dark, profound,
Which walls of polished ebony surround
With mystic characters engrav'd—and signs
Of constellations,—every star that shines—
I'll go. (23)

The lovelorn plot and some maritime references suggest Wilmer had seen Gluck's *Île de Merlin* in theater-rich Philadelphia or Baltimore, though apart from Merlin the characters are different. But this is also an American story: Merlin lives in Wales, but Elmira's home, where she gives her sad lament, is on "The Banks of the Hudson" (6). Merlin sends his spirits there at the start and then crosses the Atlantic to bring the lovers' problem to a satisfactory conclusion.

Ralph Waldo Emerson, familiar with German culture, transplanted the continental Romantic initiative more fully when in a number of poems he took Merlin, in characteristic Transcendentalist mode, as a figure of the poetic muse with wide impact. In his essay on "Poetry and the Imagination," published in 1844, he, like Wieland and Immerman, refers to Merlin's last conversation from his grave. This may have personal meaning—David Porter comments that the "similarity to Emerson's leaving the ministry and his later ostracism...is striking" (1978, 88)—but he centrally celebrates the general power of the voice of the poet, as in "Merlin I," published in *Poems 1847*:

The kingly bard
Must smite the chords rudely and hard,
As with hammer or with mace;
That they may render back
Artful thunder, which conveys
Secrets of the solar track,
Sparks of supersolar blaze
Merlin's blows are strokes of fate. (1994, 91)

"Merlin II," published in the same collection, specifies the poet's major role: as Monika Elbert notes, Emerson is combining the Celtic bard idea with the medieval French practitioner of engaged knowledge (1992, 118) and the concept of Merlin is as a major wise educator, deploying the claim from Shelley's *A Defence of Poetry* (written in 1821) that the poet is the "unacknowledged legislator" of the world. In the title poem of his collection *May-Day and Other Pieces* (1867) Emerson imagines Merlin locked inside a harp so that his pain was "pillowed all on melody As fits the griefs of bards to be" (1994, 145): when in the 1876 *Selected Poems* "May-Day" was rewritten this section was saved and used, with four new lines, as a new poem, "The Harp" (224). Also in the 1867 collection, the short, distilled "Merlin's Song" sums up Emerson's sense of Merlin as the figure of inspiring and educational poetry:

> Of Merlin wise I learned a song,—
> Sing it low, or sing it loud,
> It is mightier than the strong,
> And punishes the proud.
> I sing it to the surging crowd,—
> Good men it will calm and cheer,
> Bad men it will chain and cage.
> In the heart of music peals a strain
> Which only angels hear;
> Whether it waken joy or rage,
> Hushed myriads hark in vain,
> Yet they who hear it shed their age,
> And take their youth again. (172)

The poem written as "Motto to 'Consideration by the way'" (249) similarly deploys Merlin as being "Of keenest eye and truest tongue," and advising us "to live well" with each other. In the 1903–04 *Complete Works* most of this poem was, with four new lines, reused as "Merlin's Song" (591).

While Emerson made Merlin a sage artist-educator, a new kind of poetic knowledge for the power of American self-confidence, some Americans established their separate position by excluding Merlin. Nathaniel Hawthorne's story "The Antique Ring" involves a diamond ring that is alleged to have been "the property of Merlin, the British wizard" (1992, 322). But the point is that the story is a fabrication, and Hawthorne suggests that America can and should create its own new myths: the real value of the diamond is to symbolize not antique British connections but "the human heart" (331). Equally Merlin-free is *The Fortunate Island* (1882) by "Max Adeler" (Charles Heber Clarke): knowledge here is in the hands of a practical American professor who, with his daughter, strays into an Arthurian Atlantis.

Rejection of Merlin can be more specific and more structural. Mark Twain's novel *A Connecticut Yankee at the Court of King Arthur* appeared in

1889. He had been working on it for several years, after he enjoyed reading Malory's *Le Morte Darthur* and thought immediately of ways of turning its grandeur to farce, and also reversing the Anglocentric and aristocratic impact of Tennyson's *Idylls,* both in the Yankee himself and in Dan Beard's illustration—which Twain approved—of Merlin, an obvious caricature of Tennyson (fig. 23).

There is far more to Twain's Merlin than a mocking American joke. First, he is a general exponent of the power of oppressive superstition, including Catholicism. Hank Morgan, Connecticut artisan transported back through time, defeats Merlin's medieval mumbo-jumbo through a mix of technical skill, practical knowledge and Yankee showmanship, and in his triumph says "Merlin's stock was flat" (1982, 39).

But Merlin is not the only manipulator. Hank's image of business practice to dismiss the ancient sage is deliberately chosen by Twain. At first the novel seems a simple self-confident fable and some American critics like Louis J. Budd have been happy to read it as entirely in praise of democratic modernity (1962, 134–44), but as Allison R. Ensor notes, "What Morgan says about Merlin is just as true of himself" (1989, 57) and Donald L. Hoffman comments "Merlin may be what Hank detests but is also what he becomes" (1992, 46): Hank becomes acquisitive, bullying, even contemptuous of the ordinary people.

The novel finally shapes a disturbing ironic development, as American modernity—with its basis in both slavery and exploitative capitalism never far from consciousness—becomes as negative as the feudal brutality of the past. In the final battle the Yankee and his technicians take on the whole chivalry of England: it is reminiscent of the old-fashioned South versus the new North, and the outcome is a technologically driven massacre like a major battle of the Civil War.

But there is one last role for Merlin. At the core of Hank's military redoubt is a cave, with an old woman as housekeeper. She is Merlin transformed but Hank himself is also transformed into a Merlinesque, cave-located sleeper: her gestures are reminiscent of Vivien. Finally Hank is enchanted back across the ages and reveals himself to the narrator as, to quote Hoffman again, "a figure of Merlin as alien in his own time as he had been in Camelot" (1992, 54).

Twain does not only critique the political power of his own period as well as the past through their modes of misused knowledge. He also identifies a dominant new form of power, which is primarily vested in the individual, even if that individual is a king. At first Arthur is a representative of ancient folly and tyranny, but when he and Hank travel in disguise—like Merlin's transformations, a means of challenging authority—he shows real personal courage and honor, especially in the cholera crisis, and Hank celebrates his human value: "He was more than a king; he was a man" (202).

In the twentieth century, Merlin's primary meaning and the direction of his knowledge will be to educate this human and personal king. Whether Arthur is a puzzled leader attempting to guide progress or a child seeking to learn how to behave, or in many stages between the two, the essence of the knowledge Merlin imparts to him will focus on the judgment and achievement of that ultimate location of modern power, the human individual: the sage's focal role will be in education.

Where Twain finally offered searching American self-criticism, other post-Tennyson writers were content with his opening gestures of parody and the trivial theatrical Merlin reemerges. In his entertaining *The New King Arthur* (1885), a comic operetta in the style of Gilbert and Sullivan, Edgar Fawcett, "combining parody and realism," as Lupack puts it (2006, 161), gives Merlin updated power as a manufacturer of cosmetics: Vivien pursues his knowledge of hair-dye so she can become a blonde to attract Galahad. In 1886 appeared from Boston Oscar Fay Adams's *Post-Laureate Idylls,* a set of poems parodying Tennysonian style in which, though "sage Merlin" is mentioned (31), Vivien actually runs away with Tom the Piper's Son, and "The Passing of the Sages" is no Merlin tragedy but a version of the Three Wise Men of Gotham.

This was not a new or only American mode. In Australia, Melbourne had already seen W. M. Akhurst's "burlesque extravaganza" *King Arthur or Sir Launcelot the Loose,* with terrible puns: Merlin "the great neck-romancer of this big-isle, is big-eye-ld by the big eyes of Vivien" (1868, dramatis personae). For Christmas 1872 British writers led by Samuel Beeton (husband of the author of *Household Management*) in *The Coming K**** mocked the Prince of Wales, known as Guelpho (the royal family was a branch of the German House of Guelph, and was often known by that name): his magician is called Herlin, who meets the dubious Vilien and gets eighteen pounds from her for the secret of his table-rapping.

But the commonest American response to Arthur and Merlin was respectful and increasingly educational. In 1880 Sidney Lanier produced an influential modern-spelling version of Malory, *The Boy's King Arthur.* Claiming educational status, it starts with a lengthy account of the pre-Arthur story in Geoffrey of Monmouth and Layamon, putting emphasis on Merlin. But the retelling omits his end, presumably on moral grounds. When Howard Pyle turned to Arthurian stories with *The Story of King Arthur and his Knights* in 1902, his first sequence was "The Book of Merlin" and then he told the stories of "Three Worthies," namely Merlin, Pellias and Gawaine, indicating his reliance on Malory's first book. He completed the stories with three other books, drawn from the end of Malory, which lay emphasis on the knights, Lancelot, Tristram, Perceval, Geraint, and Galahad and Lancelot. Pyle's last Arthurian tale was *The Story of the Grail and the Passing of Arthur* (1910), but there is an overall lack of interest in Arthur which may, as Fox-Friedman suggests, reflect Pyle's republicanism and focus on "the democratic nature of Arthurian ideals" (1998, 140), and his treatment of Merlin also stresses knowledge, not rank, as a decisive force: in much the same way Pyle illustrates Vivien as a figure of quasi-Egyptian mystery (fig. 24), valuing antique knowledge over simplistic sexual allure.

Merlin as educator is realized specifically in the Arthurian boys' groups, notably those founded by William Byron Forbush well before the Boy Scout movement took off in Britain in 1907. Boys were encouraged to join as "Knights of King Arthur"; each group was called a "Castle," led by an adult "Merlin": a leaders' guide was *The Merlin's Book of Advanced Work* (Lupack, 1994, 54–56). Groups for girls, or "Queens of Avalon," were led by a "Lady of the Lake." This sense of Merlin as a dominating—and now fully Christian— educational advisor appears in *Excalibur: An Arthurian Drama* (1909), written in 1893 by Ralph Adams Cram, an architect and devout Anglo-Catholic. Merlin manages Arthur's coronation, which now extends to arranging the wonderful sword-drawing, and then assists the king in battle. He can handle Nimue, but only through God's help, like both Bors and Percival in Malory's grail story:

NIMUE: Give me thy groping hand!
            We two will lie beneath the little leaves
            Then will they whisper sleepy songs of love,
            And noon melts into night.
MERLIN: A mocking spell
            Is over me: my heart has ceased to beat:
            My brain is in disorder. Help me, God!
            My craft is broken!
            (He makes the sign of the cross; the vision vanishes.)
            Damn thee, witch of hell!
            I know thee now!
NIMUE: Have mercy, master!

MERLIN: Go!
> *(He hurls her down from the battlements, then slowly descends and seats himself by the table.)* (2002, 108–9)

Arthur is like "a troubled child" (150), but the devout educator Merlin makes him swear "by Christ Jesu's wounds that thou will live / A spotless knight" (152). Finally he sends Arthur on the grail quest to establish "the Kingdom of God that he will raise at thy hands." (157) Alan and Barbara Lupack see Cram's version as "inspired by an American outlook" amounting to antiroyal republicanism (1999, 103), but Merlin's powerful Christian devotion seems unusual in American writing—it helps him not only with the grail but also to defeat Morgan and Nimue.

An equally active but wider-ranging Merlin moves in an eclectic mythic world in Richard Hovey's *The Quest of Merlin* (1907). The Norns, Germanic Fates, speak first, then the more positive classical sylphs, followed by dryads, fauns, Bacchus, Oberon, Titania, and, returning to the North, Valkyrs. Finally Merlin meets the quasi-Celtic Argante, queen of Avalon, who foresees the Arthurian disaster.

Nimue, who is the Lady of the Lake, seems to be Merlin's associate rather than enemy, and when they together meet a group of angels she indicates a range of authority:

> Hearken to them O Merlin! Woman in me
> Makes my divinity bow and acknowledge their speech (75)

They hear speeches from the "Stars" of Arthur, Lancelot, and Guinevere, which foresee their separate qualities, and then Nimue and Merlin agree to observe as chorus the rest of the drama. Hovey's *Quest of Merlin* is only preliminary to the five-part Arthur story he hoped to dramatize, and it is basically a gesture-heavy masque, an optimistic testament to the value of knowledge as wide and as unfocused as the author's own: Merlin here is not so much a real educator as the organizer of a powerful curriculum.

Personal Merlin was not forgotten. In the three-act verse play *Merlin and Vivian: A Lyric Drama* of 1907, with words by Ethel Watts Mumford and music by Henry Kimball Hadley, Morgan sends Vivian "the sorceress" and princess of Northumberland to control Merlin with "the ring of love and hate" (v). She gives him a poisoned cup and he dies saying "I forgive thee Vivian." (ix). This short piece, with its femme fatale version of sexism and perhaps some whispers of the New Woman in the property-conscious enchantress and the defeated would-be Svengali, is an American and moral/tragic version of the vaguely magical and somewhat prurient medievalist plays, often about Tristan and Isolde, that occupied minor writers on both sides of the Atlantic around the turn of the century.

Different though they are in approach and indeed quality, Twain, Cram, and Hovey, and even Mumford, all share the view that the Arthur story is important enough to be reusable in America as a medium of modern meaning: Merlin plays a central role, realizing the idea of knowledge and its social application, whether academic, democratic, or merely self-constructive, as a substantial feature of American life.

The major statement of this position was by Edwin Arlington Robinson, creating a Merlin who was American, powerfully humanized, and education-oriented, a figure which was, in one way or another, to provide creative inspiration for many twentieth-century artists. A New Englander and committed poet, Robinson's major effort was three long Arthurian poems, the linked *Merlin* (1917) and *Lancelot* (1920), and the basically separate *Tristram* (1927). While at Harvard he admired Tennyson, but, according to an early biographer, in 1916 he conceived his own Arthurian epic as suitable for wartime (see Perrine, 1973–74, 346). The *Merlin* that he published the following year has clear links with Tennyson in the use of flashback, the spelling of major names, and the often flowing blank verse, though its style can be deliberately less melodic and even Modernist in its occasional arrhythmic effects and colloquialisms. The flashback is not here used, as by Tennyson, for the creation of deeply meaningful tableaux, but as part of a developing novel-like structure that creates, as an early reviewer saw, characters who "are not figures in armor: they are men and women no further removed from us than the characters in Meredith's 'Modern Love'" (Reed, 1917, 863).

The poem opens with knights discussing the rumored return of Merlin, who left ten years earlier for Brocéliande and Vivien. Their union is realized in the second sequence, but that ends with Merlin's being recalled to advise Arthur in his crisis. He does so ineffectively and returns once more to Brocéliande; finally he returns to observe the Arthurian catastrophe and to walk off alone, with Dagonet (representing "the common man" as W. R. Thompson notes, 1970, 245), "a groping way / Down through the gloom together" (2616–17), a scene appropriate both to 1917 and the future of Modernist, but not quite isolated, alienation.

Robinson's version of Merlin and Vivien is in part a happy one, drawing on the 1895 critical analysis of the Vulgate *Merlin* story by S. Humphreys

Gurteen—who felt Tennyson had "a strangely distorted view of Vivien's character" (1895, 203). For Robinson "the Lady Vivian" (889) is beautiful and intelligent and in her company Merlin escapes being a mage: he shaves off his beard and, he says, begins to live "in Time" (990). In this way the human is dominant: Yvor Winters said that Robinson's Merlin is essentially "an extremely intelligent man in middle age, at the height of great mental and physical power" and that Vivien is neither magical nor menacing, but "a beautiful, witty and self-centered woman" (1935, 69–70, 72). Their lively conversation, and their willing, and enjoyable, life choices enable them to create, as she puts it:

> ...a refuge
> Where two disheartened sinners may forget
> A world that has today no place for them. (1856–58)

Merlin appears to have powers: he says Fate "played with me / And gave me eyes to read of the unwritten" (1728–29), but Arthur was dismayed to realize this was only a great skill, not a superhuman gift. This human Merlin recognizes (2072–73) that he like all others is subject to both Time, its master Fate, and its agent Change:

> But now he knew that his cold angel's name
> Was Change, and that a mightier will than his
> Or Vivian's had ordained that he be there. (1871–73)

The lines invite a spiritual interpretation, but the poem as a whole resists this—Donald R. Cox comments that Christianity is "a peripheral issue" (1973–74, 497) and Lyle Domina's description of Robinson as a "transcendental naturalist" comes closer to the poem's mix of insistent realism and its suggestion of further meanings (1968, 473). Late in the poem Merlin foresees "two fires that are to light the world" (2594), which, he has told Dagonet, are "the torch / Of Woman and the light that Galahad found" (2400–2401). Some have felt that Robinson here means suffrage and Christianity; Valerie Lagorio has suggested more subtly that Robinson "is speaking of the creative force of love, human and divine" (1990, 172). But those lights are absent as Robinson ends the action with Merlin and the common man walking off together as "The King of Nowhere" and his fool (2604). The poem, as befits the year 1917, finally expresses a vision bleaker than the way in which Malory, Tennyson and even Twain ended their Arthurian stories:

Colder blew the wind
Across the world, and on it heavier lay
The shadow and the burden of the night;
And there was darkness over Camelot. (2623–26)

Between Emerson's potent statement of Merlin as poetic muse and unacknowledged legislator and Robinson's creation of an acute human intelligence facing the savagery of the twentieth century, American poetry had done
much to update and sophisticate the image of Merlin as a figure of highly
refined knowledge, capable of serving the modern citizen with deep insights,
a super-educator in reality or potential. Robinson's idea of humanist tragedy
was not repeated at such a high level, but some poets in both America and
Britain were to explore related roles for Merlin.

A positive reading of Robinson inspires Margaret Widdemer's short poem
"Merlin Is Wise" in her 1925 *Ballads and Lyrics,* which recommends that he
take a pleasing retirement with Vivien:

There is a thing more good than power—
Let the small greedy clutching hand
Break the strong wand in your tired fingers
Go with her to Broceliande. (105)

Thomas Caldecott Chubb, a young Yale poet, had in his 1920 collection
The White God taken a restricted Robinsonian line, with Merlin as "A lonely
man, his head among the stars," with a "vague mysterious power—alchemy
Of mind." The style is mildly Modernist but the image is as Romantic, even
Tennysonian, as any young poet might wish: "the waves around his feet /
Break in a fiery phosphorescence (1920, 29–30).

Clyde Furst had before Robinson written in terms of a triumphalist peda-
gogy, as suited an official of the Carnegie Foundation for the Advancement
of Teaching. His lengthy poem *Merlin,* in a blank verse that looks back unre-
servedly to Tennyson, was written in the 1890s for his college Phi Beta Kappa
society. It finds Vivien "perfidious" and feels that Merlin's "sagacity and vigi-
lance / Gave ever guidance true and sure support" (1930, 11) and he committed his "more than mortal mind and power / To work the welfare Arthur had
at heart" (12). Arthur is pleased, and when he recommends retirement it is
because "Thou hast fulfilled thy days and earned repose" (21). But Merlin's
spirit, as any teacher might wish, remains alive, and the poem ends with the
song "As once, so ever, Merlin, lead us on" (23).

Much of the American reworking of the Merlin tradition in poetry and prose had been of high quality, both technically and imaginatively, and all of it relocated the concept of knowledge in a contemporary world. The increasing personalization of poetry made Merlin and the vicissitudes of knowledge less available as a theme in this genre, however, and the major American contribution of the mid and late twentieth century was to be in narrative forms, literary and visual. But before this mode emerged there were British developments of Merlin.

Toward Education: Britain

After Tennyson's dismissal of Merlin in the *Idylls,* British poets, like the turn-of-the century verse playwrights, used the figure, as they did the even more popular Tristan and Isolt, as ways of writing in Tennyson's mode without copying him too much. They went back to earlier formations, mostly the advisory sage of the Vulgate *Merlin,* with stress either on his entanglement with Vivien or on the earlier Celtic visionary, both usually mediated by late Romanticism and involved with nature. As a result Merlin's knowledge here has little meaning beyond sentiment, either personal or vaguely Celtic. *Merlin's Youth* (1899), the work of George Bidder, a wealthy marine biologist, is a Celtic Twilight narrative poem of three lengthy parts, all in stanzaic rhyme. The young Merlin is a warrior who loves his leader's daughter, a wolf-girl, Yberha (which a note says rhymes with "guerra") (7), but they fall out and he leaves for forest exile and self-pity.

Ernest Rhys, a London Welshman of some influence, including founding the Everyman's Library series in 1906, was brought up in Carmarthen and spoke Welsh. He wrote two collections of Arthurian poems: Merlin briefly dictates in Vulgate mode to "his master Bleise" in *Lays of the Round Table* (1905, 62) but his only appearance of substance in Rhys's poems is in *Welsh Ballads* (1898). Here "The Death of Merlin" is a rousing Celtic Twilight affair, where Merlin has a sea-death, a connection with Annwn, the Welsh otherworld, and the support of a patriotic druid chorus:

> Wild Merlin's awake. The sun's on his way;
> Where the Elements heard the harp of the Stars
> That Darkness let shine, as Death does thy life,
> Oh Cymraec land! (29–37)

A different form of bravura, and a driving octosyllabic style, is found in Walter H. Mayson's *Merlin and Nivienne: A Poem in Four Cantoes* (1900)— Merlin welcomes her to the castle Vortigern has given him, where her "wondrous grace / Outshone the beauties of her face" (3). Essentially she is a contemporary femme fatale with an Italian maid Lucrezia. After betraying Merlin with a Celtic lord Banoden (sounding Gaelic), Nivienne finally entombs him. There seems to be some influence on Mumford's later *Merlin and Vivien,* and the seductress idea also appeared in Walter Flint's quite erotic illustrations for the 1910 Medici Society *Morte Darthur.*

Sexual schadenfreude was not for Alfred Noyes in "The Riddles of Merlin," published in 1920. Though the tone sounds Emersonian, the seer is evoked thorough the narrow sentimentality of Georgian nature poetry:

> Tell me Merlin—it is I
> Who call thee, after a thousand Springs,—
> Tell me by what wizardry
> The white foam wakes in whiter wings,
> Where surf and sea-gulls toss and cry
> Like sister-flakes, as they mount and fly,
> Flakes that the great sea flings on high,
> To kiss each other and die? (247)

Others linked Merlin, nature, and masculinity. Wilfred Scawen Blunt wrote a lyric "To Nimue" in which wild Merlin admires "The Vision of Nature" (1914, I. 389), but nevertheless cautiously permits Nimue to return. Without mention of Nimue, in his later long-line rhapsodic statement "The Wisdom of Merlyn" both author and character express bliss in nature after the vicissitudes of life, the world, and women: the poem ends by recommending that listeners "Lean thy lips on the Earth; she shall bring new peace to thy eyes with her healing vesture green." (II. 471) At the other end of the male growth process, "In Merlin's Wood," title-poem of the small collection by the young Oxford scholar E. H. W. Meyerstein, concludes:

> I have come to the end of the sorrow of youth
> And dance in the warmth of manhood's sun. (1922, 30)

A mixture of fairy lore and vague Celticity with a little nature and eroticism is enough for Ralph de Tunstall Sneyd, who also called himself "Teliesin Peredur Amadis"; in 1929 he published "Vivian and Merlin" which speaks of "Old Merlin, skilled in Bardic lore" and also of Vivien "the Fairy Queen." She finishes him off because he is her rival, but, Sneyd feels, they may still be together with him "loving her still and loved 'midst waters blue" (2001, 74).

Better poets did more with Merlin as a force of knowledge and possible education: in Arthur Symons's "Merlin and Mark," published in 1931, Merlin uses his inherent malice—"he was evil and cruel and had in his soul some spite" (35)—to intervene in the Mark-Tristan-Iseult triangle and forces on Mark a vision of the lovers in bed. Symons's own intervention in the Arthurian story is Modernist in both its wrenching of the tradition and its memorably open ending:

> Merlin had vanished, Mark heard the sea wail, and
> he knew that he had to give
> Life to one and death to another: but one seagull knew
> better, and shouted: "No!" (37)

John Masefield was not only a long-serving Poet Laureate but also a sailor, scholar, and pacifist. His Arthurian poem-sequence *Midsummer Night* (1928) has little room for Merlin: he is distantly involved in "The Old Tale of the Begetting" which suggests Igraine and Uther are already lovers (from Deeping, see p. 193), but this is located outside the coherent, quasi-narrative series of Arthurian poems. Uther is of Roman origin, and Masefield already has substantial interest in a post-Roman British period, but like some later novelists, his scholarly rigor prevents Merlin from playing any part in mediating this concept.

In "Merlin," published in 1937, Edwin Muir achieves an Emersonian voice, if not his certainty, by speculating in verse of bardic poise whether the sage really has power to resolve human distress:

> O Merlin in your crystal cave
> Deep in the diamond of the day,
> Will there ever be a singer
> Whose music will smooth away
> The furrow drawn by Adam's finger
> Across the meadow and the wave? (1984, 73)

The first two lines inspired the first title in Mary Stewart's later novel sequence; Muir here, and elsewhere, can briefly match the best of the Modernists as he reflects on the power of knowledge across time, though he also shares Modernist skepticism about the value of traditional wisdom.

Both the fragmentary technique and the pessimistic context of high poetic Modernism made narratives of Arthur and Merlin seem inappropriate,
but potent references were deployed. David Jones, an Anglo-Welshman, in
his powerful Modernist epic *In Parenthesis* (1937) includes Merlin among the
many references which both lament and mythicize the ordinary men of a
London Welsh regiment in trench warfare. At the start a lance corporal appears who will, like so many, die at Mametz Wood, Aneirin Merddyn Lewis
(1): he bears the names of two of the Welsh "prifeirdd," "the first poets." Jones
uses the medieval Welsh image of battle-trauma to convey postwar despair:
"Come with Merlin in his madness, for the pity of it; for the young men reaped
like green barley, for the folly of it" (66): he refers to the *Vita Merlini* in a note
on the passage (204).

Ezra Pound is another Modernist to deploy Arthurian myth as reference,
not narrative: where T. S. Eliot only used the Waste Land myth, Pound briefly
mentions Merlin in the late Canto XCI along with "Aurelie" and Stonehenge
in a context involving early Britain and the classical world of West and East
to consider the "beatific spirits" of antiquity:

> Merlin's fader may no man know,
> Merlin's moder is made a nun. (1975, 613)

A major Arthurian poem sequence of the thirties that made restricted use
of Merlin was by Charles Williams. He was, as Jones became, a devout Christian, and as Judith Kollman comments, he takes "a symbolic and theological perspective rather than a historical one" (1990, 203). In *Taliessin through
Logres* (1938) Merlin establishes the king in "The Calling of Arthur," later
sets Galahad on the grail quest, and then disappears of his own volition. As in
Tennyson, Galahad is an initiatory rather than explanatory character and for
Williams he is a figure of the material world, a symbol of time: Williams said
"Merlin is somehow apart from the whole question of sin and grace" (1961,
158; see also King, 1989, 72–75). A more elevated and explanatory power of
vision is bestowed on the arch-druidic figure of the poet Taliessin: the "ss"
spelling of his name indicates to English readers the Welsh unvoiced "s." He
largely subsumes Merlin's authority, more as a poet-visionary than a figure of
the Celtic world—indeed Merlin's limitations seem linked to Celtic wildness.
Taliessin's mission, and Williams's own position, is spiritual nationalism, encouraging and helping Arthur to defend the Christian world against infidels
Western and Eastern, and also against what Williams sees as barbarous modern practices like coinage.

After the second World War, Merlin was briefly resurrected as a poetic persona, but in negative and static form: he defines what we do not know and cannot value. For Alec Craig in *The Voice of Merlin* (1946) he is a mouthpiece for vulnerable modernity who, Craig's foreword suggests, "may trace something of the hopes and despairs of contemporary life" (1946, 5). Merlin is a difficult character, who actually fathers Arthur with Igraine, in order to bring himself power. Then he plans to marry Nimue and produce a dynasty of kings, but she escapes him. He watches the country destroy itself and the new King Constantine has him arrested and tried for sorcery and treason, but he saves his life in court, only to return to Nimue's garden and await death. A treasonous clerk reaching for power beyond the realms of knowledge seems an improbable defender of personal liberty, but Craig makes Merlin finally criticize modern social, and presumably socialist, forces:

> One thing only
> Is potent, one treachery alone effective
> To defeat our country's destiny.
> If her people, seduced by specious fraud,
> Betraying the holy name of liberty,
> Mistaking the form of virtue for its substance;
> Seek to curb and bridle the soul of man,
> And limit its free choice of good and evil. (76)

Equally negative, and equally forgotten, is Martyn Skinner, a postwar right-wing writer. *The Return of Arthur: A Poem of the Future* (1955) extends his *Merlin Part 1* or *The Return of Arthur: A Satiric Epic* (1951). The whole is a satire against "a disease called progress" (1951, 1, st.13) in a clumsily playful tone. In *Merlin Part 1,* using Byron's *Don Juan* meter, Skinner constructs a reactionary allegory in which Merlin, "A bardic Bismarck, holy H. G. Wells," will "guide King Arthur, like a second Virgil / Back to a world that sorely missed its Churchill" (2, st. 38, 42). As Part 2 develops, the Arthur myth is the basis for a critique, and fantasy destruction, of mammon and modernity which, like the verse, is sometimes witty but often crass—the postwar socialist government is figured through the hostile image of "Karl Kremlin Hengist," and the end is a return to theocratic conservative order.

A major effort to revive high Arthurian poetry with a cultural Merlin was made by John Heath-Stubbs, whose long *Artorius* (1973) combines historicist scholarship, Celtic myth, and classical traditions—including some Aeschylan drama sequences—into a rambling statement about the continuing value of myth to British culture. Merddin appears occasionally and through the "craft of his magic" (1973, 9) arranges Arthur's classical-style visit to the underworld, but he is outranked in Celtic authority as both bard and prophet by Taliesin, also known as Gwion. Admired by some, and clearly drawing on David Jones and Charles Williams, Heath-Stubbs's work, without any recurrent generic confidence, is also without interest in Merlin as a figure of organized and positive knowledge—he is not mentioned in Raymond Thompson's 1989 interview with Heath-Stubbs: the text simply offers its magpie assemblage of cultural references as an adequate version of knowledge.

Later British poetry abandoned this link between Merlin and conservative cultural politics and returned to him as a figure of the poet, as in Emerson and Muir, a mediating focus of personal wisdom. In Thom Gunn's "Merlin in the Cave: He Speculates Without a Book" (1993), Merlin reviews his life through images of nature that now surround and imprison him, and feels he must "grow back through knowledge, passing it / Like casual landmarks in a well-known land" (82). He feels negatively that knowledge has only left "a great emptiness in my brain" (83), and ends with minimal but real life in renewed existential action:

> But I must act, and make
> The meaning in each movement that I take.
> Rook, bee, you are the whole and not a part.
> This is an end. And yet another start. (84)

Gunn's sense of the surviving value of nature and animal life is re-created by Geoffrey Hill in "Merlin" (1994), apparently spoken in his voice:

> Arthur, Elaine, Mordred; they are all gone
> Among the raftered galleries of bone.
> By the long barrows of Logres they are made one,
> And over their city stands the pinnacled corn. (8)

A similar position is taken by Leslie Norris, a Welsh poet long based in America, in "Merlin and the Snake's Egg" (1978), where Merlin—referring back to the Myrddin tradition—becomes part of nature:

> Feathers sprout from his arms,
> His nose is an owl's hooked nose,

His eyes are the owl's round eyes,
Silent and soft he flies. (45)

Yet as in Gunn there are still limits: it is the natural wisdom of his dog, Glain,
that finds that totem of true wisdom, the serpent's egg.

The American Richard Wilbur writes in a similarly elegiac way in "Merlin
Enthralled," which externalizes the postwar experience through the Merlin
myth, imagining the knights as what Robert Bagg calls "fighters who have
lost the exhilaration of their vocation" (1992, 193). They ride with Gawen and,
as in the Vulgate, find Merlin's tomb. In Merlin's mind "History died" and he
moves again towards "the deep transparent dream" (1988, 245): Arthur too
realizes his strength has passed: the hand that once drew a sword now "cannot dream of such a thing to do" (245). Using rhyme as closure for this im-
mobilizing of power and aspiration, the poem ends, it seems, referring back to
manuscript illumination, but unlike in Robinson finding light, not darkness:
"The sky became a still and woven blue" (246).

For the major postwar Welsh poet R. S. Thomas, in "Taliesin, 1952"
(1955), Merlin—clearly here the Celtic Myrddin—is just one of the voices
of knowledge-free despair:

I have been Merlin wandering the woods
Of a far country, where the winds waken
Unnatural voiced, my mind broken
By sudden acquaintance with man's rage. (105)

The positive personal and natural self-knowledge of the knowledge of Uhland and Emerson are now far away.

In the 1980s the Oxford-educated Indian poet Dom Moraes found
"Merlin" in sad case, bereft of both knowledge and hope:

Centuries I waited to be called.
I am now sleeping in a midden,
Bruised with kicks, the cruses of my eyes
Once filled with holy oil by Arthur
Brimming with mucus and tears.
The Pendragon said I would never die.
This is no longer good news. (1987, 165)

If, without Emerson's vigorous faith in poetry or Robinson's steady humanist values, British poetry found no real value in Merlin's knowledge, British

drama, through its narrative thrust, was able to find positives, though they tended to be sensual or patriotic rather than educational in any orderly way. Arthurian verse plays flourished after Tennyson: Taylor and Brewer speak of "a very large number of plays, of varying quality, in the next three decades" (1983, 204). Some of these do not mention Merlin at all, like Henry Newbolt's *Mordred* (1895), or just treat him as a marginal and dispensable manipulator, much as in Malory, like Arthur Dillon's 1906 *King Arthur Pendragon*. A precursor, John S. Stuart-Glennie (sometimes just Glennie), combined Celticism and humanism in *King Arthur or the Drama of the Revolution* as early at 1867: he planned a series of plays and operas, beginning with *The Quest for Merlin*. The character list indicates combined Celtic and French sources: Merlin the Wild, Taliessin the Wise, Viviann the Lady of the Lake, and Blaize the wolf of Merlin. A substantial scholar—his book *Arthurian Topography* (1869) was reprinted in the Early English Text Society edition of the English prose *Merlin*—Stuart-Glennie is also an aggressive secularist, seeking the overthrow of religion, though he says his movement is inspired "alike with the Nature-worship of Heathenism and the Fraternal Sentiment of Christianity" (1867, xxxi).

This new world is to be focused on Merlin, a Celtic sage; he has been "to the Underworld" and now, his sister Ganieda says:

> all the people, Merlin, are seeking thee
> The bond of their new brotherhood to be. (63)

Remarkable for its confidence and scope rather than its achievement—much like Hovey's work—Stuart-Glennie's work was the harbinger of many Merlin melodramas.

Yeats provided a brief one in his dramatic poem "Time and the Witch Vivien," published in *The Wanderings of Oisin* in 1889. In a single scene, the confident and splendid Vivien—"Where moves there any as beautiful as I?" (1984, 514) she asks, and only the title identifies her as a witch—is defeated symbolically at dice and chess by Time, who seems much like a revenant Merlin, taking his vengeance as she dies.

In 1890 Ralph McLeod Fullarton, a distinguished barrister, created in *Merlin: A Dramatic Poem* a melodrama without much symbolic meaning beyond conventional Christianity found in odd places. Merlin represents nature and sings of love when visited by the spirits of Air and Earth. Vivien and Merlin squabble over a magic ring; she gets it and proclaims "Vivien shall be king." She sends Merlin to sleep, Morgan saves him with a crucifix, and they have a restrained love scene; eventually Vivien finishes him off in an essentially

Christian death and he forgives her, but she is also entombed (Mumford seems to have read this). The poetry is sometimes competent, and the emphasis on Vivien as a sort of New Woman has been found by Christopher Dean a matter for admiration (1993, 34–36).

A more common role for Merlin in verse drama is to act as facilitator, sometimes even manager, for Arthur. J. Comyns Carr's *King Arthur: A Drama* of 1895, an all-star event with Henry Irving and Ellen Terry, music by Arthur Sullivan, and design by Edward Burne-Jones, brings the grail quest in soon after Merlin helps establish Arthur, and then combines Mordred and Morgan as the enemies of the Round Table—which was to be a recurrent simplification of Arthur's problems in the twentieth century. Equally common is the return of Merlin at the very end of the story to supervise Arthur's glory as "a voice from shore to shore" presses home the patriotic message saying "England's sword is in the sea" and that

> "…in that shifting sea
> Burns a light that from afar
> Men shall hail for liberty!" (69)

Most plays are not so directly jingoistic, tending to focus on a mixture of poetry and an idealistic rendition of a heroic British past, such as *Gwenevere* (1905), written, among other Arthurian and Celtic plays, by Ernest Rhys. Near Merlin's house in Gwent, southeast Wales, Gwenevere comes maying and is abducted by Mordred, who is himself set on by Morgan. As Gwenevere's adultery lets Arthur's enemies gain power, Merlin steps in to mediate, in verse better than usual in this genre:

> Oh Gwenevere
> The passions, woes and wars of men
> To dust shall stoop at least: but then
> There is a dawn-wind wakes again! (77)

The wind he predicts blows as Arthur's host stands before the throne where the king sits "pale, like one in swoon or half asleep." The host cries out in Welsh "Deffro, deffro, deffro! Arthur vawr!" ("Awake, awake, awake! great Arthur!"). (78) He does, and they all brandish their swords.

Rhys's work was modest and focused compared with the ambition of *King Arthur: A Trilogy of Lyric Dramas* by Francis Burdett Money Coutts, culture-oriented member of a famous banking family. The trilogy, beginning with

Merlin, was produced and privately printed in 1897 and then published in revised form in 1907. The first play starts conventionally enough, if slowly, with the sword in the stone sequence supervised in correct twelfth-century mode by the archbishop, not Merlin. Nivian and Morgan are here to make trouble, but Merlin sends Nivian back to the forest and Morgan's charge that the stone is just Merlin's magic is ruled out: she still storms off with the battle-cry "Mordred and defiance" (1907, 59).

Arthur captures Morgan and Mordred and, against Merlin's advice, pardons them: Morgan tells Nivian how to entomb Merlin with his own magic rod. He does not fear her but with Morgan's help she invokes "The Spirit of Liberty"—her own—and entombs him. Taylor and Brewer find Coutts's plays "of little literary value," and feel that his style can be "absurdly operatic" (1983, 210), but he can write and plot with vigor. This is a bold presentation of the Arthurian New Woman in Morgan and Merlin's main role is to facilitate her realization, though the revised version added a lengthy poem "Uther Pendragon" to the start, where Merlin acts as a general mastermind. It was this text for which the Spanish composer Isaac Albeniz, to whom the 1897 version is dedicated, wrote music in 1902: this was published in 1906, but the opera was not produced until 2003, in Madrid.

Even grander, but less interesting today, was the Arthurian cycle written by Reginald Buckley and deployed in the music-drama performance style of Rutland Boughton as "a British equivalent to Wagner's Ring cycle" (Hurd, 1992, 208). The plays were performed in parts from 1912 on and in 1914 Buckley published the four that made up *Arthur of Britain.* Merlin is a major figure in the first part, *The Birth of Arthur,* a negative development of his Malorian role (with clear influence from Warwick Deeping's novel *Uther and Igraine,* see pp. 193–94): his "will is moved by fancies, / Dark and wayward to other men" (64). As usual in Malory-based versions Merlin soon disappears, as indeed has the work of Buckley and largely that of Boughton. Elgar's refusal to set the Buckley poems seems understandable—their basic tone is grandiose. Buckley and Boughton both shared a retrospective William Morris-like communalism (Hurd, 1992, 214), but Tennyson's reading of Merlin is dominant.

After the First World War, Arthurian themes found even less place in verse drama than in poetry itself. A rare exception, probably because he was in effect a writer of an older generation, is Laurence Binyon's *Arthur: A Tragedy* of 1923. This has no role for Merlin but in the 1920s Binyon started *The Madness of Merlin,* published posthumously in 1947. Binyon—who was aware that his name had a Welsh origin as Ap Einion, "son of Einion"—goes back to the Celtic Myrddin. In his introduction Gordon Bottomley says the play

is unfinished, but it seems complete enough, though short. As in British poetry of the period, Merlin represents the imagination in unhappy mood, and
there seems little positive to find in the text, though Himlian, a peasant version of Vivien, does bear Merlin a son. Bottomley reports Binyon's theme as
"the ardours and agonies and doubts and dilemmas of our contemporary life,
by reference to the timeless factor common to all generations" (1947, vi). No
doubt this was a credible position between the wars and Merlin explores in
quasi-humanist style "the country of my own mind" (25), but Binyon fails to
get beyond a stagy diction and self-pitying tone:

> Suddenly I heard a voice,
> A voice that accused me:
> What hast thou done, Merlin?
> Thou hast broken the beauty of the world,
> Thou hast broken the lamp and extinguished the light.
> None can recover it, none. (40)

One reviewer, the Welsh writer and academic Gwyn Jones, liked the Celticity
(1947), but another, the poet Roland Gant found the poem "rather artificial
and outmoded in form" (1947–48, 253).

Bottomley wrote his own short verse drama, "Merlin's Grave" (1929),
where a genuine wisdom with some clear educational goal emerges, and the
effect is like an overwrought version of Robinson. The play is based on the
Caledonian Merlin: Bottomley lived in northeast England and was aware of
the Scottish material, though his style here as elsewhere owes a good deal to
Japanese Noh dramas (Phillips, 1991, 217). In his cave the old exile is visited
by a Highland reincarnation of Nimue who bears "the power of nature" (67),
and he realizes that each period replays the drama of knowledge and beauty:

> Age upon age
> Have you been born,
> To turn at last to the Sage,
> Imprisoned under the thorn. (68)

Merlin is again ensnared by Nimue, but Bottomley has more than the old
fin de siècle melodrama in mind. As Margaret Reid notes, he condenses the
Myrddin setting with the dark romance of the Vulgate (1938, 82), and he goes
further: a final chorus speaks for the interwar period about the tragic weight
of history itself, and its continued transmission in the present:

Who can escape them, who can know
What things the ancients have laid on us?
A secret thing that one of us does
Can be remembered and done again
By flesh that is not yet borne of our pain. (76)

Merlin could have a more positive and less angst-ridden contemporary meaning. In darkest wartime between November 1940 and November 1941, Winifred Ashton, a prolific author of plays and novels, including mysteries, who usually worked under the pen-name of "Clemence Dane," wrote for radio a linked series of "Seven Plays on One Theme" entitled *The Saviours* (1942). She speaks of it as "the legend of a hero who helps his people to be one strong and civilized—but then disappears" (v), but it in fact involves a set of heroes. The first is Merlin, and the play briefly retells the story of his role in the war against the invading Saxons, with obvious contemporary relevance: "The German plague shall be swept away" (27). Merlin goes on to mastermind the rest of the heroes: Arthur is "The Hope of Britain," Alfred is "England's Darling," and Nelson is another hero; but, showing her own gender interest, Ashton gives Elizabeth I hero status, and her leftist sympathies bring in Robin Hood as "The May King." The last, and most moving, play focuses democratically on "The Unknown Soldier." Merlin narrates the whole sequence from his "deathless tower of air and hawthorn bloom" (274) and finally speaks in clearly educational mode for the values of English tradition and resistance:

"Love of God, love of man, love of justice, love of freedom, courage. Imagination and laughter. And to these gifts the Unknown Soldier has added—sacrifice." (302)

With less energy and much less national self-confidence, later drama continued to handle Arthurian themes including Merlin. "James Bridie" (actually Osborne Mavor, a Glasgow doctor), a writer committed to Scottish themes, both realist and symbolic, also appears to continue the national late medieval hostility to Arthur, and Merlin's only real role is satirical, as in the contemporary English poets Craig and Skinner. *Holy Isle* (1942) focuses on the distinctly northern Lot and Morgause, though the play becomes a satirical fantasy and "a study in disillusion" set on Orkney (Bannister, 1955, 162). In *Lancelot* (1945), Merlin arranges Lancelot's fathering of Galahad, while being harassed by the aggressive Nimue, who will soon imprison him. From his rocky grave he describes Arthur's court as "a parcel of bullies and strumpets ruled over by a dolt" and advises Lancelot "to find your own truth for yourself" (1944, 50, 53). The story then follows Malory with some fidelity, finally reusing Ector's eulogy for Lancelot.

A dramatically central and positive use of Merlin is by Christopher Fry, the playwright who, with T. S. Eliot, was thought at the time to have renewed the verse play as a genre of artistic and social significance. *Thor with Angels* (1948) locates Merlin in Dark Age Britain, a Christian land where Joseph of Arimathea's staff flowered at Glastonbury, but where the pagan Saxons have triumphed. They mock Merlin, but Fry's naturo-mysticism asserts that "the shape of the dream / In the ancient slumbering rock" will wake "in the open eyes / Of the sea of the love of the morning of the God" (40). So finally the Saxons decide not to "let the light of our lives / Be choked by darkness" (53), and they agree to follow Merlin's implicitly educational lead and adopt Christianity.

Fry's use of Merlin is the last theatrical deployment of him as an authority figure—in John Arden and Margaretta Darcy's *The Island of the Mighty* (1974), Merlin is seen in Arden's "Arthur's Preface One" as negative knowledge: "the liberal intellectual who no longer knows what is liberality and what is tyranny" (15). The historicism they deploy, as did Fry, however, derives from the development of another major force in the reworking of both Arthur and, to a lesser degree, Merlin. The dynamic growth in historicism about the Arthurian period, which found its most productive generic form in the novel, was the domain where Merlin the educator was to be most fully developed.

Education and the Novel: White, Lewis, and Cooper

Arthur and Merlin appear through the nineteenth century almost exclusively in elevated genres, poetic and theatrical, not in the novel. Charlotte Yonge's *The History of Sir Thomas Thumb* (1855) does add the Vulgate Merlin and Vivien love story to Merlin's creation—here with Queen Mab—of the tiny hero: she may well have been influenced by Arnold's poem of the previous year. There is little else to note. Mary Linwood's *The House of Camelot: A Tale of the Olden Time* (1858) is a post-Lytton fable of Celtic-Saxon reconciliation under Avalloc, prince of Camelot where, as in Layamon and Malory, Merlin's prophecies are remembered. *The Count of the Saxon Shore* (1887) by Alfred Church, a professor of Latin, has Lucius Aelius as "a British Caesar" and Cedric as a noble British-speaking Saxon. Arthur only appears in the final pages to win at "Badon" and with historicist caution, Merlin is absent. Dinah Craik's novel *King Arthur* (1886), subtitled *Not a Love Story,* is actually not Arthurian at all, being about a Cornish foundling boy whose mother named him Arthur, thinking of Tennyson. At the end of the nineteenth century, Merlin fiction might seem to emerge in *Merlin: A Piratical Love Story* (1896) by "Mr M————."[4] But this has nothing to do with Merlin; that is just the name of a mysterious rich adventurer, roaming between the South Seas and London's West End. This is the first of a number of books which, to the present, simply exploit the potent name. There can be a strained rationale: Peter Dickinson's *Merlin Dreams* (1988) keeps him asleep and offstage as stories loosely related to him are told. Or Merlin can be transplanted to a different setting and an entirely new story: the *Merlin's Descendants* series by "Irene Radford" (Phyllis Ann Karr) loosely links the sage and Nimue to different periods—*Guardian of the Vision* (2001) is yet another Mary Stuart and Queen Elizabeth story. Ann Chamberlin's *The Merlin of St Gilles' Well* (1991) is a Joan of Arc story where a hermit is called "heir to Merlin" (46).

The name Merlin evidently has continuing power in the publishing market and some books merely, even shamelessly, use it in the title. Eric Forbes Boyd's *Merlin Hold* is a standard Buchanesque thriller (1927); Edith Brace's *Thus Merlin Said* (1934) is simply set in medieval Wales; *Merlin's Furlong* (1953), by Gladys Mitchell, is just a place name in a standard mystery; Marcel Wallerstein's *Merlin's Forest* (1965) is the Breton location for a spy story; two novels are called *Merlin's Keep,* one a melodramatic romance set in Wales by Kate Norway (1966) and the other, by Madeleine Brent, a governess romance that starts in Tibet (1977). Some of these titular exploitations at least have some flair, like George Beardmore's spirited French resistance story *Madame Merlin* (1946) and Anne McCaffrey's *The Mark of Merlin* (1971), where Merlin is a dog.

The first actual Merlin novel of any substance is *Uther and Igraine* (1903) by Warwick Deeping. A doctor, he wrote this novel, the first of many, when only twenty-five, neatly combining Arthurian, or rather Utherian, themes with the contemporary romantic mode. The novel was innovative in focusing on Uther and Igraine and conceiving them as lovers before her forced marriage to Gorlois. A lesser novelty is making Uther not the usual royal oaf but what Conlee calls "a man of more refined sensibilities and a devout Christian" (2001, 89). Igraine starts as a nun, who is rescued by Pelleas after being tied naked to a tree; she comes to love him, but is tricked into marrying Gorlois, who brutalizes her. These are all routine adventures for turn-of-the-century romance: Pelleas turns out to be the incognito Uther. Merlin, who looks like Dante, is basically the medieval grand vizier in domestic mode, organizing the Gorlois-Igraine wedding, where he puts Igraine into a trance, supervising the final happiness of the royal lovers (after Uther kills Gorlois), and predicting their glorious child.

In spite of the relative success of this novel, modern romance proved a blind alley for Arthurian themes, though there were some exotic and largely forgotten examples like George Moore's reworking of the Perceval grail story on Breton lines in the Merlin-free *Peronnik the Fool* (1921) and *The Boy Apprenticed to an Enchanter* (1920) by Padraic Colum. In the latter work, a parable of Irish independence, a young Irish apprentice magician gains Merlin's help in resisting his cruel master.

But as on other occasions in the tradition, one writer proved able to reconceive the role of Merlin in convincing contemporary terms and shape a new genre to realize a new development. Merlin as educator had been hovering around the tradition certainly since Bulwer Lytton, even to some degree since Spenser, and had been developed more recently, mostly in America by Emerson, Robinson, and various minor figures, but it was T. H. White who both saw and realized in fiction the possibilities of this concept, essentially creating the Arthurian bildungsroman.

After success studying English at Cambridge, where he took Malory as a special subject, White became a teacher at the progressive public (i.e. private) school Stowe. He soon gave that up for full-time writing, and transmitted his wide and curious learning with a fluent, engaging style. His first major work combined Arthurian expertise with his teaching flair in *The Sword in the Stone* (1938). The idea of presenting Arthur's youthful development seems obvious in retrospect, but White imagined it first. He apparently admired A. A. Milne's success with the small boy theme (Warner, 1967, 99), but Arthur's companion is the opposite of a foolish toy bear: Merlyn, as White medievally spells the name, is a fantasy projection of himself, isolated, learned, eccentric, very amusing, but essentially serious. Martin Kellman comments that Merlyn is "the most complete self-portrait White had put in any book" (1991, 56).

White was very widely read, and appears to know the tradition of wild Myrddin and his animals, because Merlyn educates Arthur primarily through making him experience the natural world. But the development of an English *Naturmensch* has political as well as moral meaning: what Wart, or Arthur, learns as a fish or a hawk is to comprehend both the structures of power in the social world and also ways in which the individual can gain personal authority and seek to improve society. The original story was substantially different from the version in the collected *The Once and Future King:* in the 1938 version Arthur meets cannibals, a grass-snake, and a giant, and has much more to do with the unsettling Madame Mim, but this somewhat random material was cut from the 1958 tetralogy (see Brewer, 1993, 33–44).

As well as linking with nature, *The Sword in the Stone,* and Merlyn's role in it, were comic. Much of the humor both mocks and celebrates the English gentry to which White was always attracted, as in the painfully whimsical presentation of Sir Ector and his friends. But this quaintness cannot mask the drive of the book to celebrate education. Merlyn tells the young Arthur:

> "The best thing for being sad," replied Merlyn, beginning to puff and blow, "is to learn something. That is the only thing that never fails....Learn why the world wags and what wags it. That is the only thing which the mind can never exhaust, never alienate, never be tortured by, never fear or distrust and never dream of regretting. Learning is the thing for you." (1996, 193–94)

Learning is also purposive: the book ends as Arthur's education ends, and the animal agents of his natural learning attend and empower him as he draws the sword. The rest of the series will debate whether this natural education will be of any use in the face of human propensity for conflict.

White's next step was to follow his ground-breaking prequel with a version of Malory's first book. Originally published as *The Witch in the Wood* (1940), in the 1958 omnibus it was cut down to little more than half and retitled *The Queen of Air and Darkness* (though in the five-book omnibus of 1996 it regained its original title). Compared to Malory the story lacks Balin and the prequel to the grail and has a much more positive Merlyn, but it adds a number of distractions. White was living in Ireland, and he combines local comedy, focused on St. Toirdealbhach (originally spelt, as pronounced, St Torelvac), with his equally stereotypical insistence that King Lot's family are Gaelic—hot-tempered, passionate, and though brave, basically a problem. This English chauvinism tends to be overlooked because the book more alarmingly deploys both White's hatred of his mother—Morgause, with her dangerous seductive wiles, represents her—and his own interest in sadomasochism, hence unpleasant scenes like boiling the cat and beheading the unicorn, developing darkly from the Madame Mim material in the original *The Sword in the Stone.*[5]

After this book of manifold violence, White calmed down and followed Malory in what was published separately as *The Ill-Made Knight* (1941) and also in *The Candle in the Wind,* which though written during the war first appeared as the final book of the 1958 *The Once and Future King.* Merlyn is now off-stage: White follows Malory in this as well, though like many modern writers he will bring Merlyn back. He disappears at the end of *The Queen of Air and Darkness,* with a few final jokes—he tells them to psychoanalyze the questing beast ("But not too much of Freud," 326)—and, a crucial moment, forgetting to tell Arthur who was his mother (333). After Arthur meets his half-sister Morgause, Mordred will be born, and the fall of Camelot is started—and education is shown to be crucially ineffective in the face of malice and mishap, while Arthur faces the destructive effects of power across Europe, just as White did in his own lifetime.

The developing crisis is the underlying theme of the third and fourth books. Lancelot comes to court, but neither his somewhat underdeveloped love for Guinevere nor the Christian challenge of the grail story are of much weight. The issue is violence and aggression: White was writing as fascism, Stalinism, and war gathered force, and he is the first Arthurian writer to turn his mind firmly onto the politics of international violence, making explicit what is implied in Twain and Robinson. Drawing on his natural education, Arthur continually debates the conflict of Right and Might. He sums it up before the final battle, speaking to a page called—with characteristic White flair—Tom Malory:

> …the idea was that force ought to be used, if it were used at all, on behalf of justice, not on its own account. Follow this, young boy. He thought that if he could get his barons fighting for truth, and to help weak people, and to redress wrongs, then their fighting might not be such a bad thing as once it used to be. So he gathered together all the true and kindly people that he knew, and he dressed them in armour, and he made them knights. And taught them this idea and set them down at the Round Table. (693)

The boy asks what has happened: Arthur replies "For some reason, things went wrong. The Table split into factions, a bitter war began, and all were killed." (693)

It is a characteristic 1930s response, both in its moral seriousness and also, sadly, in its failure to work out any real way of opposing brutality on an international basis. The problems are inherent—the good people are only "true and kindly," not bound by international law (much like the good-hearted but ineffectively individualistic Peace Pledge Union). In this impasse White recoils into his limited personal experience and can only make Arthur suggest that all the conflict arises from a version of competitive school sports that he and Merlyn call "Games-Mania" (395).

This makes knowledge individual, in the sense that it is moral and personal, so in modern terms credible, but also crucially weak in practice because it has no general, supra-individual analytic power, no sociopolitical plans or sanctions to resolve the problems it identifies. Nevertheless the grandeur of the story and the vigor of White's retelling created an impact: the 1958 Complete Edition ended, as does the musical and film *Camelot,* with what seemed a fine open, tragic moment: "The cannons of his adversary were thundering in the tattered morning when the majesty of England drew himself up to meet the future with a peaceful heart." (697)

Though White had originally planned to end there, he decided that "Pendragon can still be saved, and elevated into a superb success" (Warner, 1967, 176)—and the key was more education of the king. White drafted a fifth book in which Merlyn returns the night before the battle—apparently in a dream—and Arthur is taken out of Malorian time to reflect on the debate the book has raised, especially "what can we learn about abolition of war from animals" (Warner, 1967, 176). Supervised by Merlyn, he will meet again the animals of *The Sword in the Stone* in the badger's den, which is just like a Cambridge dons' common room where issues can be debated at length. White's publisher William Collins declined to print this, presumably thinking such a skeptical account of power was counter to the war effort, though he claimed a shortage of paper (Warner, 1996, 825). The fifth book did not appear until 1977 in a separate edition, and it was not until the 1996 pentalogy omnibus that *The Book of Merlyn* rejoined the whole text.

Structurally it looks to belong. The educator Merlyn returns to supervise the analysis of his pupil's achievements in life, and there are strong tonal links: so much so that when Collins published the four-book *Once and Future King* in 1958 someone—apparently White himself—lifted two sequences from *The Book of Merlyn* and put them in *The Sword in the Stone* to replace the cut elements. These are Arthur's negative experience among the fascist ants and his highly positive encounter with the communal geese, including his own attraction to a female goose. Having been judged too good to abandon for the 1958 edition, they both held their place when in 1996 the *Book of Merlyn* joined it, and curiously recur in their original locations.

Critics have generally disliked *The Book of Merlyn,* feeling it wordy, inconclusive, too far from Malory: Brewer thought it "a strange ending" (1993, 151), Kellman calls it "preachy" (1991, 59) and Geoffrey Ashe regarded it as "the aborted fifth book" where "his personal convictions were...intruding" (2006, 200, 199). Not all agree: Alan Lupack sees it as "the capstone in the construction of the sequence" (2001, 104), and it is fair to note that the book we have is only a draft. White was in the habit of reworking his texts heavily in galley proof, as were many writers in a more expansive age, and he never saw this material set up in print. But even as it stands it seems to speak to the desperate early years of the war. The best of education, Cambridge plus nature, cannot resolve the threat of violence: knowledge is out of contact with power, and all that is left is courage: as Arthur leaves, the animals wish him well:

> They were saying "Good success to your majesty, a speedy and successful issue."
> He smiled gravely, saying "We hope it will be speedy."
> But he was referring to his death, as one of them knew. (803–4)

Arthur is a brave soldier, fighting on; as he, and of course Merlyn, know, sacrifice is all that seems likely—there is a resonance here with Clemence Dane's contemporary *The Saviours,* including the presence of Merlin as the source of knowledge and evaluation. But Arthur's story, and the memory of honor, will live on: in a typically, but not ignobly, sentimental moment White has the hedgehog, lowest of the animals and representative of the common people, insist that Arthur "Say not Farewell" but "Orryvoyer" (804).

It is after this long sequence, which is apparently a dream, that Arthur returns to fight, and White tells in Malorian mode the last sequences of the Arthurian story, ending as Malory does with a prayer for the author, Malory's "humble disciple, who now voluntarily lays aside his books to fight for his kind" (812). White did not manage to be taken on as a warrior, and nor would he again reach this level in writing; but he did at least have relative riches and international recognition when the musical *Camelot,* based on his work, became so successful.

White has always been famous for the brilliance and imagination of *The Sword in the Stone;* this and the quality of his transmission and updating of Malory has made his book a bestseller, still reprinting almost every year. But if *The Book of Merlyn* is considered as it was drafted, with the defining animal experiences among the ants and geese that were to be cannibalized, and with the author's direct final involvement, it seems a powerful ending to this reworking of the Arthur story in time of war, one that insists that the story of Arthur and Merlin is always more than just a fiction, and that knowledge must interact with power to educate us towards a better world.

Fortunate as he was in his biographer, the friend and writer Sylvia Townsend Warner, White has yet to receive a critical analysis of the subtlety and range that he deserves as a major Arthurian. Firstly he linked Merlin very convincingly with education, so much so that this became the default view back across the ages: the French *Larousse Encyclopédie* improbably calls the dark-age Merlin "l'éducateur d'Arthur" (1963, 7, 274); and he also established the Arthur story with style and confidence in the juvenile book market. There was to be an enormous impact from those two relocations, as Merlin's knowledge was made available for the education of the individual citizen, especially the younger ones, and there were two more major British novels with an educationally inspirational Merlin.

A successor to White—also with ethical politics in mind, if of a much more religious kind—is C. S. Lewis in *That Hideous Strength* (1945). Part of the Oxford-based circle that generated Tolkien's *The Lord of the Rings* and Charles Williams's poetry, Lewis wrote both major scholarship and also popular fiction, mostly for the young, imbued with Christian moralism. Early in his career he drafted a poem, now lost, about "Nimue" (2000, 466, 482–83), but there seems no link to his later Merlin. After two science fiction allegories, *Out of the Silent Planet* and *Perelandra* (published as *Voyage to Venus* in the United States), about a cosmic conflict of good and evil forces, the trilogy directs its moral allegory into largely satirical mode in contemporary England, especially in its uncut original version. In *That Hideous Strength* the forces of modern and malign bureaucracy, called NICE (National Institute for Co-ordinated Experiments) are gaining power over the country, and especially over a university town very like Lewis's Oxford. The only opponents are a small group of wise Christians led by Ransom (the name implies redemption), hero of the earlier novels, who is also known as Mr. Fisher-King (Lewis, like White and Tennyson, can be banal at times). As Nan Arbuckle notes (1989, 79), devout Lewisians have disliked the contemporaneity of the novel, with the notable exception of Charles Moorman (1956–57 and 1960), perhaps because he was himself a distinguished medievalist.

In the story, discussed in some detail by Traxler (2003), Merlin is an ancient figure of great power and tricksterish spirit who is entombed in a wood owned by a college (a neat natural-intellectual condensation). The land is sought by NICE, who are keen to use Merlin's power in their own operations. Lewis outlines with some skill how the college dons are mostly swayed by modernity, and also how the young couple at the core of the story are divided: Mark's ambition takes him towards NICE while Jane's intuition—she is a visionary—leads her towards Ransom. Merlin remains largely offstage and his role can seem obscure: Dean sees him as only "a character of convenience" to assist the plot (1988, 74) but he is meant to represent knowledge alone, *scientia,* which Lewis, with theological precision, always insisted, as in his contemporary essay *The Abolition of Man* (1947), was secondary to wisdom, *sapientia.* Accordingly Merlin appears as at best a facilitator for Ransom (as also for Arthur) and a coarse weapon, as when he makes all the guests at a NICE dinner talk in gibberish. *That Hideous Strength* relies for its central meaning on Lewis's faith in theocratic rule, but this is less clear since, like White's Arthuriad, the book has suffered in publication: the first version was cut (by the author) to less than half when it reappeared in 1955 and the stress on adventure rather than dark social commentary has tended to obscure both the book's moral and social allegory and its similarities to George Orwell's later and much more famous antimodernity tract, *Nineteen Eighty-Four* (1948). There may even be influence, as Orwell reviewed Lewis's book favorably, approving its "horror of modern machine civilisation" and saying "it sounds all too topical" (1998, 250), though he demurred at the spirituality and optimism: much as his own novel admires the human past, its own figure of old knowledge, Mr. Charrington, turns out to be a spy for modernity.

Less political, less complex, and much more popular than Lewis's book has been Susan Cooper's *The Dark is Rising* series (1965–77). This is targeted firmly at the juvenile market as it, like Lewis's Narnia series, presents middle-class British children encountering excitement and mystery. Cooper, an English writer who moved to the United States, deploys the Merlin myth in the children's literature tradition for what Goodrich calls "rational and developmental purposes" (1989, 188). She constructs a myth from fragments of Celtic story that is closer to Lewis's alarmist allegory than White's attempt at real-world analysis. The forces of the Dark are in conflict with those of the Light, led by the Old Ones. Professor Merriman Lyon, whose name encodes Merlyn, is "first of the Old Ones, the strongest and wisest" (*The Grey King,* 1975, 37); he has "lived in every age" (*The Dark is Rising,* 1973, 86) and as Spivack and Staples comment, he has "an immortal role as a great lord of the forces of the Light, with power over time and nature" (1994, 21).

In *Over Sea, Under Stone* (1965) the three Drew children are normally, if bravely, human: in *The Dark is Rising* (1973) Will Stanton, though adolescent and humble in class, is also himself an Old One and becomes a warrior for the Light. Two short novels develop matters: *Greenwitch* (1974), where the Drews meet Will, and *The Grey King* (1975) a more Welsh-oriented story introducing another youthful warrior, Bran Davies, also Arthur's son. Then in *Silver on the Tree* (1977) the story realizes its mythic core as Arthur and his astral army come to fight the Dark. They win, but although Bran will remain with the children and their world, Merriman Lyon tells them Arthur will not be back and the world is left to humans. Where medieval Merlin departed so that the Arthurian tragedy can ensue, now he is a professional educator who passes on humanist hope to brave children: power is both demoticized and optimistic.

Merlin's insightful authority, and his extended if also marginal role in the story, distinguish the moralized stories of the twentieth century from the darker and more intermittent presences of Merlin in the past. No longer entombed or otherwise excluded from the story, he can regularly survive to the end or reappear in time for the resolution. He still engages with power, but now the power involved is that of the individual character, and so the reader and book buyer. Just as the novel itself has been shown persuasively to be a means of constructing the knowing subject (Belsey, 1980), Merlin imparts, as an educator, knowledge to the subjective central figure or figures. The idea of accumulating knowledge towards ultimate comprehension is structural to the form of the novel itself and so Merlin gains strength: as Taylor and Brewer comment, there develops a "later twentieth century fascination with the figure of Merlin" (1983, 274).

This happens in the historicist Arthur fictions, which are in chronological terms the next subgenre to develop after White and Lewis, overlapping with Cooper. There can be exceptions when the novel is rigorously historical and Merlin is excluded from the Arthurian dark age, as in Rosemary Sutcliff's *Sword at Sunset* (1963) but usually the modern reconstruction of Merlin as an educator-adviser and the knowledge-focused form of the novel itself together permit him to remain in the historicist novels, usually as a guide to the personalized central figure of Arthur, and this role develops first in juvenile and fantasy fiction.

Education and the Novel: Historicism, Juveniles, and Fantasy

The "historical" Arthur is a product of recent history. Gibbon had discussed "the illustrious name of Arthur" but on historicity merely refers to "Nennius": he is much more interested in "the singular revolutions of his fame" in later years, which he explores, in literary and folkloric mode, for several pages (1910, 94–96). Through the nineteenth century scholars were aware that there were early references that could be taken as memories of a historical Arthur, but the original *Dictionary of National Biography* essay, by Charles Kearney, a numismatist and historian at the British Library, discussed these issues in 1885 with some skepticism, not going beyond "Nennius" and a possible "northern Arthur" on the Scottish border. Apart from Alfred Church's 1887 novel *The Count of the Saxon Shore* (see pp. 192–93), nothing more was made of this issue, not even by the usually patriotic E. K. Chambers or the Celtic John Rhŷs.[6] But in the first volume of the *Oxford History of England* (1936), R. G. Collingwood, an Oxford scholar of wide influence, ended his account of the Roman-British period with a few pages of fantasy, suggesting that Arthur was "the last of the Romans" (324), a Romanized Celt who confronted and delayed the Germanic invaders using heavy cavalry on the imperial model—so linking medieval knights back to the Roman empire. The ideological impact of this was to separate England from solely Germanic origins though the argument that the Arthurian resistance enabled a fictional melding of the Celtic and the Germanic to create the unique English—a version of the "reassurance of fratricide" linking the modern British Empire back to Roman grandeur. This idea of Arthur as historical and essentially Roman became fascinating to the English, especially after the Second World War, though Collingwood's own impetus may well have been the First World War, and Una O'Farrell-Tate (2004, 17) has noted that Merlin's return "features in a number of short stories written around the period of the Second World War," with instances from 1931 to 1948.

Such patriotism was not only English: Fritz Lienhard's *König Arthur* (1900) is a five-act play with Merlin as Arthur's bard in the German Romantic tradition (and Vivien as a charcoal burner's daughter), but it ends with the Anglo-Saxon Horsa exulting "Heil: The German Victory Banner over the *Blachfeld* ("battlefield") of Britain" (1900, 112). English Arthurian jingoism was both more subtle and much more widespread. A link between war and historicism is clear in the poem by Francis Brett Young "Hic Jacet Arthurus" which was published in his poem sequence starting with the creation of the world and focusing on great moments in British history up to the Battle of Britain, *The Island* (1944). In lines that Rosemary Sutcliff would later use as epigraph to *Sword at Sunset,* Collingwood's fantasy is fully realized:

> ...when Rome fell, like a writhen oak
> That age had sapped and cankered at the root,
> Resistant, from her topmost bough there broke
> The miracle of one unwithering shoot.
> Which was the spirit of Britain—(56–57)

Arthur is a sort of Churchill; a British origin legend from Rome is imagined. But as Young goes on to note, in the context of historicity and quasi-empiricism, "lost is Merlin's magic" (56): the historicist myth springs up as a compensation for England's postimperial weakness.

Edward Frankland, a scientist turned writer, produced *The Bear of Britain* (1944), a Rome-oriented, war-focused novel with a patriotic foreword by David Lloyd George, the veteran Welsh-born politician. Merlin is absent, as is Celtic accuracy—Uther's elder son is Modron, the Welsh for "mother." Other post-Collingwood novels avoid Arthur as well as Merlin in constructing their Romanized English historicity, like Meriol Trevor's *The Last of Britain* (1956)—though in 1957 she produced a children's story, *Merlin's Ring*—and Warwick Deeping's *The Sword and the Cross* (1957). This latter novel, published seven years after Deeping's death, like *Uther and Igraine* is focused on Igerne, but now partners her with Gerontius, presumably linked to John Henry Newman's 1865 poem about this Christianized Celtic hero. But Arthur is the usual focus of classicized patriotism. In John Masefield's *Badon Parchments* (1947) the Arthur of his poem sequence *Midsummer Night* is now re-formed through the use of fictional Latin archives, with no place for Merlin. As Myrddin, he makes a forceful appearance in John Cowper Powys's *Porius,* a firmly Celticized and quasi-historical novel (Thompson called it one of his "didactic fantasies," 1990, 229), which appeared in 1951 in a cut version.[7] Powys had included Merlin in *Morwyn* (1937) as one of the book's authorities—Socrates and the Marquis de Sade are others—but now a greater devotion to both Celticism and historicism surrounds the invented Porius with a richness, perhaps even an embarrassment, of detail, events, and ideas—Dean suggests there is some lack of clarity in the novel (1988, 70). Myrddin Wyllt, almost primeval in form, is a visionary across time, an earth spirit, and a major channel for the freewheeling cultural speculations of the text: Lindstedt sees him as "both prophet/god and herdsman/counsellor" (2004, 32), while Taylor and Brewer describe him in Powysian terms as a symbol of "the life-principle" (1983, 286). Many of his features, except his capacity to represent Saturn/Chronos/Time and a taste for white magic (Goodrich, 2000, 104), are close to the early Welsh: Goodrich notes his resemblance to the Giant Herdsman figure who survives in Chrétien's *Yvain* (1989, 185). Powys heaps more yet into his novel: Porius rescues Myrddin from Nineue, and, as W. J. Keith notes (2004, 11), Arthur is presented as a Collingwoodesque cavalry leader. In this last context the figure of knowledge is also called Merlin the Emperor's Counsellor, again an adviser, but now in a wide-ranging educational mode.

Henry Treece, a poet of the heavily symbolic "New Apocalypse" style and also a schoolmaster, controlled his Celtic and historicist interests more than Powys did, in a series of novels, several of them dealing with Arthur. In his short, child-oriented *The Eagles Have Flown* (1952) two boys meet Artos and this story is told more fully and with more sex and violence in *The Great*

Captains (1956). Treece took a Collingwood position, seeing the Arthurian period as "the growing pains of our country" (Fisher, 1969, 24): his interest in historicity restricts a role for Merlin, but his complementary interest in Celticity does permit a druidic "Merddin" to appear briefly in both books and in the later *The Green Man* (1966).

A less somber sensationalist tone is struck by the American adventure writer and big game hunter Edison Marshall, who took the semihistorical Arthur as a point of departure in *The Pagan King* (1959). "The whitebeard gaffer, Merdin" is a "fierce old man with burning eyes" (8–9), and a lively unhistorical story ensues in which Arthur is the son of Igerne of Aberffraw, a fishermaid, and Merdin, though he is involved with Vivain, as she is here spelled, and is eventually stabbed to death by Elaine.

Rosemary Sutcliff is a major force in Arthurian historical fiction, but she is too scholarly to include Merlin, either in *The Lantern Bearers* (1959), a prize-winning juvenile reader's book with Arthur (as Artos) a minor figure, or in the major success *Sword at Sunset* (1963): indeed, for all the novel's aura of romance and mystery, it is in fact, as Dean notes, without any magic at all (1991, 64). A theatrical parallel was R. C. Sheriff's 1954 play *The Last Sunset,* highly successful in London, combining a historical and so Merlin-free Romano-British setting with a romance based on invented characters.

Novelists were rarely as historically rigorous as Sutcliff. *Twilight Province* (1967), by an Australian naval officer, George Finkel, published in Sydney, is set mostly in the northeast of England—historically accurate for early British-Saxon encounters. Mylan, also known as Aneurin, is the Merlin figure, who plays a facilitating role in a somewhat downbeat story—the narrator at the end doubts Arthur's survival.

Patriotic English politics can actually downgrade Merlin's knowledge: in *The Emperor Arthur* (1968) by the prolific English author and lexicographer Godfrey Turton, Merlin has a major, but negative role as a druid who has conspired with the Saxons. The link back to Richard Blackmore in the 1690s is presumably a coincidence, as there are many other inventions. Vivien's mother Niniane has been killed—with Excalibur—and Merlin is a suspect; nevertheless Vivien becomes Merlin's mistress, but knowing his pro-Saxon plans, arranges for the Saxons to burn him in a wicker cage (reversing the Roman allegation of what the druids did to their victims). Vivien marries the narrator Pelleas, who wrote this story. In addition to mild eroticism (Pelleas makes love to his lady actually in the lake), the book offers anti-Celtic prejudice in Merlin's treachery.

This negative feature is also found in *Artorius Rex* (1977) by John Gloag, an English writer and businessman. He claims historical and Celtic knowledge, but is consistently pro-Saxon: the historical Maelgwn Gwynedd has a court bard and tutor called "Myrddin (or Merlin as I shall call him henceforth in preference to his barbarous native name)" (49). Merlin espouses the cause of the Roman-Saxon alliance (fighting the Picts) and comes to feel that the British "however mixed their blood becomes, will always be mostly fools" (192).

American Arthurian historical novels tend to be less anxiously political or fussily historicist than the British: they usually offer a mix of romanticism and antiquarianism and see a more positive role for Merlin's knowledge, itself advisory or directly educational. Catherine Christian's *The Pendragon* was first published in 1978 in the United States as *The Sword and the Flame* but adopted the more Arthurian name on its British appearance in 1979 (not, as some sources say, the other way round). Quite learned in its details, the story is, as is common in historical fiction, told by a minor character, here Bedivere. He is a bard and will end the story as the new "Merlin"—no more than "a title of honour" (1979, 34)—since the previous one, Celidonius (a northern reference), is now "in some dark corner" in Brittany (499) after exercising a public role, both medieval, as Arthur's spokesman, and modern, running a spy network against Medraut. Like many of the inherently educational Merlins, his knowledge never conflicts with political power, and like a good teacher he simply retires, having taught Bedivere to replace him to transmit his "memory and the memory of the truths he lived by" (500).

Even more inventive and at greater distance from the tradition—the author calls it "a fantasy" in the acknowledgments—is Parke Godwin's *Firelord* (1980), to be the first in a trilogy. A regular writer of historical fiction, including some capable novels on Robin Hood, Godwin here makes Arthur part-Roman, with a mother named Flavia, but he also spends time north of the Hadrian's Wall where he becomes involved with Morgana, a Pict. Merlin does little in the action except predict and observe events and behave oddly: he addresses Arthur as "boyo" as if both are Dylan Thomas characters, and he appears finally in Avalon to entertain Arthur as a golden-haired boy juggling three balls in the air. The lack of conflict in Merlin's role vis-à-vis power is in part replaced by the suggestion that he is part of an internalized individual conflict: Raymond Thompson sees him as "a creation of Arthur's own imagination" (2000, 121), but this interesting development (in line with the notion that White's fifth novel is mostly a dream) is not elaborated in the text. There are American touches, both direct—Arthur addresses the historical prince

Maelgwn as Mal—and further-reaching, as Godwin develops a multicultural eclecticism as his characters and plot lines roam across ancient Europe. Where the English tend to realize their own politics, anti-German or even anti-Welsh, the Americans often have a more relaxed, Europe-wide, even melting-pot, approach to knowledge in the text.

The range of historicist novels is wide, including the low-temperature trilogy *The Crimson Chalice* (1976–80) by the British pot-boiler Victor Canning, which elaborates the "Arthur as cavalry leader" concept in a slow-moving narrative and uses an immortal Merlin principally as a plot device to save Arthur from difficulties—in a quaintly English touch, it leaves him at the end with Arthur's horse and dog. A livelier if barely historicist American treatment is Quinn Taylor Evans's *Merlin's Legacy—Dawn of Camelot* (1999), one of a five-book series in a well-known U.S. romance format. Marcus Merlinus is young and handsome: the charming Meg of Avalon sucks poison from his body when Morgan tries to murder him. But this is no common bodice-ripper: Meg dies, and returns for Merlin as an immortal, but also as a deer. A mix of sex and sorcery gives this novel vigor, if no special connection to knowledge or power beyond a shrewd aim at the market.

A more positive, though inherently subordinate, role is allotted to Merlin in a rewriting both knowledgeably historicist and seriously feminist, Marion Zimmer Bradley's *The Mists of Avalon* (1982)—Larrington calls it "path-breaking" (2006, 192). Here, as in Christian, "Merlin" is only a title, and the aged Taliesin hands it on to Kevin, who has two roles: one is to indicate that Morgaine has womanly generosity as well as feminist strength—though he is crippled she gives herself to him—and also to represent the rising power of the Christian church (one of the book's major historical themes), to which he defects, letting its clergy posses the regalia of Avalon. But in the surprising ending where Bradley adapts feminist paganism to Christianity through the figure of Mary, Kevin's actions as a Christianizing Merlin are seen as valid in historical terms.

The same period saw less powerful and less historicist feminist treatments. *The King's Damosel* (1976) by Vera Chapman is a Malory-based story about Lynett: she is raped by Bagdemagus (whose son abducted Guinevere back in Chrétien de Troyes' *Lancelot*), Merlin's advice helps her, she becomes a warrior, has Bagdemagus beheaded, and then goes on to achieve the grail. In a final feminist touch, it is the Sibyl, not Merlin, who is the concluding authority in the story. Sharan Newman's *Guinevere* (1981) is a more straightforwardly gendered text, realizing the story from the viewpoint of a woman whose pains and powers, some of them knowledge-linked, have been largely overlooked: to permit this focus Merlin is reduced to a somewhat oppressive relative with limited powers, but like most in feminist romance he comes to admire the heroine and her spirit. Fay Sampson's five-book series *Daughter of Tintagel* (1989–92) deploys her knowledge of Cornish tradition and a skillfully managed set of different viewpoints to give Guinevere for once a privileged viewpoint, but Merlin plays no major role, negative or positive: as in Malory he merely helps to establish Arthur before being disposed of off-stage by Nimue.

The modern masculinist bestseller, combining as it does some historicism with sadistic combat, has not neglected Merlin. Stephen Lawhead, an American living in Britain, has produced a series mixing history and myth with an eclectic hand. In *Merlin* (1988) the future sage, also known as Myrddin, studies early Welsh poetry with Blaise, his mother is the daughter of the Lady of the Lake (her father is King Avallach of Avalon), his father is Taliesin, he sings brilliantly and has foresight. Merlin's range of knowledge, here and elsewhere in the series, is only used to support, not in any way challenge, secular power. His adventures indicate the author knows the *Vita Merlini* and the early Welsh poems. Reasonably learned in Celticity, and meshing this with a firm Christian belief, vigorously structured and written, *Merlin* has an energy that overrides oddities like the potatoes that are anachronistically consumed (97). Lawhead's later *Pendragon* (1994) has Merlin, as Myrddin Emrys, tell the story of Arthur from kingship to passing: here Merlin has many powers—he arranges the sword in the stone, is a bard and Christian quasi-druid, he supervises Arthur's grail-like end—but he is effectively no more than a wise mediator of the narrative.

Less scholarly and more military has been the equally successful series by Bernard Cornwell, a prolific producer of battle fiction across the centuries. Starting with *The Winter King* (1995), part of a trilogy called *The Warlord Chronicles,* he makes Merlin a druid who is himself a warlord, with a territory based on the Glastonbury area, but in keeping with the violent and sensational tone of the series, his household is composed of deranged and physically impaired people: the caged mad king Pellinore speaks for the author and apparently the audience as "loving the horror" (85). Vivien, here known as Nimue, is always close to Merlin: at first as a troubled but not unsympathetic girl who is of Irish origin but, with some historical credibility, comes from an Gaelic kingdom in south Wales. She becomes Merlin's helper, rival, and eventually enemy in his quest to bring "the gods" back to an increasingly Christian Britain, but where Bradley saw this theme in terms of British religious history, Cornwell creates through the second novel, *Enemy of God* (1996), a hyper-real and often grisly quest for the thirteen pagan treasures of Britain, an idea also found in Patricia Kennealy-Morrison's 1980s Keltiad series.

Through a series of brutal battles, the warrior Arthur's story is told by Derfel, a bastard son of the Saxon King Aelle who is raised to become Arthur's right-hand warrior (and was once sworn brother to Nimue), an improbability itself realizing the "reassurance of fratricide" in Celtic-Saxon integration. Merlin's role in the story is similarly hyperbolic, both as demonic enemy and ultimate protector: as the trilogy ends in *Excalibur* (1997) his body, sacrificed by Nimue, floats behind Arthur's ship, protecting it in a storm as it sails off to the Otherworld. Finally he is simply a supportive spirit for the king, where previously, at least until Nimue ousted him from this role, he has been a proponent of pagan values in conflict with Arthur's Christianizing mission. The idea may be derived from Bradley, but it does make Merlin's knowledge a challenge to power that embeds some level of complexity in what otherwise seems merely a skillfully sensationalist set of action novels.

Merlin can be central at times and his knowledge more purposively educational. Mary Stewart, a successful writer of thrillers, chose Geoffrey of Monmouth as her source and Merlin as her focal figure in a series beginning with *The Crystal Cave* (1970). She offers both rationalism—Merlin is the son of Ambrosius and is trained as an engineer in the Roman army (hence Stonehenge)—and some mysticism. Though as Dean comments, Merlin is "clearly and unambiguously human" (1991, 68–69), he does have private visions, especially in his cave above Carmarthen where he communicates with "the sky-god Myrddin, he of the light and the wild air" (*The Last Enchantment,* 1979, 70): Watson has noted the frequent connection between the wind and "the presence of the god" (1989, 160).

The god gives Merlin occasional magical power as when he embeds in a stone altar a mythic sword for Arthur's eventual drawing, and on this basis Hildebrand has argued for "the importance of religion in Stewart's trilogy" with Merlin's "deeply personal" commitment to his own god central to the meaning of the texts (2001, 91–92), but this seems too narrow a focus. Rather, Stewart interweaves medieval ideas, including vague spirituality, the Arthurian narrative, Merlin's love for Nimue from the Vulgate, and his retirement from the *Vita,* into the Roman-origin historicism of modern England. The idea of the magic cave, Stewart has said,[8] comes from Edwin Muir's poem and she uses it as her epigraph. But in the mode of the realist novel the story tends to cover every plodding detail—the second book, *The Hollow Hills* (1973), is a notably slow account of Merlin's fostering of Arthur up to the point of kingship. Stewart spends much time speculating on motives for events and actions that romance could leave mysterious, suggestive: Merlin's lengthy debate with Igraine seems particularly banal (1973, 365–71) and Maureen Fries has noted "the bathos which occasionally envelops Stewart's Merlin" (1977, 261).

The Last Enchantment has at least more action to focus its progress, and it is largely without the currently popular levels of violence. Nimue, Lady of the Lake, is Merlin's lover and equal—Herman identifies her as "another of Stewart's strong women" (1984, 111) and while she does take his power, it is slipping from him and it is Morgause who ends his life with poison, but he escapes from his tomb to help Arthur defeat her and Morgan. By focusing on the story of Merlin as a clever, sometimes visionary figure, with his own wisely gratified ending, Stewart has substituted humanist romance for the myth of Arthurian power, and her thoughtful research and fluent writing do not replace the drama of a conflict between knowledge and power: Merlin as hero of his own bildungsroman is not very interesting or educational. Diana Wallace has seen Stewart more positively as making an "appropriation" which permits women writers "to ventriloquise male voices" (2005, 168) and suggests "it is precisely Merlin's 'otherness' that makes him a superlatively appropriate figure for the woman historical novelist, herself reassembling the mosaic of the past." (2005, 172)

Stewart filled the narrative gap the trilogy left with one more novel leading to the catastrophe. *The Wicked Day* (1983) begins with the words "Merlin is dead" (11), but though he escapes both his debilitation and his apparent tomb, he plays no role in a story that is itself a remarkably low-temperature transmission of the end of Arthur, notable only for treating Mordred with some sympathy.

Another British writer made Merlin central, but here the mode is more postmodern than humanist, entertaining rather than educational. Robert Nye, who had written a children's book *Taliesin* (1966), gained praise and a major prize for *Falstaff* (1976) and with even more bravura produced *Merlin* (1978). As in Stewart, Merlin is the central figure and plays no role in challenging power, but Nye incorporates other excitements, both sexual and sacrilegious, and jokes from learned to adolescent. John Matthews has taken the book seriously as "a subtle alchemy" that "plumbs the depths of Merlin's character" (1995, 322–23), but the ultimate impact of both Nye's learning and his wish to shock is thoroughly humanist: the sage teaches Arthur, outwits Nimue, knows all, and stays to the passing of Arthur as a hero of anarchic knowledge—Merlin figured as an author as fluent as Nye in a firmly Celtic context:

> Now, without sail, without oars, the draped barge
> passes out from the shore.
> It is black upon the waters and then gold.
> Little pig, listen.
> The wind in the reeds.
> *The laughter of Merlin!* (220)

One strongly educational element in Merlin fiction aims only at the younger market.[9] In England this starts as a cross between bourgeois children's adventures and a more myth-oriented approach. *Merlin's Magic* (1953) by "Helen Clare" (Pauline Clarke), is an example: Merlin is a young man who arranges an adventure hunt for his professor's children: effectively he is a tutor. They go back through time and, with some resonance of *That Hideous Strength* and *Nineteen Eighty-Four* help both King Arthur and Sir Walter Raleigh fight "the machine people" along "The Power River" (158). But the tone is less noble: "Nimue, in a fit of spite, had shut poor Merlin up under the stone" (123). More recent examples have more to say educationally: Margaret Mann's *The Merlin Set Up* (1997) is juvenile enough, with a tree-sprite and a jovial Merlin, but he possesses an informative interest in Teillard de Chardin's Christian quasi-theology. *Merlin's Mound* (2004) by Nigel Bryant (the translator of Robert de Boron) in essence teaches the inquiring young by linking the Iron Age artificial mound at Silbury Hill, Wiltshire, with the grail tradition.

Mythic intensification of that kind has been a feature of British children's Merlin fiction, whether in displaced form as in Alan Garner's *The Weirdstone of Brisingamen* (1960), which uses a magician called Cadellin Silverbrow, or Peter Dickinson's vigorous *The Weathermonger* (1968), set in a future Britain depopulated and severely damaged by "the change" caused by "the Necromancer" who lives on the Welsh borders on Mynydd Merddin ("Merlin Mountain"). This is an anti-Merlin story, apparently aimed against *That Hideous Strength,* as a boy and girl save the modern world from dangers deriving from medieval knowledge.

The mythic approach can move to America as in *Steel Magic* (1967) by "André Norton" (the prolific and often thoughtful Alice Norton). This translates the English "children in another world" model to the American Northeast, where the mysterious Mr. Brosius (clearly suggesting the ur-Merlin Ambrosius) welcomes two ordinary kids into an American Avalon where

Arthur fights with local help—Huon is a Native American version of Robin Hood: for the displaced Celtic warriors iron is as usual magic against fairies, but so, as the title suggests, is modern American steel.

Equally, the Americans to be educated can move to Merlin's own world, as in Edward Eager's *Half Magic* (1954) where a Toledo family and their children enjoy magic and instructive adventures in Arthurian Britain, and that pattern continues in more elaborate form in Molly Cochran and Warren Murphy's *The Forever King* (1992), where Al, a trouble-oriented youth, time-shifts to England and fulfills himself as Arthur's champion. Merlin is the facilitator in both these appropriation-by-travel books, and the pattern is strong: the 2007 film of Cooper's *The Dark is Rising* refocuses on an American boy relocated to Britain.

Some British examples combine Celticism with historicism as in Roy Turner's *King of the Lordless Country* (1971), an effectively structured narrative leading up to a triumphant battle against the Saxons led by the hero, here called Aruthr, not a name but an adjective meaning "terrible" in Welsh, with Gwenhwyfar as an Old Irish–style woman leader of warriors and Myrddin as a constant adviser. But American children's fiction is the main location for historicist Merlin, some in best-selling series form. In Robert Newman's amusing *Merlin's Mistake* (1970) and the rather more serious *The Testing of Tertius* (1973) Tertius is Merlin's godson in an invented Celtic Britain populated by Maloryesque characters like Princess Lianor and Sir Owain of Caercorbin. As usual the child is endangered but courageous, and the senior figures, notably Blaise and Merlin, are tolerant to youthful promise: as Newman's titles suggest, the old can be mistaken and the young can triumph.

Jane Yolen started a varied series where Merlin represents education towards self-development with *Merlin's Book* (1986), a collection of stories in which Merlin "is a different character in each tale" (xii). As usual, Yolen combines scholarship and imagination in a clear and attractive style, with a good deal of positive role models for girls—in "Evian Steel" the maternally strong Argente and the magically potent Morgan help a girl grow under the supervision of a Merlin who is friendly to feminism.

Yolen regenders the object of benign supervisory knowledge in *The Dragon's Boy* (1990), with a Merlin figure called Old Linn, and in the impressive *Young Merlin* trilogy, *Passager* (1996), *Hobby* (1996), and *Merlin* (1997), she represents Merlin as a boy with strange skills in a medieval world where events are a creative mix of the context of both Geoffrey of Monmouth and T. H. White—for example Vivien, a charming bard, sings a song about "Robin o' the Wood" when they are near Carmarthen. Yolen has said that she understands the inner meaning of Merlin as "a metaphor for the Maker" (1987, 21), and in this story she seems to combine, with characteristic subtlety, the meanings of maker as both poet and god.

One of the major rewriters of the Merlin tradition, directing the concept of knowledge into the empowerment of children, Yolen has been followed by others like T. A. Barron. His *The Lost Years of Merlin* series (1996–2000) combines an eclectic, or perhaps just imprecise, range of Celtic material—Irish as well as Welsh—and his philosophy is equally general: in the preface to the second book in the series, *The Seven Songs of Merlin* (1997), he comments: "Merlin's mythic powers sprang from both the conscious and the unconscious, just as his wisdom flowed from both nature and culture" (4).

Emersonian transcendence of this kind is foreign to the all-action style of another major producer, Jack Whyte, whose series *The Camulod Chronicles,* starting with *The Sky Stone* (1998), is an Irish-Welsh mix in which Merlin is Arthur's uncle-in-law, married to the Irish Ygraine's sister. Whyte's success stimulated his imagination: in *The Sorcerer: Metamorphosis* (2000) the wise man has become Caius Merlin Britannicus who is protected by King Derek of Ravenglum in the fortress of Mediobogdum. Merlin catches leprosy, but Arthur still becomes High King, with ethnically varied ladies, Shelagh, Ludmilla, and Turga.

Whyte moves Arthurian juvenile historicism across the border into Arthurian fantasy, another subgenre that has flourished, sometimes impressively, in America. The earliest moves in this direction were made within the modes of science fiction. As with the American appropriation stories, "André Norton" is again an initiator: *Merlin's Mirror* (1975), a book described by Taylor and Brewer as "one of the most competent" in this kind (1983, 317), is a classic science fiction text with Myrddin/Merlin the son of a Star Lord, born in Vortigern's time in a cave where an intergalactic beacon is located, as is an electronic mirror through which his distant family educates him, a pattern like that in Stewart's earlier *The Crystal Cave.* Merlin is a major figure in a conflict against Nimue, who represents those who feel the Star Lords just played with the earthly people.

Through this classic science fiction plot major elements of the whole Arthurian story are skillfully woven, including the cocooning of both Merlin and Arthur for the future in a life-preserving box. Other elements of the film *2001* appear in what Spivack and Staples call "an ingenious tour de force," but they also note its theme as "male rationalism and technology versus female intuition and nature" (1994, 26), a conflict where, as in the film *2001* itself, Nimue's side may seem the better, and Merlin's scientist knowledge may not seem triumphant. *Merlin's Mirror,* in this narrativizing of conflict as well as its polished style, is more searching than the science fiction use of the mage by Roger Zelazny. In his long story "The Last Defender of Camelot" (1980), Merlin is, as Goodrich puts it, "a dangerously atavistic and power-mad wizard" (1992, 48) and what at first seems a Californian tough guy called Du Lac fights one more time for the Arthurian ideal. Even more ultramodern but now bearing positive knowledge is the Merlin of Zelazny's second series of "Amber" novels where as a computer scientist he defends the world of Amber against the world of Chaos.

The move from science fiction to fantasy was easy for Merlin: Raymond Thompson commented in 1985 that his appearances in fantasy fiction were "about twenty to date" (49). H. Warner Munn, a writer who goes back to the days of H. P. Lovecraft and *Weird Tales,* had early work repackaged as *Merlin's Godson* after his *Merlin's Ring* (1974) was quite successful.[10] The first novel extended the transatlantic appropriation of Merlin by linking Atlantis as well as him to America. The second novel is, as Dean notes, both anti-English and pro-Catholic (1988, 73), but actually focuses on a godson to Merlin, Gwalchmei. His rapid and underrationalized adventures are classic fantasy fiction, but appropriation eventually appears; his last encounter is with Christopher Columbus, and so the power of Merlin's ring passes to the land that so much developed fantasy fiction.

In another part of the fantasy forest, the master of Merlin Gothic is the well-known British author Robert Holdstock. *Merlin's Wood* (1994) is a mystical account of Merlin's imprisonment in Brocéliande, where his knowledge transcends "the pain at the heart of the world" (145) and Vivien is "the vision of Magic" (158), all inset skillfully into a modern story of a family that is splitting up. His later *Celtika* (2001) is part 1 of *The Merlin Codex,* a drastically eclectic fantasy where Merlin is focus for the interweaving of Irish, Welsh, and classical traditions in a spirit more mind-expanding than just educational.

In Merlin fantasy his knowledge tends to become submerged in the author's own claims on imaginative excitement, as in the entertaining multiple-possibility narrative by Michael Coney, *Fang the Gnome* (1987), from his *The Song of Erith* series, where Merlin and Nimue tell highly improbable, even contradictory, Arthur stories. More focused is Fred Saberhagen's *Merlin's Bones* (1995), part-set in the near future of scientific manipulation, at the Stonehenge laboratory of Dr. Elaine Brusen, whose first name links with the Lady of Shalott (and Brusen was the handmaid to Elaine of Carbonek, mother of Galahad). But most of the action is back in the Dark Ages where the boy Amby (from Ambrosius) is being prompted by the buried Merlin to restore the lost Arthurian civilization. Saberhagen writes with vigor and clarity, both in battle scenes and mythic moments: the characteristic American syncretism is present—Vikings are involved—and Merlin's mystic knowledge is a lasting value against the power of secularist threats.

This kind of political theme is unusual in Merlin fantasy, including Saberhagen's earlier *Dominion* (1982), an energetic grotesque about vampirism and magic set mostly in modern Chicago, involving at some distance both Merlin, known as Falcon or Hawk, and an underdeveloped version of Vivien. More amusing is Peter David's *Knight Life* (2002, expanded from the 1987 version), set in New York. Morgan is a bag lady, Merlin an overgrown youth working in the Camelot Building for businessman Arthur Penn who is elected mayor. The sequel *One Knight Only* (2003) makes Penn president after 9/11, but modern tensions are elided into the epic of Gilgamesh, with an ending including both Merlin and the grail.

Merlin fiction for grown-ups can itself seem close to fantasy. In James Branch Cabell's *Jürgen* (1919) Merlin is the Arthurian prophet-magician, friendly to the learned and adventurous hero of this exotic compromise between Rabelais and sheer fantasy. Cabell's *Something about Eve* (1927) is a more mandarin fable where Merlin advises the devil-possessed but truth-seeking hero about chivalry—but only persuades him it too is an illusion. Walker Percy's *Lancelot* (1977), a realistic antiromance, has Robert Merlin as an elderly but sexually active film director, seen as malignant by the cuckolded but equally self-indulgent hero. A subtler version of this subgenre, where the Arthurian structure is used to isolate the inadequacies of modernity, including education, is by the Canadian Robertson Davies in *The Lyre of Orpheus* (1988). The Arthur-Guinevere-Lancelot triangle is readily identifiable in the modern university, and the plot involves the recreation of an imaginary E. T. A. Hoffman opera *Arthur of Britain, or the Magnanimous Cuckold*. The central story wryly implies how the narrator, both priest and academic, is, through his self-seeking use of uncertain knowledge to retain, or rescue, his own authority, a sadly reduced self-knowing modern form of Merlin, the image often deployed by twentieth-century poets.

Merlin has been seen as behind Morgan the old Welsh adviser in John Steinbeck's *The Cup of Gold* (1929) and the figure of Doc in *Cannery Row* (1945) (see Mathis, 2002, 31, 68), but his most overt appearances have been in modernizations. He appears in Steinbeck's unfinished rewriting of Malory, *The Acts of King Arthur and His Noble Knights* (1976), as a figure with some modernity both psychological—"Merlin knew the winding channels of the human mind" (4), and banal—he describes himself to Arthur as "the powerful and learned man that gets his come-uppance from a stupid, clever little girl" (332). Thomas Berger's reworking of Malory, *Arthur Rex* (1978) further diminishes Merlin's knowledge to "craft," "japes," and "a unique sense of irony" (3, 5, 18). He recognizes that Vivien's "powers far exceeded his own" (105) and his achievements are limited, more what Thompson calls Berger's "literary legerdemain" (1989, 146) than real magic, though he does give Arthur a magical beard and his "cave of alchemy" (109) is equipped with a gramophone, telephone, and cinema. While Berger's approach might well seem no more than opportunistic joking, an abandonment of knowledge, it has been seen as postmodern wisdom by Suzanne MacRae (1992), and by Thompson, via its "comic distancing," as providing a "lesson in comedy" (1989, 150).

A negatively ironic Merlin appears in Naomi Mitchison's satirical fable *To The Chapel Perilous* (1955), in which two modern journalists investigate the possible appearance of the holy grail. Merlin is the monarchist editor of the *Camelot Chronicle,* always planning to join his mistress Nimue, the Paris correspondent, and write his novel. A Scot, a radical, and a feminist, Mitchison sees little value in a conservative English editor, however knowledgeable, and Merlin is a figure of fun and weakness, in a novel full of challenging ideas, including a sense of religion as a value against vulgar modernity.

Merlin's knowledge appears more validly educational in the North American subgenre of semi–fantasy fiction for grown-ups. Robert Nathan's *The Elixir* (1971) is a curiously dated piece of Anglophilia in which in the early twentieth century a Harvard graduate meets a modern version of Niniane: she drove a car in the desert in the First World War. After a romance, she rescues him from a plane hijack and with the help of a Mr. Jones, called Myrdin (*sic*), the American has adventures stretching back through British history. More thoughtful American modernity is the focus of *Triad* (1973) by the actress and journalist Mary Leader, which presents a young woman in Michigan who is psychically possessed by her analyst, Dr. Ambrose. As his name suggests, he is a Merlin figure and she is herself in a way Rhiannon/Niniane, looking back to earlier texts and scholarship. This is in part a psycho-thriller in the tradition of Margaret Millar, a successful Americanization of the Merlin, and also the anti-Merlin, tradition. Alike in innovation is *Morlock Night* (1979) by the American K. W. Jeter. In London in 1892, Dr. Ambrose, that is Merlin, creates a new Arthur to fight the Morlocks who have hijacked the time machine from H. G. Wells's novel, to which this is a sequel. The novel is crisply written, with some thoughtful elements. Modern knowledge is shown to be valid, as the narrator Edward Hooker remains a rationalist, but with limited success—and he finally loses the New Woman whom he loves.

Merlin on Screen

By contrast with the riches—and sometimes the poverty—of the novel, film has not as a genre been very welcoming to Merlin. He does appear in highly negative form in the many versions of Twain's *Connecticut Yankee*—Kevin Harty lists fourteen of these in various formats, almost all comedies (1999). The Yankee can have the vigor of Will Rogers or the charm of Bing Crosby (in 1931 and 1949), but Merlin is only a comic villain as the films avoid both the searching satire of the novel and its terrible climax. The fairly distant 1998 version, *A Knight at Camelot,* with Whoopi Goldberg as Dr. Vivian Morgan, is of some interest, combining as it does recognition of scientific knowledge with the possibilities of female and African American self-empowerment—and finally, directly contrary to Twain, showing Merlin as actually behind Dr. Morgan's progressive actions.

Merlin has suffered on the screen in part because there have been so few major Arthurian films. The word "Morte" itself must have been a handicap, nor has Arthur's regal status helped in antimonarchist America. Merlin does make appearances in various American Arthurian films, but he tends to be a bearded ancient, either a wise man or, as in the 2004 *King Arthur,* a wild one, without any of the humanist modernization that surrounds the often cowboy-like Lancelot as played by Robert Taylor in *Knights of the Round Table* (1953) or Richard Gere in *First Knight* (1995).

John Boorman's *Excalibur* (1981) does give a major educational role to the magician, and in the planning stages "Merlin" was the film's title (Umland and Umland, 1996, 143–44). He is the first figure seen, stalking the world when Uther attains the kingship; his magic is potent, as in the scene where Uther rides a mist—"the dragon's breath"—into Tintagel to impregnate Igraine. He is also thematically central, bearing like a national *Naturmensch* the New Age quasi-Jungian mantra that the land and the king are one. He also suffers from it: when Arthur drives Excalibur into the earth between the lovers Lancelot and Guinevere (a moment borrowed from the Tristan and Isolde story), the sword enters "the spine of the dragon," the core of creation, and also goes right through creation's priest, Merlin. He was about to destroy Morgana, and she triumphs as a result. But as in many modern versions Merlin comes back, in a dream—White's *The Book of Merlyn* was published not long before the film was made—and helps Arthur in battle, as he once did in the Vulgate, with a protective mist.

As a figure of natural harmonic wisdom and eco-national seriousness (fig. 25), Merlin looks towards modern concerns, though Nicol Williamson's playing of him as an eccentric bully—he apparently based the characterization on his English master at school—tends to reduce the figure's impact, as does the on-screen power of Helen Mirren as his rival Morgan. The inherent counterrationalism of those presences itself meshes with the modern interest in superrational knowledge, and the film conceptually and stylistically looks towards fantasy. Presumably as a response to this success, 1982 saw *Merlin and the Sword,* with a strong cast and directed by the capable Clive Donner, but, Harty comments, "one of the silliest films ever made about the Arthurian legend" (1999, 25). A later challenger for this title is *Merlin: The Return* (2000), a clumsy effort, with the fatuous English comedian Rick Mayall as Merlin.

Television has never treated Merlin with the seriousness film has at times reached, whether as Twain's villain or Boorman's conveyer of mythic wisdom. The small screen has minimized his role, as in the U.S. *Mr Merlin* series (1982) where a wise garage owner supervises the development of a young mechanic as a demoticized Arthur—Goodrich calls the series "trivialized" (1989, 185). Though the man of knowledge was the hero of the 1998 television series *Merlin,* written by Edward Khmara (also found in trilogy novel form, 1999, by James Mallory), and Arthur is of little interest, Merlin's role is merely comic, especially in the sense of having a happy ending. He leaves his entombment with Nimue to see the end of Arthur's world (Robinson seems an influence), and after Camlan, with the help of a magical horse, he finds Nimue again, and with one last piece of self-helping, knowledge-free magic, changes himself back to youth and her wizened face becomes the beauty of Isabella Rossellini.

Baudry saw this series as having "infantile and boy-scout moralizations" (2007, 355), but this romanticized Merlin was so successful—in part because it was very well made—it generated a weak sequel, *Merlin's Apprentice* (2000), stressing the possible knowledge of youth. That was the major focus of the 2008 series *Merlin* through which the BBC sought to exploit the youth-oriented (and so advertiser-pleasing) success of its recent *Doctor Who* and *Robin Hood* series. With a conceivably knowing link back to Geoffrey of Monmouth, Merlin is a young boy whose magical capacities are pressed into royal service, but the program emphasizes modern electronic substitutes for knowledge: its website offers games and stresses the cast members' televisual histories; it is extremely difficult to identify the writers of the series. In spite of, or because of, this banality, the new series has proved highly acceptable to television channels and viewers around the world, as have many other modern and not always very searching formations of Merlin and his myth.

International Merlin

Peter H. Goodrich, in a scholarly and tolerant essay, has outlined the fortunes of what he calls "The New Age Mage" (1992), where Merlin is a totem of psychic self-improvement, a substitute for education. He notes that Merlin's value has not been only as a means of access to a world beyond the self, but also, being essentially a Western European figure, as a way of letting writers, notably Anglophone ones, avoid the distinctly Eastern character of much mystical thought (1992, 44). While the occult Merlin can be traced back to the Renaissance mage, he has recently flourished as an alternative to, or just an extension of, individualism, at times with sources in one of the founders of that personalized science, psychiatry, Jung himself. Emma Jung and Marie Louise von Franz, in *The Grail Legend,* devote their last five chapters to Merlin. Taking him as "the archetypal image," who hybridizes a number of "semi-human nature beings" (1986, 350, 352), they see his function as "a form of projected consciousness" (355) which "opens up a direct and personal approach to the collective unconscious" (360). They see the red and white dragons having alchemical significance as "the psychic problem of the opposites" (357) and though his trickster element comes from the Devil (355), his laugh is "the result of his more profound knowledge of invisible connections" (363).

This may seem free-ranging enough, but later they connect him with Jung's reading of Mercury, with the Celtic Cernunnos, with medieval Joachite visionary material, with Solomon, and with himself being a version of the grail. But while these might be seen as a set of self-contradictions, the views nevertheless cohere in the concept of the multiple potential of the individual: the ultimate connection is to see Merlin, with Heinrich Zimmer, as "the Self, the inner wholeness to which Percival should attain through the quest of the Grail" (1939, 150).

The Jungian approach has been popular on an academic level, as in *The Death of Merlin* (1989) by the Rudolf Steiner follower Walter Johannes Stein, and in Charlotte Spivack's essay collection *Merlin versus Faust* (1992), including Goodrich's thoughtful survey "The Alchemical Merlin." Jean Markale's work has developed from quite scholarly analyses of Celtic culture, as in *Women of the Celts* (1975), into the esoteric mythicism of his *Merlin l'Enchanteur* (1981), translated as *Merlin, Priest of Nature* (1995), not to mention his *La Fille de Merlin* (2000), a post-Arthur novel about Merlin's daughter Gwendolyn, who is loved by Taliesin—with almost no mention of her father. More popular projections of this submerging of knowledge in and through the sensitive self are by well-known figures in the field like Deepak Chopra—the preface to his novel *The Return of Merlin* (1995) speaks of "waking up the wizard that sleeps deep within all of us" (1995, "The Key to Merlin," unpaginated)—and R. J. Stewart, both in his own *The Prophetic Vision of Merlin* (1980) and in his leadership of the "Merlin Conference" essay collection series, starting with *The Book of Merlin* (1987). This approach is also found in much of John Matthews's work, especially *Merlin: Shaman, Prophet, Magician* (2004).

There is a wide spectrum of subscholarly mystical Merlin publications (many, puzzlingly, coming from southern England), ranging through the sorcery self-help guide *The Way of Merlyn: The Male Path in Wicca* (1990) by Ly Warren Clarke and Kathryn Matthews to the admittedly lightweight *Merlin the Immortal* (1984) by Courtney Davis and Peter Quiller, which at least has one of the best Merlin jokes: a moral discussion by Myrddin is entitled "Anyone for Tenets?" (1984, unpaginated). Presumably not a joke is Dave Gannaway's *The Merlin Connection* (1997): the connection is "to experience the flow of good into your life" (3), nor even Charles E. Smith's *The Merlin Factor: The Key to the Corporate Kingdom* (1995). This offers business workshops in "successful and satisfying change for individuals and organizations alike" (2) and cites a successful consultation with a food products company where Smith advised them on optimal ways of inserting broccoli into cans: this sequence is titled "The Sword in the Soup." In contrast, there seems some possible sense in Douglas Monroe's Minnesota-based *The Lost Books of Merlyn* (1998), a bumper collection of very broadly educational pamphlets, recipes, advice about magic, Celticity, and curiosa, all focusing on a Merlin who is buried in Mexico.

As in the last three works, the mystical and the empirical can collide, and the real Merlin industry is another example of reductive modernity. Finding the bones of a mythical hero has been in recent decades a myth of true knowledge, combining and empowering as it does the modern obsessions with personalized identity and empirical fact. Like the real Robin Hood and King Arthur and scores of other yet unlocated mythic cadavers, Merlin's historicity and resting place have been a matter of concern. There may well be some elements of historicity in the Cumbrian Myrddin, as there surely is in his context, and this led Nikolai Tolstoy to produce *The Quest for Merlin* (1985). This mix of real scholarship and pure speculation, characteristic of this kind of hero-hunting, not only feels Myrddin was "a pagan druid or bard" who was present at Arfderydd "where paganism made its last fiery stand" but goes so improbably far as to assert that "It is possible to identify Merlin's sylvan retreat" (29, 52, 53), and offers photographs of the site, in Hart Fell in southern Scotland. Tolstoy generally proceeds via the chain of dubious argument and rapidly cumulating assumptions that can pass in the media for intensive research, but the book has at least a sense of focus not found in his long, learned, but also rambling sub-Tolkien novel *The Coming of the King* (1985), the first, and so far only, in a promised series of four to comprise "The Tale of Myrddin." Tolstoy does build his castles on a base of credible scholarship, unlike Norma Lorre Goodrich, whose *Merlin* (1987) asserts the historicity of both Arthur and Merlin, "who was probably his junior by twenty-five years" (5). In *Merlin and the Discovery of Avalon in the New World* (2000) Graham Phillips claims with an air of improbability not found even in his work on King Arthur and Robin Hood that Merlin settled in North America. The alleged proof involves Freemasons, Rosicrucians, and the Old Irish *Voyage of Mael Dun:* Phillips confides not only that Merlin had a vision of the Statue of Liberty but also that "Shakespeare was killed because of what he knew about Merlin" (11).

International as he has become as a quasi-educational figure representing historicity and its fantasy projections, wide-ranging Celticity, the training of the sensitive self, and the imaginative child, as well as films from banal to romantic, Merlin can still have powerful localized meaning. In Germany Tankred Dorst, meshing the power of Brechtian theater with the sense of visionary values that the German Romantics created in the myth, has created with Ursula Ehler the major performance piece *Merlin oder Das wüste Land* (1981), which has had varied produced versions. In this spectacular dystopian epic Merlin "seeks refuge from the horrors of history in the timelessness of nature" (Schwab, 1989, 105). However, Merlin finally retires with Vivien, and so there is retained "a little bit of the usual Arthurian hope," if only in personal terms (Müller, 2003, 227). A more quietist politics is at the heart of Alvaro Cunqueiro's engaging *Merlin and Company* (1996, in Spanish, 1955), about Don Merlin who, after Arthur's death, is a generous host to Donna Guinevere. He has Europe-wide status as a medical graduate of Montpellier (he matriculated at eight), and his knowledge is special whether low-level—he teaches a dog to whistle and mends an hourglass—or more exotic, when repairing the bishop of Paris's magical parasol (it banishes rain) and saving Lady Aquitaine from demonic enchantment as a hind.

The French retain a special interest in the myth as major creators of Merlin the romantic enchanter, and Baudry has explored their continuing productivity with enthusiasm (2007). A Breton sense of resistance to modernity is coded in Théophile Bryant's *Le Testament de Merlin* (1975) about "Merlin, l'immortel commandeur de la Celtie" (266) who goes so far as to kill Mordred in the final battle and then retires to Brocéliande with Vivien. Michel Rio's novels

Merlin (1989) and *Morgana* (1999) rework the Arthurian traditions further in the French tradition, with Merlin as a figure of love, subtlety, and artistic insight. René Barjaval in *L'Enchanteur* (1984) deploys the full medieval French connection rather than its nineteenth-century Breton and aesthetic developments. Here Merlin has established the Round Table, initiated the grail quest, and (looking back to the Didot *Perceval*) has even been Perceval's adviser. But Barjaval does not ignore the modern Merlin: after he finally states that the grail knights will return, "not in blood but in light" and that the grail "always remains nearby" (469–70), in an Apollinaire-like ending he joins Vivien on an isle in the lake, among birds and flowers, to live "since that day in an invisible room, a room of air, a room of love" (470–71). The opposite to this serious sensitivity is the very successful television comedy series *Kaamelott* (2005), a cross between Monty Python and French peasant comedy with Merlin as a shape-shifting joker. A more fully modern and European Merlin as *Naturmensch* is produced by the Dutch writer Ron Langenus in *Merlin's Return* (1993). He combines themes from White, fantasy and ecology, where Myrdinn (*sic*), living in a Britain here democratically named "Scowaleng," teaches the knights that "a tree is worth more than a pot full of money" (154).

Music has been a medium of some international Merlin activity as in Elmer Bernstein's only moderately successful 1983 musical *Merlin* (the *New York Times* felt that the splendid magical illusions were its only "strong suit," Ross, 1983); in 2003 the Spanish first production of Coutts's 1895 *Merlin* with Isaac Albeniz's 1902 music; and the equally substantial but less grand *Merlin the Rock Opera* (1999) by the English writer/director Victoria Heward, scored by the "progressive rock musician" Fabio Zuffanti (Nastali, 2002, 151).

The name Merlin has often become a worldwide unproblematized modern shorthand for the power of science, whether in the name of the engine that powered the Spitfire or the more peaceable Medical Emergency Relief International—and in a staggering variety of lesser instances, gathered by Goodrich (2002). In personalized terms Merlin figures tend today to advise and so validate the subjective identity of the modern person, not the socialized human set among nature of the early Celtic material of German Romanticism. The white beard that medievalizing Romanticism gave Merlin has made him an educationally transgenerational grandfather figure in the time of Freudian dissent with parents, as seen in his multicultural avatars Obi-Wan Kenobi, Dumbledore, and Gandalf. It is true that the modern Merlin's knowledge can still be political, as it was in the Middle Ages through to the eighteenth century, but the politics tend now to be personal, and his value is educational, developmental, and transferable to modern individuals, not to any larger formation of power as in the past: the constant modern image of Merlin as old, bearded, and eccentric, is the way in which the power of the modern individual controls through irony the force of knowledge which it so patently lacks.

But if modern culture tends to individualize and ironize knowledge as education, structures of public authority still exist as they ever did, and they still interrelate dialectically with knowledge, both relying on it and attempting to control it. The pressure on knowledge to conform is everywhere. Teachers and academics are now forever writing documents to explain their methods and intentions, undergoing various controls and assessments, required to be useful to business and to public bodies, pressed to bring in research funding but only able to access it within certain externally constructed parameters: such people have a clear sense of the extent to which knowledge is still under constraint. And the effect of those pressures can go well beyond pedagogical irritation. In recent years people including a Turkish historian, a Russian investigative journalist, an Iranian feminist, an Israeli pacifist, an Islamic secularist, have all felt the heavy, sometimes brutally heavy, hand of power as a result of their intended contributions to knowledge. And should that range of negative examples seem ethnocentrically Western, the Anglophone world has its modern Merlins. Robert Oppenheimer's long harassment by officialdom would seem to qualify him, let alone his friendship at Berkeley with Jean Tatlock, daughter of the Merlin scholar discussed in chapter 1. Even closer to home, and even more troubling, is to ask just what Dr. David Kelly, the Welsh-born British weapons inspector in Iraq, knew and was going to say in 2003 that led to the government pressure that caused his suicide—if that was indeed why he was found dead in a wood near Oxford: a Merlinesque end that the Internet is still debating (Baker, 2007).

If knowledge is of value it must bear danger to someone who will be discomforted by it, or wants to profit by it secretly, and so would prefer it not to remain in the hands of those who have developed it. Knowledge is, like the club carried into the royal court by the ragged child Merlin, a weapon of disproportionate power. The story of Myrddin/Merlin across a thousand years is the story of constant re-formations of the conflict of knowledge and power, re-formations made in terms of—and so revealing—the institutions that mediate knowledge and power in those periods, and also re-formations governed by the changing production of both knowledge and power across time.

To study the development and the variety of the Myrddin/Merlin myth over a thousand years is not only to explore an intriguing variety of literary forms and symbolic stories: it is also to trace the consistent conflict between knowledge and power, and to see how changing cultures and their contexts represent and evaluate that conflict in constantly changing, sometimes disturbing, but always dynamic ways. Merlin may appear as a boy, a peasant, an old woman, or in modern times an as an East Coast gentleman, an eccentric professor, a rural exile, but those transformations are forms of camouflage, not evidence of weakness. He is still Merlin, and knowledge, however much it is pressured by power, is still knowledge. Its possessors remain capable, at their own danger, like Socrates or Galileo or Martin Luther King, and many lesser but still crucial practitioners of knowledge, of speaking truth to power.

Notes

Chapter 1. British Myrddin-Merlin

1. Comment on and translations of the Myrddin poems can be found in Bollard, 1990, 13–54. The translations used here are more literal and closer to the original. The poem "Afallen" ("Apple Tree") is often called "Afallennau," "Apple Trees," because a series of stanzas starts with the word "Apple Tree": but only one tree is discussed throughout, and the plural title is misleading. "Oian" or "Hoian" ("Little Pig") is similarly often called "Oianau," "Little Pigs." Bollard avoids this confusion by translating the Welsh plurals as "The Apple Tree Stanzas" and "The Little Pig Stanzas."

2. The most recent discussion of the texts and the people and events possibly connected to them is in the wide-ranging Koch, 2006; the entry on Myrddin, 1322–26, is by Brian Frykenberg.

3. Rachel Bromwich discusses this matter and doubts the assumption that Rhydderch was Gwenddolau's opponent, see Bromwich, 1978), 504–5; Rowland, 1990, 108, notes that no source before Geoffrey of Monmouth places Rhydderch at Arfderydd; see for a full discussion Miller, 1975, 98–117; see also Koch, 1997, xxxii–xxxiii n. 3, and Koch, 2006, 1652–53.

4. The poems have not been edited together nor are all yet fully annotated and glossed. For a recent discussion of them see Frykenberg, in Koch, 2006, 1322–23. "Myrddin and Taliesin," "Apple Tree," and "Little Pig" (and "Birch Tree") are all in *Llyfr Du Caerfyrddin* ("The Black Book of Carmarthen," 1982. For "Myrddin and Gwenddydd," see Williams, 1924, 114–21; for "Commanding Youth," see Jarman, 1951–52; for "Myrddin in the Grave," see *The Red Book of Hergest,* 1911, 5: this poem's title was formerly translated as "The Separation Song of Myrddin in the Grave," but Marged Haycock has recently argued for "Diffuse Song" (2004, 898).

5. The Cornish scholar O. J. Padel has resurrected the idea of Geoffrey shaping much, especially the Cumbrian Myrddin/Merlin, see Padel, 2006, 37–65. His case relies on stating that "Afallen" and "Oian" are the earliest Cumbrian poems and Myrddin is not named in them (41). But they are Myrddin's own monologues; three other Cumbrian-related poems, not spoken by him, all name him, as he does himself in the dialogue with Taliesin. Padel also asserts (37–38) that Jarman did not associate the name Myrddin with the Cumbrian material, but this is quite contrary to Jarman's final essay on the topic, in *The Arthur of the Welsh,* where among other Cumbrian Myrddin references things he sees "Afallen" as "the oldest existing document of the Myrddin legend" (Bromwich and Jarman, 1991, 118).

6. There is another possible transitional name Ceidyaw: he was father to Gwenddolau, and the name persisted in south Wales, see Bromwich, 1978, 307: this as a version of Cedfwy is supported by the linguistic data cited in Jarman, 1951, 34.

7. For a text of these stories, see Galyon and Thundy, 1980, 3–11; also see Geoffrey of Monmouth, 1973, Appendix 1, 277–34. The most recent discussion of the Kentigern material is in Koch, 1997, lxxvi–xxx.

8. "Llallogan," taken by the editor to mean "dear one," also appears in a poem dated as early as the ninth century in the *Canu Llywarch Hên* ("The Poetry of Llywarch the Old," 1935), 155; Jenny Rowland has improbably suggested that it is the northern Lailoken "before his madness" and on a visit to Powys, recognized by Llywarch, himself originally from the north, 1990, 539.

9. One of the key features, and difficulties, of Welsh (and Irish) is the recurrent change of initial consonants under a range of circumstances, called mutation. The change from *m* to *f* is only one of these.

10. The Breton Conan Meriadoc, called Cynan in *Armes Prydein* and Welsh tradition, was the traditional Welsh founder of Brittany and is given a substantial role by Geoffrey: he is thought the most likely bearer of this name, or a version of it, to be the traditional prophesied protector of the Welsh, by Griffiths, 1937, 118; and Clarke agrees, 1973, 175–76. Bromwich supports Cynan Meriadoc on the grounds of a deliberate Breton-pleasing emphasis in the influential early prophetic poem *Armes Prydein,* 1978, 317–18.

11. On place-names in Wales see Davies, 1957; and Richards, 1998.

12. This summary is based on Basil Clarke's edition and translation (Geoffrey of Monmouth, 1973).

13. The Morrígan has a malign avatar as a raven, and in Welsh tradition Owain, Morgan's son by Urien of Rheged (a surprising connection as both men are historical figures), is attended by a flight of warrior ravens in the Mabinogion story *Breuddwyd Ronabwy* ("The Dream of Rhonabwy").

Chapter 2. Medieval Merlin

1. Wace, 1999.

2. See Section 5, "From Epic to Romance," in Southern, 1953.

3. The number of lines in the *Merlin* has been variously interpreted: Paris had 502 in his edition, a number of commentators say, as if vaguely, 500, but there are 504 in Alexandre Micha's recent edition, Robert de Boron, 1979.

4. French authors have tended to be skeptical of the Bleddri-Blaise link: Villemarqué (1862, 147) favored the Breton St. Loup, via the Breton for wolf, as being behind the name, while Micha (1980, 190) expressed his doubts on the somewhat unimaginative grounds that while Bleddri was an oral storyteller, Blaise was a writer of narratives: this may, however, be the point of the contact, both to preserve and change the tradition. The best recent summary of the pro-Bleddri position is by the Welsh scholar Rachel Bromwich (1991, 273–98), see especially 286–88.

5. Rupert T. Pickens (1984) is against Robert's authorship, but it is supported by Linda M. Gowans (1987)

6. The 1953 film *Knights of the Round Table,* starring Robert Taylor and Ava Gardner, ends much like this, with Perceval in the context of the achieved grail after the death of Arthur—except that it is Lancelot (Taylor), not Merlin, who is still alive to share this spiritualized chivalric future with him.

7. For a discussion of this period and its events see Baldwin, 1986, especially Chapter 9, "Narrative: The Great Conquests and the Victory at Bouvines," 191–219.

8. When referring directly to a text, its spelling of this character's name will be used, but in general references to the figure character she will throughout be called Vivien.

9. There were some Merlin loyalists among the *Lancelot* scribes: Kennedy reports that a number of the manuscripts replace the brisk account of his birth to a girl and an incubus with Robert's fuller, more Christian account of Merlin's birth (2003, 22).

10. John Rhŷs suggested that behind Niniane was the potent, man-controlling Rhiannon of the *Mabinogion* (1891, 284). W. A. Nitze rejected this idea (1943, 78), then rejected Niniane itself in favor of the Irish name Béfind (1954); Eric P. Hamp saw "no way of getting *Niannonn* from *Riannon* via established and accepted channels" (1954). But the Vulgate says she had "a name in Welsh that sounds in French as if she said 'I will do nothing.'" (I.281). If the words heard as "ferai rien" were "feerie Rhian," Rhys's suggestion might be back in operation. Jean Markale comments on this, 1995, 205 n. 4.

11. The pioneer Celticist Skene thought "hwimleian" was a woman's name and Villemarqué argued that this could give a form in French like "Vivleian" which could adapt to the classically shaped Vivian/Vivienne. However, A. O. H. Jarman, the most recent editor of the poems, is clear that this is in fact merely a compound word translatable as "pale wild wanderer." It would seem Paris was right when he traced the source to the Celtic nature of the Ninian version of the name—though the recorded holder of it is a male saint. Nitze pointed this out in his skeptical review of the issue, but he later accepted Ninian as the most likely source. See Skene, 1868; Villemarqué, 1842, 1:49; *Llyfr Du Caerfyrddin,* 1982, 151; Paris, 1886, xlv n. 1; Nitze, 1943, 78–79 and 1954.

12. Lucy A. Paton says that "the Guinebaut theme stands nearer the early Celtic material" than the Merlin-Niniane story, see the chapter on "Niniane and Merlin" in Paton, 1960, 207.

13. The French word is in fact "astrenomie" but the translator comments in an earlier note that as this would have involved operations much closer to astrology, that is the more appropriate translation, *Lancelot-Grail,* 1.179 n. 8.

14. See Vinaver, 1956, and 1990, 1269 (on Torre and Pellinore); Muir, 1957; Nitze, 1936; and Roussineau, 1996, xvi–vii.

15. Some scholars felt the post-Vulgate author was inventing a text to avoid elaborating his story, and a Spanish author later provided it, but recent scholarship tends to assume there was a now lost French version. See Bogdanow, 2006, 342–52.

16. *Arthour and Merlin*, 1973, 1979. The work is often titled *Of Arthour and Merlin,* a title given at the beginning of the text, but this apparent reference to Latin *de,* "concerning" seems unnecessarily complex and *Arthour and Merlin* seems the most sensible title. That appears on the cover of Macrae-Gibson's two volumes, while inside "Of" is added.

17. The word "woned" in 4446 is a problem: taking it as meaning "dwelled" and "withouten" as "outside" gives the improbable sense of Nimiane as a place name; "woned" can have more general meanings like "inhere in" and "be accustomed to" but these do not make sense either. It could be a scribal error, perhaps for "I wene."

18. The philosopher and his contexts, mostly classical, are discussed by Mary Hamel (1984, 42– 44), though she does not link him with Merlin.

19. Lovelich, 1913, 1932, and 1932. Two remaining volumes, with introduction and notes, never appeared.

20. On Malory's relation to his period see "Fifteenth Century History," in Field, 1998, 47–71; "A grete angur and unhappe: Sir Thomas Malory's Arthuriad," Chapter 3 of Knight, 1983; Riddy, 1996; and Hanks and Brogdon, 2000.

Chapter 3. English Merlin

1. See Cervantes, 2000: a butler impersonates a hell-derived Merlin to terrify Sancho Panza, 727–78; Rabelais, 1955: a monk comments on a letter that its "style is like Merlin the Prophet. You can read all the allegorical and serious meanings into it that you like," 163.

2. Shakespeare, 2002, 3.1, 144–46; 1992, 3.2, 79–93; the speech is not in the Quarto and its authenticity has been doubted, but John Kerrigan argues for its being an authentic insert parodying prophecies as they became less admired (1983, 195–245, 221–26).

3. See Michelsson, 1999, 105–10, and Strong, 1983, 133–35. For Cumberland's role and Pendragon Castle see Williamson, 1920, 106–10: Michelsson and Strong give 1590 as the date but the archive cited in Williamson indicates 1592.

4. Harington also wrote a book about the water closet, which he apparently designed, called *The Metamorphosis of Ajax* (1596), punning on the long-lasting slang

term for a lavatory, "a jakes": Harington sometimes called himself Ajax and he is probably the original for Shakespeare's Jacques in *As You Like It*.

5. Jonson had some enthusiasm for the Arthur myth in his 1619 conversations with Drummond of Hawthornden, see "Ben Jonson's Conversations with William Drummond of Hawthornden." Jonson, 1925, 136. But by 1640, when his "An Execration on Vulcan" was published, he felt the medieval material, including "Errant Knighthood" and "Merlins Marvailes," was "proper stuffe," (1947, 205–6, lines 66–67 and 71). Jonson's acceptance of Camden's skepticism about the Arthur and Merlin myth is discussed in Peacock, 1987, 173.

6. In the Latin poem *Mansus* of 1639 the young Milton imagined himself writing a national epic focused on Arthur and the heroic Britons, see Milton, 1931, 293. A more general reference in the following year in *Epithaphium Damionis* includes a dismissive comment on Merlin and his deceptive treatment of Igraine (Milton, 1931, 296). Any pro-Arthur position weakened as Milton grew more radical and more aware of the historiographical problems with Geoffrey of Monmouth; see on the historiography, Brinkley, 1932, 126–31; and on the politics, Hill, 1977, 360–61.

7. Dearing suggests (Dryden, 1996, 288) he was influenced by Bouchaut's Emine, Arthur's sister; but as they are lovers in Dryden, this seems as unlikely as the occasional favoring, as a source, of Emiline, the mother of Tristram, found in *The Faerie Queene*, 6.2.29, 2.

8. Dearing states that this title only belonged to a pirate version, Dryden, 1996, 283.

9. The first edition was in fact only attributed to "the author of *The New Timon*," which had also been issued anonymously, but Lytton claimed authorship in the 1849 reprint.

10. Percy insists on the Northern origins of chivalry in his "Essay on the Ancient Metrical Romances," Appendix II of Percy, 1966 [1765]), 3, 341–51.

11. The plan is reprinted in Ricks, 1987, 256.

12. Tennyson's concerns with gender and the "feminization" of the male are discussed Carol Christ (1987) and Margaret Linley (1992).

13. On the motive for writing "Balin and Balan" see Staines, 1982, 134 and Ricks, 1987, 261. The inserted line (actually two half-lines), found in the first complete edition of *Idylls of the King* (London: Macmillan, 1892), is at "Guinevere," 97–98: "Vivien, lurking, heard. / She told Sir Modred."

14. The idea was common in the period: Scott refers to it in *Anne of Geierstein* (1829) by making the ill-fated Lady Hermione wear a great opal; Queen Victoria is thought to have worn opals to rebut the negative connotations of the stone and so help the new Australian opal trade.

15. See *The Story of Merlin and Vivien*, 1879, 110: the collection is anonymous, but its preface is signed G. R. E.

16. See the discussion of Merlin in Pre-Raphaelite art by Linda K. Hughes (1989): she mentions the significance of "ME" in the Beardsley Merlin roundel;

Chapter 9, "Tennyson and the Artists," in Whitaker, 1995, 207–36; Larrington, 2006, 157–65.

17. See the headnote to the poem in Tennyson, 1987, 205, which also suggests a link to Wordsworth's "Peel Castle"; also Haight, 1947. John Killham (1958, 509) suggests as a source John Veitch's poem "Merlin," very recently published in April 1889, because this, also drawing on Skene, refers to "Hwimleian" as "the Gleam," see Veitch, 1889, 9.

Chapter 4. International Merlin

1. An actor and son of an actor, Claude-Ferdinand Guillemay Du Chesnay is usually called Rosidor, but is cited in the 1691 edition of *Les Amours de Merlin* as "le Sieur de Rozidor."

2. For the five Merlin-as-valet plays, see Dancourt, 1711 and 1721, *La Folle Enchère* ("The Mad Bid"), vol. 1 (played in 1690); *L'Impromptu de Garnison* ("The Garrison Impromptu"), vol. 2 (played in 1693); *Les Enfans de Paris* ("Children of Paris"), vol. 5 (played in 1699); *La Déroute de Pharaon* ("The Rout of Pharaoh"), vol. 7 (played in 1718); and *Madame Artus* vol. 7 (no playing date given; and without Arthurian connection in spite of the name).

3. On this important source for medievalism, see Martin, 1985.

4. The author was Julian Croskey, who wrote several adventure stories set in Asia; the title page actually reads "A Piratical Love Study" but this is presumably a printer's error.

5. On White's treatment of the female, see Worthington, 2002.

6. E. K. Chambers devotes a chapter to the possible evidence for "The Historicity of Arthur" (1927, 168–204), but remains firmly agnostic in the matter; Rhŷs had reviewed the "historical Arthur material from 'Nennius'" in his long introduction to the widely read 1893 Dent reprint of the 1817 Malory (with illustrations by Beardsley), but he had put the emphasis on the Welsh literature Arthur. For a discussion of Collingwood's move see Knight, 1983, 209–11; a recent discussion of the historicist Arthur is Chapter 5, "The Rise and Fall of the 'Historical' Arthur," in Higham, 2002, 218–66.

7. The uncut manuscript has also been published: Powys, 1994.

8. See the interview with Raymond Thompson on the University of Rochester Camelot website, www.lib.rochester.edu/camelot/intrvws/stewart.htm.

9. For a general discussion see Alan Lupack, "Merlin in Juvenile Fiction," in Lupack, 2006, 359–62; and Stephens and McCallum, "An Affirmation of Civilization against Barbarism," 1998, chap. 5, 127–64.

10. For a discussion of this material see Carter, 1974, vii–xi.

Primary Bibliography

Adams, Oscar Fay. *Post-Laureate Idylls and Other Poems.* Boston: Lottrap, 1886.

"Adeler, Max" (= Charles Heber Clark). *The Fortunate Island.* Boston: Lee and Shepherd, 1882.

Akhurst, W. M. *King Arthur or, Launcelot the Loose, Gin-ever the Square and the Knights of the Round Table and Other Furniture.* Melbourne: Bell, 1868.

Aneirin. *Canu Aneirin,* ed. Ifor Williams. Caerdydd: Gwasg Prifysgol Cymru, 1966.

Apollinaire, Guillaume. *L'enchanteur pourrissant.* Paris: Kahnweiler, 1909.

——. *Alcools.* trans. Anne Hyde Greet. Berkeley: University of California Press, 1965.

——. *L'enchanteur pourrissant,* ed. Jean Burgos. Paris: Lettres Modernes, 1972.

Arden, John and Margaretta Darcy. *The Island of the Mighty.* London: Eyre Methuen, 1974.

Ariosto, Ludovico. *Orlando Furioso,* see under Harington, Sir John.

Armes Prydein ("The Prophecy of Britain"). Edited by Ifor Williams. Translated by Rachel Bromwich. Dublin: Institute for Advanced Studies, 1972.

Arnold, Matthew. "Tristram and Iseult." In *The Poems,* 2nd ed., ed. Miriam Allott. London: Longman, 1979, 206–37.

Arthour and Merlin. Edited by O. D. Macrae-Gibson, 2 vols. Early English Text Society, O.S. 268 and 279. Oxford: Oxford University Press, 1973 and 1979.

Arthur: the Hididdle-diddles of the King. By "our own Poet Laureate," London: privately published, 1859.

Bannerman, Anne. "The Prophecy of Merlin." In *Tales of Superstition and Chivalry.* London: Vernor and Hood, 1802, 124–26.

——. *Poems.* Edinburgh: Mundell, Doig and Stevenson, 1807.

Barjaval, René. *L'Enchanteur.* Paris: Denoel, 1984.

Barron, T. A. *The Seven Songs of Merlin.* New York: Philomel, 1997.

Beardmore, George. *Madame Merlin.* London: Macdonald, 1946.

Beeton, Samuel O., Aglen A. Dowy, and S. R. Emerson. *The Coming K***.* London: *Beeton's Christmas Annual,* 1872, 1–47.

Berger, Thomas. *Arthur Rex: A Legendary Novel.* New York: Delacorte, 1978.

Bibliothèque Universelle des Romans, vol. 1. Paris: Lacombe, 1775. Reprinted Geneva: Slatkine, 1970.

Bidder, George. *Merlin's Youth.* London: Constable, 1899.

Binyon, Laurence. *Arthur: A Tragedy.* London: Heinemann, 1923.

———. *The Madness of Merlin.* London: Macmillan, 1947.

Blackmore, Richard. *Prince Arthur: An Heroick Poem in Ten Books.* London: Awnsham and Churchil, 1695.

———. *King Arthur: An Heroick Poem in Twelve Books.* London: Awnsham and Churchil, 1697.

Blake, William. *Jerusalem.* In *Complete Works,* ed. Geoffrey Keynes. London: Oxford University Press, 1972, 620–747.

———. "Merlin's Prophecy." In *Complete Works,* ed. Keynes, 177.

Blanchard, E. L. *Tom Thumb and Merlin the Magician and the Good Fairies of the Court of King Arthur.* London: The Music-Publishing Company, 1861.

Blunt, Wilfred Scawen. "To Nimue." In *Poetical Works,* vol. I. London: Macmillan, 1914, 388–90.

———. "The Wisdom of Merlyn." In *Poetical Works,* vol. II, 451–71.

Bottomley, Gordon. "Merlin's Grave." In *Scenes and Plays.* London: Constable, 1929, 61–76.

Boyd, Eric Forbes. *Merlin Hold.* London: Jarrold, 1923.

Boyle, John Magor. *Gorlaye: A Tale of the Olden Time.* London: Baldwin; Truro: Cradock and Brokenshir, 1835.

Bradley, Marion Zimmer. *The Mists of Avalon.* New York: Knopf, 1982.

Brent, Madeleine. *Merlin's Keep.* London: Souvenir Press, 1977.

Brereton, Jane (as "Melissa"). *Merlin: A Poem, Humbly Inscrib'd to Her Majesty.* London: Cave, 1735.

"Bridie, James" (= Osborne Mavor). *Lancelot* and *Holy Isle.* In *Plays for Plain People.* London: Constable, 1944, 3–78 and 81–153.

Browne, Edith Ophelia. *Thus Merlin Said.* London: Hutchinson, 1934.

Brut y Brenhinedd ("The Brut of the Princes"). Edited by Brynley F. Roberts. Dublin: Institute of Advanced Studies, 1971.

Bryant, Nigel. *Merlin's Mound.* Oxford: Mandrake, 2004.

Bryant, Théophile. *Le Testament de Merlin.* Nantes: Bellanger, 1975.

Buchanan, Robert. *Fragments of the Table Round.* Glasgow: Murray, 1859.

Buckley, Reginald. *Arthur of Britain.* London: Williams and Norgate, 1914.

Buile Suibhne, Being the Adventures of Suibhne Geilt: A Middle-Irish Poem. Edited by J. G. O'Keefe. Irish Texts Society, vol. 12. London: Irish Texts Society, 1913.

Cabell, James Branch. *Jürgen.* New York: McBride, 1919.

——. *Something About Eve.* New York: McBride, 1927.

Campion, Thomas. *The Masque at Lord Hays Marriage.* London: Windet, 1607. Reprinted London: Scolar, 1973.

Canning, Victor. *The Crimson Chalice.* London: Heinemann, 1976.

——. *The Circle of the Gods.* London: Heinemann, 1977.

——. *The Immortal Wound.* London: Heinemann 1978.

Canu Llywarch Hên ("Poetry of Llywarch the Old"). Edited by Ifor Williams. Caerdydd: Gwasg Prifysgol Cymru, 1935.

Carr, J. Comyns. *King Arthur: A Drama.* London: Macmillan, 1895.

Cervantes, Miguel de. *Don Quixote,* trans. John Rutherford. London: Penguin, 2000.

Chamberlin, Ann. *The Merlin of St Gilles' Well.* New York: TOR, 1991.

Chapman, Vera. *The King's Damosel.* London: Collins, 1976.

Chester, Robert. *Loues Martir: or Rosalins Complaint.* London: Blount, 1601. Reprinted, ed. Alexander Grosart. London: Trübner, 1878.

Chopra, Deepak V. *The Return of Merlin.* New York: Harmony Books, 1995.

Chrétien de Troyes. *Erec et Enide,* ed. Mario Roques. Paris: Champion, 1970.

Christian, Catherine. *The Sword and the Flame.* New York: Knopf, 1978. Reprinted as *The Pendragon.* London: Pan, 1979.

Chubb, Thomas Caldecott. "Merlin." In *The White God and Other Poems.* New Haven: Yale University Press, 1920, 29–30.

Church, Alfred J., with Ruth Putnam. *The Count of the Saxon Shore, or The Villa in Vectis: A Tale of the Departure of the Romans from Britain.* London: Seeley, 1887.

"Clare, Helen" (= Pauline Clarke). *Merlin's Magic.* London: Bodley Head, 1953.

Cochran, Molly and Warren Murphy. *The Forever King.* New York: Tor Books, 1992.

Cocteau, Jean. *Les Chevaliers de la Table Ronde.* Paris: Gallimard, 1937.

——. *The Knights of the Round Table.* Trans. W. H. Auden. In Jean Cocteau, *The Infernal Machine and Other Plays.* New York: New Directions, 1967.

Cokayne, Sir Aston. *The Obstinate Lady: a new comedy.* London: Pridmore, 1657. Reprinted, ed. Catherine M. Shaw, in *The Renaissance Imagination,* vol. 17. New York: Garland, 1986.

Coleridge, Samuel Taylor. "The Pang More Sharp than All." In *The Collected Works, Poetical Works,* vol. 1 *Poems (Reading Text),* pt. 2, ed. J. C. C. Mays. Princeton N.J.: Princeton University Press, 2001, 82.

Colum, Padraic. *The Boy Apprenticed to an Enchanter.* New York: Macmillan, 1920.

Coney, Michael. *Fang the Gnome.* New York: New American Library, 1987.

Cooper, Susan. *Over Sea, Under Stone.* London: Cape, 1965.

——. *The Dark is Rising.* London: Chatto & Windus, 1973.

——. *Greenwitch.* London: Chatto & Windus, 1974.

——. *The Grey King.* London: Chatto & Windus, 1975.

——. *Silver on the Tree.* London: Chatto & Windus, 1977.

——. *The Dark is Rising* (pentalogy). London: Puffin, 1984.

Cornwell, Bernard. *The Winter King.* London: Michael Joseph, 1995.

——. *Enemy of God.* London: Michael Joseph, 1996.

——. *Excalibur.* London: Michael Joseph, 1997.

Coutts, Francis. "Merlin." In *King Arthur: A Trilogy of Lyric Dramas.* London: Privately printed (Lane), 1897; revised as *The Romance of King Arthur.* London: Lane, 1907.

Craig, Alec. *The Voice of Merlin.* London: Fortune Press, 1946.

Craik, Dinah. *King Arthur: Not a Love Story.* London: Macmillan, 1886.

Cram, Ralph Adams. *Excalibur: An Arthurian Drama.* Boston: Badger, 1909. Reprinted Whitefish, Mont.: Kessinger, 2002.

Cunqueiro, Alvaro. *Merlin and Company,* trans. Colin Smith. London: Dent, 1996.

Curll, Edmund. *The Rarities of Richmond.* London: Curll, 1736.

D'Avenant, Sir William. *Britannia Triumphans.* In *The Dramatic Works.* London: Sotheran, 1872, vol. 2, 245–300.

Dancourt, Florent. *Oeuvres,* 9 vols. Paris: Robin, vols. 1–6, 1711; vols. 7–9, 1721.

"Dane, Clemence" (= Winifred Ashton). *The Saviours.* London: Heinemann, 1942.

Darley, George. "Merlin's Last Prophecy." *The Athenaeum,* 14 July 1838, 495–96.

David, Peter. *Knight Life.* Rev. ed. New York: Ace, 2002 [1987].

——. *One Knight Only.* New York: Ace, 2003.

Davies, Robertson. *The Lyre of Orpheus.* New York: Viking, 1988.

Davy, Humphrey. "The Death of Merlin." In Roger Simpson, "An Unpublished Poem by Humphrey Davy: Merlin in the Late Eighteenth Century." *Notes and Queries,* n.s. 35 (1988): 195–96.

Deeping, Warwick. *Uther and Igraine.* London: Richards, 1903.

——. *The Sword and the Cross.* London: Cassell, 1957.

Desmarres, Officier. *Merlin Dragon.* La Haye: Foulque, 1696.

Dibdin, Charles. *Wizard's Wake: Harlequin and Merlin.* London: Glendenning, 1803.

Dickinson, Peter. *The Weathermonger.* London: Gollancz, 1968.

——. *Merlin Dreams.* London: Gollancz, 1988.

Dillon, Arthur. *King Arthur Pendragon.* London: Elkin Matthews, 1906.

Dorat, Claude Joseph. *Merlin Bel Esprit.* Paris: Monory, 1780.

Dorst, Tankred and Ursula Ehler. *Merlin, oder Das wüste Land.* Frankfurt: Suhrkamp, 1981.

Drayton, Michael. *Polyolbion.* In *Works of Michael Drayton,* ed. J. William Hebel. 5 vols. Oxford: Blackwell, 1933, vol. 4.

Dryden, John. *King Arthur, or The British Worthy: A Dramatick Opera.* London: Tonson, 1691. Reprinted in *The Works.* vol. 16, ed. Vinton A. Dearing. Berkeley: University of California Press, 1996.

——. "Prologue" to Fletcher's *The Pilgrim.* In *The Poems,* ed. James Kinsley, 4 vols. Oxford: Clarendon Press, 1952, vol. 4.

——. "Discourse concerning the Original and Progress of Satire." In *The Works,* vol. 4: *Poems 1693–1696,* ed. Vinton A. Dearing. Berkeley: University of California Press, 1974.

Eager, Edward. *Half Magic.* London: Macmillan, 1954.

Emerson, Ralph Waldo. *Collected Poems and Translations,* ed. Harold Bloom and Paul Kane. New York: Library of America, 1994.

The English Prose Merlin, ed. Henry B. Wheatley, ed., 5 vols., Early English Text Society, O.S. 10, 21, 27, 36, and 119. London: Kegan, Paul, Trench and Trübner, 1865–99; selected edition, ed. John Conlee. Kalamazoo: University of Western Michigan Press, 1998.

Evans, Quinn Taylor. *Merlin's Legacy: Dawn of Camelot.* Unity, Me.: Five Star, 1999.

Fabyan, Robert. *New Chronicles of England and France,* ed. Sir Henry Ellis. London: Rivington, 1811.

Fawcett, Edgar. *The New King Arthur.* New York: Funk & Wagnalls, 1885.

Fielding, Henry. *Tom Thumb: A Tragedy.* London: Roberts, 1730.

——. *The Tragedy of Tragedies: The Life and Death of Tom Thumb the Great.* London: Roberts, 1731.

Finkel, George. *Twilight Province.* Sydney: Angus & Robertson, 1967. As *Watch Fires to the North.* New York: Viking, 1968.

Flood, Eloise. *The Legacy of Merlin.* New York: Pocket Books, 1999.

Frankland, Edward. *The Bear of Britain.* London: Macdonald, 1944.

Fry, Christopher. *Thor with Angels.* London: Oxford University Press, 1948.

Fullarton, Ralph McLeod. *Merlin: A Dramatic Poem.* Edinburgh and London: Blackwood, 1890.

Furst, Clyde. *Merlin.* New York: Updike, 1930.

Garner, Alan. *The Weirdstone of Brisingamen.* London: Collins, 1960.

Garrick, David. *Cymon: A Dramatic Romance.* London: Theatre Royal, 1766.

Gascoigne, George. *The Princely Pleasures at Kenelworth Castle.* In *The Complete Works,* ed. J. W. Cunliffe. Cambridge: Cambridge University Press, 1907–10, vol. 2, 101–31.

Geoffrey of Monmouth. *The History of the Kings of Britain,* trans. Lewis Thorpe. London: Penguin, 1966.

——. *Vita Merlini,* ed. Basil Clarke. Cardiff: University of Wales Press, 1973.

——. *The Prophetia Merlini of Geoffrey of Monmouth: A Fifteenth Century English Commentary,* ed. Caroline D. Eckhardt. Cambridge, Mass. The Medieval Academy of America, 1982.

——. *Historia Regum Britanniae,* vol. 1: *The Berne Manuscript,* ed. Neil Wright. Cambridge: Brewer, 1984.

——. *Historia Regum Britanniae: A Variant Version,* ed. Jacob Hammer. Cambridge, Mass.: Medieval Academy of America, 1951.

——. (as Jeffrey of Monmouth). *The British History,* trans. Aaron Thompson. London: Bowyer, Clements and Innys, 1718.

Gerald of Wales. *The Journey Through Wales/The Description of Wales,* trans. Lewis Thorpe. London: Penguin, 1978.

Gibbon. Edward. *The Decline and Fall of the Roman Empire.* 6 vols. London: Dent, 1910, vol. 4, 94–96.

Gloag, John. *Artorius Rex.* London: Cassell, 1977.

Gluck, Christoph Willibald. *Merlins Insel/L'Île de Merlin.* In *Sämmtliche Werke,* pt. 4, vol. 1, ed. Günter Hausswald. Kassel: Bärenreiter, 1956.

Godwin, Parke. *Firelord.* Garden City, N.Y.: Doubleday, 1980.

Goldmark, Carl and Siegfried Lipiner. *Merlin: Oper in Drei Akten.* Leipzig: Schuberth, 1886.

Gunn, Thom. "Merlin in the Cave: He Speculates Without a Book." In *Collected Poems.* London: Faber, 1993, 82–84.

Gunnlaug Leifsson. *Merlinus-Spá or The Prophecy of Merlin.* In *Corpus Poeticae Boreale: The Poetry of the Old North Tongue,* ed. Gudbrund Vigfusson and F. York Powell, 2 vols. Oxford: Clarendon Press, 1883, vol. 2, 372–79.

Hardyng, John. *The Chronicle,* ed. Henry Ellis. London: Rivington, 1812.

Harington, Sir John. *Ludovico Ariosto's Orlando Furioso,* ed. Robert McNulty. Oxford: Clarendon Press, 1972.

Hauptmann, Gerhart. *Nachgelassene Werke und Fragmente.* In *Sämmtliche Werke,* ed. Hans-Egon Hass, vol. 10. Frankfurt am Main: Propyläen, 1970.

Hawthorne, Nathaniel. "The Antique Ring." In *Modern Arthurian Literature,* ed. Alan Lupack. New York: Garland, 1992, 319–31.

Haywood, Eliza and William Satchell. *The Opera of Operas; or Tom Thumb the Great.* London: Rayner, 1733. Reprinted in *Selected Fiction and Drama of Eliza Haywood,* ed. Paula R. Backscheider. Women Writers in English 1350–1850. New York: Oxford University Press, 1999.

Heath-Stubbs, John. *Artorius: A Heroic Poem.* London: Enitharmon Press, 1973.

Heber, Reginald. "The Book of the Purple Faucon." In *The Poetical Works.* London: Murray, 1840, 262–66.

———. "Fragments from the Masque of Gwendolen," In *Poetical Works,* 205–21.

———. *Morte D'Arthur: a Fragment.* In *Poetical Works,* 147–202.

Heine, Heinrich. "Postscript to the Romancero." In *The Complete Poems of Heinrich Heine: A Modern English Version,* trans. Hal Draper. Berlin: Suhrkamp/Insel, 1982, 693–98.

———. "Katharina, 3." In *Neue Gedichte,* in *Werke,* vol. 2, ed. Elisabeth Genton. Hamburg: Hoffman und Campe, 1983, 66–67.

Henry of Huntingdon. *Historia Anglorum: The History of the English People,* ed. and trans. Diana Greenway. Oxford: Clarendon Press, 1996.

Heywood, Thomas. *Troia Britannica, or, Great Britaines Troy.* London: Jaggard, 1609.

———. *The Life of Merlin Sirnamed Ambrosius.* London: Emery, 1641.

Higden, Ranulph. *Polychronicon,* trans. John de Trevisa. 9 vols., vols. 1–2 ed. Churchill Babington, vols. 3–9 ed. J. R. Lumby. London: Longman, 1865–85; vol. 1, 1865, vol. 5, 1874.

Hill, Aaron. *Merlin in Love, or Youth Against Magic: A Pantomime Opera.* In *The Dramatic Works,* 2 vols. London: Lownds, 1760, vol. 1, 319–42.

Hill, Geoffrey. "Merlin." In *New and Collected Poems, 1952–92.* Boston: Houghton Mifflin, 1994, 8.

Hoffman, L. A. and Philip Rüfer. *Merlin: Grosse Oper in drei Akten.* Leipzig: Breitkopf und Härtel, 1887.

Holdstock, Robert. *Merlin's Wood.* London: HarperCollins, 1994.

——. *Celtika.* New York: Doherty, 2001.

Hole, Richard. *Arthur, or The Northern Enchantment.* London: Robinson, 1789.

Hovey, Richard. *The Quest of Merlin: A Masque.* New York: Duffield, 1907. Reprinted Amsterdam: Fredonia, 2003.

Hughes, Thomas. *The Misfortunes of Arthur.* London: Robinson, 1587.

Immerman, Karl. *Merlin: Eine Mythe.* Düsseldorf: Schaub, 1832.

——. "Merlins Grab." In *Gedichte,* in *Immermans Werke,* ed. Harry Maync, 5 vols. Leipzig: Bibliographisches Institut, 1936, vol. 4, 433–38.

——. "Merlin im tiefen Grab." In *Gedichte,* vol. 4, 439–40.

Jarman, A. O. H. "Peiryan Vaban." *Bulletin of the Board of Celtic Studies* 14 (1951–52): 104–8.

Jeter, K. W. *Morlock Night.* New York: DAW, 1979.

Johnson, Richard (as R.I.). *The History of Tom Thumbe, the Little.* London: Langley, 1621. Reprinted, ed. Curt F. Buhler, for the Renaissance English Text Society, Evanston, Ill.: Northeastern University Press, 1965.

Jones, David. *In Parenthesis.* London: Faber & Faber, 1937.

Jonson, Ben. "Ben Jonson's Conversations with William Drummond of Hawthornden." In *Ben Jonson, The Works,* ed. C. H. Herford and Percy and Evelyn Simpson. Oxford: Clarendon Press, 1925, vol. 1, 128–78.

——. *The Speeches at Prince Henries Barriers.* In *Ben Jonson, The Works,* ed. C. H. Herford and Percy and Evelyn Simpson. Oxford: Clarendon Press, 1941, vol. 7, 321–36.

——. "An Execration of Vulcan." In *Ben Jonson, The Works,* ed. C. H. Herford and Percy and Evelyn Simpson. Oxford: Clarendon Press, 19417, vol. 8, 205–6.

Katzleben, The Baroness de. *The Cat's Tail: Being the History of Childe Merlin: A Tale.* Edinburgh: Blackwood, 1831.

Keats, John. "The Eve of St Agnes." In *The Poems,* ed. Miriam Allott. London: Longman, 1970, 450–80.

Kennealy-Morrison, Patricia. *Silver Branch.* New York: New American Library, 1988.

Kinkel, Gottfried. "In der Winternacht." In *Gedichte.* Stuttgart: Gotta, 1851, 267–68.

Lancelot do Lac: The Non-Cycle Old French Romance, 2 vols. Edited by Elspeth Kennedy. Oxford: Clarendon Press, 1980.

Lancelot-Grail: The Old French Arthurian Vulgate and Post-Vulgate in Translation, ed. Norris J. Lacy, 5 vols. New York: Garland, 1993–96.

Langenus, Ron. *Merlin's Return,* trans. Niesje C. Horsman Delmonte. Dublin: Wolfhound, 1993.

Lanier, Sidney. *The Boy's King Arthur, being Sir Thomas Malory's History of King Arthur and his Knights of the Round Table.* London: Sampson Low, 1880.

Lawhead, Stephen. *Merlin.* Oxford: Lion, 1988.

——. *Pendragon.* Oxford: Lion, 1994.

Layamon. *Layamon's Arthur: The Arthurian Section of Layamon's* Brut, ed. and trans. W. R. J. Barron and S. C. Weinberg. London: Longman, 1989.

Leader, Mary. *Triad.* New York: Coward, McCann and Geoghan, 1973.

Le Franc, A. *Merlin et Viviane.* Villeneuve-le-Roi: Librairie Générale des Oeuvres, 1930.

Leigh, Joseph. *Illustrations of the Fulfilment of the Prediction of Merlin Occasioned by the Late Outrageous Attack of the British Ship of War the* Leopard, *on the American Frigate,* Chesapeake. Portsmouth, N.H.: privately published, 1807; available at http://www.sacred-texts.com/neu/arthur/art096.htm.

Leland, John. *Assertio Inclytissimi Arthurii Regis.* London: Herford, 1544. See also under Robinson, Robert.

"Lenau, Nicolas" (= N. F. Nembsch von Strehlenau). *Waldlieder und Gedichte.* Stuttgart: Gotta, 1878.

Lewis, C. S. *That Hideous Strength.* London: Lane, 1945. Rev. ed., London: Pan, 1955.

——. *Collected Letters,* vol.1: *Family Letters 1905–31,* ed. Walter Hooper. London: HarperCollins, 2000.

Lienhard, Fritz. *König Arthur.* Leipzig: Meyer, 1900.

Lilly, William. *Merlinus Anglicus Junior.* London: Lilly, 1644.

——. *Merlinus Anglicus Ephemeris.* London: Lilly, 1647.

Linwood, Mary. *The House of Camelot: A Tale of the Olden Times,* 2 vols. London: Hope, 1858.

Lives of St Ninian and St Kentigern. Edited by A. P. Forbes. Edinburgh: Edmonston and Douglas, 1874.

Llyfr Du Caerfyrddin ("The Black Book of Carmarthen"). Edited by A. O. H. Jarman. Caerdydd: Gwasg Prifysgol Cymru, 1982.

Lovelich, Henry. *Merlin,* ed. J. Koch, 3 vols. *Early English Text Society,* E.S. 93 and 112, O.S. 185. London: Oxford University Press, 1913 (E.S. 112), 1932 (E.S. 93) and 1932 (O.S. 185).

Lytton, Sir Edward Bulwer. *King Arthur.* London: Colburn, 1848.

"M———, Mr" (= Julian Croskey). *Merlin: A Piratical Love Story.* London: Beeman, 1896.

Mallory, James. *The Old Magic.* London: Voyager, 1999.

——. *The King's Wizard.* London: Voyager, 1999.

——. *The End of Magic.* London: Voyager, 2000.

Malory, Sir Thomas. *The Byrth, Lyf and Actes of Kyng Arthur.* London: Longman, 1817. Reprinted, illustrated by Aubrey Beardsley, London: Dent, 1893; illustrated by Walter Flint, London: Medici Society, 1910–11.

——. *The Works of Sir Thomas Malory.* ed. Eugène Vinaver, 3 vols., 3rd ed., rev. P. J. C. Field. London: Oxford University Press, 1990.

——. *Le Morte Darthur,* ed. Helen Cooper. Oxford: Oxford University Press, 1998.

Mann, Margaret. *The Merlin Set-Up.* Bath: Tayar, 1997.

Mannyng, Robert. *Chronicle,* ed. Idelle Sullens. Medieval and Renaissance Texts and Studies, vol. 153. Binghamton: State University of New York Press, 1996.

Markale, Jean. *La Fille du Merlin.* Paris: Pygmalion, 2000.

Marshall, Edison. *The Pagan King.* Garden City, N.Y.: Doubleday, 1959.

Masefield, John. *Midsummer Night and Other Tales in Verse.* London: Heinemann, 1928.

——. *Badon Parchments.* London: Heinemann, 1947.

Mayson, Walter H. *Merlin and Nivienne: A Poem in Four Cantoes.* Manchester: Privately printed, 1900.

McCaffrey, Anne. *The Mark of Merlin.* San Francisco: Brandywine, 1971.

Merlin's Life and Prophecies...from Vortigern down to his present Majesty [and] His Prediction relating to the late Contest about the Rights of Richmond Park. London: Cooper, 1755.

Meyerstein, E. H. W. *In Merlin's Wood.* Oxford: Blackwell, 1922.

Milman, H. H. *Samor, Lord of the Bright City.* London: Murray, 1818.

Milton, John. *Epithaphium Damionis.* In *The Complete Works,* vol. 1, ed. W. P. Trent. New York: Columbia University Press, 1931, 294–317.

——. "Mansus." In *Complete Works,* vol. 1, 284–95.

——. *History of England.* In *The Complete Prose Works,* vol. 5, ed. French Fogle. New Haven, Conn.: Yale University Press, 1971.

Minot, Laurence. *The Poems 1333–52,* ed. Richard H. Osberg. Kalamazoo: University of Western Michigan Press, 1996.

The Mirror for Magistrates. Edited by Lily B. Campbell. Cambridge: Cambridge University Press, 1938.

Mitchell, Gladys. *Merlin's Furlong.* London: Michael Joseph, 1953.

Moore, George. *Perronik the Fool. The Dial* 70 (1921): 497–537. Reprinted in slightly revised form, New York: Boni and Liveright, 1924.

Moraes, Dom. "Merlin." In *Collected Poems.* London, Penguin, 1987, 161–65.

Morte Arthur: A Critical Edition. Edited by Mary Hamel. New York: Garland, 1984.

Moultrie, John. "La Belle Tryamour." In *Poems.* London: Pickering, 1837, 252–357.

Muir, Edwin. "Merlin." In *The Collected Poems.* London: Faber and Faber, 1963, 73–74.

Mumford, Ethel Watts. *Merlin and Vivian: A Lyric Drama.* New York: Schirmer, 1907.

Munn, H. Warner. *Merlin's Ring.* New York: Ballantine, 1974.

——. *Merlin's Godson.* New York: Ballantine, 1976.

Myerstein, E. H. W. *In Merlin's Wood.* Oxford: Blackwell, 1922.

Nathan, Robert. *The Elixir.* New York: Knopf, 1971.

Nennius: British History and The Welsh Annals. Edited by John Morris. London: Phillimore, 1980.

Newbolt, Henry. *Mordred.* London: Fisher Unwin, 1895.

Newman, Robert. *Merlin's Mistake.* New York: Atheneum, 1970.

——. *The Testing of Tertius.* New York: Atheneum, 1973.

Newman, Sharan. *Guinevere.* New York: St Martin's, 1981.

Norris, Leslie. "Merlin and the Snake's Egg." In *Merlin and the Snake's Egg.* New York: Viking, 1978, 45.

"Norton, André" (= Alice Norton). *Steel Magic.* Cleveland: World Publishing, 1965.

——. *Merlin's Mirror.* New York: DAW, 1975.

Norway, Kate. *Merlin's Keep.* London: Mills and Boon, 1966.

Noyes, Alfred. "The Riddles of Merlin." In *The Elfin Artist and Other Poems.* Edinburgh: Blackwood, 1920, 135–37.

Nye, Robert. *Taliesin.* London: Faber & Faber, 1966.

——. *Falstaff.* London: Hamilton, 1976.

——. *Merlin.* London: Hamilton, 1978.

O'Hara, Kane. *Tom Thumb: A Burletta, Altered from Henry Fielding.* London: Baxter, 1805.

Ordericus Vitalis. *The Ecclesiastical History,* ed. and trans. Marjorie Chibnall, vol. 6. Oxford: Clarendon Press, 1978.

Parker, Martin. *The Famous History of that most Renowned Christian Worthy ARTHUR, King of the Britaines.* London: Coles, 1660.

Peacock, Thomas Love. *The Misfortunes of Elphin.* London: Hookham, 1829.

——. "Sir Calidore," In *Sir Calidore and Miscellanea,* in *The Works,* ed. Richard Garnett, 7 vols. London: Dent, 1891, vol. 7, 32–47.

——. *Poems.* In *The Works of Thomas Love Peacock,* vol. 6, ed. H. F. B. Brett-Smith and C. E. Jones. London: Constable, 1926.

Percy, Walker. *Lancelot.* New York: Farrar, Strauss and Giroux, 1977.

Phillips, Edward. *The Royal Chace, or Merlin's Cave.* London: Wood, 1736.

Pope, Alexander. *Peri Bathous: A Treatise of the Art of Sinking,* in *The Complete Prose,* vol. 2: *The Major Works, 1725–42,* ed. Rosemary Crowley. Oxford: Blackwell, 1986, 171–276.

——. *Poems,* ed. Pat Rogers. Oxford: Oxford University Press, 1993.

Pound, Ezra. "Canto XCI." In "Section: Rock Drill De Los Cantares LXXXV–XCV (1955)," in *The Cantos, Revised Collected Edition.* London: Faber & Faber, 1975, 613.

Powys, John Cowper. *Morwyn, or The Vengeance of God.* London: Cassell, 1937.

——. *Porius: A Romance of the Dark Ages.* London: Macdonald, 1951.

——. *Porius* (complete manuscript version), ed. Wilbur T. Albrecht. Colgate, N.Y.: Colgate University Press, 1994.

Les Prophécies de Merlin. Edited by Lucy Allen Paton. New York: Modern Language Association Monograph Series, no. 1, 1926.

Les Prophécies de Merlin. Edited by Anne Berthelot. Coligny and Genève: Fondation Bodmer, 1992.

The Prophetia Merlini of Geoffrey of Monmouth: A Fifteenth-Century English Commentary. Edited by Caroline D. Eckhardt. Cambridge, Mass.: The Medieval Academy of America, 1982.

Pyle, Howard. *The Story of King Arthur and His Knights.* New York: Scribner, 1902.

——. *The Story of the Grail and the Passing of Arthur.* New York: Scribner, 1910.

Quinet, Edgar. *Merlin l'Enchanteur,* 2 vols. Paris: Lévy, 1860.

Rabelais, François. *Gargantua and Pantagruel,* trans. J. M. Cohen. London: Penguin, 1955.

"Radford, Irene" (= Phyllis Ann Karr). *Merlin's Descendants: The Guardian of the Vision.* New York: DAW Books, 2001.

The Red Book of Hergest. Edited by J. Gwenogvryn Evans. Series of Old Welsh Texts, 9. Llanbedrog: Privately printed, 1911.

Rhys, Ernest. "The Death of Merlin." In *Welsh Ballads and Other Poems.* London: Nutt, 1898, 29–40.

——. *Gwenevere: A Lyric Play.* London: Dent, 1905.

——. *Lays of the Round Table.* London: Dent, 1905.

"Rider, Cardanus" (= Richard Saunders). *Riders Brittish Merlin.* London: Leybourn, 1656.

Rio, Michel. *Merlin.* Paris: Seuil, 1989.

——. *Morgana.* Paris: Seuil, 1999.

Robert de Boron. *Merlin,* ed. Alexandre Micha. Geneva: Droz, 1979.

——. *Joseph of Arimathie,* ed. Richard O'Gorman. Toronto: Pontifical Institute, 1995.

——. *Merlin and the Grail: Joseph of Arimathea, Merlin, Perceval,* trans. Nigel Bryant. Cambridge: Brewer, 2001.

Robinson, Edwin Arlington. *Merlin.* New York: Macmillan, 1917.

Robinson, Robert. *The Assertion of Arthur.* London: Wolfe, 1582. Reprinted in Christopher Middleton, *The Famous Historie of Chinon of England,* ed. William Edward Mead, Early English Text Society, O.S. 165. London: Oxford University Press, 1925, Appendix, 1–151.

"Rozidor" (= Claude-Ferdinand Guillemay du Chesnay). *Les Amours de Merlin.* Rouen: Besongne, 1691.

Rowley, William ("with William Shakespeare"). *The Birth of Merlin.* London: Kirkman and Marsh, 1662.

——. *A Critical Old-Spelling Edition of The Birth of Merlin,* ed. Joanna Udall. London: Modern Humanities Research Association, 1991, 89–111, 101–2.

Saberhagen, Fred. *Dominion.* New York: Pinnacle, 1982.

——. *Merlin's Bones.* New York: TOR, 1995.

"Samivel" (= Paul Gayet-Tancrède). *La Grande Nuit de Merlin.* Paris: IAC, 1943.

Sampson, Fay. *White Nun's Telling.* London: Headline, 1989.

——. *Wise Woman's Telling.* London: Headline, 1989.

——. *Black Smith's Telling.* London: Headline, 1990.

——. *Taliesin's Telling.* London: Headline, 1991.

——. *Herself.* London: Headline, 1992.

Schuré, Edouard. *Merlin l'Enchanteur: Légende dramatique.* Paris: Perrin, 1924.

Scott, Sir Walter, *The Bridal of Triermain.* In *The Poetical Works,* ed. J. Logie Robertson. London: Oxford University Press, 1904, 553–84.

Shakespeare, William. *The Tragedy of King Lear,* ed. Jay L. Halio. The New
    Cambridge Shakespeare. Cambridge: Cambridge University Press, 1992.
———. *King Henry IV, Part I,* ed. David Bevington. The New Arden Shakespeare.
    London: Methuen, 2002.
Shelley, P. B. *Charles the First.* In *The Complete Works,* ed. Thomas Hutchinson.
    London: Oxford University Press, 1923, 488–507.
Sheriff, R. C. *The Last Sunset.* In *Plays of the Year 1954–5,* ed. J. C. Trewin. London:
    Elek, 1955.
Silence: A Thirteenth-Century French Romance. Edited and translated by Sarah
    Roche-Mahdi. East Lansing: Michigan State University Press, 1992.
Skinner, Martyn. *Merlin Part 1: The Return of Arthur: A Satiric Epic.* London:
    Muller, 1951.
———. *The Return of Arthur: A Poem of the Future.* London: Chapman & Hall, 1955.
Sneyd, Ralph de Tunstall. *Vivian and Merlin.* Chesterfield: Edmunds, 1929.
    Reprinted in *Poems,* vol. 1. Huddersfield: Hilltop Press, 2001, 74–77.
Southey, Robert. *Madoc.* In *The Poetical Works 1793–1810,* vol. 2, ed. Lynda Pratt.
    London: Pickering and Chatto & Windus, 2004.
Spenser, Edmund. *The Faerie Queene.* In *The Works,* ed. J. C. Smith and E. de
    Selincourt. Oxford: Oxford University Press, 1912.
Steinbeck, John. *The Acts of King Arthur and His Noble Knights.* London:
    Heinemann, 1976.
Stewart, Mary. *The Crystal Cave.* London: Hodder & Stoughton, 1970.
———. *The Hollow Hills.* London: Hodder & Stoughton, 1973.
———. *The Last Enchantment.* London: Hodder & Stoughton, 1979.
———. *The Wicked Day.* London: Hodder & Stoughton, 1983.
*The Story of Merlin and Vivien Gathered from the Old British and British Christian
    Poems, and Modern Versions of the Ancient Legend.* London: Moxon, 1879.
Stuart-Glennie, J. S. *The Quest for Merlin.* In *King Arthur or the Drama of the
    Revolution,* vol. 2. London: Trübner, 1867.
La Suite du Roman de Merlin. Edited by Gilles Roussineau. 2 vols. Paris: Droz, 1996.
Sutcliff, Rosemary. *The Lantern-Bearers.* London: Oxford University Press, 1959.
———. *Sword at Sunset.* London: Hutchinson, 1963.
Swift, Jonathan. *Miscellanies in Verse and Prose.* London: Morphew, 1713.
Swinburne, Algernon. *Tristram of Lyonesse.* London: Chatto & Windus, 1882.
———. "The Tale of Balen." In *Algernon Charles Swinburne,* introd. James P. Carley.
    Arthurian Poets Series. Woodbridge: Boydell Press, 1990, 161-237.
Symons, Arthur. "Merlin and Mark." In *Jezebel Mort and Other Poems.* London:
    Heinemann, 1931.
Taliesin. *The Poems of Taliesin,* ed. Ifor Williams, trans. J. E. Caerwyn Williams.
    Dublin: Institute for Advanced Studies, 1968.
Tennyson, Alfred. "Merlin and Vivien." In *The Poems of Tennyson,* ed. Christopher
    Ricks, 3 vols., 2nd ed. London: Longman, 1987, vol. 3, 393–422.
———. "Merlin and the Gleam." In Ricks, ed., *The Poems of Tennyson,* vol. 3, 205–9.

Theobald, Lewis. *Merlin or, The Devil of Stonehenge.* London: Watts, 1734.

Thomas, R. S. "Taliesin, 1952." In *Song at the Year's Turning.* London: Rupert Hart-Davies, 1955, 105.

Tieck, Ludwig. *Die Geburt des Merlin.* In *Shakespeare's Vorschule,* 2 vols. Leipzig: Brockhaus, 1823–29, vol. 2, 219–366.

Tolstoy, Nikolas. *The Coming of the King.* London: Hamilton, 1985.

Tom a Lincoln. Edited by G. R. Proudfoot and H. R. Woudhuysen. London: Malone Society Reprints, 1992.

Treece, Henry. *The Eagles Have Flown.* London: Bodley Head, 1952.

———. *The Great Captains.* London: Bodley Head, 1956.

———. *The Green Man.* London: Bodley Head, 1966.

Trevor, Meriol. *The Last of Britain.* London: Macdonald, 1956.

———. *Merlin's Ring.* London: Collins, 1957.

Turner, Roy. *King of the Lordless Country.* London: Dobson, 1971.

Turton, Godfrey. *The Emperor Arthur.* London: Allen, 1968.

Twain, Mark. *Adventures of a Connecticut Yankee at the Court of King Arthur.* New York: Norton, 1982 [1889].

Uhland, Ludwig. "Merlin der Wilde." In *Gedichte.* Stuttgart: Gotta, 1854, 308–12.

Veitch, John. *Merlin and Other Poems.* Edinburgh: Blackwood, 1889.

Vergil, Polydore. *English History from an Early Translation,* trans. Thomas Loughey (though name given on 1663 edition is that of his brother John), 2 vols., ed. Sir Henry Ellis. Camden Society. London: Nichols, 1846.

The Vulgate Version of the Arthurian Romances. Edited by H. Oskar Sommer, 8 vols. Carnegie Institution Publications, no. 74. Washington: Carnegie Institution, 1908–16.

Wace. *Le Roman de Brut.* ed. Ivor Arnold, 2 vols. Paris: Société des Anciens Textes Français, 1938–40.

———. *Roman de Rou,* ed. A. J. Holden, 3 vols. Paris: Picard, 1970.

———. *Roman de Brut: Text and Translation,* ed. and trans. Judith Weiss. Exeter: University of Exeter Press, 1999.

"Waldmüller, Robert" (= Édouard Deboc). *Merlins Feiertage.* Hamburg: Meissner und Schirze, 1857.

Wallenstein, Marcel. *Merlin's Forest.* London: Constable, 1965.

Warner, William. *Albions England.* London: Moore, 1589.

Warton, Thomas. *Poems.* London: Becket, 1777.

White, T. H. *The Sword in the Stone.* London: Collins, 1938.

———. *The Witch in the Wood.* London: Collins, 1940.

———. *The Ill-Made Knight.* London: Collins, 1941.

———. *The Once and Future King* (tetralogy). London: Collins, 1958.

———. *The Book of Merlyn.* Austin: University of Texas Press, 1977.

———. *The Once and Future King* (pentalogy). London: Voyager, 1996.

The Whole Prophecies of Scotland, England, France, Ireland and Denmarke. Prophecied by Marueilous Merling, Beid, Bertlington, Thomas Rymer, Waldhave, Eltraine, Banester, and Sybilla. Edinburgh: Hart, 1617.

Whyte, Jack. *The Sky Stone.* New York: Forge, 1996.

———. *The Sorcerer.* New York: Viking, 1997.

Widdemer, Margaret. *Ballads and Lyrics.* New York: Harcourt Brace, 1925.

Wieland, Christoph Martin. *Die Abentheur des Don Sylvio von Rosalva.* Ulm: Bartholomai, 1764.

———. "Merlin der Zauberer." In *Sämmtliche Werke,* 36 vols. Leipzig: Göschen, 1855–58, vol. 35, 364–66.

———. "Merlins weissagende Stimme aus seiner Gruft im Walde Broseliand." In Ludwig Preller, ed., *Ein fürstliches Leben.* Weimar: Böhlau, 1859, 101–3.

Wilbur, Richard E. "Merlin Enthralled." In *New and Collected Poems.* New York: Harcourt Brace Jovanovich, 1988, 245–46.

Williams, Charles, *Taliessin through Logres.* London: Oxford University Press, 1938.

———. *The Region of the Summer Stars.* London: Nicholson & Watson, 1944.

Williams, Ifor, ed. "Myrddin a Gwenddydd." *Bulletin of the Board of Celtic Studies* 4 (1924): 114–21.

Wilmer, Lambert A. *Merlin.* Baltimore: North American, 1827. Reprinted, ed. Thomas Ollive Mabbot. New York: Scholar's Facsimiles and Reprints, 1941.

Wordsworth, William. *Artegall and Elidure.* In *The Poetical Works,* ed. Ernest de Selincourt and Helen Darbyshire, 3 vols. Oxford: Clarendon Press, 1946, vol. 2, 14–22.

———. *The Egyptian Maid or The Romance of the Water Lily.* In *The Poetical Works,* vol. 3, 232–43.

———. *The Prelude,* ed. Ernest de Selincourt, 2nd rev. ed., ed. Helen Darbyshire. Oxford: Clarendon Press, 1959.

Yeats, W. B. "Time and the Witch Vivien." In *The Poems,* ed. Richard J. Finneran. Dublin: Gill and Macmillan, 1984: 514–16.

Ymddiddan Myrddin a Thaliesin ("The Conversation of Myrddin and Taliesin"). Edited by A. O. H. Jarman. Caerdydd: Gwasg Prifysgol Cymru, 1951.

Yolen, Jane. *Merlin's Book.* New York: Ace, 1986.

———. *The Dragon's Boy.* New York: Harper & Row, 1990.

———. *Hobby.* San Diego: Harcourt Brace, 1996.

———. *Passager.* San Diego: Harcourt Brace, 1996.

———. *Merlin.* San Diego: Harcourt Brace, 1997.

Yonge, Charlotte. *The History of Sir Thomas Thumb.* Edinburgh: Constable, 1855.

Young, Francis Brett. *The Island.* London: Heinemann, 1944.

Zelazny, Roger. *The Last Defender of Camelot.* New York: ibooks, 2002.

Secondary Bibliography

Note: Essay collections which only appear once are entered fully under the name of the essay taken from them; others have a separate entry and cross-references are made from essays cited.

Ackerman, Robert W. "Herry (sic) Lovelich's *Merlin*." *Proceedings of the Modern Language Association of America* 67 (1952): 473–84.

Adams, Alison, *et al.*, eds. *The Changing Face of Arthurian Romance.* Cambridge: Boydell, 1986.

Adolf, Helen. "The *Esplumoir Merlin:* A Study in its Cabbalistic Sources." *Speculum* 21 (1946): 172–93.

Alexander, Victor. *The Life of Edward Bulwer, First Lord Lytton.* 2 vols. London: Macmillan, 1913.

Allen, B. Sprague. *Tides in English Taste (1619–1800).* Cambridge, Mass.: Harvard University Press, 1937.

Anderson, Benedict. *Imagined Communities,* rev. ed. London: Verso, 1999.

Anglo, Sidney. "The *British History* in Early Tudor Propaganda." *Bulletin of the John Rylands Library* 44 (1961): 17–48.

Arbuckle, Nan. "That Hidden Strength: C. S. Lewis's Merlin as Modern Grail." In Watson and Fries, 1989, 79–99.

Archibald, Elizabeth and A. S. G. Edwards. "Beginnings: *The Tale of King Arthur* and *King Arthur and the Emperor Lucius.*" In Archibald and Edwards, 1996, 133–51.

——, eds. *A Companion to Malory.* Cambridge: Brewer, 1996.

Arden, John. "Author's Preface (1)." In John Arden and Margaretta Darcy, *The Island of the Mighty*. London: Eyre Methuen, 1974, 9–16.

Ashe, Geoffrey. *Merlin: The Prophet and His History*. Stroud: Sutton, 2006.

Asher, Martha, trans. "The Post-Vulgate Merlin." In *Lancelot-Grail,* 1993–96, vol. 4, 3–109.

Bagg, Robert. "Merlin and Faust in two Post-War Poems." In Spivack, 1992, 189–98.

Baker, Norman. *The Strange Death of David Kelly*. London: Methuen, 2007.

Baldwin, John W. *The Government of Philip Augustus: Foundations of French Royal Power in the Middle Ages*. Berkeley: University of California Press, 1986.

Bannister, Winifred. *James Bridie and Theatre*. London: Rockliff, 1955.

Barber, Richard. "Chivalry, Cistercianism and the Grail." In Dover, 2003, 3–12.

Barnes, Geraldine. *Counsel and Strategy in Middle English Romance*. Cambridge: Brewer, 1991.

Barron, W. R. J., ed. *The Arthur of the English: The Arthurian Legend in Medieval Life and Literature*. Cardiff: University of Wales Press, 1999.

Barron, W. R. J. and Françoise le Saux. "Two Aspects of Lazamon's Narrative Art." *Arthurian Literature* 9 (1989): 25–56.

Baswell, Christopher. "Marvels of Translation and Causes of Transition in the Romances of Antiquity." In Krueger, 2000, 29–44.

Batt, Catherine. "Malory's Questing Beast and the Implications of Author as Translator." In *The Medieval Translator: The Theory and Practice of Translation in the Middle Ages,* ed. Roger Ellis. Cambridge: Brewer, 1989, 143–66.

——. *Malory's Morte Darthur: Remaking Arthurian Tradition*. London: Palgrave, 2002.

Baudry, Robert. "La Vita Merlini ou les Métamorphoses de Merlin." In Hüe, 2000, 177–91.

——. *Le Mythe de Merlin*. Rennes: Terre de Brume, 2007.

Baumgartner, Emmanuèle. "Approches littéraires." In Emmanuèle Baumgartner and Nelly Andrieux-Reix, *Le "Merlin" en Prose*. Paris: Presses Universitaires de France, 2001, 19–74.

Belsey, Catherine. *Critical Practice*. London: Methuen, 1980.

Berger, Harry, Jr. "The Structure of Merlin's Chronicle." In *Revisionary Play: Studies in the Spenser Dynamics*. Berkeley: University of California Press, 1988, 118–30.

Bernard-Griffiths, Simone. *Le Mythe Romantique de Merlin dans l'oeuvre d'Edgar Quinet*. Paris: Champion, 1999.

Berthelot, Anne. "Robert le Diable: Instances d'énonciation et figures d'économie dans le suite Merlin." In Hüe, 2000, 11–25.

Blackburn, William. "Spenser's Merlin." *Renaissance and Reformation,* n.s. 4 (1980): 179–98.

Blacker, Jean. "'Ne vuil sun livre translater': Wace's omission of Merlin's Prophecies from the *Roman de Brut*." In *Anglo-Norman Anniversary Essays,* ed. Ian Short. London: Anglo-Norman Text Society, 1993, 49–59.

Blacker-Knight, Jean. "Transformations of a Theme: The Depoliticisation of the Arthurian World in the *Roman de Brut.*" In *The Arthurian Tradition: Essays in Convergence,* ed. Mary Flowers Braswell and John Bugge. Tuscaloosa: University of Alabama Press, 1988, 54–79.

Bloch, R. Howard. *Etymologies and Genealogies: A Literary Anthropology of the French Middle Ages.* Berkeley: University of California Press, 1983.

———. "Le rire de Merlin." In Hüe, 2000, 39–50.

Bogdanow, Fanni. *The Romance of the Grail.* Manchester: Manchester University Press, 1966.

———. "The *Vulgate Cycle* and the *Post-Vulgate Roman du Graal.*" In Dover, 2003, 33–51.

———. "The Arthurian Material in Maistre Richart d'Ireland's *Prophecies de Merlin.*" In Bogdanow and Trachsler, "Rewriting Prose Romance," in Burgess and Pratt, 2006, 352–57.

———. "The Post-Vulgate *Roman du Graal.*" In Fanni Bogdanow and Richard Trachsler, "Rewriting Prose Romance." In Burgess and Pratt, 2006, 342–92.

Bollard, John K. "Myrddin in Early Welsh Tradition." In Goodrich, 1990, 13–54.

Bottomley, Gordon. "Introduction." In Binyon, 1947.

Brewer, Elisabeth, *T. H. White.* Cambridge: Brewer, 1993.

Brinkley, Roberta Florence. *Arthurian Legend in the Seventeenth Century.* Johns Hopkins Monographs in Literary History, 3. Baltimore: Johns Hopkins University Press, 1932.

Bromwich, Rachel. "Y Cynfeirdd a'r Traddodiad Cymraeg" ("The Early Bards and Welsh Tradition"). *Bulletin of the Board of Celtic Studies* 22 (1966): 30–57.

———. *Trioedd Ynys Prydein* ("Triads of the Island of Britain"). 2nd ed. Cardiff: University of Wales Press, 1978.

———. "First Transmission to England and France." In Bromwich and Jarman, 1991, 273–98.

Buckler, William E. *Man and His Myths: Tennyson's* Idylls of the King *in Critical Context.* New York: New York University Press, 1984.

Budd, Louis J. *Mark Twain: Social Philosopher.* Bloomington: Indiana University Press, 1962.

Burgess, Glyn and Karen Pratt, eds. *The Arthur of the French: The Arthurian Legend in Medieval French and Occitan Literature.* Cardiff: University of Wales Press, 2006.

Burgos, Jean. "Introduction." In Apollinaire, 1972, v–clxii.

Burns, E. Jane. *Arthurian Fictions: Rereading the Vulgate Cycle.* Columbus: Ohio University Press, 1985.

———. "Introduction." In *Lancelot-Grail,* 1993–96. vol. 1, xv–xxxiii.

———. "Vulgate Cycle." In Lacy, 1996, 496–99.

Capp, Bernard. "Almanacs and Politics." Chapter 3 of *Astrology and the Popular Press: English Almanacs 1500–1800.* London: Faber, 1979, 67–101.

Carman, James Neale. *A Study of the Pseudo-Map Cycle.* Lawrence: University of Kansas Press, 1973.

Carter, Lin. "Introduction." In Munn, 1974, vii–xi.

Chadwick, H. M. and N. K. Chadwick. *The Growth of Literature.* Cambridge: Cambridge University Press, 1932.

Chadwick, Nora K. *Celtic Britain.* London: Thames & Hudson, 1963.

Chambers, E. K. *Arthur of Britain.* London: Sidgwick & Jackson, 1927.

Christ, Carol. "The Feminine Subject in Victorian Poetry." *English Literary History* 54 (1987): 385–401.

Clarke, Basil. "Proem" and "Introduction." In Geoffrey of Monmouth, 1973.

Clarke, Margaret A. *Rimbaud and Quinet.* Sydney: Simmons, 1945.

Cohen, Walter. *Drama of a Nation: Public Theater in Renaissance England and Spain.* Ithaca: Cornell University Press, 1985.

Collingwood, R. G. "Roman Britain." In R. G. Collingwood and J. N. L. Myres, *Roman Britain and the English Settlements.* Oxford: Clarendon Press, 1936.

Colton, Judith. "Merlin's Cave and Queen Caroline: Garden Art as Political Propaganda." *Eighteenth Century Studies* 10 (1976): 1–20.

Conlee, John. "Introduction." In *English Prose Merlin,* 1998, 1–18.

———. "Warwick Deeping's *Uther and Igraine.*" *Arthuriana* 11 (2001): 88–95.

Cooper, Helen. "Introduction." In Malory, 1998, vii–xxx.

———. "The *Lancelot-Grail Cycle* in England: Malory and His Predecessors." In Dover, 2003, 147–62.

———. "Appendix: Medieval Romance in English after 1500." In Helen Cooper, *The English Romance in Time: Transforming Motifs from Geoffrey of Monmouth to the Death of Shakespeare.* Oxford: Oxford University Press, 2004, 409–29.

Cooper, J. P. D. *Propaganda and the Tudor State: Political Culture in the West Country.* Oxford: Clarendon Press, 2003.

Coote, Lesley A. *Prophecy and Public Affairs in Later Medieval England.* York: York Medieval Press, 2006.

Cox, Donald R. "The Vision of Robinson's *Merlin.*" *Colby Library Quarterly,* ser. 10 (1973–74): 495–504.

Crane, R. S. *The Vogue of Medieval Chivalric Romance during the English Renaissance.* Menasha, Wis.: Collegiate Press, 1919.

Crick, Julia C. *The Historia Regum Britanniae,* vol. 3: *Summary Catalogue of the Manuscripts.* Cambridge: Brewer, 1989.

———. *The Historia Regum Britanniae,* vol. 4: *Dissemination and Reception in the Later Middle Ages.* Cambridge: Brewer, 1991.

Crossley, Ceri. *Edgar Quinet (1803–75): A Study in Romantic Thought.* Lexington, Ky.: French Forum, 1983.

Cumming, Mark. "Allegory and Comedy in Bulwer-Lytton's *King Arthur.*" In Mancoff, 1992, 31–51.

Dakyns, Janine R. "Second Empire." In Lacy, 1996, 412–13.

Dalrymple, Roger. "'Evele knowen ye Merlyne jn certein': Henry Lovelich's Prose *Merlin.*" In *Medieval Insular Romance,* ed. Judith Weiss, Jennifer Fellows, and Morgan Dickins. Cambridge: Brewer, 2000, 155–67.

Daniel, Catherine. *Les prophéties de Merlin et la culture politique (XIIe–XVIe siècle).* Turnhout: Brepols, 2006.

Davis, Courtney and Peter Quiller. *Merlin the Immortal.* Reading: Spirit of Celtia, 1984.

Dean, Christopher. "The Many Faces of Merlin in Modern Fiction." *Arthurian Interpretations* 3 (1988): 61–78.

——. "The Metamorphosis of Merlin: An Examination of the Protagonist of *The Crystal Cave* and *The Hollow Hills.*" In Gollnick, 1991, 63–75.

——. *A Study of Merlin in English Literature from the Middle Ages to the Present Day.* Lewiston, N.Y.: Mellen, 1992.

——. *The Lady of the Lake in Arthurian Legend.* Lewiston, N.Y.: Mellen, 1993.

Dee, John. *The Limits of the British Empire,* ed. Ken MacMillan with Jennifer Abeles. Studies in Military History and International Affairs. Westport, Conn: Praeger, 2004.

De la Croix, Arnaud. *Arthur, Merlin et le Graal.* Monaco: Rocher, 2000.

Dennis, John. *Remarks On a Book entituled Prince Arthur, an Heroic Poem.* London: Heyrick and Sare, 1696.

Denoyelle, Corinne. "Le prince et le prophète: Une politique du secret et de la révélation." In Hüe, 2000, 192–205.

Dobin, Howard. *Merlin's Disciples: Prophecy, Poetry, and Power in Renaissance England.* Stanford, Calif.: Stanford University Press, 1990.

Domina, Lyle. "Fate, Tragedy and Pessimism in Robinson's *Merlin.*" *Colby Library Quarterly* 8 (1968): 471–78.

Dominik, Mark. *William Shakespeare and the Birth of Merlin.* Beaverton, Ore.: Alioth Press, 1991.

Doob, Penelope. *Nebuchadnezzar's Children: Conventions of Madness in Middle English Literature.* New Haven, Conn.: Yale University Press, 1974.

Dover, Carol, ed. *Companion to the Lancelot-Grail Cycle.* Cambridge: Brewer, 2003.

Dunlop, John. *The History of Fiction.* 2 vols. London: Longman, 1814.

Echard, Siân. "'For Mortals are Moved by these Conditions': Fate, Fortune and Providence in Geoffrey of Monmouth." In *The Fortunes of King Arthur,* ed. Norris J. Lacy. Cambridge: Brewer, 2005, 13–28.

Eckhardt, Caroline D. "Introduction." In *The Prophetia Merlini of Geoffrey of Monmouth: A Fifteenth Century English Commentary.* Cambridge, Mass: The Medieval Academy of America, 1982.

Eggers, J. Philip. *King Arthur's Laureate: A Study of Tennyson's* The Idylls of the King. New York: New York University Press, 1971.

Elbert, Monika. "From Merlin to Faust: Emerson's Democratization of the 'Heroic Mind.'" In Spivack, 1992, 113–35.

Ellis, George. *Specimens of Early English Metrical Romance,* 3 vols. London: Longman, 1805.

Elton, G. R. *England Under the Tudors,* 3rd ed. London: Routledge, 1991.

Ensor, Allison. "The Magic of Fol-de-Rol: Mark Twain's Merlin." In Watson and Fries, 1989, 51–63.

Faral, Edmond. "Geoffrey de Monmouth: Les faits et les dates de sa biographie." *Romania* 53 (1927): 1–42.

Field, P. J. C. *The Life and Times of Sir Thomas Malory.* Cambridge: Brewer, 1993.

——. *Malory: Text and Sources.* Cambridge: Brewer, 1998.

Fisher, Margery. *Henry Treece.* London: Bodley Head, 1969.

Fletcher, Robert Huntington. *The Arthurian Material in the Chronicles.* Harvard Studies in Arts and Literature, 10. 1896 [1906].

Fogle, French. "Introduction to *The History of Britain.*" In Milton, 1971, xiv–xlix.

Forbes, A. P. "Introduction to *Life of Kentigern.*" In *Lives of St Ninian and St Kentigern,* 1874, lxiii–cv.

Fox-Friedman, Jeanne. "The Chivalric Order for Children: Arthur's Return in Late Nineteenth- and Early Twentieth-Century America." In Mancoff, 1998, 137–57.

Fries, Maureen. "The Rationalization of the Arthurian 'Matters' in T. H. White and Mary Stewart." *Philological Quarterly* 56 (1977): 258–65.

Galyon, Aubrey and Zacharias P. Thundy. "Merlin in the Dark Ages." In Goodrich, 1990, 3–11.

Gannaway, Dave. *The Merlin Connection: the Magic of a Second Reality.* Southampton: Solomon, 1997.

Gant, Roland. Review of Binyon, 1947. *Poetry Quarterly* 9 (1947–48): 252–53.

Garten, Hugh F. *Gerhart Hauptmann.* Cambridge: Bowes & Bowes, 1954.

Gaunt, Simon. "Romance and Other Genres." In Krueger, 2000, 45–59.

Gillingham, John. "The Context and Purposes of Geoffrey of Monmouth's *History of the Kings of Britain.*" In *Proceedings of the Battle Conference, 1990,* ed. Marjorie Chibnall. Anglo-Norman Studies 13. Woodbridge: Boydell, 1991, 99–118.

Given-Wilson, Chris. *Chronicles: The Writing of History in Medieval England.* London: Hambledon, 2004.

Glencross, Michael A. *Reconstructing Camelot: French Romantic Medievalism and the Arthurian Tradition.* Cambridge: Brewer, 1995.

Gollnick, James, ed. *Comparative Studies in Merlin from the Vedas to C. G. Jung.* Lewiston, N.Y.: Mellen, 1991.

Goodrich, Norma Lorre. *Merlin.* New York: Franklin Watts, 1987.

Goodrich, Peter H. "Modern Merlins: An Aerial Survey." In Watson and Fries, 1989, 175–97.

——. "Introduction to *Vita Merlini.*" In Goodrich, 1990, 71–73.

——. "The Alchemical Merlin." In Spivack, 1992, 91–109.

——, "The New Age Mage: Merlin as Contemporary Occult Icon." *Journal of the Fantastic in the Arts* 5 (1992): 42–73.

——. "The Erotic Merlin." *Arthuriana* 10 (2000): 94–115.

——. "Merlin in the Public Domain." In Sklar and Hoffman, 2002, 219–32.

——, ed. *The Romance of Merlin: An Anthology.* New York, Garland, 1990.

Goodrich, Peter and Raymond H. Thompson. "Introduction." In Goodrich and Thompson, 2003, 1–102.

——, eds. *Merlin: A Casebook.* New York: Routledge, 2003.

Gossedge, Rob. "Thomas Love Peacock's *The Misfortunes of Arthur* and the Romantic Arthur." *Arthurian Literature* 23 (2006): 157–76.

Gossedge, Rob and Stephen Knight. "Arthur in the Sixteenth to Nineteenth Centuries." In *The Cambridge Companion to King Arthur,* ed. Elizabeth Archibald and Ad Putter. Cambridge: Cambridge University Press, 2009, 103–19.

Gowans, Linda M. "New Perspectives on the *Didot-Perceval.*" *Arthurian Literature* 7 (1987): 1–22.

Grande Larousse Encyclopédie, 10 vols. Paris: Larousse, 1963.

Gray, J. M. *"Thro' The Vision of the Night": A Study of Sources, Evolution and Structure in Tennyson's* Idylls of the King. Edinburgh: Edinburgh University Press, 1980.

Griffith, Richard R. "The Authorship Question Reconsidered." In Takamiya and Brewer, 1981, 159–76.

Griffiths, M. E. *Early Vaticination in Welsh.* Cardiff: University of Wales Press, 1937.

Grimbert, Joan Tasker and Norris J. Lacy. "Arthur in Modern French Fiction and Film." In Burgess and Pratt, 2006, 546–70.

Grosart, Alexander B. "Introduction" In Chester, 1878, v–lxxiii.

Gurteen, S. Humphreys. *The Arthurian Epic: A Comparative Study of the Cambrian, Breton, and Anglo-Norman Versions of the Story and Tennyson's* Idylls of the King. New York: Putnam, 1895.

Haight, G. S. "Tennyson's Merlin." *Studies in Philology* 44 (1947): 549–66.

Hamel, Mary. "Introduction." In *Morte Arthur,* 1984, 3–99.

Hamilton, A.C., ed. *The Spenser Encyclopedia.* Toronto: University of Toronto Press, 1980.

Hamp, Eric P. *"Viviane* or *Niniane*—A Comment from the Keltic Side." *Romance Philology* 8 (1954): 91.

Hanks, D. Thomas, Jr. and Jessica G. Brogdon, eds. *The Social and Literary Contexts of Malory's Morte Darthur.* Cambridge: Brewer, 2000.

Hartung, Albert E., ed. *A Manual of the Writings in Middle English.* New Haven, Conn.: Connecticut Academy of Arts and Sciences, 1975, vol. 5.

Harty, Kevin J. *The Reel Middle Ages.* Jefferson, N.C.: McFarland, 1999.

Haycock, Marged. "Merlin." In *Oxford Dictionary of National Biography.* Oxford: Oxford University Press, 2004, vol. 37, 898–99.

Heber, Amelia. *The Life of Reginald Heber,* 2 vols. London: Murray, 1830.

Henry, archdeacon of Huntingdon. *Historia Anglorum: The History of the English People,* ed. and trans. Diana Greenway. Oxford: Clarendon Press, 1996.

Herman, Harold J. "The Women in Mary Stewart's Merlin Trilogy." *Interpretations* 15 (1984): 101–14.

Higham, N.J. *King Arthur: Myth-Making and History.* London: Routledge, 2002.

Hildebrand, Kristina. *The Female Reader at the Round Table: Religion and Women in Three Contemporary Arthurian Texts.* Studia Anglistica Upsaliensia, 115. Uppsala:, Upsaliensis S. Academiae, 2001.

Hill, Christopher. *Milton and the English Revolution.* London: Faber & Faber, 1977.

Hodder, Karen. "Henry Lovelich's *Merlin* and the Prose *Merlin.*" In Barron, 1999, 80–83.

Hoffman, Donald L. "Mark's Merlin: Magic vs. Technology in *A Connecticut Yankee in King Arthur's Court.*" In Slocum, 1992, 46–55.

——. "Seeing the Seer: Images of Merlin in the Middle Ages and Beyond." In *Word and Image in Arthurian Literature,* ed. Keith Busby. New York: Garland, 1996, 105–22.

Holbrook, S. E. "Nymue, the Chief Lady of the Lake in Malory's *Le Morte Darthur.*" *Speculum* 53 (1978): 761–77.

Houck, Margaret. *Sources of the Roman de Brut of Wace,* University of California Publications in English, 5. Berkeley: University of California Press, 1941.

Hüe, Denis, ed. *Fils sans père.* Orléans: Paradigme, 2000.

Hughes, Linda K. "Illusion and Relation: Merlin as Image of the Artist in Tennyson, Doré, Burne-Jones and Beardsley." In Watson and Fries, 1989, 1–33.

Hurd, Michael. "Rutland Boughton's Arthurian Cycle." In Mancoff, 1992, 205–29.

Jackson, K. H. "O achaws nyth yr ychedydd" ("Because of a lark's nest"). *Ysgrifau Beirniadaeth* 10 (1977): 45–50.

Jarman, A. O. H. "Lailoken a Llallogan" ("Lailoken and Llallogan"). *Bulletin of the Board of Celtic Studies* 9 (1939): 8–27.

——. "Rhagmadroddiad" ("Introduction"). In *Ymddiddan Myrddin a Thaliesin,* 1951.

——. *The Legend of Merlin.* Cardiff: University of Wales Press, 1960. Rev. ed., 1976.

——. "Rhagmadroddiad" ("Introduction"). In *Llyfr Du Caerfyrddin,* 1982, xiii–lxxii.

——. "The Merlin Legend and the Welsh Tradition of Prophecy." In Bromwich and Jarman, 1991, 117–45.

Johnson, Lesley. "Medieval Chronicles." In Barron, 1999, 38–46.

Jones, Ernest. *Geoffrey of Monmouth 1640–1800.* University of California Publications in English 5, no. 3. Berkeley: University of California Press, 1941.

Jones, Gwyn. Review of Binyon, 1947. *Life and Letters* 54 (1947): 74–76.

Jump, John D., ed. *Tennyson: The Critical Heritage.* London: Routledge, 1967.

Jung, Emma and Marie-Louise von Franz. *The Grail Legend,* trans. Andrea Dykes, 2nd ed. Boston: Sigo, 1986.

Kay, Sarah. "Courts, Clerks and Courtly Love." In Krueger, 2000, 81–90.

Kearney, Charles Francis. "Arthur." In *The Dictionary of National Biography.* London: Smith, Elder, 1885, vol. 1, 598–601.

Keeler, Laura. *Geoffrey of Monmouth and the Late Latin Chroniclers, 1300–1500.* University of California Publications in English, 17, no.1. Berkeley: University of California Press, 1946.

Keith, W. J. "Reading the Complete *Porius.*" *The Powys Journal* 14 (2004): 8–26.

Keller, Hans-Erich. "Le mirage Robert Wace." *Zeitschrift für Romanische Philologie* 106 (1990): 465–66.

Kellman, Martin. "T. H. White's Merlin: A Flawed Prophet." In Gollnick, 1991, 55–61.

Kendrick, T. D. *British Antiquity.* London: Methuen, 1950.

Kennedy, Elspeth. "The Making of the *Lancelot-Grail* Cycle." In Dover, 2003, 13–22.

Kerrigan, John. "Revision, Adaptation and the Fool in *King Lear.*" In *The Division of the Kingdoms: Shakespeare's Two Versions of King Lear,* ed. Gary Taylor and Michael Warren. Oxford: Oxford University Press, 1983.

Killham, John. "Tennyson and the Sinful Queen: A Corrected Impression." *Notes and Queries,* n.s. 5 (1958): 507–11.

Kincaid, James R. *Tennyson's Major Poems: The Comic and Ironic Patterns.* New Haven, Conn.: Yale University Press, 1975.

King, Roma A. "Charles Williams' Merlin: Worker in Time of the Images of Eternity." In Watson and Fries, 1989, 65–77.

Kirby, I. J. "Angles and Saxons in Lazamon's *Brut.*" *Studia Neophilologica* 36 (1964): 51–62.

Knight, Stephen. *Arthurian Literature and Society.* London: Macmillan, 1983.

——. "From Jerusalem to Camelot: King Arthur and the Crusades." In *Medieval Codicology, Iconography, Literature and Translation: Studies for Keith Val Sinclair,* ed. Peter Rolfe Monks and D. D. R. Owen. Leiden: Brill, 1994, 223–32.

Koch, John T., ed. *The Gododdin of Aneirin: Text and Context from Dark-Age North Britain.* Cardiff: University of Wales Press, 1997.

——. ed. *Celtic Culture: A Historical Encyclopedia,* 5 vols. Santa Barbara, Calif.: ABC Clio, 2006.

Köhler, Erich. "Le rôle de 'coutume' dans les romans de Chrétien de Troyes." *Romania* 81 (1960): 385–97.

Kollman, Judith. "Charles Williams's *Taliessin through Logres* and *The Region of the Summer Stars.*" In Lagorio and Day, 1990, 2, 180–203.

Krueger, Roberta, ed. *The Cambridge Companion to Medieval Romance.* Cambridge: Cambridge University Press, 2000.

Lacour, Léopold. *Les Maitresses de Molière.* Paris: Société Française d'éditions littéraires et techniques, 1932.

Lacy, Norris J. "Preface." In *Lancelot-Grail,* 1993–96, vol. 1 (1993), ix–xiii.

——, ed. *The New Arthurian Encyclopedia,* rev. ed. New York: Garland, 1996.

——and Geoffrey Ashe. *The Arthurian Handbook.* New York: Garland, 1988.

Lagorio, Valerie M. "Edwin Arlington Robinson: Arthurian Pacifist." In Lagorio and Day, 1990, 2, 165–75.

——and Mildred Day, eds. *King Arthur through the Ages,* 2 vols. New York: Garland, 1990.

Larrington, Carolyne. *King Arthur's Enchantresses: Morgan and Her Sisters in Arthurian Tradition.* London: I. B. Tauris, 2006.

Lavender, Philip. "Merlin and the Völva." *Viking and Medieval Scandinavia* 2 (2006): 111–39.

Le Gentil, Pierre. "The Work of Robert de Boron and the Didot *Perceval.*" In Loomis, 1959, 251–62.

Le Saux, Françoise. *Layamon's Brut and Its Sources.* Cambridge: Brewer, 1989.

——. *Layamon's Brut: Text and Tradition.* Cambridge: Brewer, 1994.

——. *A Companion to* Wace. Cambridge: Brewer, 2005.

Lewis, C. S. *The Abolition of Man: Reflections on Education.* London: Oxford University Press, 1943.

——. *Arthurian Torso.* Oxford: Clarendon Press, 1948.

——. "The English Prose *Morte.*" In *Essays on Malory,* ed. J. A. W. Bennett. Oxford: Clarendon Press, 1963, 17–28.

Lida de Malkiel, María Rosa. "Arthurian Literature in Spain and Portugal." In Loomis, 1959, 408–9.

Lindstedt, Eivor. "Chroniclers and Prophets: Time and Genre in *Porius.*" *The Powys Journal* 14 (2004): 27–44.

Linley, Margaret. "Sexuality and Nationality in Tennyson's *Idylls of the King.*" *Victorian Poetry* 30 (1992): 365–86.

Lloyd, J. E. *A History of Wales from the Earliest Times to the Edwardian Conquest,* 3rd ed. London: Longman, 1939.

Loomis, R. S. *Celtic Myth and Arthurian Romance.* New York: Columbia University Press, 1927.

——. *Arthurian Myth and Chrétien de Troyes.* New York: Columbia University Press, 1949.

——, ed. *Arthurian Literature in the Middle Ages: A Collaborative History.* Oxford: Clarendon Press, 1959.

—— and Laura Hibberd Loomis. *The Arthurian Legend in Medieval Art.* New York: Modern Language Association of America, 1938.

Lupack, Alan. "Merlin in America." *Arthurian Interpretations* 1 (1986): 64–74.

——. "American Arthurian Authors: A Declaration of Independence." In Mancoff, 1992, 155–73.

——. "Visions of Courageous Achievement: Arthurian Youth Groups in America." In *Medievalism in North America,* ed. Kathleen Verduin. Cambridge: Brewer, 1994, 50–68.

——. *The Oxford Guide to Arthurian Literature and Legend.* Oxford: Oxford University Press, 2006.

—— and Barbara Tepa Lupack. "From Twain to the Twenties." In Alan Lupack and Barbara Tepa Lupack, *King Arthur in America.* Cambridge: Brewer, 1999, 93–124.

——. "*The Once and Future King:* The Book That Grows Up." *Arthuriana* 11 (2001): 103–14.

MacCallum, Mungo. *Tennyson's* Idylls of the King *and Arthurian Story from the Sixteenth Century.* Glasgow: McLehose, 1894.

Macdonald, Aileen Ann. *The Figure of Merlin in Thirteenth Century French Romance.* Lewiston, N.Y.: Mellen, 1990.

——. "Merlin in the Vulgate and Post Vulgate: A Study in Contrasts." In Gollnick, 1991, 3–20.

MacRae, Suzanne H. "Berger's Mythical *Arthur Rex.*" In Slocum, 1992, 85–95.

MacRae-Gibson, O. D. "Introduction." In *Arthour and Merlin,* 1979, vol. 2, 1–75.

——. "Wynkyn de Worde's *Marlyn.*" *The Library,* ser. 6 (1980): 73–76.

Mancoff, Debra N., ed. *The Arthurian Revival: Essays on Form, Tradition, and Transformation.* New York: Garland, 1992.

——. ed. *King Arthur's Modern Return.* New York: Garland, 1998.

Mann, Jill. "Taking the Adventure: Malory and the *Suite de Merlin.*" In Takamiya and Brewer, 1981, 71–91.

Markale, Jean. *Women of the Celts,* trans. A. Mygird, C. Hauch, and P. Henry. London: Gordon Cremonesi, 1975.

——. *Merlin l'Enchanteur.* Paris: Retz, 1981. Translated by Belle N. Burke as *Merlin: Priest of Nature.* Rochester, Vt.: Inner Traditions, 1995.

Martin, Angus. *La Bibliothèque universelle des romans 1775–89.* Oxford: Voltaire Foundation, 1985.

Matheson, Lister M. "Historical Prose." In A. S. G. Edwards, ed., *Middle English Prose: A Critical Guide to Major Authors and Genres.* New Brunswick, N.J.: Rutgers University Press, 1984, 209–48.

——. "King Arthur and the Medieval English Chronicles." In Lagorio and Day, 1990, 1, 248–74.

Mathis, Andrew A. *The King Arthur Myth in Modern American Literature.* Jefferson, NC.: McFarland, 2002.

Matthews, John. "Merlin in Modern Fiction and Cinema." In *Merlin through the Ages.* ed. R. J. Stewart and John Matthews. London: Blandford, 1995, 310–25.

——. *Merlin: Shaman, Prophet, Magician.* New York: Mitchell Beazley, 2004.

Matthews, Timothy. *Reading Apollinaire: Theories of Poetic Language.* Manchester: Manchester University Press, 1987.

Mead, W. E. "The Literary Value of the *Merlin.*" In *The English Prose Merlin,* vol. 1 (republished in vol. 5), ccxlii–ccxlviii.

Meale, Carol M. "The Manuscripts and Early Audience of the Middle English *Prose Merlin.*" In Adams et al., 1986, 92–111.

Meehan, Bernard. "Geoffrey of Monmouth, *Prophecies of Merlin:* New Manuscript Evidence." *Bulletin of the Board of Celtic Studies* 28 (1980): 37–46.

Merriman, James Douglas. *The Flower of Kings: A Study of the Arthurian Legend in England between 1485 and 1835.* Lawrence: University Press of Kansas, 1973.

Micha, Alexandre. "Les Sources de la Suite Vulgate du Merlin." *Le Moyen Age* 57 (1952): 299–346. Reprinted in Alexandre Micha, *De la Chanson de Geste au Roman.* Geneva: Droz, 1976, 319–65.

——, ed. *Étude sur le "Merlin" de Robert de Boron.* Geneva: Droz, 1980.

——. "Robert de Boron's Merlin." In Goodrich and Thompson, 2003, 296–307.

Micha, Hugues. "Reflets du monde contemporain." In Micha, 1980, 111–38.

Michelsson, Elisabeth. *Appropriating King Arthur: The Arthurian Legend in English Drama and Entertainments, 1485–1625.* Studia Anglistica Upsaliensis, 109. Uppsala: Upsaliensis S. Academiae, 1999.

Michon, Patricia. *A la lumière du* Merlin *espagnol.* Genève: Droz, 1998.

Miller, Barbara D. "The Spanish 'Viviens' of *El baladro del sabio Merlín* and Benjamín Jarnés's *Viviana y Merlín:* From Femme Fatale to Femme Vitale." *Arthuriana* 10 (2000): 82–93.

Miller, Molly. "The Commanders at Arthuret." *Transactions of the Cumberland and Westmoreland Archaeological Society* 76 (1975): 98–111.

Millican, Charles Bowie. *Spenser and the Table Round.* Harvard Studies in Comparative Literature, 8. Cambridge, Mass.: Harvard University Press, 1932.

Moll, Richard J. *Before Malory: Reading Arthur in Late Medieval England.* Toronto: University of Toronto Press, 2003.

Monroe, Douglas. *The Lost Books of Merlin.* St Paul, Minn.: Llewellyn Publications, 1998.

Moorman, Charles. "Space Ships and Grail: The Myths of C. S. Lewis." *College English* 18 (1956–57): 401–5.

——. *Arthurian Triptych.* Berkeley: University of California Press, 1960.

Morris, Rosemary. *The Character of King Arthur in Medieval Literature.* Cambridge: Brewer, 1982.

Muir, Linette Ross. "The Questing Beast: Its Origin and Development." *Orpheus* 4 (1957): 24–32.

Müller, Ulrich. "Merlin in German Literature." In Goodrich and Thompson, 2003, 219–29.

Nastali, Dan. "Arthurian Pop: The Tradition in Twentieth Century Popular Music." In Sklar and Hoffman, 2002, 138–67.

Newstead, Helen. "Arthurian Legends." In *A Manual of the Writings in Middle English, 1050–1500,* ed. J. Burke Severs, vol. 1. New Haven, Conn.: The Connecticut Academy of Arts and Sciences, 1967, 38–79.

Nitze, William A. "The Beste Glatissante in Arthurian Romance." *Zeitschrift für romanische Philologie* 56 (1936): 409–18.

——. "The *Esplumoir* Merlin." *Speculum* 18 (1943): 69–79.

——. "Messire Robert de Boron." *Speculum* 28 (1953): 279–96.

——. "An Arthurian Crux: Viviane and Ninian?" *Romance Philology* 7 (1954): 326–30.

Noble, James. "Patronage, Politics and the Figure of Arthur in Geoffrey of Monmouth, Wace and Lazamon." *Arthurian Yearbook* 2 (1992): 159–78.

O'Farrell-Tate, Una. "The Return of King Arthur in Twentieth-Century Fiction." Ph.D. thesis, University of London, 2004.

O'Gorman, Richard. "Robert de Boron." In Lacy, 1996, 385–86.

Orwell, George. Review of *That Hideous Strength. Manchester Evening News,* August 16, 1945. Reprinted in *The Complete Works of George Orwell,* vol. 17, *I Belong to the Left,* ed. Peter Davison. London: Secker & Warburg, 1998, 250–51.

Padel, O. J. "Geoffrey of Monmouth and the Development of the Merlin Legend." *Cambrian Medieval Celtic Studies* 51 (2006): 37–65.

Paris, Gaston. Review of Arthur de la Borderie, *Les véritables Prophéties de Merlin. Romania* 12 (1883): 367–76.

———. "Introduction." In *Merlin: Roman en Prose du XIIIe Siècle,* ed. Gaston Paris and Jacob Ulrich, 2 vols. Paris: Firmin Didot, 1886, vol. 1, i–lxxx.

Parry, John J. *The Vita Merlini. University of Illinois Studies in Language and Literature* 10, no. 3 (1925). (1925a)

———. "Celtic Tradition and the *Vita Merlini.*" *Philological Quarterly* 4 (1925): 193–207. (1925b)

Paton, Lucy A. "The Story of Grisandole: A Study in the Legend of Merlin." *Proceedings of the Modern Language Association of America* 22 (1907): 234–76.

———. "Notes on Manuscripts of the *Prophécies de Merlin.*" *Proceedings of the Modern Language Association* 28 (1913): 121–39.

———. *Studies in the Fairy Mythology of Arthurian Romance.* 2nd ed. New York: Burt Franklin, 1960 [1927].

Peacock, John. "Jonson and Jones Collaborate on *Prince Henries Barriers.*" *Word and Image* 3 (1987): 172–94.

Pelan, Margaret M. *L'influence du Brut de Wace sur les romaniers français de son temps.* Genéve: Slatkine, 1974.

Percy, Thomas. "Essay on the Ancient Metrical Romances." Appendix II of *Reliques of Ancient English Poetry,* 3 vols. London: Dodsley, 1765. Reprinted New York: Dover, 1966, 341–51.

Perrine, Laurence. "The Sources of Robinson's Arthurian Poems and His Opinions of Other Treatments." *Colby Library Quarterly* 10 (1973–74): 336–46.

Phillips, Graham. *Merlin and the Discovery of Avalon in the New World.* Rochester, Vt.: Bear, 2000.

Phillips, Helen. "Gordon Bottomley and the Scottish Noh Play." In *English Studies 3: Proceedings of the Third Conference of Literature and Nation,* ed. J. J. Simon and Alain Sinner. Luxembourg: Publications du Centre Universitaire de Luxembourg, 1991, 214–33.

Pickens, Rupert T. "'Mais de Çou ne parole pas Chrestien de Troies...': Re-examination of the Didot-*Perceval.*" *Romania* 105 (1984): 492–510.

———, trans. "The Story of Merlin." In *Lancelot-Grail,* 1993–96, vol. 1, 167–425.

Porter, David. *Emerson and Literary Change.* Cambridge, Mass.: Harvard University Press, 1978.

Porterfield, Allen Wilson. *Karl Lebrecht Immerman: A Study in German Romanticism.* New York: Columbia University Press, 1911.

Prescott, Sarah. "The Cambrian Muse: Welsh Identity and Hanoverian Loyalty in the Poems of Jane Brereton (1685–1740)." *Eighteenth-Century Studies* 38 (2005): 587–603.

Putter, Ad. "Finding Time for Romance: Medieval Arthurian Literary History." *Medium Aevum* 63 (1994): 1–16.

Quinet, Edgar. *Rapport à M. le Ministre des travaux publiques sur les épopées françaises du XIIe siècle.* Paris: Levrault, 1831.

Ramsey, Lee C. *Chivalric Romance: Popular Literature in Medieval England.* Bloomington: University of Indiana Press, 1983.

Rathbone, Isabel E. *The Meaning of Spenser's Fairyland.* New York: Columbia University Press, 1937.

Reed, Edward Bliss. Review of E. A. Robinson, *Merlin. Yale Review,* n.s. 7 (1917): 863–64.

Reed, John R. *Perception and Design in Tennyson's* Idylls of the King. Athens: Ohio University Press, 1969.

Reid, Margaret J. C. *The Arthurian Legend.* Edinburgh: Oliver and Boyd, 1938.

Revel, Thierry. "Diversité et unité: Le *Merlin* de Robert de Boron." In *Merlin: Roman du XIIIe Siècle,* ed. Danielle Queruel and Christine Acher. Paris: Ellipsis, 2000, 105–21.

Rhestr o Enwau Lleodd ("A List of Place-Names"). Edited by Elwyn Davies. Caerdydd: Gwasg Prifysgol Cymru, 1957.

Rhŷs, John. *Studies in the Arthurian Legend.* Oxford: Clarendon Press, 1891.

Richards, Melville. *Enwau Tir a Gwlad* ("The Names of the Land and Country"), ed. Bedwyr Lewis Jones. Caernarfon: Gwasg Gwynedd, 1998.

Ricks, Christopher. "Introduction." In Tennyson, 1987, vol. 3, 255–62.

Riddy, Felicity. "Contextualizing *Le Morte Darthur.*" In Archibald and Edwards, 1996, 55–73.

Robbins, Rossell Hope. "Poems Dealing With Contemporary Conditions." In Hartung, 1975, 1521–22.

Roberts, Brynley F. "Introduction." In *Brut y Brenhinedd,* 1971, ix–lx.

———. *Studies on Middle Welsh Literature.* Lampeter: Mellen Press, 1992.

Roberts, Brynley F., Rachel Bromwich, and A. O. H. Jarman, eds. *The Arthur of the Welsh: The Arthurian Legend in Medieval Welsh Literature.* Cardiff: University of Wales Press, 1991.

Robinson, Robert. *The Assertion of Arthur.* London: Wolfe, 1582. Reprinted as appendix to Christopher Middleton, *The Famous Historie of Chinon of England,* ed. William Edward Mead. Early English Text Society, O.S. 165. London: Oxford University Press, 1925.

Rosenberg, John D. *The Fall of Camelot: a Study of Tennyson's "Idylls of the King."* Cambridge, Mass.: Harvard University Press, 1973.

Roussineau, Gilles. "Introduction." In *La Suite du Roman de Merlin,* 1996, i–cxxxix.

Rowland, Jenny. "Y Beirdd Enwog" ("The Famous Bards"). In *Cyfoeth y Testun: Ysgrifau ar Llenyddiath Gymraeg yr Oesedd Canol* ("The Authority of the Text: Writings on Welsh Medieval Literature"), ed. Iestyn Daniel, Marged Haycock, Dafydd Johnston, and Jenny Rowland. Caerdydd: Gwasg Prifysgol Cymru, 2003, 31–49.

———, ed. *Early Welsh Saga Poetry.* Cambridge: Brewer, 1990.

Ryals, Clyde de L. *From the Great Deep: Essays on the* Idylls of the King. Columbus: Ohio University Press, 1967.

Salter, H. E. "Geoffrey of Monmouth and Oxford." *English Historical Review* 34 (1919): 382–85.

Saunders, Corinne. *The Forest of Medieval Romance—Avernus, Brocéliande, Arden.* Cambridge: Brewer, 1993.

Savage, Roger. "The Theatre Music." In *The Purcell Companion,* ed. Michael Burden. London: Faber & Faber, 1995, 313–83.

Schlegel, Friedrich, ed. *Geschichte des Zauberers Merlin.* Leipzig: Junius, 1804.

Schwab, Hans-Rüdiger. "Tankred Dorst." In *Literatur Lexicon: Autoren und Werke Deutscher Sprache,* ed. Walther Killy, 15 vols. Munich: Bertelsman, 1989, vol. 3, 104–6.

Schwyzer, Philip. *Literature, Nationalism and Memory in Early Modern England and Wales.* Cambridge: Cambridge University Press, 2004.

Shaw, Marion. *Alfred Lord Tennyson.* New York: Harvester, 1988.

Shichtman, Martin B. and Laurie A. Finke. "Profiting from the Past: History as Symbolic Capital in the *Historia Regum Britanniae.*" *Arthurian Literature* 12 (1993): 1–35.

Shires, Linda M. "Rereading Tennyson's Gender Politics." In *Victorian Sages and Cultural Discourse: Renegotiating Gender and Power,* ed. Thaïs E. Morgan. New Brunswick, N.J.: Rutgers University Press, 1990, 45–65.

Simpson, Roger. *Camelot Regained: The Arthurian Revival and Tennyson.* Cambridge: Brewer, 1990.

Skene, W. F. *The Four Ancient Books of Wales,* 2 vols. Edinburgh: Edmonston and Douglas, 1868.

Sklar, Elizabeth S. and Donald E. Hoffman, eds. *King Arthur in Pop Culture.* Jefferson, N.C.: McFarland, 2002.

Slocum, Sally K., ed. *Popular Arthurian Tradition.* Bowling Green, Ohio: Bowling Green State University, 1992.

Smallwood, T. M. "The Prophecy of the Six Kings." *Speculum* 60 (1985): 571–92.

Smiles, Sam. *The Image of Antiquity: Ancient Britain and the Romantic Imagination.* New Haven, Conn.: Yale University Press, 1994.

Smith, Charles E. *The Merlin Factor: Keys to the Corporate Kingdom.* Aldershot: Gower, 1995.

Smith, Roland M. "*King Lear* and the Merlin Tradition." *Modern Language Quarterly* 7 (1946): 153–74.

Snider, Clifton. "Merlin in Victorian Poetry: A Jungian Analysis." *Victorian Newsletter* 72 (1987): 51–54.

Southern, R. W. "From Epic to Romance." Part 5 of *The Making of the Middle Ages.* London: Hutchinson, 1953, 209–44.

Southey, Robert. "Preface." In Malory, 1817, vol. 1, i–lxiii.

Speed, Diane. "The Saracens of King Horn." *Speculum* 65 (1990): 564–95.

Spivack, Charlotte, ed. *Merlin Versus Faust: Contending Archetypes in Western Culture*
Lewiston, N.Y.: Mellen, 1992.

—— and Roberta Lynne Staples. *The Company of Camelot: Arthurian Characters in
Romance and Fantasy.* Westport, Conn.: Greenwood, 1994.

Staines, David. *Tennyson's Camelot: The Idylls of the King and Its Medieval Sources.*
Waterloo, Ontario: Wilfred Laurier University Press, 1982.

Stein, Walter Johannes. *The Death of Merlin: Arthur Myth and Alchemy.* Edinburgh:
Floris Books, 1989.

Stephens, John and Robin McCallum. *Retelling Stories, Framing Culture: Traditional
Story and Metanarratives in Children's Literature.* New York: Garland, 1998.

Stern, Karen. "The Middle English *Prose Merlin*." In Adams et al., 1986, 112–22.

Stewart, R. J. *The Prophetic Vision of Merlin: Prediction, Psychic Transformation, and
the Foundation of the Grail Legends in an Ancient Set of Visionary Verses.* London:
Arkana, 1986.

——. *The Book of Merlin: Insights from the Merlin Conference.* Poole: Blandford, 1987.

Strong, Roy. *The Artists of the Tudor Court.* London: Victoria and Albert
Museum, 1983.

Stuart-Glennie, J. S. *Arthurian Topography.* Edinburgh: Edmonston and Douglas,
1869. Reprinted as "Arthurian Localities" in Mead, ed., *Prose Merlin,* xviii–clvi.

Summers, David A. *Spenser's Arthur: The British Arthurian Tradition and the Faerie
Queene.* Lanham, Md.: University Press of America, 1997.

Takamiya, Toshiyuki and Derek Brewer., eds. *Aspects of Malory.* Cambridge:
Brewer, 1981.

Tatlock, J. S. P. "Geoffrey of Monmouth's *Vita Merlini*." *Speculum* 18 (1943): 265–87.

——. *The Legendary History of Britain.* Berkeley: University of California
Press, 1950.

Taylor, Beverly. "Re-Vamping Vivien: Reinventing Myth as Victorian Icons." In
Mancoff, 1998, 65–81.

Taylor, Beverly and Elizabeth Brewer. *The Return of King Arthur.* Cambridge:
Brewer, 1983.

Thomas, Keith. *Religion and the Decline of Magic: Studies in Popular Belief
in Sixteenth and Seventeenth Century England.* London: Weidenfeld &
Nicholson, 1971.

Thompson, Raymond H. "The Enchanter Awakes: Merlin in Modern Fantasy." In
Death and the Serpent: Immortality in Science Fiction and Fantasy, ed. Carl B. Yoke
and Donald M. Hassler. Westport, Conn.: Greenwood, 1985, 49–56.

——. "The Comic Sage: Merlin in Thomas Berger's *Arthur Rex*." In Watson and
Fries, 1989, 143–53.

——. "The Arthurian Legend in Science Fiction and Fantasy." In Lagorio and Day,
1990, 2, 223–39.

——. "Rationalizing the Irrational: Merlin and His Prophecies in the Modern
Historical Novel." *Arthuriana* 10 (2000): 116–26.

——. Interview with Mary Stewart. University of Rochester Camelot website: www. lib.rochester.edu.camelot/intrvws/stewart.htm.

——. Interview with John Heath-Stubbs. University of Rochester Camelot website: www.lib.rochester.edu.camelot/intrvws/heath.htm.

Thompson, W. R. "Broceliande: E. A. Robinson's Palace of Art." *New England Quarterly* 43 (1970): 231–49.

Thorpe, Lewis. "Gerald of Wales and King Arthur." In *Gerald of Wales,* 1978, 280–88.

Tolstoy, Nikolai. *The Quest for Merlin.* London: Hamilton, 1985.

Trachsler, Richard. *Merlin l'enchanteur: Étude sur le Merlin de Robert de Boron.* Paris: Sedes, 2000.

Traxler, Janina P. "Pendragon, Merlin and Logos: The Undoing of Babel in *That Hideous Strength.*" *Arthurian Literature* 20 (2003): 191–206.

Turville-Petre, Thorlac. *England the Nation: Language, Literature and National Identity, 1290–1340.* Oxford: Clarendon Press, 1996.

Udall, Joanna. "*The Birth of Merlin* and the English History Play," in William Rowley, *A Critical Old-Spelling Edition of The Birth of Merlin,* ed. Joanna Udall. London: Modern Humanities Research Association, 1991, 89–111.

Umland, Rebecca A. and Samuel J. Umland. *The Use of Arthurian Legend in Hollywood Film: From Connecticut Yankees to Fisher Kings.* Westport, Conn.: Greenwood, 1996.

Villemarqué, Théodore Claude Henri, vicomte Hersart de la. *Contes populaires des anciens Bretons.* 2 vols. Paris: Coquebert, 1842.

——. *Myrdhin ou Merlin l'enchanteur.* Paris: Didier, 1862.

Vinaver, Eugène. "The Dolorous Stroke." *Medium Aevum* 25 (1956): 175–80.

——. "Introductions." In Books 1–8, *The Works of Sir Thomas Malory,* 1990, vol. 3.

Wallace, Diana. *The Woman's Historical Novel: British Women Writers, 1900-2000.* London: Palgrave Macmillan, 2005.

Walter, Philippe. *Merlin ou le Savoir du Monde.* Paris: Imago, 2000.

Walton, Brad. "Merlin and the Divine Machinery of Dryden's King Arthur." In Gollnick, 1991, 41–52.

Warner, Sylvia Townsend. *T. H. White.* Oxford: Oxford University Press, 1967.

——. "Afterword." In White, 1996, 813–25.

Warren-Clarke, Ly and Kathryn Matthews. *The Way of Merlyn: The Male Path in Wicca.* Bridport: Prism, 1990.

Warton, Thomas. *The History of English Poetry,* 3 vols. London: Dodsley, 1774.

Watson, Jeanie. "Mary Stewart's Merlin: Word of Power." In Watson and Fries, 1989, 155–73.

Watson, Jeanie and Maureen Fries, eds. *The Figure of Merlin in the Nineteenth and Twentieth Centuries.* Lewiston, N.Y.: Mellen, 1989.

Weiss, Adelaide Marie. *Merlin in German Literature: A Study of the Merlin Legend in German Literature from Medieval Beginnings to the End of Romanticism.* Washington, D.C.: Catholic University of America Press, 1933.

Whitaker, Muriel. *The Legends of King Arthur in Art.* Cambridge: Brewer, 1995.

Williams, Charles. "Malory and the Grail Legend." *Dublin Review, no.* 214 (1944): 144–53. Reprinted in *Charles Williams: Selected Writings,* ed. Anne Ridler. London: Oxford University Press, 1961, 151–62.

Williams, Glanmor. "Prophecy, Poetry and Politics in Medieval and Tudor Wales." Chapter 3 of *Religion, Language and Nationality in Wales.* Cardiff: University of Wales Press, 1979, 71–86.

Williams, Ifor. "Introduction." In Aneirin, 1966.

——. "Introduction." In *Armes Prydein,* 1972.

Williamson, G. C. *George, Third Earl of Cumberland (1558–1605): His Life and His Voyages.* Cambridge: Cambridge University Press, 1920.

Winn, Mary Beth. *Anthoine Vérard: Parisian Publisher 1485–1512: Prologues, Poems and Presentations.* Genéve: Droz, 1997.

Winters, Yvor. *Edwin Arlington Robinson.* New York: Macmillan, 1935.

Worthington, Heather. "From Children's Story to Adult Fiction: T. H. White's *The Once and Future King.*" *Arthuriana* 12 (2002): 97–119.

Wright, Neil. "Introduction." In Geoffrey of Monmouth, 1984, ix–xx.

——. "The Place of Henry of Huntingdon's *Epistola ad Warinum* in the Text-History of Geoffrey of Monmouth's *Historia Regum Britanniae:* A Preliminary Investigation." In *France and the British Isles in the Middle Ages and the Renaissance: Essays by Members of Girton College, Cambridge, in Memory of Ruth Morgan,* ed. Gillian Jondorf and David N. Dumville. Woodbridge: Boydell, 1991, 71–113.

——. "Angles and Saxons in Lazamon's *Brut:* A Reassessment." In le Saux, 1994, 161–70.

Yarndell, Stephen. "Prophetic Authority in Adam of Usk's *Chronicle.*" In *Prophet Margins: The Medieval Vatic Impulse and Social Stability,* ed. E. L. Risden, Karen Moranski, and Stephen Yarndell. New York: Peter Lang, 2001, 79–100.

Yolen, Jane. "Interview" with Rozalyn Levin, Tom Holberg, and David Bachi. *Avalon to Camelot* 2 (1987): 20–23.

Zimmer, Heinrich. "Merlin." *Corona* 9 (1939): 133–55.

Zumthor, Paul. *Merlin le prophète.* Lausanne: Payot, 1943.

Index

Characters' names are entered under the commonest forms; titles are abbreviated, and only creative ones inserted; pseudonyms are used for entries; anonymous texts are entered under title; co-authors are entered separately. Page numbers in italics indicate illustrations.